Adventure Therapy

Adventure Therapy

Theory, Research, and Practice

Michael A. Gass

H. L. "Lee" Gillis

Keith C. Russell

Routledge
Taylor & Francis Group
New York London

Routledge
Taylor & Francis Group
711 Third Avenue
New York, NY 10017

Routledge
Taylor & Francis Group
27 Church Road
Hove, East Sussex BN3 2FA

© 2012 by Taylor & Francis Group, LLC
Routledge is an imprint of Taylor & Francis Group, an Informa business

Printed in the United States of America on acid-free paper
Version Date: 20111216

International Standard Book Number: 978-0-415-89289-6 (Hardback) 978-0-415-89290-2 (Paperback)

Library of Congress Cataloging-in-Publication Data

Gass, Michael A.
    Adventure therapy : theory, research, and practice / by Michael Gass, H. L. Lee Gillis, Keith C. Russell. -- 1st ed.
       p. cm.
    Includes bibliographical references and index.
    ISBN 978-0-415-89289-6 (hardback : alk. paper) -- ISBN 978-0-415-89290-2 (pbk. : alk. paper)
    1. Adventure therapy. I. Gillis, H. L. Lee. II. Russell, Keith C. III. Title.

RC489.A38G374 2012
616.89'165--dc23
                                                    2011033323

Visit the Taylor & Francis Web site at
http://www.taylorandfrancis.com

and the Routledge Web site at
http://www.routledgementalhealth.com

Printed and bound in the United States of America by
Edwards Brothers Malloy on sustainably sourced paper

Names with metaphorical connections are often given to individuals for attributes they possess or societal roles it is hoped they will fill. Such an action is not a dictatorial mandate, but a gift given with the hope and support that the individual can achieve this objective in a manner that best suits her and the needs of a particular culture and society.

In an article in Science *(1977), amaranth was described as "the crop of the future." In many cultures in the Americas, the grain amaranth not only represented the actual staple in the diet of these civilizations, but also served as an interpretive symbol of being nurtured by growth and strength. Any item, concept, or person with the name amaranth represented the idea of holding a critical nurturing role in society.*

Serving as a nurturing food source for the Incas, Aztecs, Mayans, and other cultures, amaryth holds modern significance as an entity that is highly productive, tolerant in difficult environments, contains large amounts of strength building elements, and requires small amounts of support to grow rapidly. Adding honey or chocolate to amaryth makes a treat called alegría, meaning "joy" in Spanish.

Contents

Foreword

I went to my first Association for Experiential Education (AEE) conference in 1995, in Lake Geneva, Wisconsin. I had just received a score and written feedback on a grant application I had submitted with my colleague, Kathy Konrad, where we proposed to use outdoor adventure as a method to diffuse binge drinking in college fraternities and sororities. Our application did not score high enough to be considered for funding, so we set out to address the concerns of the reviewers, with the goal of resubmitting. A main criticism of the application was that, beyond a loose anthropological explanation linked to rites of passage, we did not provide a well-developed theory about how outdoor adventure might actually change the drinking behavior of college students; another concern was that we needed to clearly articulate the operational processes necessary to standardize and establish the quality implementation of outdoor adventure experience across groups of participants. Kathy figured that, given we were going to the AEE conference anyway, we should just go ahead and talk directly with the outdoor adventure researchers we had referenced extensively in our proposal, to figure out how to address the reviewers' feedback. I thought it was a great idea myself, until we actually got to the conference and had to go up and introduce ourselves to those folks who wrote so eloquently on the topic and did the best research in the field. I was quite intimidated and scared by this adventure—a sort of rite of passage!

Much to my surprise, the adventure researchers, Mike Gass and H.L. "Lee" Gillis, were extremely approachable (I didn't meet Keith at this conference—he was too young at the time to be an established researcher). In addition to being approachable, they were also both completely willing to question the effectiveness and universal application of adventure approaches for different groups of people—in the same way the reviewers of my grant application were. As I have followed Mike and Lee's work and have gotten to know the work of their colleague, Keith, I have found that all three are able to reconcile their personal passion for adventure approaches with their curiosity about how adventure works, when it works, and for whom. Their book represents the state-of-the-art for building an evidence-informed approach to what works in adventure therapy, an approach that translates across theory, practice, and research.

Although my own career path now focuses on building the knowledge base for how to take evidence-based approaches to scale, across a broad range of strategies and for multiple health and well-being outcomes, I am still highly energized and motivated to learn about adventure and its potential for facilitating long-term behavior change across contexts. Few approaches provide the opportunity to combine lived experience with real-time reinforcement and consequences in the natural environment. By reading this text, you will learn what is currently known about adventure therapy and how to do it well, as well as feed your own curiosity for understanding more about how it works, for whom, and under what conditions.

Aleta L. Meyer, PhD
Senior Social Science Research Analyst
Office of Planning, Research, and Evaluation
Administration for Children and Families

Preface

EQUIFINALITY: A STORY OF THREE
PATHS OF ADVENTURE THERAPY

One of the key concepts in systems theory first identified by Bertalanffy (1968) is the concept of equifinality. This term advances the notion that a goal or "given end-state" can be achieved through more than one, if not many, potential means, methods, or paths. The following three stories illustrate the beginning paths each of us underwent in our professional careers in adventure therapy. They are presented here in the beginning of this text to show emerging professionals how different individuals can reach the requisite proficiencies of adventure therapist through a myriad of methods and pathways. We hope that, by sharing these stories, readers will become educated to choose the right path that works best for them and the clients they serve.

STORY 1: MIKE

In the fall of 1978, I was a graduate student at the University of Northern Colorado, studying outdoor education with noted colleagues such as Alan Ewert, Ed Raiola, Don Mendence, and other emerging professionals. As I was looking for ways to subsidize my graduate school expenses, I applied for and was offered a weekend shift position in a group home for adolescents. I also was appointed as the recreation director for all four group homes in the small city of Greeley, Colorado. Little did I know, the first weekend of my work there would forever change the direction of my professional career.

On Saturday of the first weekend, one of the young men in one house ran away, stole a tractor, and drove it into the side of the church. The only "saving grace" of this incident was that the church services were held on Sunday for this particular religion and therefore the church was empty at the time. On Sunday, we received our first opportunity to go to the local pool to swim. Unfortunately, within the first 10 minutes of our arrival a fight broke out between members of our group home and local adolescent boys. We were summarily kicked out of the pool and had our swimming privileges revoked for the remainder of the summer by the city of Greeley.

As my shift ended on Monday morning, I was asked to go speak with the Director of our program. As easily as I had started my job on Friday, I thought I was being called into the Director's office to lose my job. As I entered his office, he was hanging up the phone after receiving a call from one of the city counselors in Greeley. He stated, "You had quite a weekend!" I sheepishly agreed, and then his next statement took me by surprise. Recalling several items from my application and resume, he asked, "Don't you know a little bit about this outdoor adventure programming stuff?" I said yes, and he responded in the following manner:

"Here's what I want you to do. I want you to take this group of young men out every weekend for the remainder of the summer and do that outdoor stuff with them. I don't really care what you do, but bring them back by Sunday evening. Because if we have another weekend like the one we had this past one, the city will probably revoke our license to operate."

So began my first experience using adventure experiences with a therapeutic population. Unlike current requisites and necessary directives from sources such as evidence-based practices and expected outcomes, our program truly was a form of "divergent therapy" or alternative programming for these young men. Despite my lack of experience, the staff and I found that the success orientation and supportive yet challenging environment of our experiences led to positive effects on several individuals and kept us off tractors and away from community swimming pools! One of the key individuals who came to assist me that summer was a colleague named Craig Dobkin, who would become a fixture in my ability to think creatively and in innovative ways with responsibility for the rest of my professional career.

While not all of these young men benefited from these experiences in a therapeutic manner, some of them found beneficial insights from the adventure experiences. As I have previously highlighted in a *Ziplines* article (Gass, 1998), one of these young men experiencing success was named "Charlie." Charlie found he enjoyed the adventure experiences and looked forward to our weekend experiences. I also enjoyed working with Charlie much more in the outdoors than I did in the confines of the group home. Charlie's successes on the weekends actually earned him early integration from the group home back into his home community and his family. Unfortunately, Charlie's family was experiencing high levels of dysfunctional behavior, and his efforts to utilize any functional gains from our adventure experiences were quickly dismissed or sabotaged by his family and peer group in his home environment. This transition became extremely frustrating to him, as he was incapable of creating the successes he had accomplished in his outdoor experiences in his home environment. This experience "planted the seeds" of my professional pathway to become a marriage and family therapist.

Much of what I observed and experienced that year also created a lasting impression on how I view adventure therapy at that time as well as now. I saw the need to help individuals like Charlie integrate positive changes into their returning environments. This led to three years of researching how other professionals in the adventure programming field created positive transfer into their clients' lives. The basis of my findings led to my first publication in 1986, in the *Journal of Experiential Education,* on programming the transfer of learning in adventure programs (Gass, 1986). I became further interested in systems thinking, especially the role of family and other social structures in supporting (or at least tolerating) beneficial change in returning adolescents. From 1988 to 1990, I combined efforts with Marianne Scippa and John Stephen in the state of Connecticut (and with the staff at Eagleville Hospital in Eagleville, Pennsylvania) to implement this type of thinking and to evolve facilitation styles that worked best with adolescents who were addicted to abusive substances. While on sabbatical leave from the University of New Hampshire in 1990–1991, in Boulder Colorado to serve as President of the Board of Directors of the Association for Experiential Education (AEE), and to complete the requirements for my marriage and family therapy license, I rejoined collaborative efforts with Craig Dobkin, who was working at West Pines Hospital in Wheatridge, Colorado. This further expanded my thinking about metaphors and client-centered focuses for facilitation.

At the 1984 AEE conference, my eye caught an early Sunday morning workshop on adventure family therapy conducted by a Ph.D. psychologist by the name of H.L. "Lee" Gillis. I saw his insightful thinking and respectful approach to clients to be incredibly caring and effective. From that day forward, our joint interests would develop into over 20 years of professional collaborative efforts that extended my thinking beyond any individual capabilities I individually possessed. Our joint article in 1993, in the *Journal of Marriage and Family Therapy,* became the first of over 15 joint publications we have completed on adventure therapy topics. His efforts with Dr. Jude Hirsch to coordinate and capture the innovative developments at the 1995 "Food for Thought" workshop is what I consider to be one of the most productive professional gatherings ever produced by the field.

During this time, I also strove to integrate systems thinking on an even broader level into adventure therapy programs. I found that the methods of client facilitation in adventure therapy experiences provided the greatest influences on whether or not clients benefitted from these experiences, as well as on how long these benefits lasted. Two sources of client interaction served as mediums to test out my beliefs. The first sources were two federal grants Project Impact (1987–1990) and the Family Expedition Program (1993-1996). Both brands served as a maturing influence on my ability to prescriptively design adventure experiences for client change. The second source, which served as a rich medium for developing innovative adventure practices and facilitation, arose from my work with Simon Priest, with corporate clients around the world in several different cultures who were experiencing dysfunctional behaviors in their workplace. Just as my work with H.L. "Lee" Gillis expanded my thinking beyond anything I ever could have accomplished alone, my work with corporate and other client populations with Dr. Priest, from 1986 until today, has greatly influenced my thinking.

As I began to share my learning with others through various writings and workshops, I was invited by Larry Stettler to speak at the annual Mental Health of Montana Association Conference in Butte, Montana, in May 2001. At the end of the conference, I remember being incredibly struck by an insightful conversation with Dr. Keith C. Russell about his efforts to bring together a collaboration of the leading wilderness therapy programs to advance the field's practices and research. His dedicated efforts to coordinate these often-competing programs created the Outdoor Behavioral Healthcare Research Consortium (OBHRC). The programs of OBHRC (http://obhrc.org) are simply some of the best examples of professional collaboration and integrity our field has witnessed. Their efforts, combined with AEE's development of its accreditation program, "saved the field" from several abusive practitioners and their inappropriate and abusive programs by advancing the field's risk management and research-driven practices.

STORY 2: H.L. "LEE" GILLIS[*]

Other than having the good sense in the summer of 1965 to go to camp (as a 10 year old), meeting and knowing Karl Rohnke for 30 years is one of the most significant events in my life as an experiential-adventure-educator-researcher-psychologist-psychotherapist. I attended and later worked at Camp Monroe in the pine tree, sandspur, copperhead snake, blackwater-infested part of the southeastern portion of North Carolina every year through my undergraduate experience, ending in 1977. I learned so many valuable things experientially—not just how to paddle and camp, but how to trust the group process, how to rearrange your entire day's cabin plan when the weather would turn electric from the powerful thunderstorms, and how to handle a group of scared kids in aluminum boats paddling through the North Carolina swamps.

Camp led me to a wonderful experience of an instructor's course at the now defunct Wolfcreek Wilderness (GA) (with "Crazy" Dave & Dr. Don) and to an incredible experience through Davidson College's (my alma mater) summer program at Broughton Hospital in Morganton, NC. In the summer of 1976, I was fortunate to rock climb each Wednesday, at Table Rock, with male

---

[*] This material is based on an article I wrote for the AEE Old Folks & Allies Elder Roster, at http://tinyurl.com/3gvmasv.

adolescents who were patients at western North Carolina's mental hospital. I spent time each week with these young men—in school, at their "recreation therapy," and on their ward.

In the parking lot of Table Rock, they would horse play and goof around as teenage boys are know to do. However, when they went "on belay" on the two and three pitch climbs, "something happened." As I sat with each kid on the rock shelves overlooking western North Carolina, our conversations "changed" to a reality base that I had not experienced in other milieus. And my relationship with each of these young men changed in a positive way. I did not know the term "therapeutic alliance" at the time, but I knew something was different. I had no idea, when having conversations with these young men to connect their observations and thoughts to how they were behaving on the rock and back at the hospital, that I was applying the principles of cognitive behavioral therapy on the side of that mountain. But I was learning the power of the relationship formed with conducting adventure experiences. I have spent my career trying to understand what "happened" when those kids went on belay. It has been quite a journey.

In that same summer, while at Wolfcreek Wilderness, I saw a book titled *Physical Education: Adventure Curriculum*. I ordered it but received instead the book *Cowstails and Cobras*! Little did I know how the use of this book with high school kids would impact my career. This well-used book led me to a Project Adventure training in Hamilton, MA in the fall of 1978. At the time, I was working with "second chance" adolescents at The Glade Valley School in Sparta, NC, and together, the youth and I built and explored low initiatives. Karl came down to Glade Valley and ran a workshop. This became one of the many times I would learn so much from simply carrying his bag of tricks and having FUN with such a master. My journey led to The Webb School in Bell Buckle, TN, where I developed an outdoor program ("Outer Limits") and began to understand the power of adventure + therapy. I worked with many youth from the southeast who had some dysfunctional family dynamics. When we were out on the challenge course, climbing in Savage Gulf, or rafting the Oconee River, I would see the progress these young men and women made in their own lives. These positive changes seemed to be dashed when they went home on long holiday breaks or over the summer. I wanted to know more about how to impact larger systems.

An accident also got my attention! This occurred on one of my many trips to Savage Gulf (not too far from where Bonnaroo now occurs), at the end of the day. After belaying the long rappel for most of the afternoon, the youth on the trip wanted me to go and enjoy the ride. With my loose flannel shirt, I clipped in using a Figure 8 descender, and about halfway down, my shirt jammed in the device. I was stuck 75 feet up. With my prussik loop, I was able to self-rescue, but one week later I could not walk due to a herniated disk. The doctor said, "I'd like to avoid surgery and have you rest for two weeks at home, in bed." This existential crisis—"if I cannot run outdoor programming, what am I going to do?"—led me to those wise words, "when the going gets tough, the tough go back to school!"

Curiosity of how to impact family systems and my lingering existential angst led me to graduate school in Counseling Psychology at The University of Georgia. I was blessed to be with supervisors who had no experience in adventure or wilderness, but who had tremendous knowledge of and respect for experiential and metaphorically based therapy. They challenged me to know why experiential methods were so powerful in therapy. I was trained in Ericksonian hypnosis while at Georgia. I thought I had invented metaphorical introductions to adventure programming until I met, read, and received some training from Steve Bacon back in the early 1980s. I framed my dissertation (naively) to compare metaphorical introductions to challenge course activities with traditional activities. Surprisingly, I found no differences. I should have been researching the impact of the challenge course as a therapeutic intervention back in 1985, not trying advanced techniques that were so new in the field. I received one gift at that time, from my family supervisor, mentor, and running buddy, Don Randall, who one day noted that what I was engaged in seemed to him to be kinesthetic metaphors. How right he was!

Georgia College has been my academic home since 1986. In that time, I have had the opportunity to start and end an adventure therapy based masters in psychology (1994–1998) program; host a "metaphorical potluck" (1996) with my dear friends Mike Gass, Karl Rohnke, Jude Hirsch, Simon Priest, Jim Schoel, Laurie Frank, Scott Bandoroff, and Christian Itin; speak as keynote at the first and second International Adventure Therapy Conferences, put together by the multi-talented Martin Ringer; consult as a psychologist, since 1991, at Project Adventure's Covington GA site with many wonderful (and challenging) young people; write and present with Mike Gass in multiple places around the world; conduct research and evaluation with Keith Russell, and meet and work with my wonderfully talented wife, Jude Hirsch!

My path as a psychologist has not been a traditional one, but has been fueled by curiosity for what changes when one engages in adventure. Sometimes I wonder how adventure therapy might have been different had I (or someone!) sought out a research position in psychology at a university and tried to obtain grants and train adventure therapists. The few adventure therapy students I had at Georgia College and the countless participants in trainings I have been part of have gone on to do great things. I hope this book encourages you, the reader, to find your own path in the many choices for your consideration.

STORY 3: KEITH C. RUSSELL

In 1995, I was fortunate to be involved with a wilderness experience program called Wilderness Discovery (WD) while working as a graduate assistant with the Wilderness Research Center at the University of Idaho. I was a lead guide and trainer on the two year pilot program, which was launched at three Job Corps Centers in the Northwest in 1994, with a fourth Job Corps Center in downtown Atlanta added for the summer of 1995. Although I had run trips with various organizations, been a commercial river guide, and had worked in outdoor education for years at that point, I realized that this was a unique opportunity, and I embraced it.

WD was a soft skills, low stress, and low challenge wilderness experience program aimed at enhancing self-efficacy, personal control, confidence, and awareness that empowered and strengthened student performance in the ongoing training they receive in Job Corps. The focus of the experience was a 20–25 mile hiking trip, including camping for six nights on the trail, sharing of camp and cooking chores, and completing some wilderness trail work to show appreciation for use of the wilderness by the group. The students at the Atlanta Job Corps, 98% of whom were African American young women ages 16–24, many with children, posed a new challenge to Wilderness Discovery. Nearly all of the students had been hardened by intense urban environments, and all trip participants had never been exposed to a wilderness setting or been hiking or camping.

On my first trip to the center, I drove my old Subaru down Martin Luther King Boulevard and became slightly lost. I stopped at a gas station to ask for directions. A man replied, as he eyed me with skepticism, "Why do you want to go there?" I smiled and said I was working there this summer. He cracked a wry grin and simply said, "Well good luck to you then." I was late and was quickly ushered into Mr. Lonnie Smith's office, a charismatic 6'5" center director, dressed in an immaculate pin striped suit. He told me I was just in time, and that there was an "all center" meeting and to follow him. As we emerged into the steamy basement, 500 faces quickly smiled, and all began chatting, as my pending arrival had been discussed for some time by Mr. Smith. After a 20-second introduction, I was handed a microphone and told to do my thing. I pitched the wilderness program to them and asked for eight brave volunteers who would come with me on our first trip to the Joyce Kilmer Slick Rock Wilderness Area in North Carolina, scheduled to leave in 10 days. There was an extremely long silence, punctuated by the whrrrrrrrrrrrrr of the slow spinning fans. A brave young woman named Barbara raised her hand and said "With all due respect Mr. Wilderness, there are bad things in those woods up in North Carolina." I looked her in the eye and said, "Yes there are some bad things out there, but I got your back, trust me." A hand shot up. "Where do we go to the bathroom?" Laughter ensued as I explained the process. I knew at that point that I had them.

Ten days later, I was sweating buckets, packing the final gear into our van, and rounding up my crew for the first trip. A staff member walked up to me and said, "Mark my words, those damn girls will be back here tonight by the latest; they ain't going to make a 25-mile hike." Though slightly taken a back by his prediction, I simply said "We'll see." Well, needless to say, the trip was a huge success, and all eight women made the 25-mile hike through the wilderness area to our destination. Of course there were tears, arguments, endless stops to put on second skin to ward off blisters, packs thrown down the draw into the creek in frustration, and wild boars paying visits late in the evening under the nearly deafening cadence of the cicadas that kept us up at night. There were also amazing discussions, singing (lots of singing), laughter, incredible views of the Appalachia Mountains, cool creeks, and amazing sweet and sour chicken cooked by young women who had never before camped, hiked, or spent an evening under a tarp in a sleeping bag.

Barbara, the woman who asked that first question, was the first student to sign up for the first trip. A 17-year-old mother of two who had struggled with her weight for years, she blossomed under the sweat and tears, and the joy and laughter, of the experience. As we were reflecting on the experience on the last evening of the first trip, she thanked me for believing in her, and thanked her group for supporting her. I looked at Barbara and thanked her for believing in herself, because that is always the first step. There is simply nothing you can't do if you put your mind into it and believe in yourself. The ladies all got up and did a big group hug and unanimously said that this was the most important thing they had ever done in their lives. Upon arrival at the Center, the ladies poured out of the van, laughing and singing (always singing), and were greeted by a huge reception by the Center staff and students. I caught the eye of the staff member who said they wouldn't make it and winked at him. To his credit, he smiled back with a thumbs-up and shook his head, as if to say "I can't believe it."

It was at this point that I decided to dedicate my future work in the field to designing, implementing, evaluating, and leading wilderness experience programs for young people. The remarkable transformations I was seeing in people needed to be systematically studied—not to "prove" their worth, but to better understand how the process works and what can be realized from the experience. I was lucky enough to have been surrounded by amazing mentors and wonderful people in this journey. You all know who you are and I thank you. I also thank my amazing wife and best friend, Sheri, and my two little girls for their continued support and smiles. Finally, I thank Barbara, who ended up going on a second trip later in the summer as my special leader assistant. I kept up with Barbara for a year or two and found out that she went on to community college, where she studied medical records; she still lives in Atlanta with her family. I hope one day her kids will get to experience a trip like their mother did.

Acknowledgments

It is difficult to express the level or amount of gratitude we owe others in the production of this text. So much of our work extends beyond as well as between us; our work is much more of a composite of numerous individuals rather than three authors.

In many ways, our clients (i.e., the individuals and groups with whom we have worked in therapy) are the originating authors of this text, and we have served as "copy editors" of their processes. We are grateful for being invited into their lives, often at extremely critical and vulnerable moments. We are humbled by the courage they showed to grant us permission to research their efforts. We are indebted by their willingness to share appropriate elements of their life stories. We cannot wholly express the value of their patience with us as we refined our therapeutic approaches to enhance their growth processes, as well as adapted our research approaches to more accurately understand their realities.

In a parallel vein we are also grateful for the support we received from programs, institutions, organizations, and associations around the world to advance adventure therapy practices and research their effectiveness. These programs often devoted valuable time and hard earned resources so we could conduct our work to advance the field. We are grateful for their trust and investment toward such goals.

Special thanks go to Dr. Will White, for sharing and writing about the history of adventure therapy in Chapter 2. While several authors have written about the history of adventure/ wilderness therapy, no one else has gone to the level of depth, accuracy, or original sources as Dr. White. We commend him for his diligence in understanding this area and fairly representing both the positive as well as the negative elements in the field's evolution.

We extend additional thanks to several featured authors in Chapter 6 who contributed edited program descriptions and logic models describing their programs. This includes Jenn Jevertson and Sky Gray from the Santa Fe Mountain Center, Stephen Glass from the Wendigo Lakes/DARE program;

Lorri Hanna from Soltreks; John Conway from Omni Youth Services; Matt Chisholm with the UNH Operation Integration Program; and Jessa Hobson with the Longview Alternative School. In addition, the 14 adventure therapy professionals featured between each chapter merit additional recognition for their contributions in this book as well as to the field. Each one of these individuals, identified with their respective contributions in the manuscript, represent the present as well as the future standards of practice in the field.

In his usual imbuing and positive manner, Dr. Simon Priest freely contributed to several portions of the book with his advice and collegial input. He is also recognized for his evolving work with Figure 10.5 in Chapter 10, describing competencies. Dr. Aleta Meyer and Paula Leslie provided expertise in exploring the challenges of the future of adventure therapy.

The members of the Outdoor Behavioral Healthcare Industry Council (OBHIC), especially those involved with the research branch of the council (Outdoor Behavioral Healthcare Research Consortium—OBHRC) are to be especially recognized for their contributions to this text and the field. In a true spirit of cooperation to advance the field, these "competitors" have banded together to advance the best practices of the field of wilderness therapy. Without their efforts, much of this text (especially with research and risk management) would simply not be possible to write. It is our opinion that other adventure therapy organizations should follow their exemplary practices of professional development and advancement of the field. These programs (listed by the year they joined OBHIC) include Anasazi (1997), Aspen Achievement Academy (1997), Catherine Freer Wilderness Therapy programs (1997), Redcliff Ascent (1997), Omni Youth Services (2002), Mountain Homes Youth Ranch (2003), Soltreks (2004), Wendigo Lakes (2004), Summits Achievement (2005), Open Sky Wilderness Therapy (2006), Alaska Crossings (2007), Santiam Crossing (2009), and Second Nature Cascades (2009). We also value the support and future vision from other OBHRC research scientists DRs. Anita Tucker, Joanna Bettman-Schaefer, Christine Norton, and Ellen Behrens.

Special mention is directed to Karl Rohnke for granting permission to us, and to thousands of other professionals, to adapt the plethora of adventure experiences he created to the targeted needs of clients. His altruistic expressions of the products as well as processes of adventure programming present a wonderful model we strive to emulate.

Support from the Therapeutic Adventure Professional Group (TAPG) of the Association for Experiential Education (AEE) has remained invaluable as a professional source of growth for our own development as well as advancing the field. Combined with AEE's program accreditation process, this group remains one of the most innovative sources of professional development for adventure therapy. Through its efforts of professional conferences, its website, and the best practices initiative, we often stand in awe of the accomplishments this group regularly produces. Professional membership in this professional group is a wise choice for professional development.

The AEE's REAP and CORE initiatives remain on course as one of the most promising initiatives for the field's future. Dr. Bobbi Beale, Maurie Lung, and Tiffany Wynn represent the cornerstones of these initiatives, and we stand in deep respect of their tireless, continuous, and professional efforts.

Certainly particular aspects of the National Association for Therapeutic Schools and Programs (NATSAP) bear mentioning. The present efforts and future promise of NATSAP's research database and Practice Research Network (PRN), as well as other supporting professional practices, bodes well for the field's future.

Many of the principles and practices in this book have received invaluable feedback from other professionals through multiple national and international presentations. Probably the most notable of these were 10 years of the AEE Adventure Therapy Supervision Workshop (1999–2008), the AEE Kinesthetic Metaphor Workshop (2009–2011), and the Food For Thought Workshop coordinated at Georgia College in the February, 1996. Certainly, the feedback and input from thousands of participants utilizing the concepts in these workshops added invaluable feedback and a strong confirming evolutionary process to these professional practices. Without this input, the quality, if not the existence, of these refined techniques would not be possible. Gratitude to these participants is offered in the most genuine expression possible.

Students at our various universities remain a valuable source of inspiration and ongoing encouragement. We all feel very privileged to be involved with these individuals as the future of our field.

We would also like to thank Marta Moldvai, our senior editorial assistant at Routledge Mental Health Publications, for all her support and feedback. Her kind and thorough advice was helpful in continuing the process through its many alterations and adaptations.

Readers should interpret contributions of the authors as equal and integrated. Over the time of our work together, it became more and more difficult to determine when individual thoughts were unique to just one person. This is extremely evident in the book where concepts are often the extensions of the thinking of all three of us rather than a single individual. As colleagues, we have been blessed with professional relationships that simply make each of us better through our interactions.

Finally, we thank our families for their patience, as many of our professional endeavors to produce such a book have taken us away from them. While such support may be unknown and unnoticed to the reader, we fully recognize that without such love and encouragement of our professional endeavors this book would not occur.

About the Authors

Michael Gass, PhD, is a professor and coordinator of the Outdoor Education Program in the College of Health and Human Services at the University of New Hampshire (UNH). He received his PhD in experiential education from the University of Colorado at Boulder and completed postdoctoral studies in marriage and family therapy. Gass is a Clinical member of the American Association for Marriage and Family Therapy and a licensed marriage and family therapist.

He is the current editor of the *Journal for Therapeutic Schools and Programs*, published by the National Association of Therapeutic Schools and Programs (NATSAP). He directs two critical research initiatives in the field of adventure therapy—one as Director of the Outdoor Behavioral Healthcare Research Consortium and another as Director of the NATSAP Research Database.

In 1998, Gass received the Association for Experiential Education (AEE) Outstanding Experiential Teacher of the Year Award, and in 2002, he delivered the Kurt Hahn Address for AEE. In 2005, he received the UNH College of Health and Human Service's Distinguished Career Research Award as well the University's Award for Excellence in International Engagement in 2011.

Keith C. Russell, PhD, is an associate professor in the Recreation Program at Western Washington University. Dr. Russell's publications focus on the design, implementation, and evaluation of educational and therapeutic programs for youth. In 2011, he was awarded the Distinguished Researcher Award by the Association for Experiential Education. He is the founder and former director of the Outdoor Behavioral Research Cooperative (1999–2010) and serves as an evaluation consultant to organizations that use wilderness and adventure experiences to help youth and families create positive change. His research has appeared in the *Journal of Youth Violence and Juvenile Justice*, the *Journal of Groups in Addictions and Recovery, Child and Youth Care Forum,* the

International Journal of Wilderness, the *Journal of Experiential Education,* and the *Journal of Adventure Education and Outdoor Learning.*

H.L. "Lee" Gillis, PhD, is professor and chair of psychological science at Georgia College in Milledgeville, GA and is a licensed psychologist (#1335 GA). He received his undergraduate degree in psychology from Davidson College, his masters degree in psychology from Middle Tennessee State University, and his PHD in counseling psychology from The University of Georgia. He worked at two residential boarding schools where he ran outdoor programming: Glade Valley School (1977–1979) and The Webb School (1979–1982). He worked extensively with therapeutic programs at Project Adventure in Covington GA as a consulting psychologist from 1989 until 2010; He conducted numerous Adventure Based Counseling and advanced practice workshop for Project Adventure in the US and Europe. He has the distinction of both starting and ending a masters degree in psychology that specialized in adventure therapy (1994–1998). He has directed several videos of adventure based counseling, adventure activities (with Karl Rohnke), and metaphors (with Jude Hirsch). He has co-authored two seminal metaanalyses of adventure programming (1993 with Dana Cason and 2008 with Liz Speelman). Lee's work has appeared in the *Journal of the National Association of Therapeutic Schools & Programs, Journal of Child Sexual Abuse, Residential Treatment of Children & Youth, Journal for Specialist in Group Work, Journal of Experiential Education,* and *Journal of Group Psychotherapy, Psychodrama, and Sociometry.* He gave keynotes at the first two International Adventure Therapy conferences;1997 (Perth, Australia) and 2000 (Augsburg, Germany with Simon Priest). He was recognized by AEE with the Michael Stratton Practitioner of the year Award in 2000. He and his wife, Jude Hirsch, gave the 2010 Kurt Hahn Address at the AEE International Conference in Las Vegas, NV. Currently he continues to work on meta-analyses of adventure programming as well as measurements for both collective self efficacy and individual self efficacy.

Chapter 1

Introduction

Adventure therapy (AT), as it is defined in this book, is the prescriptive use of adventure experiences provided by mental health professionals, often conducted in natural settings that kinesthetically engage clients on cognitive, affective, and behavioral levels. Arriving at this definition was not easy, and it reflects the challenges faced by researchers, practitioners, and licensing and accrediting bodies in understanding a mental health approach that has largely been misunderstood and misinterpreted. On the one hand, AT is grounded in the Outward Bound model, which was developed in the United Kingdom by the legendary Kurt Hahn. Outward Bound uses wilderness expeditions designed to challenge participants to overcome their perceived limitations and develop an enhanced sense of self. On the other hand, AT could also use a challenge course as a tool to help families struggling with interpersonal dynamics develop new strategies to help them communicate with each other more effectively. It is for these and other reasons that multiple definitions of AT exist in the literature, leading to confusion on the part of researchers, educators, mental health practitioners, and others as to exactly what AT is and how it works to effectuate changes in individuals, groups, families, and organizations. The goal of this book is to address this ambiguity and to clearly and succinctly explore the history, evolution, theoretical foundations, current practices, and research on AT. In this way, the authors hope to incite discussion and dialogue that will strengthen and improve the design, delivery, and evaluation of AT as a viable and credible mental health approach.

The definition of AT has been a well-debated topic, if not a contentious one, due to multiple influences and widely varying applications. The evolution of the field is well chronicled in Chapter 2, with key influences being early therapeutic camping approaches, the emergence of Outward Bound in the 1960s in the United States, and the increased need for alternative programs for youth in therapeutic and correctional settings. A systematic and integrated effort on the part of researchers and practitioners emerged from these influences to more clearly define AT and identify its key characteristics. Kelly and Baer (1968) demonstrated that a 21-day standard Outward Bound course for groups of adjudicated youth was more effective in reducing recidivism and less costly than traditional treatment for adolescents in a correctional program. Programs for adjudicated youth using the Outward Bound approach dramatically increased during this time. Providing additional insight into the work by Kelly and Baer (1968), Kimball (1983) discussed the power of wilderness for young offenders in the Santa Fe Mountain Center AT program. Gillis and Bonney (1986) provided one of the early rationales for using adventure activities in group counseling, and grounded their discussion of AT in the Outward Bound process (Bacon, 1983), and Project Adventure's efforts to translate wilderness and adventure processes like Outward Bound into educational and counseling programs to be used in more urban settings (Rohnke, 1977). Gass (1993a) followed these efforts by editing the first comprehensive text on AT and discussed seven key areas that provided the basis for AT: (1) action-centered therapy, (2) unfamiliar environment, (3) climate of change, (4) assessment capabilities, (5) small group development and a caring community, (6) focus of successful behaviors (strengths) rather than dysfunctional behaviors (deficits), and (7) altered role of the therapist.

In 1997, another important event occurred when the International Adventure Therapy Committee held its first meeting in Perth, Australia, with the proceedings edited by Itin (1997). In the introduction, Itin states "there is no universally accepted definition of adventure therapy, or of what constitutes it and how it is best conducted" (p. vi). Itin did provide parameters that framed the discussion as to how AT had been defined to that point, with narrow clinical definitions consistent with sister fields like psychology, social work, and counseling on one end, and broader ones that believe AT could be any intervention that seeks to address maladaptive behaviors or support meta-level behaviors on the other end. Newes and Bandoroff (2004) later defined AT as a "therapeutic modality combining therapeutic benefits of adventure experiences and activities with those of more traditional modes of therapy" (p. 5) that integrates group-level processing and individual psychotherapy sessions as part of an overall therapeutic milieu. Newes and Bandoroff went on to discuss the implications of the debate, including asking questions as to what type of clinical and academic training best serves AT, as well as the need to explore the required qualifications and competencies of a practicing adventure therapist.

To this day, the debate and ongoing effort to define AT continues to cause a great deal of both semantic and professional confusion (Gillis, Gass, & Russell, 2008). Because of this, consumer groups, government agencies, academics, and professional councils have often created their own definitions. For example, the Bureau of Land Management (2008), which is charged with permitting programs to operate on public lands, defined wilderness/adventure therapy programs as "those programs intended to provide a less restrictive alternative to incarceration or hospitalization for youth who may require intervention to address emotional or behavioral challenges" (p. 1). The Council on Accreditation (2010), charged with accrediting and certifying AT programs operating in the United States, defined AT programs as "day or residential programs that provide an intensive, therapeutic experience based on outdoor, educational, clinical, and other activities that involve physical and psychological challenges" (p. 1). Although these definitions may suffice, the message sent to those interested in AT is clear: If we do not formally define AT ourselves, someone else may do so—and the definitions may be more harmful or distracting than they are constructive and focused.

We therefore believe it is important to define AT and, in doing so, reference and pay respect to the key historical programmatic and individual influences and efforts that have shaped AT over the past decades. For this reason, the definition proposed at the beginning of this chapter aims to be a reference point for theory development, practice, and research. Key elements found in AT that differentiate it from, or link it to, other therapeutic approaches integrated into this definition include:

- The positive influence of nature in the therapeutic healing process
- The use of eustress or the positive use of stress
- The active and direct use of client participation and responsibility in their therapeutic process
- The involvement in adventure experiences meaningful for the particular client, particularly in terms of natural consequences
- The focus on positive changes in the client's present and future functional behavior
- The strong ethic of care and support embraced throughout the therapeutic experience, particularly given the use of unfamiliar experiences in therapy

This list is meant to serve as a starting point to discuss AT, not as a definitive inventory of AT foundational elements. Certainly there are several other characteristics relevant to AT missing from this list; these are addressed elsewhere in this book in more detail. It is also important to note the use of the word *prescriptive* in this definition may raise some concerns among those historically involved with AT. We intentionally use this word to denote the ideally co-created way an adventure therapist (or treatment team promoting AT) would know their client (or client group) so well that an adventure experience would be tailored to the clients' need(s) with full attention given to the clients' affect, behavior, and cognitive abilities. We are not advocating a medical model in the pejorative sense; rather, we are advocating intention, co-creation, assessment, dosage, fidelity, and most of all the power to heal, restore, or prevent without doing harm.

We also are considering the changes in the role of the therapist in AT versus other "standard practices" psychotherapy. Adventure therapists actively design and frame adventure experiences around critical issues for clients, focusing on the development of specific treatment outcomes—and then get out of the chair! When utilizing adventure experiences with clients, adventure-based therapists are removed from serving as the central vehicle of functional change. The experience takes on the central medium for orchestrating change, freeing therapists to take on a more mobile role (e.g., for supporting, joining, confronting) in the co-construction of change processes with the client. Combined with the informal setting of adventure experiences, the dynamics of this approach remove many of the barriers limiting interaction. While still maintaining clear and appropriate boundaries, adventure therapists often become more approachable and achieve greater interaction with clients when compared to traditional therapists.

ADVENTURE THERAPY PRACTICE

Rather than break AT into a typology based on various programmatic models, we believe that AT is better understood by exploring dimensions that help situate how AT is delivered by mental health professionals, programs, agencies, and managed care organizations. In this way, we hope to curb the confusion surrounding the definition debate, where AT has been referred to by a variety of terms, such as wilderness therapy, wilderness-adventure therapy, adventure-based counseling, adventure-based therapy, wilderness challenge program, and wilderness experience program. As shown in Figure 1.1, these dimensions include:

1. The degree where the approach utilizes the "mountains speak for themselves" factor, in which nature plays a key therapeutic role in facilitating thought, reflection, and intended therapeutic change, or is facilitated more directly by the therapist
2. The degree to which AT is viewed as primary, adjunctive, or tangential to the therapeutic process
3. Practical linkages or theoretical connections to existing forms of therapy or treatment
4. How and to what degree nature or wilderness environments are used
5. The length or depth of the intervention in terms of time and resources allocated
6. Individual- or group-based milieu used in treatment

The first dimension embraces the ongoing discussion of the powerful role that nature plays in AT, referencing the phrase coined by Rustie Baillie of the Colorado Outward Bound School when he famously said, "Let the mountains

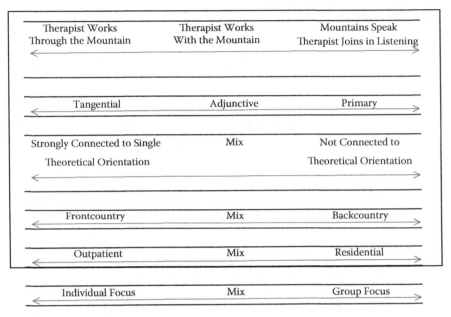

Therapist Works Through the Mountain	Therapist Works With the Mountain	Mountains Speak Therapist Joins in Listening
Tangential	Adjunctive	Primary
Strongly Connected to Single Theoretical Orientation	Mix	Not Connected to Theoretical Orientation
Frontcountry	Mix	Backcountry
Outpatient	Mix	Residential
Individual Focus	Mix	Group Focus

FIGURE 1.1 Dimensions that help distinguish adventure therapy approaches.

speak for themselves" (James, 1980, p. 1). The statement was made in reaction to a movement within Outward Bound circles to add an intellectual element to the courses through directed and guided facilitation of student experiences, rather than just letting the experience speak for itself and allowing participants to take from the course what they needed. In his famous essay on the subject, James captures the essence of the discussion in stating, "The experience happens naturally if instructors are skilled enough to take their students safely through the adventurous activities that make up Outward Bound, and when they do that, the mountains are extraordinary teachers indeed" (p. 1). Applied in an AT context, if therapists are working toward the "mountains speak" for themselves side of the spectrum, they allow the client to guide the process in reaction to what the environment and experience is providing for the client. If therapists tend toward the more active side, they will include interactive processes and working with or through the environment as a therapeutic tool and the experience as a reflecting catalyst to help the clients integrate the experiences to their lives.

The second dimension refers to whether the use of adventure and activity is primary (i.e., first in importance and direct and immediate in its utilization), adjunctive (an additional component of treatment used in conjunction with more traditional models), or tangential (indirectly related to treatment and used more as a recreational outlet for clients). This dimension reflects the idea that adventure and activity, and their subsequent use, varies widely across

AT approaches and programs. In fact, this question was used on a recent survey of residential treatment programs in the United States (Russell & Gillis, 2010), where the majority indicated that adventure and activity were adjunctive (64.4%), with slightly over a third indicating primary (33.3%), and only 2% noting their use was tangential.

The third dimension refers to the degree to which the AT approach is grounded in traditional therapeutic treatment approaches or has evolved through time-tested practice into an integrated approach unique to the populations served and treatment strategies employed. In previous discussions of theoretical foundations in AT, the approach has been referred to as eclectic (Russell, 2006b) and multimodal (Newes & Bandoroff, 2004), referring to AT practitioners integrating different theoretical frameworks like cognitive behavioral therapy and family therapy in orienting their approach. The third dimension reflects this diversity and illustrates that some programs may rely heavily on one approach, orient their programs to an eclectic approach, or operate from a position of time-tested practice.

The fourth dimension reflects how nature and wilderness or backcountry environments are used as therapeutic factors in the treatment process. Simply put, AT occurs in challenge course environments (frontcountry), city and county parks or lakes in the form of guided nature walks or paddling a canoe (frontcountry), climbing areas within a 2-hour drive from a metropolitan area (mixed), or in remote wilderness areas miles from the nearest road (backcountry). The more prominent role that wilderness and backcountry expeditions and travel play in the treatment process, the farther to the right on the spectrum the AT approach will sit.

The fifth dimension speaks to whether the treatment is residential (meaning the clients leave the normal routines of life and are wholly engaged in the treatment process) or conducted in the flow of everyday life through the use of intermittent (e.g., traditional weekly) visits to an adventure therapist. It can also be assumed that the AT residential treatment approach would involve clients who may have greater symptomology and, to work with our definition, have more work to do to strengthen functional behaviors and/or reduce dysfunctional behaviors. It may also be assumed that this spectrum also represents the continuum of care model, in that clients may move up and down the spectrum as they require less and more intensive treatment, respectively.

The final dimension reflects whether the key therapeutic milieu is based on an individual or group focus of treatment. In general, the group-focused milieu appears to be the most widely used. It originates from the Outward Bound ten-man group model, which was adopted by many AT programs that use wilderness and backcountry travel to a significant degree. However, this appears to be changing as several programs now focus on the individual and not framing treatment on the group-based approach due to the potential effects of exposing clients to maladaptive behaviors they otherwise would not be exposed to. The pros and cons of this could be a noteworthy focus for future research on process and practice.

There are no doubt other dimensions that were not included in this section. Rather than form an exhaustive list, we begin with these factors to help illustrate the variety of ways that AT can be delivered based on clients' needs, cost, risk management, practicality, and myriad other factors that shape AT approaches. It is hoped that these dimensions will serve as a springboard for future discussion in exploring how and why AT is being delivered to best meet the clients' needs.

ACCESS TO ADVENTURE THERAPY

Our discussion of AT is also centered on fundamental principles of human rights and equity in AT practice. Equitable access to mental health care has been a persistent problem presenting unique challenges to parents, school officials, youth workers, and policy makers on many levels. Where should concerned parents turn for help when their child begins exhibiting signs of depression, acting out in school, or showing signs of dependent substance use? Where should a 16-year-old girl go when she begins having doubts about her sexuality and fears her parents are not going to be able to accept her for who she is? When school officials are concerned that a student is withdrawing further and further into a dark and violent place, to whom do they bring their concerns? On the surface, the answer does not seem complicated; in fact, it should not be complicated, as access to mental health treatment should be basic and fundamental human right. For example, if a youth is having trouble, then a counselor or therapist would be consulted and a plan would be established to get the necessary help and support needed to address the personal or social issues causing the problem. Unfortunately, this rarely happens because youth, parents, and concerned professionals are often confronted with a dizzying array of challenges and barriers as they seek what should be a basic service that should be provided to all youth in need.

This issue is a growing concern, especially for young people at the lower end of socioeconomic status, as research and trend data suggest that six to nine million youth in the United States have mental or behavioral problems (Kataoka & Zhang, 2002). More than 40% of this population do not receive treatment when services are warranted and/or referred (U.S. Department of Health and Human Services, 2005), and the majority of those who do receive treatment are typically seen in nonspecialized settings that may not be appropriate for their specific age or diagnosis (Burns et al., 2004). In one study, youth identified two common barriers to accessing care: "I thought the problem would go away" and "I didn't want my parents to know" (Samargia, Saewyc, & Elliot, 2006, p. 21).

Affordable and accessible mental health services should be available equally to all clients, regardless of race, socioeconomic status, or any other characteristic that presents additional barriers to appropriate and affordable care. We believe this is a basic human right. Adventure therapists and related professionals have an obligation to create access points and facilitate interventions to help address many of the barriers and stigmas associated with traditional models of youth mental health service delivery. Adventure therapists can (and should) be vital partners in helping to realize the objectives of increased adolescent health and well-being proposed by the U.S. Department of Health and Human Services' (2005) Healthy People 2010 initiative. Clients need to be safe and protected. This declaration clearly illustrates "the engagement and advocacy for those in our society who are economically, socially, politically, and/or culturally underresourced" (p. 11).

Underresourced groups include, for example, minority adolescents who have poorer health status as reflected by a broad range of health outcomes and behaviors, including diet, physical activity, obesity, substance use, sexually transmitted diseases, and, not surprisingly, mental health symptoms. Groups of special concern include Native American youth, who have very high suicide and substance abuse rates; African American youth, who have very high homicide rates; and recent war veterans, who have suicide rates currently exceeding the national average. There are many underlying causes for the disparities in health status of minority youth, including prejudice and stereotypes that underlie a healthcare system that systematically works against them. AT programs and settings can play a dynamic role in reducing these injustices by actively providing a gateway to programs and services to all individuals, regardless of their age, race, color, veteran status, religion, disability, marital status, ethnicity, gender, sexual orientation, or national origin. We encourage adventure therapists to follow the guidelines established in the ethical principles of the Association for Experiential Education (AEE).

ORGANIZATION OF THE BOOK

The goal of this book is to present the reader with an extensive review of the history, guiding theoretical frameworks, current practices, research and evaluation, and ethical considerations of AT. The outline of the book is as follows.

Chapter 2. A History of Adventure Therapy

Chapter 2 explores the historical origins and evolution of AT theory and practice. Our friend and colleague, Dr. Will White of Summit Adventures in Stow, ME, did extensive research and spent an untold amount of time interviewing the living legends of AT to craft an authentic history of the field. He graciously condensed his work into this chapter, in which he identifies the start date, name, information about the organization, and the significance of the organization to the evolution of AT. He also reveals the extensive history of the use of adventure for character development and treatment of young people in the United States; identifies the origins of the three areas of implementation of AT (i.e., therapeutic camps, wilderness therapy, adventure-based therapy); highlights significant organizations and leadership influencing the field; and presents some of the controversies related to adventure programs for youth.

Chapter 3. A Psychotherapeutic Foundation for Adventure Therapy

Chapter 3 presents an AT response to Paul's (1967) ultimate question—what treatment, by whom, is most effective for which individual with what specific problem, under which set of circumstances?—by offering an integrative approach to psychotherapy. This approach begins with what the client presents to the therapist in terms of affect, behavior, and cognition. It then connects this to the relationship of therapist to client, client to peer group, and client to larger systems (e.g., family, school, community) that are part of the change maintenance process.

Chapter 4. Foundations

Chapter 4 explores how AT works. Key theoretical and practical foundations relevant to the AT process are reviewed and presented. A conceptual foundation of AT is presented, which includes the integration of the Walsh and Golins Outward Bound Process model within an AT context to illustrate how AT works in therapeutic settings. It is argued that the AT process provides an autonomy-supportive atmosphere conducive to participants finding an internal source of motivation to begin thinking about change, and establishes the framework where three basic psychological needs of participants in therapy can be met by the subsequent social milieu and adventure-based activities that occur in this environment. The three psychological needs being met through these experiences are autonomy (through nondirective inquiry and reflection), competence (through provision of activity, demonstrated skill acquisition, and other factors), and relatedness (through a relationship with self, peers, therapists, and leaders characterized by relationships that are facilitated in the environment by genuineness, unconditional positive regard, empathy, and concreteness).

Chapter 5. Exploring the Foundation of Nature's Role in Adventure Therapy

Chapter 5 presents a theoretical framework that supports the role of nature in AT. AT has been criticized for not recognizing and discussing the value and role that nature and wilderness play in therapeutic contexts. In fact, many researchers argue that the main therapeutic power in outdoor AT interventions is nature, and the work of therapists and leaders simply supplements the power of nature to heal. Chapter 5 directly addresses this issue and explores the philosophical, theoretical, and practical dimensions of nature's role in AT. When delving deeper into nature's restorative role, fundamental questions arise that form the foundation for this chapter and frame the discussions about why spending time in nature is inherently therapeutic for individuals. We approach this chapter from the perspective of citizens of a Western industrialized nation, but recognize that other cultures, in place and time, hold the view that nature and humans are not separate from one another.

Chapter 6. Adventure Therapy Models

Chapter 6 provides examples of current AT programs and how they are implemented with various clients. Some AT programs primarily address issues of **prevention** (e.g., adolescent substance abuse prevention, high school dropout prevention, underachieving adolescents, reintegration program for soldiers returning from combat situations), whereas others are more **treatment oriented** (e.g., adjudicated populations, adolescent sex offenders, alternative public schools). Under current evidence-based practices and accountability, many programs have been required to explain program practices through the use of logic models. Logic models are typically constructed along a linear continuum as shown in Figure 6.1. Programmers create these models by either identifying the resources professionals use in the treatment of clients (also sometimes referred to as inputs), the clients' needs, or both. These needs and resources are used to intentionally design adventure activities and experiences for clients' treatment and interventions. When properly conducted, client treatment should produce positive outputs and outcomes that result in immediate, intermediate, and long-term productive changes. Logic models are presented in Chapter 6 for several program models to illustrate the intentional program design process of AT (e.g., resiliency programs for adolescent substance abuse prevention, dropout prevention programs, reintegration programs for combat soldiers, adjudicated youth, programs for struggling adolescents, alternative high schools).

Chapter 7. Assessment in Adventure Therapy

Chapter 7 begins with a quotation from one of the earliest adventure therapists, Rocky Kimball, on his reflection of using the wilderness. In comparing the wilderness to a Rorschach ink blot test, we find that he was partly correct. Since that time, we have learned that AT assessment is not a one-time snapshot projective experience, but a fluid continuous cycle that continually feeds information to the joint therapeutic relationship of client and therapist. The CHANGES model (from a macro level) and the original GRABBS model (from a micro level) seek to inform the client and therapist on which pathway functional behavior seems to reside. The seven steps that make up the CHANGES model are Context, Hypotheses, Action, Novelty, Generating, Evaluation, and Solutions. This model possesses the three elements of AT assessment: Diagnosis and Design, Delivery, and Debrief.

Chapter 8. Practicing Adventure Therapy

Chapter 8 outlines how adventure therapists connect positive and functional changes in adventure experiences with positive and functional changes in clients' lives using kinesthetic metaphors. Through the use of double entendres occurring in language as well as behavior, facilitators are able to proactively use double entendre structures from clients' lives with guidance from clients, match them with a parallel structure (i.e., isomorphic structure) from an appropriate experience before the AT experience begins, and use this information to join intervening experiences and clients' lives. The goal is the provision of a parallel kinesthetic structure where successful resolution of the intervening experience mirrors and provides guidance and meaning to a successful resolution of the clients' issue.

Chapter 9. Risk Management of Adventure Therapy Programs

The concept of risk is incredibly important for the AT field. Actual risks taken by clients through adventure experiences are often critical and key factors in the process of functional change. In fact, many adventure therapists would argue that not incorporating some form of risk in AT undermines some of the most critical elements (e.g., eustress, contrast, structured challenges) of this psychotherapeutic approach. It is also important to remember that the types of risks in AT are not only physical ones. Certainly social and emotional risks, when applied appropriately, provide an important milieu for functional change with the right client. Conversely, when applied inappropriately, these risks can also be quite damaging. In many ways, the concept of risk is the ultimate paradox in the AT field. Too much risk or inappropriate risk places clients in unnecessary positions of danger and overwhelms clients to a point where functional change fails to become an outcome. With too little risk, clients remain in a state of homeostasis, failing to be motivated to change dysfunctional behaviors and gather new perspectives. Just as AT interventions need to be tailored to specific individual or group needs, so do levels of risk. Therefore, in many ways, managing risk at physical, psychological, emotional, and social levels is one of the most important abilities of an adventure therapist. To demonstrate how to appropriately manage risks as an adventure therapist for constructive client change, Chapter 9 examines categories of physical, psychological, and medication risks. This chapter emphasizes that the appropriate use of risk, not its elimination (even if this was humanly possible), is the goal of risk management as an adventure therapist.

Chapter 10. Adventure Therapy Competencies

Many professionals are drawn to the practice of AT for the advantages of using adventure experiences in therapy, its solution-oriented approach, the richness found in the assessment process, and its effectiveness in reaching clients with whom other approaches may have failed. In order to use AT appropriately, professionals must be competent in both the adventure and therapeutic aspects of the field. Chapter 10 addresses the following questions:

- What qualities should competent adventure therapists possess?
- What type of training do they receive?
- How are they different or similar to other mental health therapists?

In seeking answers to these questions, four sources have informed the development of AT competencies: adventure programming competencies, mental health therapist competencies, specific therapeutic population competencies, and past explorations into the development of AT competencies. Chapter 10 provides an overview of the development of each of these four sources, presents a current model for assessing levels of competency in appropriate areas, and offers an additional model inviting adventure therapists to achieve new levels of excellence and enrichment beyond basic competency levels.

Chapter 11. Supervision

Chapter 11 discusses supervision in AT, as well as specific supervision models that could be used in AT practice. Supervision of therapeutic practice is one of the cornerstones of mental health professions and is intended to provide professional growth for therapists, more effective therapy for clients, and some measure of protection for the welfare of clients and the public. The main purpose of supervision is to provide a source of information on the content, processes, and insights into situations that have become difficult, if not problematic, for therapists and their clients.

One active experiential supervision model that has emerged to address these issues is the ENHANCES model (Gass & Gillis, 2010). The ENHANCES model was designed to use unique sources of cognitive, affective, and kinesthetic insights to create structurally relevant experiential events that enhance the effectiveness of the supervision and feedback process. The model has been refined over the years through presentations of the model with case studies at the Association for Experiential Education's annual international conferences, as well as through pilot testing and feedback from other professionals from their use of the model. Three case studies are included in Chapter 11, as well as links to online video clips.

Chapter 12. Adventure Therapy Ethics

Chapter 12 addresses the many decisions that are made on a daily basis by adventure therapists concerning what is right, best, or appropriate for their clients. Many of these decisions involve possible and differing choices in the selection of professional behaviors, and sometimes these choices conflict with one another. Adventure therapists often face the following questions:

- How should I interact with my client?
- What should I do for my client's specific issues as an adventure therapist?
- What is the right technique to use with my client?
- Is this the most appropriate AT experience to use with my client?
- What is an example of good behavior in this AT experience?
- What is the best way to care for my client given his or her needs?

For each of these questions, a variety of answers could be provided. When one of these answers is selected as the best answer, when the answer fits most appropriately into the relative context of the client's life, and when the resulting actions for the client are decided to be better than other choices, then we are concerned with ethics. This can be difficult and potentially contentious, but some of the most important professional decisions made in AT deal with ethics. The field of ethics covers a wide variety of issues and subjects. Whole cultures and countries make important ethical decisions every day based on their belief systems. This is also true for professional organizations intersecting with AT programs, such as like the American Psychological Association, American Alliance of Marriage and Family Therapists, National Association of Social Workers, American Counseling Association, and Association for Specialists of Group Work. Chapter 12 centers its attention on how adventure therapists should prepare themselves for ethical situations and respond to ethical dilemmas.

Chapter 13. Research and Evaluation

Chapter 13 presents an overview of critical issues in AT that research and evaluation should address by asking the hard questions about process and outcomes in AT. In addition, the role that research and evaluation plays in the development of AT theory is presented, citing a historical lack of theory development as noted in the AT literature. The challenges that researchers face when researching the practice of AT from a clinical perspective are also discussed. Chapter 13 concludes with a brief overview of the the outcomes or effects of AT on participants and a call for a more systematic and active research agenda in the field.

Chapter 14. A View of the Future for Adventure Therapy

The questions that stem from Chapter 14 are many. The question that begins the chapter—will AT remain or return to being an application of other therapies or will it emerge as a profession unto itself? (Gass, 1993a, p. 415)—remains unanswered. Will government control of reporting structures for any alleged or real incidents in residential treatment come to fruition and provide hardships that shut down wilderness therapy programs? Will land access become so restrictive for those who take groups into the wilderness that programs have no place to go and thus have to close? Will wilderness therapy go the way of corporate adventure and price itself out of the market, becoming the "boutique therapy" it does not want to be? Will clear academic and internship training paths in adventure and wilderness therapy emerge for social workers, professional counselors, marriage and family therapists, psychologists, and psychiatrists? Will there be lifelong career paths in adventure and wilderness therapy that extend to direct care practitioners beyond their 20s that do not have to involve going into administration? Will technology enhance our safety in the wilderness or become an attractive nuisance? Will social networking provide ongoing support for participants and parents of wilderness therapy clients so that there is sustained positive aftercare that supports changes made while in treatment? Many of these issues have surfaced since Gass asked the previously stated question in 1993.

Other questions asked in this chapter include: Will there be more widespread acceptance of AT as a valid, research-supported treatment? Will multiple graduate training opportunities exist for budding adventure therapists who can help refine this prevention and treatment approach for a variety of diagnoses? Will funded opportunities exist to help researchers provide undeniable evidence of this powerful approach to treatment? Can the reader make a commitment to influence public policy and the acceptance of AT as a viable approach to healing and health? It only takes a spark—or perhaps a sustained flame—from passionate professionals and eager students joining together to offer valid answers to these questions.

HOW TO USE THIS BOOK

This book is written for several audiences, and each audience will extract different levels of knowledge from the text. As you reread certain sections, you may find yourself discovering different perspectives and deeper applications of what is being offered for consideration. Readers are invited to debate, challenge, agree, disagree, and even dismiss what we have offered as they experience this book. But most importantly, as writers and professionals who are deeply invested in AT, we sincerely hope that you will take the elements of what we offer, adapt and expand on them accordingly, and use your efforts productively to further the field not only for AT professionals, but for the clients we are invited to work with in co-creating better lives for them. We wrote this book with the sincere hope that the next generations of adventure therapists will be much more effective for clients than we ever were or could ever imagine being. If the book results in this accomplishment, we will have succeeded.

Using the paradigm from the AT competencies in Chapter 12, there are elements in this book that emerging professionals will find new, exciting, and instructive to follow as they work with clients in the first few years of their professional development. Other elements may add to the proficiency of more seasoned adventure therapists. It is not so much that many of the ideas in this book will be radically novel, but they will add new and sometimes multiple perspectives on current practices and the way AT professionals work with clients.

This text seeks to create the next platform of AT for future professionals to use. Although some chapters may seem basic for the experienced adventure therapist, other chapters will encapsulate certain concepts bound to affect the field and its current practices. Risk management may not be the same for the AT field building on the concepts presented in this book. AT competencies may not be as open as they have been in the past. New considerations around ethics and social justice will guide the field to examine its approaches differently. The concept of evidence-based practices may no longer be a fallacy and fiction, but more of the future reality and guiding principles.

This book may create controversy. Who gets to write the history of AT? Who says this technique works better than others? Who says this is what emerging adventure therapists should be taught, what qualities represent competency in AT, and what qualities should stand for an exemplary adventure therapist? Who are we to say what is the future of AT? Certainly, no single source can represent a comprehensive perspective of an entire field. We welcome the forthcoming discussions from this text, with the sincere hope that such discussions will not just to lead to deconstructive analysis alone, but an evolving and constructive process that makes AT more effective for clients. This is our intent and the pragmatic value on which this book will be judged.

THE BEAUTY OF NEW IDENTITIES

Mark Ames

It was the last night in the field for the boys. Seven students from a residential treatment program in Wyoming were completing a 26-day wilderness expedition in the Teton and Snake River Mountain ranges. Tonight was their ceremony night—a night when field staff, therapists, and students gathered to feast on fresh food, tell stories, celebrate accomplishments, and reflect on their group's month-long wilderness journey. My pickup truck was filled with all the essentials: BBQ grill, marinated ribs, salads, soda, chips, and a few props for the celebration. As I drove up to the campsite smiling, students eagerly greeted me to help unload, get a hug, and quickly share the most recent events and discoveries. They were a wilderness group, totally comfortable with their wild greasy hairdos, sweaty smelly t-shirts, smudged faces, stiff socks, and variety of scratches and bug bites. I could feel their pride in all of it.

After feasting, the charcoal turned into campfire and the boys were asked to get ready for the evening's group. We all found our place around the fire in a moment of collective silence. The field staff then took the boys back through their journey by reflecting on a special event or two from each day, hoping to trigger students' own reflection of the experience. As the staff talked, I took notice of the boys' faces in the firelight and their collection of beads, woven necklaces, and feathers—all symbols and representations of goals, commitments, friendships, and connections they had made. When the reflection brought us to the present moment, the boys were asked to answer four questions.

The questions were based on themes we believe serve the purpose of reminding us of what the essential qualities and touchstones are for journeying well through life. People are universally propelled or drawn toward mystery, beauty, and community. The fourth question was based on the Hero's Journey tale and asked the boys to share a glimpse of the new identity they wanted to carry over to their family and community back home. During the course of their 26-day trip, the field staff had guided the boys toward these themes, drawing from a quiver of personal experiences, activities, traditions, and knowledge of the boys' issues. The ceremony was their payoff, hearing what the boys were taking away from the trip.

The responses to **beauty** brought on descriptions of waterfalls, triple rainbows, and views from high places. One boy shared that the view of the Tetons and the clouds from the top of Starvation Peak made it feel like everything was perfect and he broke into tears.

With the question of **mystery** and what made them wonder, most of the boys turned to nature, wondering what the mother bear and her cubs were feeling, how the mountains were formed, what made weather, or what they would see over the next hill. One boy wondered about how they all could live out in the wilderness without the usual things.

Development of **community** was a big focus of the trip and the boys easily recalled times when it felt good to help each other out and accomplish what they set out to do, stick together as a team, circle up and talk about things, and develop friendships despite their differences.

The final question about a glimpse of a **new identity** pushed the boys to be a little more insightful. Their answers were thoughtful. They talked about discovering self-esteem, perseverance, determination, patience, trust in others, and helpfulness. Some realized they needed to take action for things to change. One boy thought about how small he was in the big picture.

The boys sat around the fire and shared their stories for over 2 hours. What amazed me most is how well they had learned to listen to each other. At the end, there was no fighting over chocolate, marshmallows, and graham crackers—just sharing. This is what I would call adventure therapy.

My path to becoming an adventure therapist started with my outdoor experiences growing up and wanting to be outdoors. My education in college started in environmental sciences and forestry and ended in outdoor education. For my senior internship in outdoor education in 1981, I worked in the Alpha House, which was an early residential/wilderness program run by the Department of Corrections in Corvallis, Oregon. From there I moved to Wyoming and started working for Red Top Meadows, a new residential treatment program where I had the opportunity to start doing wilderness trips on weekends with the students. Over the course of the next 30 years, Red Top expanded and developed a wilderness therapy program that was an integral part of the overall residential/school program. We learned as we went along, and we still learn with the students by spending about 50 days in the field during their stay. Red Top has been an Association for Experiential Education accredited program since 1999. I have served as Chair of the Therapeutic Adventure Professional Group within the Association for Experiential Education and currently am a member of the Accreditation Council.

Chapter 2

A History of Adventure Therapy

Will White

This chapter presents a brief history of the evolution of the field of adventure therapy (AT). It is only a brief history because an all-encompassing history of the field could fill several volumes of books. The many venues where AT has operated are full of innovations, challenges, setbacks, and growth. At its core, the history of AT is about organizations and leaders who often began their practices outside the behavioral health mainstream. This chapter reveals the extensive history of the use of adventure for character development and treatment of young people in the United States and highlights significant organizations and leadership influencing the field. In addition, we discuss the origins of the three areas of implementation of AT, as initially identified by Gass (1993a): long-term residential camping, adventure-based therapy, and wilderness therapy. This chapter updates these terms and refers to therapeutic camps (which include both long- and short-term camps), adventure-based therapy, and wilderness therapy (which includes mountaineering and primitive skills-based programs). We also present some of the controversies surrounding adventure programs for youth, including reports that are related to cases of participant abuse and death, because AT professionals should be well versed in all aspects of the field's history to avoid the problems of the past.

In this chapter, organizations were chosen for discussion because their models, actions, or activities served as catalysts for change in the AT field. It should be noted that each organization influenced the field in different ways and not always for the better. Also, the focus in this chapter is on AT for youth, although we do include some adult organizations as well.

THE ORIGINS OF ADVENTURE THERAPY

The origins of AT can be traced back to the 1800s, when organized summer camps for youth emerged in the United States. According to McNeil (1957, p. 3), the initial aim of organized summer camping was about therapy for young people. The first summer camps came into being because "deeply rooted in our cultural conception of mental hygiene (health) for the developing child has always been the view that 'idleness' or 'undirected activity' is destructive to character." Summer camps were designed to create communities focused on physical and mental growth for young people under the direction of healthy adult role models. They evolved as an antidote to the perceived physical and moral decline of youth due to the changing industrial society and its movement toward mechanization and urban living. The first organized summer camp originated at a New England boarding school in 1861 called the Gunnery School. Along with the second organized summer camp at Camp Chocorua, the camps marked the beginning of theories that would shape future thinking in the field of organized camping and set the foundation for AT. During the late 1800s and early 1900s, organized summer camps flourished in the United States and around the world. However, it was not until the 1920s that the first therapeutic camps specifically designed for psychologically challenged youth opened in the United States.

1881: Camp Chocorua

Camp Chocorua was established in 1881 on Burnt Island on Squam Lake in New Hampshire. This program, unlike the Gunnery School, was independent of any organization or school, and its explicit purpose was to change young peoples' behavior. According to Eells (1986), Camp Chocorua began as an experiment by its founder, Ernest Balch, a deeply religious man and Dartmouth College student who had strong opinions on the perils of wealthy American youth. During his time as a professional, Balch was considered by many educators to be a radical because he used the outdoors for character training. Balch and his brothers were raised in New Hampshire, where their minister father encouraged his children to learn how to live off the land and survive in the wilderness. At Dartmouth College, Balch was exposed to wealthy boys who did not have the same value system related to work and did not have any knowledge of the outdoors. Balch developed the camp in order to combat "the miserable existence of wealthy adolescent boys in the summer when they must accompany their parents to fashionable resorts and fall prey to the evils of life in high society" (Eells, 1986, p. 7).

Balch wanted campers to become "responsible, independent, and resourceful" and so there were "no servants, no class distinctions, and no snobbery" at his camp (Eells, 1986, p. 7). The camp did not have a mess hall or cooks as all meals were made over an open fire by the campers. Every camper had to learn how to swim, sail, and paddle a canoe in all types of weather. Not only were outdoor skills essential, but Balch believed each boy should learn the value of money in a capitalist society; therefore, each boy had an allowance of 25 cents per week, which was earned by completing chores. The camp ran like a small community with a church, bank, court system, and a camp newspaper. The camp also possessed an intricate system to develop responsibility in campers, as well as written objectives referred to as the Camp Chocorua Principles. These principles focused on: "1) the development of a sense of responsibility in the boy, both for himself and others and 2) appreciation of the worthiness of work" (Eells, 1986, p. 8).

The critical ideas of addressing the overindulgence of youth and increasing personal responsibility for young people via time in the wilderness originated at Camp Chocorua with Ernest Balch. Camp Chocoura closed after 8 years when Balch felt he proved his point about the value of outdoor experiences to other educators. Balch would continue to be contacted throughout his life by other educators, camp founders, and directors for his theories and experiences in running Camp Chocorua. His radical ideas would later become the foundation of summer camps across the United States. A majority of early organized summer camps used Camp Chocorua principles as an outline for their organizations, including the first summer camp for girls, Camp Arey in Arey, New York, which first enrolled girls in 1892 (Eells, 1986).

The development of Camp Chocorua was critical to the evolution of AT because it was the beginning of the organized summer camp movement that would eventually include campers with psychological issues. This was the first organization that intentionally used adventure to impact adolescents so that they would become responsible, independent, and resourceful young adults.

1910: Boy Scouts of America

While organized summer camps were expanding in the United States, a systematic program of character development based on a military model came into being in the early 1900s. The Boy Scouts of America was founded in 1907 in England by Lieutenant-General Robert Baden-Powell, a former war hero and author (Rowan, 2005). As an advisor to the British Empire, Baden-Powell recognized that many English youth performed poorly in the military because they had no outdoor skills and did not respect authority. Baden-Powell wanted to "do something to improve the character of boys," so he developed a "comprehensive scheme for boy training" (p. 24). In August 1907, he brought an economically diverse group of 22 boys for a 2-week camping experience on Brownsea Island on the southern tip of England to teach them outdoor skills, character education, and military training. The experience was published in 1908 in the book *Scouting for Boys,* which became quite popular in England. In 1910, Baden-Powell retired from the military to work full time promoting scouting in Britain and abroad. Baden-Powell started Girl Guides (later known as Girl Scouts in the United States) with support from his sister in 1910 after requests from numerous girls for a program for them.

Scouting came to America because of a scout's random encounter with an American traveler in 1909 by the name of William D. Boyce. Boyce was a wealthy publisher who was visiting London when an unknown Boy Scout offered to help him cross a busy street (Rowan, 2005). So impressed by the boy's refusal of a tip, Boyce learned all he could about scouting and brought the organization to the United States. Boyce incorporated the Boy Scouts of America (BSA) in 1910, but he did not have the time or platform to make the organization grow. Shortly thereafter, Boyce had a meeting with Edgar M. Robinson, the secretary for the international department of the Young Men's Christian Association (YMCA), to discuss ways to expand scouting in the United States. Robinson decided with Boyce that the YMCA would be a good organization to help promote the Boys Scout movement in the United States. Boyce then turned the organization over to Robinson, who opened the first BSA office in June 1910 at a YMCA in New York City. With the financial support of Boyce, the BSA was developed through YMCA affiliates and spread rapidly across the United States (Rowan, 2005).

Ernest Seton and Daniel Beard were also pivotal to the evolution of the BSA. An author and naturalist, Seton developed the Woodcraft League in 1902 after his house in Connecticut was vandalized by local boys (Rowan, 2005). The Woodcraft League was an outdoor program consisting of "tribes" of boys who practiced Native American primitive outdoor skills they learned from Seton's book, *The Birchbark Roll*. Seton met Baden-Powell in 1907 and gave him a copy of *The Birchbark Roll*. Seton was influential in the adoption of Native American primitive skills by the BSA, and served as the author of the first Boy Scout Handbook and as the first Chief Scout. Some of the significant additions Seton added to the BSA were Native American primitive skills and rituals that differentiated the organization from Scouting in England. Beard, a naturalist, artist, and devout Christian, founded the Sons of Daniel Boone in 1905 to expose boys to nature and "instill the spirit of the pioneers" (Rowan, 2005, p. 26). Beard folded the Sons of Daniel Boone into the BSA and founded the first scout troop (Troop 1); he also was a national scout commissioner for 30 years. All the men involved in the early days of the Boy Scouts in America and Britain had "a common goal—to develop character in boys" (Rowan, 2005, p. 30).

BSA was one of the earliest and largest organizations to combine the use of the outdoors to help develop the character of adolescents. The BSA still currently places more teenagers into the outdoors than any other single organization in the United States (Eells, 1986). The BSA also has well-publicized controversies including cases of sexual abuse and exclusion of atheists or gay participants (Boyle, 1994; Greenhouse, 2000; Sudetic, 2000). Yet the BSA also remains the largest and arguably most successful volunteer organization focused on character development for adolescents in the United States. The largest sponsor of the BSA is the Church of Jesus Christ of Latter-day Saints, based in Utah (Sudetic, 2000), which is also home to a large number of wilderness therapy programs (Krakauer, 1995).

The BSA and its leaders influenced the field of AT in several ways. The BSA was the first systematic program to incorporate adventure as an avenue for character development. BSA goals for youth have always been about increasing personal responsibility and service to others. The BSA incorporated the use of Native American skills and rituals, which subsequently have been used by many therapeutic camps and wilderness therapy programs. It is important to note that the use of Native American skills and rituals by non–Native Americans is a continually debated and contentious subject in the AT field. The first BSA summer camp opened in 1910 and started a massive movement of scout camps throughout the United States (Eells, 1986). However, BSA camps were focused on character development for "normal" campers. It was not until the early 1920s that the first summer camp for psychologically challenged youth would open and thus mark the origins of therapeutic camps.

1922: Camp Ramapo

The first therapeutic camp developed specifically for emotionally challenged young people was founded in 1922. Camp Ramapo opened in upstate New York with the specific purpose of working with "delinquent and problem children" in a summer camp setting (Galkin, 1937). The camp was "sponsored by an independent committee of interested and influential men" and affiliated with "the Jewish Board of Guardians, an agency concerned with the treatment of behavior and personality problem children and adults" (Galkin, p. 474). Ramapo had accommodations for 120 boys who were all in active treatment with the Jewish Board of Guardians. From its inception, Ramapo's staff included psychiatrists, psychiatric social workers, and counselors. Camp Ramapo, which still operates today in Rhinebeck, New York, is now referred to as Ramapo for Children and provides services for both boys and girls. Ramapo for Children is significant to the field because it is the longest running therapeutic summer camp in the United States and has always been staffed with numerous mental health providers.

Camp Ramapo was the first of many therapeutic camps that opened in the 1900s, including Camp Wawokiye in Ohio, founded by the Cleveland Child Guidance Clinic in 1926 (Rademacher, 1928); Province Lake Camp in New Hampshire (later renamed Camp Wediko), founded in 1935 by the Psychiatric Clinic of Massachusetts General Hospital (Cockerill & Witmer, 1938); and the University of Michigan's Fresh Air Camp, which started working with "maladjusted children" in 1944 (Morse, 1947). Some previously published histories of the field (e.g., Davis-Berman & Berman, 1994) cite Camp Ahmek as the first therapeutic camp; however, the camp, which opened in Canada during the 1920s, did not serve "delinquent and problem children" and did not include therapeutic staff. The majority of early therapeutic camps developed out of mental health (referred to as *mental hygiene* in the early 1900s) and civic organizations wanting to integrate the summer camps into treatment. Those organizations included the Jewish Board of Guardians, Massachusetts General Hospital, the Cleveland Child Guidance Clinic, and the University of Michigan. The founders of these early camps were mental health professionals including psychiatrists, social workers, and psychologists who staffed their camps with similar professionals. Some camps are still in existence today, including Ramapo for Children and Camp Wediko, both of which continue to employ an extensive array of mental health professional staff.

1946: Dallas Salesmanship Club Camp

In the 1940s, a camp emerged that operated not just in the summer but also for long-term residential stays and without an extensive mental health staff. Camp Woodland Springs, later renamed the Dallas Salesmanship Club Camp, was founded in 1946 with the explicit goal of treating boys with emotional problems. The Salesmanship Club Camp was directed by Campbell Loughmiller, who possessed a bachelor's degree in philosophy, a certificate in social work, and master's degree in education. Similar to Ernest Balch, Loughmiller grew up on a family farm with a strong work ethic and commitment to his church. He wrote several books about his experiences at the camp, including *Wilderness Road* (1965) and *Kids in Trouble* (1979), which would be used by others to start their own long-term therapeutic camps. The Dallas Salesmanship Club Camp was critical to the evolution of therapeutic camps because it did things differently than previous therapeutic camps.

Loughmiller (1979, p.22) wrote about the campers, "All kinds of boys come—aggressive, delinquent, neurotic, schizophrenic; with brain damage, asthma, epilepsy, dyslexia and so on: but as we see it, they are not *sick* and we are not *therapists*." The Dallas Salesmanship Club Camp staff included "no specialists: no psychologists, no psychiatrist, no waterfront man, no special teachers. Our services are channeled as fully as possible through the two counselors in charge of each group" (Loughmiller, 1979, p. 25). The facilities at the camp were minimal, with only a kitchen-dining room (used several nights a week), bath house, warehouse, and office. Each group of boys and their leaders (called *chiefs,* a Native American reference) built their own shelters, latrines, fire pits, and camp-cooking-eating facilities. The camp also had a strong family focus with regular sessions that parents of campers were required to attend: "The full involvement of parents throughout a boy's stay is the best insurance we have found against post-camp regression" (Loughmiller, 1979, p. 33). Loughmiller (1979, p. 33) summarized the effectiveness of the camp, bolstered by a study done by the University of Texas: "85% of the boys who leave the camp are able to lead responsible and successful lives."

Unlike previous therapeutic camps, the Dallas Salesmanship Club Camp did not send its campers home at the end of summer; they were instead enrolled for 18 consecutive months. The majority of the time they resided at camp, yet on occasion the boys would go on 3- to 6-day canoe or raft expeditions with their counselors. These expeditions were some of the earliest documented multiday wilderness trips, outside of a camp setting, with psychologically challenged young people.

The Dallas Salesmanship Club Camp is a significant organization in the development of AT as it marks the origins of the first long-term residential camp. The organization is significant in that unlike previous therapeutic camps, it did not employ a variety of mental health professionals. The camp is valuable to the evolution of the field as it was the first documented use of extended wilderness trips with psychologically challenged youth. Loughmiller (1979, p. 26) was also one of the first to identify the power of the relationship between camper, counselor, and group: "We are not therapists treating boys with an illness; we are friends helping boys with problems—problems that manifest themselves in ways that are obvious to everyone in the group." The organization was one of the first to have a strong family focus in its model.

Loughmiller died in 1993, and the Dallas Salesmanship Club Camp was closed in 2004 due to funding issues after almost 60 years of helping young people. The Dallas Salesmanship Club Camp is the model for many of the year-round therapeutic camps still in existence today, including Eckerd Youth Alternatives, Three Springs, members of the Wilderness Road Camping Association (which are primarily Christian-based camps), and some of the members of the National Association of Therapeutic Wilderness Camps. The most controversial long-term therapeutic camp opened in 1962.

1962: Anneewakee

Anneewakee, a Cherokee word for "land of the friendly people," was founded, directed, and owned by Louis "Doc" Poetter (although he did not have a doctorate or medical degree) in 1962 in Georgia (Corvette, 1986). The program would expand to have two camps (one for girls) in Georgia and one in Florida. The model was a long-term therapeutic wilderness camp, similar to the Dallas Salesmanship Club Camp, where youth would construct campsites and live for up to 16 months. Unlike the Dallas Salesmanship Club Camp, the program was staffed with mental health professionals—and was also surrounded by controversy.

As reported by Corvette (1990), Poetter pleaded guilty to 19 counts of sodomy of patients in 1988 and was sentenced to 8 years in prison. Poetter had first been accused of abuse in the 1970s. Other Anneewakee staff were also charged and found guilty of sexual abuse. Further, the Anneewakee facility was found guilty of fraud as they overbilled insurance companies and families for treatment provided by psychologists. Former clients won a successful lawsuit against Anneewakee, claiming they were forced to build and repair the facilities as well as cheated out of the thousands of dollars their parents paid for education and therapy. In 1987, Anneewakee was ordered by the Georgia Department of Human Resources to be turned over to the Hospital Corporation of America, which began managing the day-to-day operations. The facility is now called Inner Harbour. Anneewakee is one of the most controversial long-term wilderness therapy camps in the history of the field.

1962: Outward Bound USA

The year that Anneewakee opened was the same year that Outward Bound came to the United States. The Outward Bound organization had a profound impact on the field of AT. It originated in England and was founded by Kurt Hahn. Hahn was born to a wealthy Jewish German family and attended Oxford University in England in 1910 to study philosophy of education, where he made many friends and influential contacts (Flavin, 1996). These contacts would be useful to Hahn later in life when he was forced to leave Germany. After World War I, Hahn became secretary to Prince Max Von Baden, the last imperial chancellor of Germany, who helped him to open the Salem School in 1920. It is there that Hahn wrote the "Seven Laws of Salem" in 1930, which included "make the children meet with triumph and defeat" and "free the sons of the wealthy and powerful from the enervating sense of privilege" (Flavin, p. 15).

Hahn's laws were similar to the philosophy of the Camp Chocorua Principles. Hahn emphasized that the goal of the school, similar to the Boy Scouts, was "character training" (Flavin, 1996, p. 17). At the Salem School, he divided the staff into two categories: teachers and character trainers. He believed strongly in educating youth in areas of character, yet, similar to Loughmiller, he did not have high regard for mental health professionals. Hahn "is said to have taken charge aggressively in cases of serious illness: He would cause a doctor a great deal of woe if he felt any doubt about his ministrations, and knew where all the best specialists were to be found and how to get them interested—except for psychiatrists, whom he thoroughly distrusted" (Flavin, p. 117). Hahn's Salem School could be viewed as one of the first character-based boarding schools in the world, yet his time at the school was short lived.

In 1933, Hahn wrote a letter to Salem School alumni and parents asking them to terminate their relationship with either Hitler and the Nazi movement or the school (Flavin, 1996). This infuriated the newly elected Nazi regime and Hahn was briefly jailed. Shortly thereafter, he was exiled to Great Britain with help from his influential friends. It was there that he conceived of a whole series of new educational ventures, including the

Gordonstoun School and Outward Bound. Hahn became a British citizen in 1938 and converted to the Church of England in 1945. If not for Hahn's dislike of Hitler and the Nazi regime, Outward Bound may never have existed, as its origins lie in the mission of helping to develop character and fortitude in British youth.

In 1938, Hahn had been trying to "launch a 'County Badge scheme' that fostered physical fitness, enterprise, tenacity, and compassion among British youth" (Miner & Boldt, 1981, p. 35). This organization was similar to the Boy Scouts with its emphasis on earning badges, but possessed a greater emphasis on physical challenges. The County Badge did not gain a large following until Lawrence Holt, a Gordonstoun parent who was also a partner in a large shipping company, approached Hahn about the loss of life of young seamen in the Battle of the Atlantic. Holt wanted to develop a program to train young people, especially sailors, to have "reliance on their own resources, and selfless bond with their fellows." So Hahn and Holt joined forces to start a "new kind of school offering one-month courses that would use Hahn's County Badge scheme to implement Holt's quest for training to turn attitudes around" (Miner & Boldt, p. 35). On Holt's insistence (much to Hahn's dislike, but Holt's financial resources backed the program), they named the program Outward Bound, a nautical term for when a ship is leaving port to the open ocean, and opened operations in 1941 in Aberdovey, Wales. The first Outward Bound program was a rigorous monthlong course of small boat training, athletic experiences, map and compass skills, rescue training, an expedition at sea, a land expedition across three mountain ranges, and service to local people. This began a movement that would not only impact youth in Britain, but also youth all around the world. Despite Outward Bound's success, the first theories and philosophies that drove the program were not well documented and can only be found in several speeches done by Kurt Hahn.

On July 20, 1960, 2 years before Outward Bound arrived in the United States, Kurt Hahn gave a lecture to the Outward Bound Trust outlining the origins and philosophy behind Outward Bound. In the lecture, Hahn pointed out several key historical influences to the evolution of Outward Bound, including Baden-Powell (Boy Scouts) and Plato. Hahn (1960) also described how Outward Bound addressed the challenges of the "five social diseases of the young":

> There is the decline in fitness due to the modern methods of locomotion, the decline in initiative, due to the widespread disease of spectatoritis, the decline in care and skill, due to the weakened tradition of craftsmanship, the decline in self-discipline, due to the ever-present availability of tranquilizers and stimulants, the decline of compassion, which William Temple called "spiritual death."

These social diseases are as relevant today as they were when Hahn delivered the lecture in 1960. Hahn's cure for the social diseases was the four elements of Outward Bound—namely the fitness training, expeditions, projects, and rescue service (Hahn, 1960). Outward Bound was the first adventure program to promote the idea of vigorous expeditions to challenge youth to increase self-reliance and self-discipline. This belief was further advanced by the early staff of Outward Bound USA, who were not sailors but mountaineers and boarding school faculty.

Outward Bound was brought to the United States by Josh Miner, who had been introduced to the concept while working with Hahn as a teacher at the Gordonstoun School (Miner & Boldt, 1981). The first school, Colorado Outward Bound, opened on June 16, 1962. The 26-day course (which was not nautical due to the location) started at a base camp in the Rocky Mountains, where participants were trained in requisite skills such as map and compass, backpacking, first aid, knots, rock climbing, firefighting, and mountain rescue and then went out on several multi-day expeditions (Miner & Boldt, p. 104). The staff was a mix of boarding school faculty who had their summers off and experienced mountaineers who were happy to have paying jobs teaching outdoor skills. The first course included a 6-mile run (called a marathon) at the end of the course and one night alone. During the second course of the fledgling program, the cook informed chief instructor Tap Tapley that their food supplier would not be there for several days due to difficulties on the mountain roads. Tapley gathered the staff around and told them, "Tonight we'll get the group together, and I'll give them a talk on edible plants and berries, and what kinds of game and fish they can find to eat, and we'll tell them they're going on a 3-day solo survival" (Miner & Boldt, p. 109). Thus, the tradition of participants spending 3 days by themselves in the wild (referred to as the "solo") first started in the United States during this second Outward Bound course. The solo, as well as the final run, are now long-standing traditions in Outward Bound courses and many other AT programs.

Outward Bound expanded rapidly in the United States throughout the 1960s and 1970s, when six schools opened in Colorado, Maine, Minnesota, Oregon, North Carolina, and New Hampshire. In 1965, Bob Pieh, director of Minnesota Outward Bound, offered the first girls' course (Miner & Boldt, 1981, p. 164). Although Outward Bound was expanding in the United States, it often was associated with private boarding schools because Miner was also a faculty member at the prestigious Philips Academy in Andover, Massachusetts. Hahn and Miner had always been involved in independent schools, and many of their instructors also worked at boarding schools during the academic year. Miner was concerned that the "movement would acquire a 'preppie' stigma" and would only be available to teens with wealthy parents (Miner & Boldt, p. 38). To combat this, they started a policy that half of a school's enrollment should be given scholarships. Miner went about implementing this policy by developing programs for adjudicated and troubled youth who had limited resources. Its model is at the core of many wilderness therapy and adventure-based therapy organizations. Outward Bound had less influence on therapeutic camps because their existence predated the start of Outward Bound.

Controversies at Outward Bound

Since its inception, Outward Bound USA has experienced some controversies related to staff training. Similar to Hahn, Miner was great at motivating young people but had little outdoor experience. To address this issue, he went about hiring some of the most skilled mountaineers so he could work on developing the organization. The most famous, and perhaps most opinionated, of these employees was Paul Petzoldt, who became the chief instructor of the Colorado Outward Bound in 1963 (Ringholz, 1997). Petzoldt soon became disenchanted with Outward Bound because he felt the instructors were poorly trained: "I practically told them their school was never going to amount to a goddamn unless they had an instructor's training program" (Ringholz, p. 180). In 1965, Petzoldt left Outward Bound to start the National Outdoor Leadership School with the intent of creating a school to train Outward Bound instructors as well as other outdoor leaders.

Ketcham (2007) examined the circumstances surrounding the death of an Outward Bound student while enrolled in a Utah desert course. The student, 16-year-old Elisa Santry, "was the first Outward Bound student to die in almost a decade and the 24th fatality in the nonprofit's 46-year history in the U.S." (Kectham, p. 49). Elisa died of heat exhaustion after getting lost in the canyons of Utah on a 110-degree day. Ketcham reported that most of the 24 deaths at Outward Bound USA happened prior to the 1980s, yet some former Outward Bound instructors believed that the organization's management was not training its new instructors or retaining older more seasoned staff (Ketcham, 2007).

This criticism of poor staff training at Outward Bound would also be directed at therapeutic camps and wilderness therapy programs (Government Accounting Office, 2007). Ironically, many AT program participants were in the same area where Elisa died, but due to State of Utah licensure regulations they were not permitted to hike as the temperature was over 90 degrees. A day after Elisa's death, a 29-year-old man participating in the Boulder Outdoor Survival School died of dehydration in Utah (Ketcham, 2007). However, before any these controversies, Outward Bound was adapted to a variety of populations and was used as a catalyst to start other types of programs.

Outward Bound Programs for Adjudicated Youth, Mentally Ill, and Chemically Dependent Participants

In the summer of 1966, several Outward Bound schools enrolled 60 adjudicated youth, who were under the custody of the Massachusetts Department of Youth Services, to see if the experience would lead to less recidivism when compared to a control group of adjudicated delinquent youth who did not attend Outward Bound. This was the first of numerous research studies looking at the effectiveness of Outward Bound on reducing recidivism in adjudicated delinquent youth. The experiment was a relative success, with 20% of the Outward Bound group reoffending compared to 37% of the control group (Kelly & Baer, 1968). The research outcome caused a surge in requests for Outward Bound to provide more courses for adjudicated youth. Outward Bound began to offer courses all over the country for adjudicated youth and spawned several 26-day organizations that are still in existence today, including the STEP program in Florida, the Wilderness School in Connecticut, and the Homeward Bound program in Massachusetts. Outward Bound was subsequently adapted to other populations, including mental health and substance abuse treatment.

The first documented integration of Outward Bound for mentally ill adolescents and adults occurred in 1975 at the Dartmouth-Hitchcock Mental Health Center in Hanover, New Hampshire. Stich (1983) reviewed the collaborative Outward Bound Mental Health Project between Dartmouth Medical School and Hurricane Island Outward Bound School. In this model, the Outward Bound organization was integrated into outpatient, inpatient, and residential mental health treatment programs: "The purpose of the Dartmouth Outward Bound Mental Health Project is to develop a unique patient education program that utilizes not only traditional concepts of patient education but also experiential learning" (Stich, p. 30). The organization did not take participants on overnight trips, but would conduct 6- to 8-hour experiences including cross-country skiing, canoeing, or rock climbing facilitated by Outward Bound staff. The Outward Bound staff would include psychiatrists, social workers, and counselors to develop and implement treatment plans for patients. This adaptation of Outward Bound lasted until the middle 1980s.

The first documented integration of the Outward Bound program and inpatient adolescent substance abuse treatment occurred at Beech Hill Hospital located in Dublin, New Hampshire, starting in 1983 (McPeake, Kennedy, Grossman, & Beaulieu, 1993). This program consisted of several phases facilitated by Outward Bound instructors (trained by Outward Bound) and clinical staff (master's level clinicians). The phases included a 3-day assessment phase occurring at the hospital, which helped to develop the treatment plan, and a 22-day wilderness phase with Outward Bound, in which participants hiked or canoed in the New Hampshire or Maine wilderness and which culminated in a 48-hour solo. This unique collaboration between Outward Bound and a substance abuse facility was relatively short lived as the program ended in the early 1990s. The Beech Hill Hospital closed in 2001 due to lack of reimbursement of substance abuse treatment by health insurance companies.

Outward Bound created a movement that exposed many individuals to the idea of personal growth through challenging adventure experiences. Outward Bound USA is the birthplace of the mountaineering-based wilderness therapy model because it can be traced directly to the majority of organizations integrating this style of expedition. While Outward Bound continued to offer courses for "at-risk" youth, it also expanded into other areas of mental health. Although many of the above-mentioned programs were directly connected to the Outward Bound organization, there were also many who would be inspired by their experiences at Outward Bound and would subsequently adapt the Outward Bound curriculum to start new organizations.

1968: Brigham Young University 480, Youth Leadership Through Outdoor Survival

One person's experience with Outward Bound created a movement in the West that brought the integration of primitive survival skills to AT. In 1967, Larry Dean Olsen graduated from Brigham Young University (BYU) with a degree in elementary education and published the book *Outdoor Survival Skills* (White, 2008). Olsen learned about primitive skills as a boy after finding an obsidian arrowhead. With the publication of *Outdoor Survival Skills* (Olsen, 1997) and his instructional classes in outdoor survival skills at BYU, Olsen became one of the country's leading experts in the area of primitive survival skills and its potential use in wilderness programs. In the summer of 1967, Olsen was invited by the Colorado Outward Bound School to teach their staff about survival skills. As Olsen explained, "I took a month or two that summer and went to their school and watched. I was not particularly interested in their curriculum, but I watched their ways of doing things and they did have a lot of success with getting people out in the wilderness and bringing them back safely" (White, p. 11). Olsen had been taking people out on survival trips for 10 days at a time, whereas Outward Bound trips were typically 26 days. After teaching at Outward Bound, Olsen recognized that he could safely take students out for longer periods of time. He added some of the Outward Bound practices to his primitive survival trips, including solos and a final marathon run.

In 1968, the Academic Standards Committee at BYU asked Olsen to take 26 students who had failed out of BYU the previous semester on a month-long primitive skills experience. This class was titled the Youth Leadership through Outdoor Survival, but was known primarily by its course number of 480. Unlike Outward Bound, which provided food, backpacks, and sleeping bags for students, BYU 480 students started the program with 1 day of training at the school and a 3-day hike with a small amount of food, one canteen of water, the clothes they were wearing, a knife, and a blanket. During the majority of the 28-day desert expedition, BYU 480 students lived off the land and would hike for miles at a time. During the first program, a student named Ezekiel Sanchez, who had grown up living off the desert, helped Olsen when a staff member had to drop out. Sanchez became critical in the continuation and implementation of BYU 480 and other outdoor programs at BYU.

The first BYU 480 program was deemed a success, and Olsen and Sanchez were asked to help run numerous outdoor survival courses for BYU. BYU opened the 480 class to anyone who wanted to learn primitive survival skills. Word of the challenging wilderness experience spread through the Church of Jesus Christ of Latter-day Saints (LDS) community, as a majority of BYU students are LDS. The BYU survival programs became popular with BYU students, scout leaders, probation officers, and others interested in having a challenging experience as well as those interested in promoting character development in youth through primitive survival skills. By the 1970s, Olsen, Sanchez, and the BYU 480 class were seen as inspirations for many of the wilderness therapy programs that emerged in the western United States using primitive survival skills as a therapeutic tool for working with troubled adolescents.

BYU 480 was quickly adopted by participants and spread throughout the western USA. According to Krakauer (1995, p. 76), its popularity may be because

> BYU is closely affiliated with the Church of Jesus Christ of Latter-day Saints, and at the core of its wilderness programs was a spiritual component that had no equivalent in Outward Bound. They were intended, first and foremost, to be deeply religious experiences that promoted faith in the Mormon ideal. As one result, graduates of BYU courses established similar programs across the West with evangelistic zeal.

Although it is possible that primitive skills programs grew because of this connection to the LDS religion, they may also have grown because individuals saw the possibility to make a living doing something they loved. Many of those involved in the early days of AT had strong religious affiliations, including Ernest Balch of Camp Chocorua (Eells, 1986), Daniel Seton of the Boy Scouts (Rowan, 2005), Kurt Hahn of Outward Bound (Flavin, 1996), and Campbell Loughmiller of the Dallas Salesmanship Club Camp (Loughmiller, 1979).

A majority of the primitive survival skills-based wilderness therapy programs emerging in the western United States in the 1980s and 1990s were directly or indirectly connected to the BYU 480 class. The primitive survival skills model of BYU 480 had minimal startup costs compared to Outward Bound and the challenge for participants was far greater. Outward Bound, with its mountaineering influence, had participants use backpacks, camp stoves, sleeping bags, tents, and other camping supplies. BYU 480, with its primitive skills influence, had participants live off the land with nothing but the clothes on their backs, a blanket, and a knife. They would learn to build fires with bow-drills to heat the wild game they killed, or might use occasional supplements of rice and beans from a food drop that could be a hundred miles from their starting point. Although an incredible challenge with simplicity of design, the BYU 480 primitive skills model would enable many people who had knowledge of primitive skills to start organizations with little to no startup costs.

In 1975, a young woman died of dehydration during a BYU 480 trip (Seymour, 1976). BYU stopped offering the course in the late 1970s, although a similar course was offered by the private sector. In 1978, Doug Nelson, who had been a Boy Scout, BYU 480 student, instructor, and then BYU professor, started the Boulder Outdoor Survival School (BOSS). The first BOSS courses were based on the BYU 480 model. BOSS continues to operate today and is known as the oldest primitive skills survival school in the United States.

1971: Project Adventure

While BYU 480 was beginning in the West, another organization inspired by Outward Bound was starting on the East Coast that would subsequently create a movement toward the use of AT in school and hospital settings using a variety of tools, including experiential activities and ropes courses. The explicit use of adventure for counseling purposes began at Project Adventure, founded in 1971 by Jerry Pieh, former Outward Bound instructor and son of the founder of Minnesota Outward Bound, in Massachusetts (Schoel, Prouty, & Radcliffe, 1988). Pieh felt that most young people could not afford the cost and duration of Outward Bound, so he wanted to adapt Outward Bound concepts to be used in traditional school settings. Although Project Adventure's original focus was on all student populations, it soon developed an alternative form of curriculum for at-risk students called adventure-based counseling. Project Adventure started to use experiential activities such as initiatives and ropes courses, spawning a movement toward their integration into hospital settings. This movement marked the origin of the current adventure-based therapy movement.

Adventure-based counseling was first practiced in a mental health program in 1974 in an outpatient therapy group at Addison Gilbert Hospital and an action seminar at Hamilton-Wenham Regional High School in Massachusetts (Schoel, Prouty, & Radcliff, 1988). In 1979, Project Adventure offered its first adventure-based counseling workshop in Massachusetts, which it still offers today. The advent of adventure-based counseling sparked a movement of integrating experiential activities into outpatient and inpatient treatment programs in order to create change. This was accelerated by Project Adventure's decision to expand their services to other parts of the country.

Project Adventure opened another office in Georgia in 1980. In 1981, Cindy Simpson, a school psychologist, developed a program integrating adventure-based counseling with academic support, parent counseling, and career guidance for adjudicated youth in the care of the Georgia Department of Services (Prouty, 1999). Simpson led the organization's expansion in the South that provided numerous services for the Georgia Department of Juvenile

Justice and later the development of the Behavioral Management through Adventure curriculum (Gillis et al., 2008). The southern office would expand to include group homes and a 70-acre treatment facility.

In 1988, Jim Schoel, Dick Prouty, and Paul Radcliffe published the book *Islands of Healing: A Guide to Adventure Based Counseling.* The book was the first publication to be focused on experiential activities as a process for change and is the forerunner of what would later be referred to as adventure-based therapy. They explained that Project Adventure's plan was to become "small Outward Bound 'outposts' near major cities and international borders" (p. 4). Project Adventure recognized that many young people and their families could not afford the time or expense of a multiday Outward Bound program, so the idea was to bring the Outward Bound experience into schools and programs. They defined adventure-based counseling as a "dynamic, adaptive process" (p. xii) and explained

> Since the first Adventure Based Counseling workshop in May of 1979, over 2000 counselors, special needs teachers or therapists have been trained. Residential treatment centers, substance abuse clinics, state and county youth rehabilitation programs, school special needs departments and psychiatric hospitals have all turned to [Project Adventure]. Because of this trend the need for a text to help others think about and plan an effective Adventure Based Counseling adoption became increasingly obvious. (p. 8)

By 1989, Project Adventure had helped more than 100 hospitals and residential settings implement a variety of adventure-based counseling programs, including high and low ropes courses (Prouty, 1999). Project Adventure's significance to the field includes its training of numerous facilities and individuals in the use of adventure-based therapy, its development of many ropes courses at hospital settings, and its books about the use of adventure-based counseling. Unfortunately, by the early 1990s hospitals were beginning to close their ropes courses due to a variety of factors, including liability issues and changes in insurance coverage policies with mental health facilities. Project Adventure is still in existence today; however, in June 2010 the organization closed its southern facilities, including 16 group homes and the treatment facility.

1971: Expedition Outreach

The first primitive skills-based wilderness therapy expedition program for adjudicated youth started in 1971 in Challis, Idaho, with a program named Expedition Outreach. According to the book by Stephen Watts (2003), a former sheriff, Expedition Outreach was founded as a private nonprofit organization to help struggling young people via primitive survival expeditions, with Larry Wells as the first executive director. Watts first became acquainted with Wells in the 1960s after he arrested him. Watts kept track of Wells during his time in prison and subsequent rehabilitation. Watts was so impressed with Wells that he requested a pardon for Wells from the Governor of Idaho, which was granted. Wells went on to work for the U.S. Forest Service and then attended a BYU 480 instructor's class. After the class, Wells approached Watts and Darroll Gardiner, a probation officer, to develop a program for adjudicated youth. These individuals worked together to start Expedition Outreach.

The program's goal was to provide experiences and challenges under positive circumstances to members of the group through primitive survival skills training. An Expedition Outreach course lasted 30 days, during which students were "marched into the wilderness areas and taught to live off the land, fend for themselves, and rely on partnerships with others to survive" (Watts, 2003, p. 121). The model was based on the BYU 480 curriculum. This organization was open to people over the age 15 and included adjudicated youth referred from Idaho State Prison, the state reformatory, and probation, as well as nonadjudicated participants. The organization combined adults and adolescents into one group to go out on the trips. Expedition Outreach was the first of numerous programs that Larry Wells would either start or assist others in starting, one of the largest of which was VisionQuest. Wells closed Expedition Outreach in the early 1980s due to lack of state reimbursements and other financial challenges.

1973: VisionQuest

VisionQuest was formed in 1973 as one of the first private for-profit organizations that integrated the outdoors for rehabilitation of adjudicated and behaviorally challenged youth. This was a departure from previous adjudicated programs developed by Outward Bound and others, which were primarily not-for-profit organizations. The history of VisionQuest is illuminated by Dennis Adams (1987), a former superior court judge who referred youth to the program, in his book. Bob Burton, a former corrections worker, founded the program because he was tired of the lack of innovation in the field and saw little success with the way state-run corrections facilities were working with youth. Burton, who had been a volunteer with the Crow Tribe, felt that Native American rituals would benefit adjudicated youth.

Burton established VisionQuest as a for-profit organization because he wanted the employees to be stockholders and thus also control the company. Burton approached Phoenix Youth Corrections out of financial desperation and proposed a pilot project in which he would take adolescents out of lockup for a 7-day mountain expedition without charge. The Phoenix Youth Corrections program agreed to Burton's offer and, with the help of Larry Wells, the first VisionQuest expedition set out on a hundred-mile journey. Wells taught the students basic survival skills, map and compass, how to eat snakes, and how to rappel down cliffs. The trip was a difficult one, but the youths came back beaming and expressing their newfound insights to their corrections officers. Shortly thereafter, VisionQuest received $36,000 from the State of Arizona for special juvenile justice projects. This first trip allowed the organization to grow and add others to its startup team.

Burton and VisionQuest's startup team included Dr. Herbert Lazarus, a psychiatrist and author of the book *How to Get Your Money's Worth Out of Psychiatry*. Lazarus believed psychiatry was not helping anyone and that most outpatient mental health professionals were "just out to make a buck" (cited in Adam, 1987, p. 120). Lazarus liked VisionQuest's treatment focus because it was action oriented and, at the time, could be summed up in a few words: confront and then support (Adam, p. 120). VisionQuest expanded quickly, adding group homes and other innovative outdoor programs for adjudicated youth across the nation. Some of the innovative outdoor programs included sending staff and students on a cross-country trip in horse-driven wagon trains, as well as on sailing ships that would travel up and down the coast, referred to as OceanQuest.

In 1974, VisionQuest became the first outdoor program to receive accreditation from the Joint Commission on Accreditation of Hospitals. This allowed VisionQuest to seek insurance reimbursement for behaviorally challenged adolescents, as Burton was intent on not relying solely on state-run contracts. During the 1970s, VisionQuest grew by expanding beyond Arizona to other states including Colorado and New Mexico. VisionQuest's influence on the field of wilderness therapy is seen in several ways, including being one of the first programs to be accredited by the Joint Commission, being one of the first for-profit organizations, and for having different methods (wagon trains, tall ships) to integrate the outdoors into working with youth.

Controversies at VisionQuest

VisonQuest was first involved with controversy in the 1970s because of its use of confrontation with teens. In 1978, the Arizona Department of Economic Security had received 127 allegations of wrongdoing related to VisionQuest. After a 12-month investigation, despite these complaints, VisionQuest was reconfirmed with its licensure by the State of Arizona (Adam, 1987, pp. 181–185). A 1988 report by the television news program *60 Minutes* focused on the VisionQuest program. On the program, journalist Diane Sawyer stated:

> Dozens of people, present and former staff members included, told us that the majority of the staff who actually spend time with kids comes to the program with virtually no training and no experience in handling kids, much less severely delinquent ones. (Eisen, 1988)

Sawyer confronted Bob Burton about lack of training and low pay. Burton stated, "The entry staff is paid at the lowest that I could possibly pay them because I want to find out whether they can do this or not. Half the people that I hire cannot even do this job.... No college is teaching anybody how to do this."

Inadequate staff skills and training were not the only complaints in the report. Sawyer interviewed Burt Johnson of the San Diego probation office, which had referred 390 juveniles to the VisionQuest program. Johnson stated:

> I think that VisionQuest does not do what they purport to be able to do. I think they have an unqualified staff, they take unnecessary risk with children, they manipulate finances, and in general I feel they're irresponsible.

Sawyer also cited a study of the first 100 adjudicated boys sent to VisionQuest by San Diego probation, which revealed that 92% were rearrested after discharge from the program (Eisen, 1988).

VisionQuest was identified in 1995 as having 16 deaths, some of which were staff, associated with the program (Krakauer, 1995). Nine of the deaths occurred in one sailing accident in November 1980. According to the *60 Minutes* report, the Coast Guard did not cite VisionQuest for negligence in the sailing accident but did say the vessel was not inspected, had too many people aboard, and was run by an inexperienced crew (Eisen, 1998).

VisionQuest currently operates in six states and provides services for adjudicated youth as well as nonadjudicated behaviorally challenged youth. Some of the criticisms leveled at VisionQuest would be directed at the field in general in 2007. First, however, it is important to recognize the establishment of Woodswomen, Inc. and the Santa Fe Mountain Center. Both programs had a decidedly different approach from VisionQuest to working with young people.

1977: Woodswomen, Inc.

As seen in this chapter, the majority of influences and models in the field of AT were male dominated. In 1977, Woodswomen, Inc., located in Minnesota, was founded by three women—Judith Neimi, Denise Mitten, and Elizabeth Barnard—as a nonprofit adventure organization for women and children.

Woodswomen was a unique organization that pioneered several important programmatic aspects of AT and adventure education from an ecofeminist perspective, according to Denise Mitten (personal communication, September 27, 2010). The overarching paradigm at Woodswomen was an ethic of care. From the office to the field, Woodswomen staff reinforced the importance of clients feeling supported and emotionally safe. Consideration of emotional safety is common today, but in the 1970s it was a radical concept. Woodswomen was one of the first organizations to advocate for the emotional safety of participants in all areas of the program.

With this model, Woodswomen pioneered working positively with women survivors of abuse. While the majority of AT programs were using the physical and emotional challenge components found in the Outward Bound model, Woodswomen focused on teaching participants stress management while on trips. This is common practice today, but not in the early days of the field. The organization closed in 1999, but the philosophy and theories behind it were elaborated on in the book *Wilderness Therapy for Women: The Power of Adventure* (Cole, Erdman, & Rothblum, 1994).

1979: Santa Fe Mountain Center

The Santa Fe Mountain Center evolved out of the state of New Mexico's Bureau of Mental Health and the Health and Environment Department to become a private nonprofit organization in 1979. This transition was facilitated by Richard "Rocky" Kimball. Kimball, who had been an instructor at Colorado Outward Bound in the early 1970s, was awarded a fellowship to attend the University of Colorado, where he received his Ph.D. in education. His first job after receiving his doctorate was for the State of New Mexico, where, according to Kimball, "what we were trying to do was to inject Outward Bound into the schools and the mental health centers" (personal communication, August 18, 2010). Kimball recognized that the program might be eliminated due to state budget concerns, so he believed the only way for the program to survive was to become independent from the state through innovations and private initiatives. This created a unique organizational model of a nonprofit emerging out of a state agency.

Instead of hiring other former Outward Bound instructors, Kimball focused on hiring professionals with a mental health background who possessed strong outdoor and group skills. Kimball encouraged the staff to see the evaluative/diagnostic strengths of the AT model. The Santa Fe Mountain Center staff encouraged the organization to broaden its focus, beyond the youth at risk, to work with other vulnerable populations. This allowed Santa Fe Mountain Center to grow even during challenging economic times.

The Santa Fe Mountain Center currently provides programs to meet the needs of a variety of populations, including:

- Emergence Program, which provides community mobilization and training programs focused on Native American communities
- Adventure Out, which offers an HIV/AIDS prevention program serving high-risk populations
- The New Mexico Gay/Straight Alliance Network, serving lesbian, gay, bisexual, transgendered, and questioning young people
- The Courage to Risk Program, serving trauma survivors

- The Therapeutic Adventure Program, serving adjudicated youth; survivors of sexual, physical, or emotional abuse; substance abusers; youth at risk of entering the system; youth in treatment; and displaced youth from a diversity of backgrounds and cultures

The organization also provides services for leadership development for schools, businesses, and universities. What is unique about Santa Fe Mountain Center has been its ability to successfully adapt to meet the needs of a variety of mental health populations and other vulnerable populations. The integration of social change and social justice concepts also permeates the current work and mission of the Center.

1981: School of Urban and Wilderness Survival

The first for-profit, private-pay, primitive skills-based wilderness therapy program (initially referred to as a wilderness experience program) was the School of Urban and Wilderness Survival (SUWS), which was opened in 1981 by L. Jay Mitchell and George Church in Idaho (White, 2008). As a former BYU 480 student, Mitchell approached Larry Olsen, who had departed from BYU, to develop the philosophy, curriculum, and staff training for SUWS. SUWS also employed Larry Wells to assist in the primitive skills programming; he conducted trips in Northwest Washington and Central Idaho. During the organization's early years, it did not employ psychotherapists. The 21-day program was based on the BYU 480 curriculum, but it was focused on teenagers who had been in trouble at home and/or school. In the first years of the program, participants would go out on expeditions while learning primitive skills in order to find and heat food and build shelters.

SUWS is a significant organization for several reasons. The program was the first to take escorted adolescents (i.e., unwilling participants brought to the program against their will but with parents' permission), had a national focus (would enroll adolescents from all over the country), and was profitable according to Larry Wells (personal communication, September 12, 2009). Unlike earlier organizations, which had contracted with government agencies, SUWS focused on private pay participants and its profits enticed others to enter the field. Both Olsen and Wells would subsequently leave SUWS to start their own programs. The SUWS program was purchased from Mitchell and Church in June 1994 for an undisclosed sum by College Health Enterprises (later renamed Aspen Education Group, which would become the largest owner of for-profit adventure programs, and would subsequently be purchased in November 2006 by CRC Health Group). SUWS currently operates programs in Idaho and North Carolina.

1983: Wilderness Treatment Center

Another long-standing private pay organization opened shortly after SUWS, and its model was the first for-profit organization that included licensed substance abuse counselors. The Wilderness Treatment Center (WTC), located in Montana, is one of the first and longest running mountaineering style wilderness therapy organizations in the United States that has licensed chemical dependency counselors working with participants while on wilderness expeditions (Brekke, 2005). This organization was founded in 1983 by John Brekke, a certified chemical dependency counselor. Brekke had participated in several Outward Bound courses and developed the curriculum with assistance from the mountaineer and creator of the National Outdoor Leadership School, Paul Petzoldt.

WTC is a private-pay program that is often reimbursed by health insurance companies. The program works with adolescent males and has always been licensed as an inpatient substance abuse center. A participant enrolls for 60 days, with 30 days of intensive substance abuse counseling in a residential setting followed by a 28-day wilderness expedition, and then returns back to the base for debriefing the experience with family. WTC has wilderness expeditions similar to Outward Bound with backpacks, stoves, sleeping bags, and tents.

WTC can be directly traced to the mountaineering model due to Brekke's involvement with the Outward Bound organization and Paul Petzoldt. Four years after the opening of WTC, a multitude of private-pay programs opened in the western United States. The majority of these programs initially were not licensed (Utah did not have licensure until July 1990) and did not include mental health professionals on staff. The exception to this was the Catherine Freer Wilderness Survival School (later renamed Catherine Freer Wilderness Therapy Expeditions), which opened in Oregon in 1988 as a licensed residential alcohol and drug program and had licensed substance abuse counselors on all trips (Woodbury, 1991). This organization was co-founded by Rob Cooley, Ph.D., and was influenced by the mountaineering style as the program's namesake inspiration was an established mountaineer.

1988–89: Anasazi Foundation, Wilderness Quest, Aspen Achievement Academy

The majority of new for-profit organizations that opened during 1988 and 1989 can be directly traced to BYU 480 and the primitive skills style. By 1987, the SUWS program was quite busy. Olsen departed and within a year started the Anasazi Foundation by joining again with Ezekiel Sanchez in Arizona (White, 2008). After Anasazi's first year, Olsen and Sanchez decided that they wanted the organization to be available to all individuals without regard to their ability to pay, so they changed the program to a not-for-profit. Not only was the Anasazi Foundation a nonprofit organization, but it actively sought licensure in order to get insurance reimbursement for services to lower costs for families (White, 2008).

Also in 1988, Larry Wells started Wilderness Conquest (later renamed Wilderness Quest), a private for-profit primitive skills-based AT program specifically for substance-abusing teens (Wells, 2008). Wilderness Academy (later renamed Aspen Achievement Academy) was co-founded in 1988 by Doug Nelson (the founder of BOSS), Dr. Keith Hooker, Doug Cloward, and Dr. Madolyn Liebing, all former BYU 480 students or instructors (Stednitz, 1991). Aspen Achievement is significant because it was the first primitive skills-based wilderness therapy organization to include a full-time doctoral level licensed psychologist, Dr. Liebing, who provided individual therapy and psychological evaluations to participants in the field. The addition of a licensed mental health professional and its clinical focus created an upsurge in referrals to Aspen. This organization was sold by its original founders and was featured in a book about the field called *Shouting at the Sky: Troubled Teens and the Promise of the Wild* (Ferguson, 1999) as well as the third season of the British reality television series *Brat Camp*.

EXPANSION OF THE FIELD

In the late 1980s and 1990s, private for-profit AT programs for adolescents exploded in the western United States, as well as other parts of the country. This rapid expansion of the field was due, in part, to increased demand for adolescent treatment by desperate parents after the closure of many adolescent inpatient psychiatric hospitals and substance abuse treatment centers due to managed care and new medications to treat mental health disorders (Santa, 2007). Another reason for closure of many hospitals was due to questionable referral and admissions procedures not validated by research (McManus, McCarthy, Kosak, & Newacheck, 1991). With this expansion came more controversy by those who were enticed to the field by the potential high profits and low startup costs—something that was best personified by the Challenger Foundation and its founder, Steve Cartisano.

1988: Challenger Foundation

The Challenger Foundation was founded by Steve Cartisano in 1987, with its first course occurring in Hawaii. Jon Krakauer (1995), a mountaineer and outdoor writer, chronicled the history of the Challenger Foundation and other abusive AT organizations for *Outside Magazine*. In January 1988, Cartisano brought the Challenger Foundation program to Utah, where he began to charge $15,900 for a 2-month wilderness therapy program while, at the same time, other organizations were charging $500 for a 1-month course. A former BYU student, Cartisano had worked as an instructor in one of the school's wilderness courses (there is no evidence that it was the 480 class) and was a former military man; he promoted an approach of dealing with students by an "in-your-face" style of confrontation. An experienced self-promoter, Cartisano hired a publicist and went on a national marketing campaign, including many television talk shows that highlighted the impact of Challenger on participants. According to Krakauer (1995, p. 77):

> Like Outward Bound, most Mormon-run wilderness schools offered kids tough challenges but generally treated them with care and sensitivity. Cartisano disdained this approach as too "touchy-feely." Instead, he ran Challenger with the in-your-face discipline of a boot camp.

In 1990, a death occurred at the Challenger program, when 16-year-old Kristen Chase collapsed while hiking in 100-degree weather and was accused of faking it by staff. Cartisano and other staff members were charged with negligent homicide and abuse but were later acquitted by a jury. Although the Challenger program was closed down by the State of Utah, several of Challenger's former staff went on to open other organizations.

The Challenger Foundation is the most documented example of an abusive culture (e.g., Gregory, 2000; Krakauer, 1995; Morganstern, 1995; Szalavitz, 2006), taught by leadership and accepted by staff, in an AT program. Also significantly, this culture was replicated by the former staff of Challenger who went on to start other organizations, such as Summit Quest and North Star Expeditions, where other deaths would occur as well. For example, at Summit Quest in May 1990, 15-year-old Michelle Sutton died from dehydration while staff taunted her (Krakauer). In July 1990, the State of Utah enacted a law that regulated wilderness therapy programs in Utah. Unfortunately, even with the regulations in effect in 1994, 16-year-old Aaron Bacon died while attending the state-licensed North Star Expeditions in Utah. Bacon repeatedly expressed feeling ill and being unable to eat but was neglected by the staff who accused him of faking it (Krakauer). All of these organizations are closed, but the impact on the field (as well as those parents whose children died in the care of AT organizations) continues to this day.

Development of AT from the 1990s to Present Day

The 1990s saw a rapid expansion of programs that today exemplify modern-day residential AT programs (Russell, Gillis, & Lewis, 2008). This expansion was coupled with several important influences that helped shape the AT field from the 1990s to present day. A key influence was the development of associations and professional organizations to help develop standards of practice in the field. The Therapeutic Adventure Professional Group (TAPG), a special interest group of the Association of Experiential Education (AEE) committed to the development of adventure-based programming principles in therapeutic settings, was first formed in the 1980s. Professionals in the fields of health, mental health, corrections, education, and other human service fields met annually to share information, techniques, and concerns regarding the therapeutic use of adventure- based experiences. The text *Adventure Therapy: Therapeutic Applications of Adventure Programming* (edited by Michael Gass, 1993) constituted the first major comprehensive effort of TAPG members to clarify what was meant by "adventure therapy." The rationale presented in this text for the use of adventure experiences as therapeutic process, based on prior research and writing, formed key theoretical elements in the development of AT as it is practiced today.

TAPG has become the dominant voice in the push to develop best practices in AT for the last decade. TAPG has been engaged in efforts to produce a statement of best practice for AT since 2001, with writing beginning in 2007. In doing so, TAPG has coordinated several AT Best Practices conferences (in 2003, 2005, 2007, and 2010) and has developed a website that serves as an open platform "to identify appropriate practices and establish programming standards for the administration of adventure and wilderness therapy programs" (Sacksteder, 2010). The website that has been developed (http:// tapg.aee.org/tapg/bestpractices) serves as a template for best practices to be informed by research with the intent to establish AT as a research-supported treatment. It is designed to inform practitioners, consumers, and policy makers on theory, process, and outcomes guiding AT. This movement is unique in the psychological literature in that it has been driven by an open and transparent process of mostly practitioners working hand in hand with researchers and evaluators to synergistically inform one another of findings from practice and research. The open process, using a "wiki" model of writing and peer evaluation, has engaged the practitioner from the onset and embraces the years of hard work that practitioners in the field have put into refining their practice.

Another organization that has begun to examine best practices is the International Adventure Therapy Conference (IATC), which has been hosted in different locations every 3 years since the first conference held in Perth, Australia in 1997. The initial meeting stemmed from the desire to expand notions of AT beyond a purely North American perspective and bring diverse international models of practice and research together. Indeed, the delegates of the first conference (Gillis, 1998) identified tasks that would move AT forward, many of which speak to the very premise of developing an evidence-based practice. The tasks included developing and documenting a body of theory; implementing research that supports practice and the development of the field; documenting practice along with the development of standards and ethics of care; advocating for the legitimacy of AT; and finally, developing and expanding AT networks (Gillis, 1998). The 2009 IATC conference called for continued movement toward a profession of AT, complete with licensure, manualization, and a need for research that is driven by randomized controlled trials to establish efficacy in line with other treatments mentioned above. This discussion sparked a debate among delegates as to the costs and benefits of such an approach. Because an intervention or therapeutic model is being tested and manuals are being developed does not preclude it from being innovative and cutting edge—a concern that many practitioners have if AT becomes more structured and tested using randomized controlled trials (as discussed in Harper, 2010). Regardless of the next steps toward developing an evidence-based practice in AT, it is clearly being driven by practitioners through the TAPG initiative; and international models, practitioners, and researchers will continue to play a vital role in this progress. Debate is a productive endeavor that pushes stakeholders in AT to examine their belief systems and their role in helping move AT toward an evidence base.

As AT programs began to establish themselves in Utah and Arizona in the late 1980s, another major influence in the development of AT emerged. Practitioners of AT programs realized that, with recognition from state agencies and insurance companies, more families might be able to afford AT interventions and treatment. Anasazi program founders Larry Olsen and Ezekiel Sanchez first approached a number of insurance companies in Arizona in 1988 and were told that, if they could meet state requirements for adolescent residential treatment, the states would recognize AT interventions. The State of Arizona later developed standards for AT programs, which had a significant impact on program design and process at Anasazi (White, 2008). Practitioners at Anasazi worked these requirements into their therapeutic, educational, and medical health model of treatment. These standards of practice would become benchmarks for other AT programs in seeking copayments for clients from insurance companies and other mental health providers. Later in 1988, the State of Utah contracted with the Anasazi program founders to develop standards for which programs operating in Utah would comply (Utah Division of Administrative Rules, 2007). These standards became the criteria that many insurance companies would use for AT programs nationwide. Standards include developing an individual treatment plan for each client supervised by professional clinical staff, regular medical check-ups by medical staff, appropriate back-up procedures while in wilderness (radio and cell phone contact), and a required number of calories per day for each client. The emerging recognition by insurance companies and state agencies and the growing third-party copayment from insurance companies distinguished AT programs from other adventure-based programs and was a significant influence in the evolution of AT practice.

Over the past two decades, writers have explored the process and effects of AT programs, and collectively they have provided a third major influence on its development. Davis-Berman and Berman (1994) in the text *Wilderness*

Therapy: Foundations, Theory and Research, integrated the ideas of Campbell Loughmiller and therapeutic camping with those of the Outward Bound model of wilderness challenge. Davis-Berman and Berman defined wilderness therapy (Loughmiller, 1965), as "the use of traditional therapy techniques, especially for group therapy, in an out-of-doors setting, utilizing outdoor adventure pursuits and other activities to enhance personal growth" (Davis-Berman & Berman, 1994b, p. 13). The intervention is a methodical, planned, and systematic approach to working with troubled youth. wilderness therapy is not taking troubled adolescents into the woods so that they feel better. It involves the careful selection of potential candidates based on a clinical assessment and the creation of an individual treatment plan for each participant. Involvement in outdoor adventure pursuits should occur under the direction of skilled leaders, with activities aimed at creating changes in targeted behaviors. The provision of group psychotherapy by qualified professionals, with an evaluation of individuals' progress, is a critical component (Davis-Berman and Berman, 1994, p. 140). Another key influence in the development of present day AT programs was formation of the Outdoor Behavioral Healthcare Industry Council (OBHIC). This coalition of more than 12 programs was formed in 1996 to work for higher standards in wilderness and outdoor treatment programs. Meeting quarterly, the members expanded cooperation through open dialogue about methods, process, equipment, staff training and qualifications, safety, land use ethics, and public relations. In 1999, OBHIC established the Outdoor Behavioral Research Cooperative (OBHRC), directed by Keith C Russell from 1999-2010. The original founding members of OBHIC and OBHRC were Anasazi Foundation (Mesa, Arizona), Aspen Achievement Academy (Loa, Utah), Catherine Freer Wilderness Therapy (Albany, Oregon), Redcliff Ascent (Springville, Utah), and SUWS (Shoshone, Idaho). The purpose of OBHRC is to carry out a comprehensive research program addressing specific questions gleaned from the literature and to address research issues asked by specific program members. OBHRC is administered through a contractual arrangement between the Outdoor Behavioral Healthcare Industry Council (OBHIC) and the current Director, Michael Gass of the University of New Hampshire. The OBHRC plan of work is guided by a steering committee of representatives from OBHIC member programs, Michael Gass, and other AT researcher scientists. A peer review committee of scholars and practicing clinical psychologists reviews all proposals and publications from OBHRC.

In addition to annual risk assessment monitoring for OBHIC programs, OBHRC has conducted several studies since its inception in 1999, including: 1) defining the scope of the OBH industry in the United States; 2) an assessment of treatment outcomes using the Youth-Outcome Questionnaire (Y-OQ); 3) a qualitative examination of youth well-being and the role of aftercare use, two-years posttreatment; 4) risk incident monitoring; and 5) depression and substance use disorder prevalence and outcome in a sample of adolescent clients (all studies are available through http://www.obhrc.org). By singling out certain influences, programs, events, and individuals, we risk unfair oversight of many influences that have contributed to the evolution of AT. For these oversights, we apologize.

SUMMARY

This chapter provided a brief history of the evolution of AT through organizations and leaders that had a significant influence on the field. The cited organizations were founded between the 1880s and mid-1990s. Their leaders were often influenced by an experience with another organization. After the mid-1990s, the growth of AT is difficult to track as the number of programs grew at a rapid rate due to an increase in demand for services after the closure of many traditional adolescent inpatient psychiatric hospitals and substance abuse treatment centers. The story of the growth of the AT field from 1990 to present day, through the use of organizations, would be a difficult endeavor as the number of programs is in the hundreds. However, many of the organizations that opened since the 1990s can be traced directly or indirectly to one or more of the organizations reviewed in this chapter.

Today, professional AT organizations tend to be staffed with a multidisciplinary team of licensed professionals that include individuals with university degrees in AT as well as physicians, social workers, psychologists, substance abuse counselors, and nurses. Organizations are learning from the past and are constantly trying to innovate by integrating technology to keep participants safe as well as provide quality treatment.

While some segments of AT are still growing, its future may be at risk, similar to adolescent inpatient psychiatric hospitals and substance abuse treatment centers, without continued investment in research and regular evaluation of practices by multidisciplinary teams. Growth will come with greater evidence-based research focusing on the variables creating change for a participant, then translating those variables and the risk to the general public and participants. Individual AT organizations will continue to grow with regular evaluations by external review teams in order to avoid problems of the past. Contraction will occur if the field does not continue to innovate and grow to meet the current needs of participants.

RAFTING ON THE RIO CHAMA WITH YOUTH ON PROBATION

Jenn Jevertson

The group was from a local county's drug court probation program. Clients were co-ed adolescents, ages 15–19, and were all in various stages of completion of their sentenced probation for drug-related offenses (ranging from possession to driving under the influence, as well as other misdemeanor crimes). The clients were voluntarily participating in a therapeutic adventure program sequence that included single-day and overnight low and high ropes courses, hiking, climbing, and rappelling experiences. Their culminating experience was a 4-day wilderness whitewater rafting trip in the Rio Chama Canyon wilderness of New Mexico.

The water was extremely low, so the boats were often getting hung up on rocks. The boat I was guiding became stuck on a rock, and the resulting jolt popped one of the young men out of the boat. One of the young women immediately reached out and pulled him out of the water in a textbook example of what she was taught during the safety briefing. The other raft boat full of clients was busy retrieving a few lost items—paddle, water bottle, and hat—and then eddied out nearby. We tried everything to get ourselves off the rock, but nothing was working. Eventually our other gear boat came by and intentionally bumped us off the rock.

Around a campfire that evening, we discussed the experience. Each client reflected upon what happened, and how it could be a metaphor for their own lives. The responses were incredibly varied and no two were the same. A few paraphrased examples included:

- "Sometimes all you can do is wait patiently nearby while a friend is going through a hard time. The only way to help is be supportive and help pick up the pieces, like the paddles!"
- "You know, it isn't always who you expect to step in and pull you out of a jam. It can be hard to accept help, but sometimes you just have to."
- "I have to say thanks to my PO (probation officer). He's stepped in and given me a 'kick in the butt' and set me straight, just like how the gear boat helped us when nothing we were doing ourselves was working."

Witnessing the connection between the day's adventure and the change they were trying to make in their lives was an incredible gift and confirmation of the power of adventure used in an intentional way. Our clients would have probably experienced growth through just that challenging and novel experience alone. But guiding them to reflect upon it, draw a metaphoric connection, and transfer that insight is what I call therapeutic adventure.

I've always felt a strong connection that pulls me toward nature. Most of my childhood memories involve some adventure in the out of doors. To me, experiences in nature are both invigorating and peaceful. Without realizing it, I began sharing nature experiences with anyone who would let me.

My career path began when I completed my undergraduate degree in recreation management. After an internship where I learned to guide whitewater rafting, rock climbing, and low and high ropes courses, I knew I wanted to make a career out of using adventure as a tool. I knew I still needed more skills and experiences, so I pursued a master's degree in recreation, parks, and tourism management with a focus on adventure education. During my time at graduate school, I was fortunate enough to serve as the graduate assistant for a semester-long traveling expedition for undergrads that focused on the environment, conservation, and outdoor education. Through my studies and this experience, it became clear to me that I not only wanted to share adventure experiences with others, but that I wanted to do this in a way that promoted personal growth. I am now proud to be an administrator and facilitator at a progressive nonprofit that focuses on marginalized and vulnerable youth and uses adventure and experiential education as a therapeutic tool for both personal and social change.

Chapter 3

A Psychotherapeutic Foundation
for Adventure Therapy

In *The Wizard of Oz,* Dorothy and her companions embarked on a journey to a faraway land to retrieve the broom of the Wicked Witch of the West in order to satisfy a challenge imposed by the Wizard (Baum, 1900). Dorothy thought achieving this task was required in order to accomplish her goal of returning home to Kansas. In her expedition to retrieve the broom, her small group engaged in numerous challenges where they needed to demonstrate cooperation, communication, patience, kindness, and decision making to be successful.

On the surface, this well-known allegory (mostly known through the movie) appears to be quite isomorphic for adventure therapy. It certainly contains the following elements: a small group of somewhat doubting individuals unable to achieve their goals alone, an expedition with a clearly stated goal, and a facilitator who prescribes a task that appears, in the end, to help each individual find what they sought. Although Dorothy had her own purpose for embarking on the journey, Dorothy's fellow travelers also possessed their own interrelated goals of seeking knowledge (Scarecrow), feeling (Tin Man), and courage (Lion)—that is, cognition, affect, and behavior. The group's success in achieving their overall goal also required each group member's issue to be addressed. In rising to the various challenges—some of which appeared impossible to them at the time—each group member was able to learn valuable insights, skills, and processes they could transfer to other parts of their lives. This archetypal story highlights how adventure therapy can:

1. Assess and capitalize on a group member's individual strengths and perceived or real limitations

2. Provide appropriately challenging experiences in a group context that are integrated with well-accepted psychotherapy methods
3. Combine all of this into an experience that values, honors, and recognizes how a sense of belonging aids the change process

These three highlights are considered by many professionals to be some of the key foundations of adventure therapy.

Unfortunately, this story falls short. The "facilitator" in the person of the Wizard is a fraud. Clients may sometimes feel their therapist is a fraud when there is no rapport, no match, or the clinician lacks the training to be effective. Granted, the small group is directed to go see the Wizard by most everyone in Oz as someone who can help them. Like the Wizard, adventure therapists have people come to them (or be referred to them) with some expectation that change will ensue. But as Murphy (1996) warns, therapists who believe they are wizards are not only egotistical and unrealistic, they are also highly unlikely to be effective in the long run because the therapy is too much about them and not about the client. As many of us know, real change only comes when clients act for themselves; therapists can guide, direct, and clarify, but it is ultimately the client's actions and changes that produce intended outcomes—although there is a skill set related to these tasks.

Adventure therapists are intentional in their prescription of activities and challenges. They are trained to diagnose problems; assess clients' strengths, potentials, and perceived limitations; and match appropriate challenges to aid clients in the change process. The Wizard prescribed an activity to Dorothy and her band of seekers to simply get rid of them so they would not bother to him, just as some therapists attempt to remove symptoms instead of addressing the problem or opt for a solo experience when they are fed up with some of the clients. These therapists act without a theoretical basis for how change could occur or how engagement in the activity might help the clients. This chapter provides a theoretical underpinning for adventure therapy so that experiences can be matched to clients' needs in a manner that is more likely to be successful.

A focus on group activity (facilitated by a trained leader) is central to the birth of group therapy. Following World War II, Slavson and Moreno, who were pioneers in group psychotherapy, used activities in their group work as a method of change (Scheidlinger, 1995). The activity base for group work was generally forgotten for many years in favor of more extensive use of conversation. Some may say that psychodrama (Moreno, 1972) and Gestalt therapy (Perls, 1969) embraced a kinesthetically (physically) active way of working with groups, but not quite in the same manner as adventure therapy does. Still, in both of these approaches, participating in the experience is the therapeutic process (as will be discussed in Chapter 4).

ANSWERING THE QUESTIONS OF ADVENTURE THERAPY

Whether they are focused on curing mental illness or promoting mental health, adventure therapists are in a clinical relationship with their clients to seek or support positive changes in their thinking, feeling, and acting. Toward that end, the key question (Paul, 1967, p. 111) asked of therapists in creating psychological changes is "what treatment, by who, is most effective for this individual, with that specific problem, under what circumstances?" For the purpose of this book, this question can be expanded to ask the following questions:

1. What is the most effective way to work with clients who come to an adventure therapist or an adventure therapy program?
2. How are traditional psychotherapies able to interact with adventure therapy to make treatment effective?

This chapter examines these questions as they relate to the psychotherapeutic foundations of adventure therapy and discusses what is meant by treatment, how adventure therapy approaches are matched to specific problems, and how certain circumstances affect the success of the adventure therapy processes. These questions also examine how adventure therapists can assist clients in their change process toward more functional and appropriate behaviors. This chapter discusses the change processes used in adventure therapy and proposes an integrative approach to adventure therapy using what a client brings as the starting or access point for therapy, using the ABC≈R triangle: emotional response (**A**ffect), acting out or withdrawn **B**ehavior, or irrational or problematic thoughts (**C**ognition), integrated around the systemic **R**elationship(s) of the individual and their therapist, field staff, peer group, family, and community. This integrative approach links the affective–behavior–cognition elements together, symbolizing that their relationships are isomorphic with the theoretical dimensions of the model.

What types of treatment work the best for adventure therapy clients? Who is best suited to treat clients through adventure therapy? What type of adventure therapy treatment is best for a particular individual with a specific problem? And what set of circumstances best suits the treatment of a particular individual with a certain set of accompanying circumstances? Obviously, if we knew the complete answers to all of these questions, the treatment of individuals in adventure therapy settings would be much more refined than current practices. Examining each of these factors may lead us closer to this objective.

What Treatment?

The history of adventure therapy presented in Chapter 2 was framed around significant movements, programs, and individuals that helped shape what we know today as adventure therapy. There are a variety of current settings where adventure therapy takes place: outpatient private practice, inpatient hospitals, residential treatment centers, therapeutic camps, and in backcountry or wilderness settings. Adventure therapy does not operate exclusively as a psychodynamic-based approach, a cognitive behavioral approach, a humanistic/interpersonal approach, or a systems approach—it can work with any or all of these orientations. The beauty of adventure therapy—as Dr. Bobbi Beale, a clinical psychologist at Child and Adolescent Behavioral Health of Canton, Ohio, would say—is its *plasticity* (personal communication, December, 2010). Therapists with different theoretical approaches who value the active engagement of their clients through wilderness or adventure experiences use adventure therapy to connect, access, treat, and work with their clients, especially when traditional talk therapy approaches are not as successful.

The goal of adventure therapy is to assess client needs and meet them where they are by (1) being intentional in choosing and tailoring the activity that engages the client(s), and (2) achieving outcomes that allow them to function more successfully in their family, school, and work life. For example, when adventure therapy is used with adjudicated youth, many of whom present with acting-out externalizing behaviors, treatment might consist of presenting experiences that allow for natural or logical consequences to help clients learn to choose more functional behaviors. This procedure removes the adult or therapist from the clients' projection by moving out of the way of the clients' dysfunctional behaviors and allowing them to contend with the responsibility invoked by these consequences. When working with anxious or depressed clients, (internalizing), treatment might consist of intentionally designing quiet solo time in a natural setting, while practicing mindfulness techniques can help clients find a "place" they can go in the future when feeling similarly. Clients with distorted views of themselves or their actions (e.g., clients with eating disorders) might be presented with treatment experiences that bring their "thinking errors" to light for everyone to witness and process. All of these treatment experiences point to the central concept that the goal of adventure therapy is to mold the treatment to meet the client or client group.

In this book, an integrated transtheoretical approach to adventure therapy is presented that is appropriate across all of the described settings, while recognizing that various aspects of the approach need to be emphasized in different contexts. It is essential to note that the impact of the natural environment, as a significant and unique setting, is also seen as providing a tremendous benefit for specific aspects of adventure therapy. Chapter 5 examines the varying impact that nature provides when it is used in adventure therapy.

By Whom?

In a study asking psychotherapists what they looked for when choosing a therapist for themselves, the top five qualities listed were competence, warmth, caring, clinical experience, and openness (Norcross, Bike, & Evans, 2009). Three of these qualities—warmth, caring, and openness—are key characteristics of a therapist's ability to form a relationship with a client (note these may or may not be skills within a therapist that can be enhanced). The other two—competence and clinical experience—have historically been very contentious issues in adventure therapy. There have been key historical figures who possessed little formal training in mental health yet helped "discover" the field, and by all accounts they performed competently. Furthermore, history has shown that any person (or organization) who can attract enough paying clients to be financially profitable can call himself or herself an adventure therapist, get a business license, and "hang out their shingle" to practice. If they are perceived by the public to be competent and can sustain their business with a steady stream of paying customers in good and difficult financial times, they may never be questioned unless they violate the ethical standard of "do no harm." (Ethical issues in adventure therapy are dealt with specifically in Chapter 12).

However, most people are currently unable to radiate competence and clinical experience to the public without some measure of formal training. For many, competence in mental health practice results from obtaining a graduate degree from a recognized (and accredited) program and subsequently becoming licensed as a mental health practitioner in the state or province where they are working. Few programs exist that focus specifically on adventure therapy or wilderness therapy training in mental health. While a more formal model explaining five levels of professional development with adventure therapy is presented in Chapter 10, most current adventure therapy practitioners obtain a licensable mental health degree along with acquiring additional training in adventure skills from other sources. Some view the interpersonal skills required to conduct therapy as "soft" skills compared with the "hard" technical skills of working safely in the backcountry or on a challenge course or paddling, for example. Others believe the soft skills can take time to teach and may not always be possible to acquire if the therapist in training does not already possess some fundamental level of this quality. This debate will continue, perhaps not so much with programs that separate the adventure from the therapy, but certainly with programs that integrate the adventure as therapy.

Competence in adventure and wilderness technical skills for use by the adventure therapist is typically not as clear as obtaining a graduate degree in a licensable mental health field. Granted, there are a few dual-degree graduate training programs, workshops, and on-the-job training at reputable programs, but it is rare to see "one-stop shops" to obtain competence in hard skills in adventure therapy. This is especially true considering the different environmental conditions available to adventure therapy and different populations served. Many adventure therapists often partner with facilitators who are technical experts, although clearly the responsibility of providing a psychologically and physically safe therapeutic environment lies with the therapist.

Most Effective?

Most of what we know about effectiveness is covered in Chapter 13 on research and evaluation. To date, there have been no randomized control trials of any approach to adventure therapy that would measure up to the gold standard (e.g., saying a particular drug might be more successful than a placebo using a double-blind study). It should be noted that very few traditional psychotherapies live up to this standard, but many therapeutic approaches do have a body of knowledge that comes closer than adventure therapy to proving effectiveness seen in Chapter 13, At the present time, there are very few studies comparing adventure therapy approaches to traditional therapeutic approaches with specific populations. This is an area ripe for research.

For This Individual With That Specific Problem?

Many practitioners in the field of adventure therapy have used an integrative approach, but may not even know it. In illustrating this approach, the ABC≈R triangle provides a visual representation of a system that helps adventure therapists initially assess and subsequently intervene with a client or client population (see Figure 3.1). As noted, the A domain of this model represents affect (e.g., feelings, emotion), the B domain represents behavior (e.g., actions, conduct), and the C domain represents cognition (e.g., thinking, knowledge). These various modalities provide access points (represented by the arrows in Figure 3.1) for this integrated approach to adventure therapy. However, there is no single, standardized sequence or modality to engage the client after entering the model through the access point provided by the clients story. The client's actions, feelings, or thoughts help determine the "proper" path; some may need to start on the cognitive road, others on the affective road, while still others may need to be on the behavioral road. The selected path should be the one that best meets the client's needs.

This integrative approach presupposes that the therapist meets the clients where they are and with what the clients offer as an access point (whether it be affect, behavior, or cognition) instead of fitting the clients into an existing program or theory. This means that the therapist will, in most cases, help to co-create the client's path. Tailoring challenges to the clients fits more closely with Milton Erikson's nontheoretical approach—or perhaps in more modern terms, transtheoretical approach (Haley, 1993). Our approach is transtheoretical in the spirit of DiClemente, McConnaughy, Norcross, and Prochaska (1986) and Prochaska and Norcross (2002). It acknowledges, values, and uses techniques and skill sets from five foundational psychotherapy approaches in the way they match clients' presenting issues: psychoanalytic, interpersonal, cognitive, behavioral, and solution/systemic/narrative. We cover these five foundational therapies later in this chapter.

Note that relationships are central and critical to this model. This model include a general systems approach and views individual clients through the lens of their environment. The term *system* not only includes nature but also

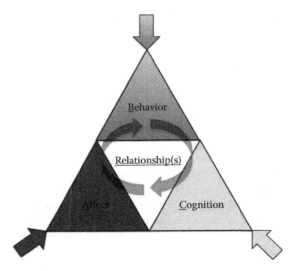

FIGURE 3.1 The ABC≈R model

peers, programs, family, schools, and community. A successful therapeutic alliance (Bachelor, Meunier, Laverdiére, & Gamache, 2010; Horvath & Symonds, 1991) is critical for effective treatment. Similarly, the relationship between the therapist and the client or client group/family is directly related to the success of treatment (Pos, Greenberg, & Warwar, 2009). How the client and the adventure therapist, or the client and the field staff, connect is critical to the success of the adventure therapy process (which will be discussed further in Chapter 4). The long-term success of this process is often dependent on how the client integrates into the family and community posttreatment systems.

Adventure therapy is primarily a group and family treatment that views the peer and family group relationships as foundational to the process of how the therapy works. A high value is placed on the milieu of the peer group, using the impact of a positive (and negative) climate of peers. A solution, choice, and positive psychology focus (Gass & Gillis, 1995b) is also embraced in adventure therapy. This approach stresses what is working for the client and attempts to increase these feelings, actions, and thoughts instead of focusing on eliminating negative thoughts, feelings, and actions.

INTEGRATION OF TRADITIONAL PSYCHOTHERAPY INTO THE ABC≈R MODEL

Affect

Foundational for much of psychotherapy are approaches emanating from the psychoanalytic and psychodynamic theories. Psychodynamic theories are thought to require more insight than behavioral theories. Ringer and Gillis (1996) presented an overview of the thinking at the time and examined theories of psychotherapy based on how much insight was required on the part of the participant. They advocated matching psychotherapy theories to the capability of insight on the part of the client. The authors felt that a more psychologically mature client might benefit from either a psychodynamic or humanistic/interpersonal approach to psychotherapy where insight was considered necessary for behavior change.

Psychoanalytic approaches generally help clients move from concerns about what others think of them to living by their own set of rules (Luborsky, O'Reilly-Landry, & Arlow, 2007). There is a predominance of therapist direction in helping clients uncover issues that were previously beyond conscious awareness. In this therapeutic approach, there is a focus on re-experiencing early family issues or trauma and uncovering buried feelings that may be related to any current anxiety or depression that the client is experiencing. This approach relies on the ability of the client to have insight into their issues as the therapist guides them. There is an assumption that insight into the source of the issue can lead to understanding and therefore a change in behavior.

Following a psychodynamic-based approach to the ABC≈R model involves using the relationship (or alliance) with the therapist and the activities themselves to unearth previously repressed patterns of thinking and behaving in clients. Because adventure therapy traditionally has involved a group component, the client's habitual patterns of interaction may become more visible during this type of intervention. They may replay the way they interact in their family of origin with their adventure therapy group. For example, the addition of stress arising from being placed out of one's comfort zone through a challenge course activity or wilderness experience may reach some clients' defenses quicker than in a traditional talk therapy format. An intense focus on solving many of the initiative problems in a group format may also prevent clients from presenting their usual false selves, and thus will allow their true selves to be utilized in the novel experience. Once these real patterns are visible, psychodynamic therapeutic processes gradually enable clients to identify the origins of these dysfunctional patterns in their early lives, which are deeper levels of psychological depth. The clients' internal representation of themselves as worthwhile people is gradually restored by repeated occasions when they find the therapist and other group members attentive, affirming, and providing reparation. Some might consider this approach as creating a corrective experience.

Interpersonal and humanistic therapies also emphasize insight on the part of the client, but also place more importance in the therapeutic relationship and less on the expertise of the therapist. The therapist is seen as more of an equal in this approach, but there is still the reliance on the clients gaining insight into why they feel or act as they do in order to make changes in their lives. The emphasis in this approach is on gaining a deeper understanding of self and a desire to be more interpersonally authentic. This approach stresses mental health over mental illness and places importance on the clients' experience and understanding of how they make sense of the world and embrace wellness. The emphasis on the client's experience provides some confusion when adventure therapists are searching the literature for the terms *experiential therapy* due to techniques of some forms of interpersonal therapy approaches being labeled as experiential. The focus on developing openness and an ability to honestly express feelings in an accepting (nonjudgmental) environment is why many use this approach when working with clients who have emotional or affective issues.

Some adventure therapists also stress that clients focus on the "here and now" in order to stay fully present in the moment (i.e., being mindful) and guide them away from speaking or dwelling on the past or future. In some cases, programs do not allow clients to have watches or other references to the current time in order to facilitate being mindful of the current situation and their place in it (e.g., not focus on what they might be doing at this time if they were back in the environment they came from before therapy). This focus on the here and now is a therapeutic technique that has its roots in Gestalt therapy (Perls, 1969).

Another concept or technique borrowed from the humanistic tradition of transactional analysis is the no-discount contract (Medrick, 1977). In current experiential education and adventure therapy, it has been renamed the full value contract. Project Adventure changed the name (but not the intent) of this contract to put a positive reframe on it (Schoel, Prouty, & Radcliffe, 1988). The intent of the full value contract is a set of positive agreements the group agrees to, such as be here, be present, be safe, let go, and move on.

Gillis and Bonney (1986) drew parallels between the stages of the psychodynamically oriented psychodrama (Moreno, 1972), the phenomenological principles of Perls' Gestalt therapy (humanistic), and adventure therapy. Instead of identifying a protagonist following warm-up activities as is done with psychodrama, an adventure therapist would use icebreakers to identify an issue common to the group and then present the activity to the group as a way to bring individual issues to the forefront and act upon them. The idea of the most pressing needs of the individual and group being right below the surface (consciousness) is consistent with the phenomenological principles of Gestalt therapy (Perls, 1969). Given the proclivity in Gestalt therapy for action/experiences, it is a natural theoretical fit for many group-oriented adventure therapists.

Hilsenroth, Blagys, Ackerman, Bonge, and Blais (2005) developed and tested the Comparative Psychotherapy Process Scale, which is based on distinguishing qualities of psychodynamic-interpersonal and cognitive behavioral therapies. Psychodynamic-interpersonal actions from their scale are listed below (note the word *patient* has been changed to *client* to be consistent with the ABC≈R model). The following list provides examples of how an adventure therapist might approach clients psychodynamically and interpersonally when working in the affective and cognitive domains of the ABC≈R model:

- Encourage the exploration of feelings regarded by the client as uncomfortable (e.g., anger, envy, excitement, sadness, happiness)
- Link the client's current feelings or perceptions to experiences of the past
- Focus attention on similarities among the client's relationships repeated over time, settings, or people
- Focus discussion on the relationship between therapist and client
- Encourage the client to experience and express feelings in the session
- Address the client's avoidance of important topics and shifts in mood
- Suggest alternative ways to understand experiences or events not previously recognized by the client
- Identify recurrent patterns in the client's actions, feelings, and experiences
- Allow the client to initiate the discussion of significant issues, events, and experiences
- Encourage discussion of the client's wishes, fantasies, dreams, or early childhood memories (positive or negative)

Psychodynamic and interpersonal techniques or interventions are suitable approaches to access clients who present with affective (emotional) issues because they are more process and relationship oriented, especially when the client is *willing* to participate and is cognitively able to gain *insight*.

Behavior

While one axis that might be used to match psychotherapy theories with client populations could be the level of insight the participants are judged to be capable of, another axis might be how willing the participants are to be involved in adventure therapy. For example, adolescents who have been sent to adventure therapy tend to be more resistant or reluctant to receive therapy than participants who choose to come voluntarily. These clients are more likely to benefit from psychotherapy approaches that initially access the behavioral aspect of the triangle.

An approach to the ABC≈R model that uses the initial access point of behavior typically takes advantage of implementing both the natural environment and the human interaction to provide concrete consequences (both positive and negative) for participants' maladaptive behavior. The hope is that participants learn to identify the triggers of their negative behaviors, as well as new or even forgotten prosocial behaviors. Through this process, they begin to behave in ways that are likely to be appropriate for the environment where they will return after the program has ended.

Purely behavioral approaches have been used with clients with impulse control issues who wish to gain rewards without consequences. Little to no insight is expected on the part of the client beyond understanding that if they engage in certain negative behaviors, consequences will follow; as well as if they engage in other positive behaviors, there will be rewards. Often the black-and-white, "no excuses accepted" approach to working with resistant adolescents provides behavioral boundaries in response to their actions in a way that helps them understand how the therapy approach works. As feedback is given to clients about their behavior and they are able to understand it, a cognitive dimension is entered and the connection between what the client is doing and the thinking (or cognitions) behind their behavior becomes the focus of treatment.

Sometimes behavioral interventions are used to establish a stable climate in the group. As an example, a wilderness therapy group may agree to meet a time limit in order to receive a special reward (e.g., dessert) that evening. The application of behavioral principles to adventure interventions is more suitable when clients' internalized sense of responsibility is diminished, when they are constantly acting out, and when they have a limited capacity for self-reflection. Many programs for offenders use behavior-oriented strategies (group applied consequences) with the intent of the externally applied rewards and consequences transferring to internalized rewards by group members. One example of this type of programming is the Behavioral Management through Adventure (BMtA) program associated with Project Adventure (Gillis & Gass, 2010). BMtA programs use a form of the full value contract. This form of the full value contract asks the group:

1. To understand and/or create safe and respectful behavioral norms under which it will operate
2. To make a commitment to those norms (by everyone in the group)
3. To accept a shared responsibility for the maintenance of those norms

The key to using the BMtA model with adolescents is structuring the peer group in a formal, constructive way for clients and staff to confront behavior, express feelings, or address the consequences of breaking behavioral rules. The group process follows a model of "control to empowerment" (Simpson & Gillis, 1998). In this model, clients are taught a process of discussing and voting for logical consequences for violations of the group contract. This move toward empowerment allows group members to conduct their own groups, with staff serving as consultants. The control-to-empowerment philosophy employs Bandura's concept of modeling (Sermabeikian & Martinez, 1994) to turn over control of the group (under staff's supervision and when appropriate) to the clients as the group demonstrates appropriate capacity.

In this process, group norms are developed by the clients, with staff adding vital elements the clients may have missed. The whole group (staff included) commit to upholding these norms, being individually responsible as well as holding the group responsible. The group checks in with their commitments through the full value contract once a day to see how they are doing. In this way, the whole group understands what behaviors are expected by hearing their peers describe their commitments in behavioral terms; group members are held to these behaviors through regular check-ins.

One overriding principle in the BMtA model is the concept of "calling group." Clients and staff may call group at any time. When group is called, all members stand in a circle, listen as the caller presents his issue, discuss the issue, and decide if a consequence is needed, and, if so, what consequence would be appropriate. Calling group enables the therapeutic cohort to learn functional behaviors by providing clients the power to care for themselves and others. Calling group is a way to explore feelings, praise peers, praise oneself, or just check-in.

Another core element of BMtA programs is the use of adventure activities. The activities are developmentally structured (e.g., a group that has just met would not do an activity that requires trust, but would build trust incrementally through activities). They also are often enjoyable (but not just fun) and require real assets that direct BMtA clients to learn skills such as patience, listening, seeing another's point of view, leading, following, planning, and acknowledging consequences.

BMTA staff often use the behavioral scanning technique called GRABBS when working with groups (Schoel et al., 1988). The acronym GRABBS was developed by Project Adventure as a scanning device for helping facilitators to remember important domains when assessing their groups in the moment. GRABBS stands for **G**oals, **R**eadiness, **A**ffect, **B**ehavior, **B**ody, and **S**tage (with an additional **S** added later for Setting; Schoel & Maizell, 2002). The acronym evolved from BASIC-ID (Lazarus, 1981), a mnemonic device to help therapists be thorough in their assessments of clients that stands for **B**ehavior, **A**ffect responses, **S**ensory reactions, **I**mages, **C**ognitions, **I**nterpersonal relationships, and **D**rugs. The GRABBS scanning device has proved invaluable to many leaders in the moment-to-moment microassessment of their groups, the individuals within their groups, themselves, and their clients (i.e., whoever is paying the bill for the service, such as parents or a government agency). Other assessment models exist for facilitators of adventure experiences, such as the wave model (Lung, Stauffer, & Alvarez, 2008).

Cognitive

Cognitive therapies use an approach that involves understanding thinking that is not correct (or is irrational), and changing it as well as the behavior that is connected to that thinking. Homework is often prescribed in which clients test beliefs they have about the world to see the accuracy and functionality of their assumptions. By identifying and understanding the distorted and unrealistic beliefs, clients are able to change the way they act upon them.

Glasser (1965) developed a cognitive behavior approach widely used in some adventure therapy programs called reality therapy. Reality therapy was an approach that could be taught to paraprofessionals and, perhaps because of the word *reality* being in the title, was thought by some to correspond with the natural and logical consequences inherent in adventure therapy. The use of natural and logical consequences, however, has its origins in the work of Alfred Adler and parenting training programs based on the work of Rudolph Dreikurs, who was a student of Adler's (Dreikurs, Greenwald, & Pepper, 1982). The reality therapy approach to problem solving focuses on the here-and-now that the client is experiencing and helps the client create a better future. It is based on the idea that humans have five basic needs: survival, love and belonging, power, freedom, and fun. An environment that embraces these five needs helps clients to get their needs met and enables them to develop a plan focused on what works. Another concept of reality therapy that appeals to many adventure therapists is the focus on no excuses, no punishment, and never giving up. This approach is still in use today, as evidenced by its explicit mention on the website of Eckerd Youth Alternatives (http://www.eckerd.org/services/out-of-home/juvenile-justice-residential/).

Cognitive behavioral strategies, as presented by Hilsenroth et al. (2005), include:

- Give explicit advice or direct suggestions to the client
- Actively initiate the topics of discussion and therapeutic activities
- Focus discussion on the client's irrational or illogical belief systems
- Suggest specific activities or tasks (homework for the client to attempt outside of session)
- Explain the rationale behind the therapist's technique or approach to treatment
- Focus discussion on the client's future life situations
- Provide the client with information and facts about his or her current symptoms, disorder, or treatment
- Explicitly suggest that the client practice behavior(s) learned in therapy between sessions
- Teach the client specific techniques for coping with symptoms
- Interact with the client in a teacher-like (didactic) manner

Again, in the previous strategies, the term *patient* was changed to *client* to be more consisted with adventure therapy approaches. The interventions are provided here as appropriate for intervening with clients in their behavioral and cognitive domains.

Behavioral and cognitive interventions are suitable approaches to access clients who present with behavioral or cognitive issues because they are more outcome and results oriented. This is especially true when the client is initially unwilling to participate and is not necessarily able to gain insight into why they are acting as they do. Starting with behavior and proceeding to cognitive base is a common path for many adventure programs. But in the timeless words of the ever-centered Mark Ames (personal communication, October, 31, 2009), "It's really all about the relationship."

Relationships

Systemic therapy attempts to address people in a relationship with others in their sphere (e.g., peer group, program staff, family, school, community) and how they interact. The field has its roots in the interactions of a client's family of origin. Systemic therapy approaches problems in a practical manner, much like cognitive behavioral approaches (whereas many psychodynamic approaches use a much deeper manner). Systemic therapy attempts to identify dysfunctional patterns of behavior and directly work with those patterns. There may be a focus on how tight or loose the boundaries were within the family, which can be determined by examining questions such as the following:

- Did everyone know everything that occurred with the family (complete permeable boundaries and an enmeshed family), so that there was no privacy?
- Was the family full of secrets, so that no one knew anything about anyone else and no one from the outside knew anything that occurred within the family (an abusive family pattern)?

These are ways of describing how family patterns influence clients (and their families) in their relationships with the adventure therapist, the staff, and peers in their group. It is not uncommon to hear an adventure therapist say the phrase "meet the parents and meet the problem" when working with adolescents. Experience tells us that there is some level of truth to this comment when examining this concept through a systems lens.

An understanding of how a client perceives relationships—especially clients who have family histories that include such things as trauma, substance abuse, divorce, and stepparents—is helpful in understanding how they will interact during the adventure therapy program. Much of the understanding of the family system, especially when the group is a family, can help the adventure therapist determine how and why the client is entering adventure therapy and how resistant or willing they are to embrace change.

WHO PARTICIPATES IN ADVENTURE THERAPY?

Using the CHANGES model (Gass & Gillis, 1995a) we described in Chapter 7, the context of how a client views their need for change and their level of insight are important factors in how they initially respond to adventure therapy. Russell (2008) examined adolescents admitted to outdoor behavioral healthcare programs. The clients in his sample were found to exhibit the characteristics listed in Table 3.1 upon admission. Participants who answered questions placing them in an *uninvolved* category were the largest group, followed by those deemed *reluctant* to engage in therapy, and finally those who were *willing* to participate were the minority. These figures mirror the clients being treated in adventure therapy programs. Russell's categorizations are by-products of a measurement of the stages of change by Prochaska and DiClemente (1983). This theory rings true to many adventure therapists as a way of conceptualizing how clients enter and engage in treatment. The stages of this model are presented in Table 3.2.

The original Stages of Change theory comes from smoking addiction research and led to a transtheoretical model of psychotherapy (Prochaska & Norcross, 2002), which has been built upon in the design of the ABC≈R model. It is one way to conceptualize where clients are as they approach treatment and allows the therapist to best match a treatment approach to the client's particular frame of reference.

Russell and Gillis (2007) also found that most clients entering adventure therapy programs meet the criteria for a substance use disorder. If this is correct and most clients who come into an adventure therapy session/program are reluctant or resistant adolescents who have substance use issues, how can the adventure therapist be most effective? Based on actual client experiences, several fictionalized case studies are presented in the following sections to illustrate the ABC≈R approach.

TABLE 3.1 Stages of Change Clusters

Cluster Name	Definition	Participants, %
Uninvolved	• Not contemplating change • Not engaging behaviors to change • Maintaining the status quo	44.1
Reluctant	• Reluctant to take action on a problem • A sense they might be thinking about it • No commitment to change	28.7
Participating	• Not ignoring the presence of a problem • Engaged in thinking about the problem • Taking some action in changing the problem • Maintaining some of these actions	27.2

TABLE 3.2 Description of Stages of Change

Stage	Description
Precontemplation	No intention to change
Contemplation	Thinking about change in the near future
Preparation	Thinking about change in the very near future
Action	Specific behaviors changed
Maintenance	Working not to relapse
Termination	Very confident change is permanent

CASE STUDIES

Three case studies are used here to highlight how adventure therapy can be tailored to clients when given their presenting issues.

Jamie

Jamie, a 17-year-old who is suffering from a mood disorder, is perhaps dealing with a combination of depression and anxiety. Jamie is referred to an adventure therapist's group who operates in an outpatient private practice. Jamie has not experienced any success in traditional one-to-one "talk-only" treatment and has been noncompliant with taking prescribed psychotropic medications. Jamie is angry at seeing yet another therapist—especially one who uses groups. The feelings that Jamie is having may provide initial access through the access point of affect. Developing an intervention through the use of an adventure experience that allows access to other feelings (e.g., going to the top of a challenge course element and having to make decisions about jumping to hit a large red ball or not) may be what the therapist chooses to tailor to Jamie's affective issues. The therapist may also intervene using the following techniques:

- Encourage the exploration of feelings regarded by Jamie as uncomfortable (e.g., anger, envy, excitement, sadness, or happiness)
- Address Jamie's avoidance of important topics and shifts in mood
- Suggest alternative ways to understand experiences or events not previously recognized by Jamie

Taylor

Taylor, age 16, has a history of outbursts with his parents, substance use issues, failure in several schools, and a lack of progress in working with his most recent counselor in an outpatient setting. Taylor would appear to present behavior as an access point to beginning adventure therapy in a wilderness program. One could initially say that nature was a behavioral therapist, focused on rewards and natural consequences. If the tent was set up securely, the stove functioned properly, and the weather was cooperative, the rewards of food and shelter would follow. If food was left in a pack or it was too dark, windy, or wet to cook, the natural consequences would be immediately obvious. Experience has shown that many adolescents like Taylor are angry at having been sent to therapy by their parents; this anger might come up when Taylor must take responsibility for the natural consequence. Therefore, identifying what triggered Taylor's angry/hurt feelings and providing more functional alternative ways to respond may result in learning that lasts. Using positive letters from parents can also work toward beginning to rebuild family relationships after Taylor has learned the boundaries (rules) of the program.

Taylor exhibits behaviors that need to be brought under control in order for the adventure therapy process to take place. The therapist may intervene using the following techniques:

- Provide Taylor with information and facts about his current symptoms, disorder, or treatment
- Explicitly suggest that Taylor practice behavior(s) learned in therapy in the coming days
- Teach Taylor specific techniques for coping with symptoms

Jordan

Jordan is a 15-year-old at a residential treatment center struggling with mood regulation related to attachment and trauma issues. Jordan is adopted and struggling with questions about being adopted. Jordan's issues are primarily cognitive. In addition, Jordan is having self-worth and identity issues. As a result, Jordan is acting out sexually and defiantly, as well as having a past dominated by substance abuse. Jordan presents with the cognitive dimension as the initial access point. Jordan wants to know why.

In the first phase of the program, Jordan should work on self-disclosure of painful past deeds and expressing anger, frustration, and sadness about being placed in treatment. As a substance abuser, Jordan is often engaging in thinking errors about the ability to maintain sobriety or lower the risk for using upon leaving treatment. Jordan is planning to return and live with the same drug-using peer group as prior to treatment. These thinking errors or errors in cognition provide an entry to this integrated approach to adventure therapy. Perhaps the adventure therapist can design an activity that will match Jordan's thinking errors and allow Jordan to understand how "rational lies" will impact the success of staying sober while going back to the same environment. The therapist can also use the following approaches:

- Give explicit advice or direct suggestions to Jordan
- Focus discussion on Jordan's irrational or illogical belief systems that are revealed in response to challenging activities

- Tailor the activities to draw out or highlight Jordan's belief systems and thoughts about the future

OTHER CONTRIBUTIONS TO UNDERSTANDING THEORY

In addition to the work of Project Adventure with adventure-based counseling (Schoel et al., 1988; Schoel & Maizell, 2002), Newes (2001) provided an extensive description of how adventure therapy intersects with several traditional psychotherapeutic theories, especially the psychodynamically oriented object relations theory and cognitive behavioral therapy. The reader is encouraged to read her full descriptions.

In her conclusion to these descriptions, Newes noted that the benefits of group experience, problem-solving activities with tangible outcomes, the use of the unfamiliar environment, immediacy of the therapeutic relationship, the opportunity to disprove negative self-evaluations, the success associated with increases in self-efficacy, and the power of modeling both therapist and peer behavior are critical factors of adventure therapy. Combined with object relations-based processing and cognitively based processing over a period of time, this combination is believed to help develop a unique and beneficial process for therapeutic change.

SUMMARY

This chapter presented an adventure therapy response to Paul's (1967) ultimate question—"What treatment, by whom, is most effective for which individual with what specific problem, under which set of circumstances?"—by offering an integrative approach to psychotherapy. This approach begins where the client is, with what they present to the therapist in terms of affect, behavior, and cognition. It then connects this information to the relationship of therapist to client, client to peer group, and client to larger systems (e.g., family, school, community) that are part of the change maintenance process.

In many ways, in *The Wizard of Oz* (Baum, 1900), the real wizard of facilitating change for Dorothy and her colleagues may have been Toto the dog. In the story, there is seemingly very little attention paid to Toto. But at critical times throughout the movie, Toto provides facilitative guidance of affective, behavioral, and cognitive support for the characters, similarly to how the adventure therapist guides clients. In addition, Toto helps to facilitate their individual as well as group development through different yet purposely structured relationships, which serves them well in strengthening their resolve for the challenges they face. Most importantly, as each group member accomplishes their goals, their success is attributed to themselves and not to Toto, the therapeutic facilitator of change.

A COOPERATIVE SAILING CHALLENGE

Lorri Hanna

A wilderness therapy program located in the Midwest enrolled six girls into their summer adventure program due to their difficulty coping with certain challenges in their lives (e.g., poor school performance, depression, low self-esteem, underachievement, family discord). As part of admitting circumstances, the girls displayed social withdrawal, poor coping, ineffective communication skills, and distorted thinking patterns. A personal development plan (treatment plan) was created with each student to include three focus areas (e.g., relationships, communication, boundaries) and action steps. The program consisted of three phases totaling 6 weeks of backpacking, rock climbing, service learning, and canoe expedition balanced with an emotional growth curriculum consisting of structure, consistency, and accountability. It was important as a group to initially establish a set of agreements (norms) as a foundation for building trust and an emotionally safe environment that would encourage the girls to take responsibility for their own process and healing. Prior to graduation, individual family sessions added to their efforts to repair and restore their family relationships and prepare for transition.

The final phase of the program was the canoe expedition. After several days on the lakes honing canoe, paddle, and portage skills, the girls were presented with a group challenge. Using only three paddles, two canoes, a large tarp, cordage, and life jackets, the group was to build a vessel to transport them as a team across the lake to their campsite. Instructors provided water-based supervision and only intervened when safety warranted.

After 45 minutes of observing old behavior patterns (e.g., activity refusal, ineffective communication), combined with their newly learned tools of problem solving and listening, the girls created a sailboat using the tarp as their sail and a paddle as their mast to successfully make their way across the bay. During the debriefing of the activity, the girls attributed their success to implementing newly learned problem-solving skills and using intentional dialogue as a way to give each girl a voice to contribute to solutions and work as a team (family). Discussion ensued as to how these behaviors could help them at home, school, and in their families. The girls expressed enthusiasm and pride in their accomplishments, and this experience became a turning point in the group cohesion and future personal processes for the remainder of the canoe expedition.

At the conclusion of the 6-week session, the girls were anxious yet excited to share their learning with their parents and took emotional risks during their 2.5-hour family sessions that demonstrated effective dialogue skills, increased confidence, accountability, and solution-focused transition goals. This ability to work cooperatively through challenging activities while demonstrating and recognizing positive behavioral change is an example of what I call adventure therapy.

I became an adventure therapist in the early 1980s while working as a wilderness counselor with at-risk and adjudicated adolescents in Virginia, my first employment during graduate school. I was passionate about backpacking and climbing and valued the self-exploration I found in the wilderness. It was important to me to share that passion with others because I believed in the therapeutic value of wilderness travel. My graduate studies in therapeutic recreation, combined with outdoor leadership and wilderness medicine courses (e.g., Wilderness

Education Association, Outward Bound, Wilderness First Responder) and my personal experiences, paved my way toward adventure therapy.

In various professional positions, resourcefulness was essential to adapting adventure activities for individuals with cognitive or physical challenges. I saw the therapeutic value of using "lobster claws" and old mattresses inside a low-element Burma bridge for clients with muscular sclerosis so that they too could have a success-oriented physical challenge while trusting the process, access skills they thought they lost, and feel empowered to make decisions. The adjudicated and high-risk youth I worked with needed to experience healthy recreational activities and a sense of belonging and connection. Adventure therapy activities provided the structure to bring about change, develop group cohesion, encourage cooperation, and create a feeling of self-worth.

I have since become a Licensed Professional Counselor and founded a wilderness therapy program providing adventure therapy practices to clients of all ages. My passion continues and is shared with colleagues, clients, and interns entering the field of adventure therapy.

Chapter 4

Foundations of Adventure Therapy

This chapter explores the question of how adventure therapy (AT) works. To address this question, the chapter examines three key theoretical and practical foundations relevant to the AT process:

1. The integration of the Walsh and Golins (1976) Outward Bound process model within an AT context
2. An overview and discussion of how adventure and experiential activities are used in therapeutic settings
3. How the process is used with different types of AT program models

CONCEPTUALIZING THE ADVENTURE THERAPY PROCESS

AT processes typically fall into one of two categories of interventions: preventive, which seek to delay or bypass the onset of psychological problems, or treatment, which focuses on alleviating symptoms, changing behaviors, or developing coping strategies for individuals who meet criteria for a mental health disorder (Hogue, 2002). In illustrating how AT interventions work to accomplish these aims, this chapter conceptualizes and illustrates the AT process and how it works in a variety of settings.

To accomplish this, the classic Walsh and Golins (1976) model of the Outward Bound process is presented here because it represents a foundational model from which many AT programs have theoretically evolved. This model remains as one of the foundational conceptual and descriptive illustrations of how the adventure-based learning process works to facilitate change in individuals. However, other authors prior to Walsh and Golins also offered models of outdoor learning that are lesser known. For example, Kesselheim (1974) presented a paper justifying the use of outdoor learning 2 years earlier at the

Conference on Outdoor Pursuits in Higher Education (the first national meeting of what was to become the Association for Experiential Education) that contained many of the same factors discussed by Walsh and Golins. These factors included environmental contrast, physical activity, intentional use of stress, small group context, and employment of newly acquired knowledge and skills.

Despite the noted standing of the Walsh and Golins models in the literature, few researchers have tested the fundamental tenets, leading to questions about whether the theory is robust enough to effectively explain the process. Critics argue that the model is linear and assumes a sequential process not reflective of an adventure-based experience like Outward Bound. But as stated by Sibthorp (2003, p. 81):

> While some readers may argue that this model is atheoretical, it has resonated with practice, a fact which longevity and popularity attest; it is difficult to find a text on adventure-based programs without the Walsh and Golins citation.

Walsh and Golins (1976) defined a process as a generalized series of conditions, events, and objects that interact to produce a desired effect. As such, the Outward Bound process model includes a *motivated* learner or program participant being placed into a prescribed physical and social/group environment where specific problem-solving tasks are presented to the learner. Problem-solving tasks, experiences, and learning are presented, sequenced, and facilitated by the leader in such a way that the participant experiences success or mastery, which leads to intra- and interpersonal growth (see Figure 4.1). The degree and mechanism to which these factors interact is not well understood. In fact, only one such study (Sibthorp, 2003) is noted in the literature. In this study, relationships were explored for 15- and 16-year-olds between antecedent variables (e.g., motivations, expectations, demographics) and characteristics of the experience (e.g., instructor support, group support, learning relevance, group and personal empowerment) to understand how they related to outcome variables (self-efficacy). The results showed a strong relationship between motives and expectations and personal empowerment and learning, which were strongly related to changes in self-efficacy. This empirical work supports the notion that being a motivated learner and having the learning be relevant to the participant directly relates to mastery (the belief in one's ability to accomplish tasks), key tenets of the Walsh and Golins model (see Figure 4.1).

Applying the Walsh and Golins (1976) model to the AT process requires some interpretation and discussion of each of these variables in a therapeutic context that is designed to promote a desire to change. In addition to variables described in the Walsh and Golins model, Gass (1993a), Newes and Bandoroff (2004), and other authors have suggested several

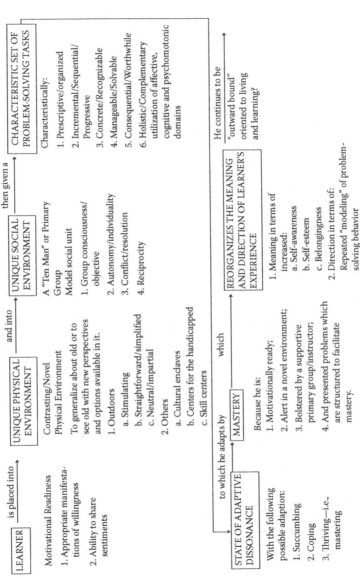

FIGURE 4.1 The Outward Bound process Model. "This model illustrates how the Outward Bound process functions, as characteristic problem-solving tasks are set in a prescribed physical and social environment, which impel the participant to mastery of these tasks and which, in turn, serve to reorganize the meaning and direction of his life experience." (Walsh and Golins, 1976, p. 16).

characteristics inherent in the AT process that are also found in the Walsh and Golins model help to further elucidate how it works. These characteristics include:

1. Provision of a group-based model
2. Use of processing and reflection during the experience
3. Sequencing of activities
4. Notion of perceived risk
5. Role of a novel and unfamiliar environment
6. Use of challenge by choice as a guiding principle
7. Concept that adventure experiences are concrete and real
8. Use of goal setting and an inherent climate of change
9. Inclusion of trust building
10. Idea that adventure experiences are fun and enjoyable
11. Role of peak experiences
12. Unique structure of the therapeutic relationship

When applying the Walsh and Golins (1976) model in a therapeutic context and weaving in these therapeutic factors to the model, these "active ingredients" in AT illustrate how the AT process uniquely works to effectuate change in individuals seeking treatment. Note that many of these assumptions, characteristics, and process variables are also common to most treatment approaches, including humanistic and cognitive behavioral treatment models. What is particularly unique to AT, however, is the use of adventure and experiential activities, as they form a central feature that melds the various factors together to create the whole that is AT.

A Metaphor to Guide Application

Gillis (1993) used a metaphor of cooking in the forward to a book on adventure therapy edited by Gass (1993a, pp. ix–x):

> Note that this book is not intended to be a cookbook; rather its strength lies in its ability to present the ingredients of [AT] for professionals, as well as a strong rationale to evaluate whether [AT] and its programs will be successful.

In many ways, this chapter is replete with evidence-based ingredients and fits well with this cooking metaphor, in that it presents a description of a process with associated ingredients with which an adventure therapist, a treatment team, or a program may work. Christian Itin, in Hirsch and Gillis (1997), suggested the metaphor of a chef who works with these ingredients to develop unique broths that are seasoned with the right spices, at the right time, with the right combinations, to create a process that will work for specific individuals and groups.

The key ingredients of AT are listed in Table 4.1. This list will not magically create change in individuals. Rather, it is intended to provide food for thought so that practitioners, researchers, and students will question these ingredients and better understand how they add to the field and practice of AT. Each of these ingredients is elaborated on throughout this chapter, which integrates the Walsh and Golins (1976) model with empirically grounded factors that make the flavor of AT come to life.

TABLE 4.1 Key Ingredients of the AT Process Integrated within the Walsh and Golins (1976) Framework

Process Factor	Ingredients
Motivated learner or program participant	Self-efficacy
	Resilience
	Stages of contemplation
	Self-determination theory
	External to internal locus of control
Prescribed physical environment	Physical exercise
	Nature as a restorative environment
	Neutral
	Disrupts familiar patterns
	Intensive and action oriented
	Appropriately challenging
	Positive stress
	Experiential
Social environment	Small group-based model
	Ten-person group dynamic
	Reciprocity dynamic
	Enriched assessment
	Therapeutic factors of group therapy
Adventure-based experience	Organized, concrete, sequential, and achievable
	Continuous and evolving
	Psychosocial and motor skill development
	Development of self
	Frame and metaphor
	Motivating
Role of the instructor	Solution focused
	Therapeutic relationship
	Core conditions of change
Success or mastery	Intra- and interpersonal growth
	Reorganization of life's meaning
Transfer	Transfer of learning

MOTIVATED LEARNER

The first variable in the model discussed by Walsh and Golins (1976) is the description of the participant as being a motivated learner. How to motivate people to change has perplexed the psychological community for centuries, and forms the basis for several major research initiatives, including that of Deci and Ryan and others in their development of self-determination theory. Self-determination theory is a macro theory of human motivation that is useful in helping to explain how to shift motivation during a therapeutic process from an external source of motivation to an internal one. This is the crux of the Outward Bound process model, quite literally, and is defined by Walsh and Golins as "thinking, feeling, and behaving as if there is something to be gained from participating" (p. 3).

Especially when working with youth or substance abuse treatment models, there are many times when participants possess considerable resistance to be in treatment, let alone be motivated to engage in the process. Several authors have suggested this comprises a significant percentage of AT clients in general, and wilderness therapy clients in particular (Russell, 2003b). When participants enter outside events or people control them more than they control themselves, most forms of treatment for these individuals has been externally recommended or mandated for them by forces outside their control (Ryan, Lynch, Vansteenkiste, & Deci, 2011). Because of this, many clients in AT have low motivation to want to be in treatment and have lower motivation to want to change, which are qualities that have been shown by researchers to lead to poor engagement in the process and less significant outcomes.

Research and anecdotal evidence suggest that AT experiences foster the development of inherent motivation in individuals to want to change despite low motivations at the onset of treatment. Gass (1993a) referred to the fact that the client is a participant rather than a spectator in therapy, and that client activities (which will be discussed later in detail) require motivation in the form of energy, involvement, and responsibility to be successfully completed. For example, Russell (2008) found that the overwhelming majority of youth in a wilderness therapy program were highly resistant and unmotivated at the onset of treatment, with motivations shifting considerably to a more participating and active involvement in the process by the midpoint of their process. Exactly how this change occurs is a major focus of the remaining sections of this chapter. Offering some theoretical support for this idea, Newes and Bandoroff (2004) suggested that AT experiences facilitate enjoyment, making the process more engaging for participants. Therefore, although an individual may not be initially motivated in an AT experience, the motivation is reasoned to manifest itself naturally, easily, and rather quickly. This leads to changes in participants' beliefs so that they believe they have control and influence over their life direction (e.g., self-efficacy).

PRESCRIBED PHYSICAL ENVIRONMENT

The prescribed physical environment used in Outward Bound experiences was characterized by Walsh and Golins (1976, p. 4) as "really nothing other than one the learner is not familiar with." Expanding on this, the *contrast* created by a novel and unfamiliar environment is the first step to shifting motivation and "reorganizing the meaning and direction of the participant's experience" (p. 4). Why and how do unfamiliar environments facilitate this shift in meaning? As was reasoned in Chapter 5 on the role that nature plays in adventure and has been expanded on by several other authors in an AT context (Kimball, 1983; Russell, 2003a; 2005; 2008), the outdoors and natural environments are particularly potent in this regard.

The variety of unfamiliar settings used in AT are endless. Key is the contrast enabling participants to see the generalities in their lives and gain a new perspective on the old, routine, and familiar behaviors to which they are accustomed and where their lives are situated. Several commonalities exist in the lives of some clients that sometimes contraindicate this phenomenon. This can include similarities in the physical setting, which is often outdoor and nature based, common to AT experiences that work to facilitate this process. It also can include the idea that an unfamiliar environment is serving as an escape from their everyday lives. Adaptations in traditional practices meant to create unfamiliarity must occur with participants with this type of background.

However, the main focus of the physical environment is to have the participant experience and create a sense of adaptive dissonance. Such a dissonance is meant to motivate and encourage people to reduce the dissonance by inherently striving to become more comfortable in their new experience by adapting to the challenges, norms, and values of the experience. Reflecting the notion of unbalancing put forth by Minuchin and Fishman (1981) and elaborated on by Gillis & Bonney (1989) in an AT context, the use of an unfamiliar and novel environment activates underlying inter- and intrapersonal processes in the hopes that participants will explore new ways of addressing them in a positive and healthier way through group and leader support. These behavioral patterns are also more tangible and can be directly addressed in real time by the group and individuals. This process is meant to reduce the defensiveness of individuals in a more natural and less contrived way, leading to a shift to more autonomous and self-promoted motivation, which in turn leads to engagement and belief in the process described by Ryan et al. (2011).

Another factor discussed by numerous researchers (but never empirically tested) is the neutrality of these unfamiliar and natural environments. As Walsh and Golins (1976, p. 4) stated, "arbitrary and consequential rules are in existence which are not made," and participants "must accept and respect these rules regardless of preconceived notions" if they are to thrive. If it rains on a particular day, everyone gets wet unless they exercise self-awareness and self-responsibility, which is often translated for each individual to provide context and meaning given their reason for being in an AT experience. For youth especially, this natural consequence is an important factor given their propensity to resist authority and contrived rules and procedures.

In summary, the prescribed unfamiliar environments where AT occurs, especially when conducted in natural settings, help to disrupt familiar patterns, create an inherent motivation to acclimate to the environment, and provide real and concrete experiences that can be drawn upon in subsequent therapeutic processes. All of these factors can help reduce defensiveness and shift client motivation. In this way, a prescribed unfamiliar environment (e.g., challenge ropes course) provides an autonomy-supportive atmosphere conducive to participants accessing an internal source of motivation to begin thinking about change. This further provides a framework in which the basic psychological needs (Self-Determination Theory) of the participants can be met by the subsequent social milieu and adventure-based activities. The three psychological needs that typically occur first in this environment—and that are elaborated on as one moves through the model—are:

1. *Autonomy* (through nondirective inquiry and reflection)
2. *Competence* (through provision of activity, demonstrated skill acquisition, and other factors)
3. *Relatedness* (through relationships with self, peers, therapists, and leaders) characterized by relationships that are facilitated in the environment by genuineness, unconditional positive regard, empathy, and concreteness

Although these factors do play a powerful role in group development activities and low/high challenge (ropes) course elements, when the prescribed unfamiliar environment is in a wilderness or backcountry setting, the factors described in Chapter 3 also manifest to create a powerful medium for therapy.

PRESCRIBED SOCIAL ENVIRONMENT

In any discussion of a therapeutic milieu, the social environment underlying the experience is one of the primary agents of change. The Walsh and Golins (1976) "ten-man group" [sic] (or primary group) is characterized as an interdependent peer group working together to complete a common set of objectives. The intentional formation of groups in the physical settings where AT occurs is incredibly diverse. AT primary groups could range from a group of women in their 50s at a retreat center who survived cancer to a group of adjudicated youth on a 50-day wilderness experience in the Boundary Waters Wilderness area of Northern Minnesota. The formation of groups in AT reflect the philosophy, goals, and expected outcomes of the AT organizations doing the prescribing for participants. In doing so, programs have underlying reasons, either evidence based or through years of experience, for choosing the groups and settings to create the experience.

Newes and Bandoroff (2004, p. 13) discussed the power of the group process to provide support, feedback, and a "potent interpersonal context." Nadler (1993, p. 61) believes a cooperative and safe environment is key to therapeutic change in that it "facilitates opportunities for clients to develop group cohesiveness." This process is predicated on a structure and belief that focuses on shared goals and objectives, as well as the generous provision of time and opportunity for interpersonal and intrapersonal communication. Several of Yalom's (1995) therapeutic factors inherent in group psychotherapy, which are often reasoned to be uniquely developed in AT settings, support these assertions. Yalom's factors include:

1. Faith in the treatment mode is a powerful therapeutic factor.
2. Universality is a process where members of a group begin to recognize that other members of the group share similar feelings, fears, desires, thoughts, and problems about their lives.
3. Social learning (the development of basic social skills) is a therapeutic factor operating in almost all therapy groups.

These factors are elaborated on in the following paragraphs using a wilderness therapy experience for youth as way to illustrate how the group process works in AT settings. Here motivation is shifted to meet the primary psychological need of *relatedness* through developed relationships with self, peers, therapists, and leaders.

Yalom (1995) asserted that the belief and confidence in the power and support of the group process reinforced by the AT therapist, and through careful explanation of the group's ability to facilitate change, is a powerful factor that makes groups inherently effective. Applied to AT experiences, this process typically occurs on the first day of any experience or wilderness trip by establishing a full value contract complete with the leader and group discussing fears and expectations (Schoel, Prouty, & Radcliffe, 1988). A "talking stick" is commonly used to graphically show that every person will be heard, and when a person is speaking others are responsible for listening and respecting that individual. The leaders model the use of the stick as well to clearly illustrate that "we are all in this together." Walsh and Golins (1976) term this factor reciprocity, and they cite Bruner (1966), who elaborates on this factor's ability to facilitate a desire to learn. Bruner stated that when cooperation is a shared value and where reciprocity is required for the group to attain an objective, "then there seems to be processes that naturally carry the individual along into learning" (p. 125). This process sets the stage for Yalom's (1995) notion of universality, a second powerful therapeutic factor that works to facilitate engagement, motivation, and therapeutic outcome.

A wilderness therapy experience provides a constant source of feedback due to the necessary and mandatory cooperation of individuals to complete daily tasks, and often through the routine process of "circling up" to reflect on or debrief an experience. Intrapersonal issues, such as feelings of inadequacy or an inability to feel a sense of empathy, are impacted by group discussions relating to the day's activities. For example, when hiking, a group member may notice that another is having a particularly hard time because of the weight of their pack. The group member might offer to carry some weight, providing a simple yet powerful example of support. The discussion that evening surrounding this simple act of helping can have powerful metaphorical application. One member showed compassion and caring by helping another out, while the other let down their barriers by asking for help and saying thank you. Each has seen that they can relate to others, show empathy, and ask for help when needed.

Many youth seeking treatment come from family environments with heightened levels of parent-child conflict and family disorganization, which lead to both acute and potentially chronic stressors (Felner et al., 1995). The effect that these stressors have on relative levels of self-esteem, depression and anxiety, and behavioral problems in home and school environments are well documented (Steinberg & Silverberg, 1986). Yalom (1995, p. 13) pointed out that the group (in psychotherapy) resembles a primary family environment, even in that the therapy team often consists of male and female members; he termed this therapeutic factor the "corrective recapitulation of the primary family unit" and believes that a cohesive group can benefit from such opportunities. This theory rests on the principle that members of a group will frequently behave in a manner similar to the way they act in their primary family. Many participants claim the group became a family during the trip (Russell, 2005) and cite this process as a key reason for their desire to change dysfunctional past behaviors. This dynamic can be a powerful one for the participants because it could be the first time in their lives they were accepted for who they are, and were allowed to be a part of a group that argued, lived, and showed compassion for other members in a manner similar to a healthy family unit.

Social learning is perhaps the most powerful therapeutic factor at work in a wilderness therapy experience in AT. The development of social skills as an objective can be traced back to the very first wilderness therapy program (Davis-Berman & Berman, 1994). Participants in a wilderness therapy experience are rewarded when positively communicating with others by the very nature of the process as described previously. This idea is often placed in a context of a caring, compassionate, and cooperative environment through the establishment of the full value contract. Peer feedback—and even confrontation—can serve as an integral part of the communication process, teaching students to confront their peers in ways that are not vindictive or demeaning. As students work through problems and issues on the trip, they practice social skills in an environment devoid of accustomed culture and practice.

The ways in which the therapeutic factors of group therapy facilitate group cohesiveness are enhanced in AT experiences. This enhanced environment offers support for why the social environment, characterized by the development of the group through these experiences, is such a powerful medium for change. This is especially important, because "the exchange of one's abilities in intimate, socially accepted cooperation with others is not readily available to people today" (Walsh & Golins, 1976, p. 6).

The final element of the Walsh and Golins (1976) model that applies to AT is the problem-solving tasks involved in the experience. Because this variable forms the essence of how AT works, it is elaborated on at length in the subsequent section.

CHARACTERISTICS OF PROBLEM-SOLVING TASKS

When describing the characteristics of the problem-solving adventure-based tasks such as rock climbing, rappelling, solo, and camping, Walsh and Golins (1976) referred to several characteristics in support of their value in adventure experiences. Tasks that are developmentally and therapeutically effective are organized, sequential, concrete, achievable, naturally consequential, and holistic. These factors are assumed to be manifest in an AT context and should guide a discussion of how adventure-based and experiential activities are used by leaders, therapists, and programs to effectuate change in clients.

Adventure-based experiences are also especially relevant to the three psychological needs presented earlier that form the foundation of self-determination theory. The integration of adventure activities is especially profound in this regard when helping individuals make this shift. The primary psychological need facilitating autonomous motivation is *competence*, which is developed through the provision of engaging activity, demonstrated skill acquisition, and real and immediate feedback. The following discussion on how adventure activity is used as a tool is strongly supported by empirical data developed in a national survey of 51 AT programs, where a director or lead clinician at each program was asked to expand on why and how adventure is used in their programs (Russell & Gillis, 2010).

A key factor discussed by Walsh and Golins (1976) is that the activities are organized to be educative (not "miseducative") by carefully matching the risks of the experience with the disposition of the participant. In exemplifying this idea, Dewey (1938, p. 38) stated the goal is in "establishing conditions that arouse curiosity, strengthen initiative, and set up desires and purposes that are sufficiently intense to carry a person over the dead places in the future." In relating this idea to AT contexts, the objectives underlying the intentional use of activity and experience are important to clarify.

Literature, practical experience, and responses from practitioners suggest several reasons for how adventure-based and experiential activities should be designed, organized, and delivered. Three key ideas provide a broader theoretical justification for their use. The first justification is that adventure and experiential activities first create a continuous and evolving therapeutic process that is dynamic and typically different from those previously experienced. In this way, therapy is not predicated on abstract ideas, but occurs on a continual basis in an unstructured and neutral environment. As one therapist stated, the "neutral environment does not allow the client access to the dependencies that have been insulating them from experiencing their respective lives in a genuine fashion" (Russell and Gillis, 2010, p. 58). This process takes clients out of their comfort zone and exposes them to incidents that occur in real time and that are not contrived. A staff member and a client working together to portage a canoe may suddenly set the canoe down because of the frustration being experienced in that moment, and then engage in a very real conversation about other types of frustrations they are dealing with in their lives.

The second important theoretical justification is that experiences are group based and involve relationship building with clients, peers, leaders, and clinicians that are shared experiences that strengthen relationships. Various activities create a shared experience with staff, students, and therapists that is central to developing the therapeutic milieu. In doing so, a more powerful medium is rapidly established that creates trust and bonding that is key to therapeutic change. As one program director stated, our shared adventure activities "create a richer and quicker experience that helps shorten the length of stay for participants" (Russell and Gillis, 2010, p. 59.)

The third justification for their use is that the activities, and the interpersonal dynamics associated with them, allow natural consequences to facilitate much of the learning. As Walsh and Golins stated, "not only will the learner recognize the problem and arrive at a solution, she will experience mentally, emotionally, and physically how well she has solved it" (1976, p. 9). Consequences are felt (naturally) in real time and the ramifications of decisions and actions play out for the entire group. If a group is out on a 2-week backpacking trip, they must ration their food and water appropriately or eventually go hungry. This factor also plays out in interpersonal situations. A clinician referenced this idea by stating, "The strategies and interventions developed in those sessions are experientially supported in the milieu by virtue of peers reminding each other throughout the day of the goals and objectives they determined for themselves with the clinicians' [?] guidance" (Russell and Gillis, 2010, p. 59).

Adventure and Experiential Activity as Therapeutic Tools

Russell and Gillis (2010) identified five key areas that illustrate how adventure and experiential activities are used to develop competence and create autonomous motivation:

1. Skill development
2. Strengthening sense of self
3. Insight
4. Motivation
5. Frame and metaphor

Activity to Develop Skills

Intentionally designed adventure-based experiences directly facilitate skill development. These include intra- and interpersonal skills and a wide variety of leisure skills that can be drawn throughout the life span. A program director commented on the value of a 2-week backpacking trip in that the experience was a "wonderful break from traditional models in that it gets our students active and using motor skills and a different set of cognitive skills that can increase buy-in to treatment and increase therapeutic gains" (Russell and Gillis, 2010, p. 60). Skill building is directly linked to developing motivation to be engaged in treatment, which leads to an increase in therapeutic gains. For youth who may be resistant to traditional models of therapy, this is a powerful tool. They are experiencing a backpacking trip in the present and gaining important skill development without it being forced. Another example of skill development is provided by a clinician who stated, "We also use some action techniques grounded in psychodrama in which through role play and role reversal, we teach skills of empathy and perspective taking" (Russell and Gillis, 2010, p. 62).

Activity to Strengthen Sense of Self

Throughout the literature, the most researched construct in support of integrating adventure and experiential activities into treatment is its role strengthening the sense of self for participants (Hattie, Marsh, Neill, & Richards, 1997). Because activities are designed to be manageable and consequential, a steady progression of self-competence is achieved by engaging in and succeeding in the activities. As one clinician who uses a challenge course in the beginning of a treatment program succinctly stated, "The student is able to learn how to take immediate accountability and ownership for his emotions and choices after a stress response elicited by an experience which has occurred within the culture of support provided by the peers and staff." (Russell and Gillis, 2010, p. 61)

Activity as Insight

Adventure and experiential activities are used to help clients gain insight into situations that are problematic for them. Clients are exposed to unique, unfamiliar, challenging situations that require them to use skills they have learned to productively respond to meet the needs of current situations. The emphasis of the experiential approach is to help clients make effective and appropriate choices when experiences are offered in order to help them gain experience, insight, and understanding. For example, one therapist stated,

> The emphasis in our use of experiential activities is to help residents make effective and appropriate choices, as we relate and re-create the experiential experiences in a variety of group-based initiatives in order to help them gain experience, insight and understanding from them and relate them to their lives (Russell and Gillis, 2010, p. 60).

In this way, activity, experience, and the subsequent personal and interpersonal learning that occur are revisited and used to help make abstract and tangential concepts, ideas, and understandings more real (which are often difficult for adolescents to relate to).

As Walsh and Golins (1976) stated, a key aspect of adventure-based experiences is that they are concrete and designed to complement learners' needs for competence, which has been identified as an intrinsic motivation for learning. A program director at a residential treatment program using adventure-based activities as a primary tool in treatment described the value of revisiting the experiences in saying,

> In order to get the most out of this program, we use (discuss) these experiences in group process after the fact, of course, and have found revisiting the 'experiences' and the intra- and inter-personal dynamics in which they are embedded to be invaluable to our students' [?] progress through the years. (Russell and Gillis, 2010, p.61)

Activity as Motivation

The integration of evidence-based treatment strategies with fun and exciting adventure-based experiences facilitates client engagement in the process and makes the experiences more active and engaging. In this way, the motivation to participate and engage in treatment is enhanced. In fact, many times clients forget they are in treatment as they are focused on accomplishing meaningful tasks. Newes and Bandoroff (2004) see this concept as a key characteristic of AT since "people are more invested in their treatment when it has positive reinforcement," which leads to increased attention on the process. Because the process typically involves a less direct or tangential approach, it is reasoned that reinforcement reduces a client's reluctance to discuss pressing issues in their lives. In addition, many AT experiences also incorporate a more intense challenge, often referred to as a peak experience, in which the individual or group is faced with a task that asks them to use all of the skills and experiences developed to that point in accomplishing the challenge. This may be an overnight solo, a particularly difficult climb, or a high element on a challenge course. The enjoyment and successful completion of the challenge combine to form a powerful motivational factor to be used in the process and treatment. One clinical director at a program stated that the staff

> often add experiential or adventure activities to evidence based treatments to make them more fun and interesting and to increase our students' willingness to participate in therapy. Even more traditional individual therapy approaches can have an experiential look and feel since our therapist may be hiking or gardening while talking to a client. (Russell and Gillis, 2010, p.59)

Activity as Frame and Metaphor

Finally, experiential and adventure-based activities serve as a frame and metaphor for therapy that relate to clients' lives. In Chapter 8, this process is discussed in greater detail in the many formats and types of metaphors that can be applied to adventure experiences. Activity as metaphor to help guide the learning experience has been discussed at length in AT contexts. Gass (1991) spelled out a seven-step framework to develop metaphors that design experiences with clients to reflect parallel structures in their lives. Schoel and Maizell (2002) also discussed ways to frame the adventure to make the experiences more meaningful to participants' lives. Bacon (1983) also discussed classic archetypal metaphors that can be elaborated on through facilitation and discussion that directly relate to the Outward Bound experience for creating stories or parables where participants place themselves.

Due to the very nature of wilderness experience trips, the opportunity to participate in a ritual rite of passage is provided by simple and practical day-to-day activities. In this way, a wilderness experience creates an environment suited for an archetypal rite of passage for individuals—an opportunity to participate in an ancient method of personal transformation that has the potential to operate quickly, mysteriously, and powerfully (Kimball & Bacon, 1993). This experience provides powerful opportunities to mirror the experience back to the participants through careful facilitation using metaphor, ceremony, group discussion, and journal writing.

THE ROLE OF THE THERAPIST AND LEADER IN ADVENTURE THERAPY

Walsh and Golins (1976) viewed the instructor as instrumental in the Outward Bound process, serving as a bridge between the learner and the experience.

Depending on the type of AT process in which a client may be engaged, several important distinctions should be made as to what is meant by an adventure therapist. For further discussion of this issue, see Crisp (2002), Russell, Gillis, and Lewis (2008), and Chapter 10, on competency. From an ethical standpoint, however, as with any mental health treatment approach, standards of care need to be adhered to based on clinical training, state guidelines for licensure, and standards of care guiding national accreditation schemes.

To simplify the discussion, as well as relate the factors present in a therapeutic context to Walsh and Golins' (1976) discussion of the instructors and their roles in facilitating the Outward Bound process, the terms *therapist* and *leader* will be used in this chapter instead of *instructor*. When important, the distinction will be made between an adventure leader and an adventure therapist. Two other important factors concerning the role of the adventure therapist/leader will be discussed:

1. The way in which genuineness, unconditional positive regard, and concreteness is facilitated when working with clients in AT therapy contexts
2. The unique development of the therapeutic relationship occurring in AT settings because these core conditions of change are present

Core Conditions of Change

A characteristic presented by Walsh and Golins (1976) in reference to the leaders is they are trainers who need to not only be proficient in the skills encountered in negotiating the physical environment, but also must be able to facilitate the affective growth of the individual through their mastery of the skills. Doing so requires them to be "empathic, genuine, concrete, and confrontational when necessary" (p. 11). This directly refers to the core conditions of change developed and discussed by Carl Rogers (1961): genuineness, positive regard, empathy, and concreteness of the therapist. The presence of these core conditions significantly contributes to treatment effectiveness regardless of the theoretical orientation of the counselor or program; they are necessary, but not sufficient, to facilitate change. These factors also connect specifically to the concept of *relatedness*, which provides support for how these core conditions meet basic psychological needs empirically shown to develop autonomous motivation in individuals in treatment. The development of these needs and consequential motivation has been linked to more pronounced positive psychotherapeutic outcomes (Ryan et al., 2011).

Genuineness occurs when therapists are congruent—that is, honest with feelings and able to communicate to the client, if appropriate, what they are experiencing at that moment (Rogers, 1961). The term *congruence* has been linked to enhancing genuineness. When someone is playing a role, faking, or saying something that is obviously not felt by the individual, it can be construed as being offensive. One key element of AT is that the therapist and the client spend time together in out-of-office experiences, where the client can observe the genuineness of a therapist or leader in her or his specific discussions and interactions, as well as interactions with other members of the group. The therapist also has an opportunity to model appropriate behaviors and emotional responses as the client and therapist go through many of the same shared experiences, whether it be a challenge course or a wilderness experience. This process also allows the therapist or leader to step back from traditional authority roles and allow natural consequences to provide the responsibility of reinforcement of behaviors. As Bandoroff (1989, p. 14) stated, "The environment assumes much of the responsibility for reinforcement and punishment, and [clients] cannot fool Mother Nature; consequences prescribed by the environment are real, immediate and consistent." Adventure experiences combined with group and communal living in nature with the therapists/leaders creates different dynamics in the client-therapist relationship, facilitating the development of genuineness on the part of the client for therapists/leaders and establishing a crucial condition for change in the therapeutic relationship.

The second condition, termed *unconditional positive regard,* refers to a warm, positive, and accepting attitude of the therapist toward the client (Rogers, 1961). Whatever feeling the client is experiencing—whether it be fear, pain, isolation, anger, or hatred—the therapist should be willing to accept these feelings and care for the client (i.e., be nonjudgmental). This nonjudgmental attitude leads the therapist to maintain positive feelings about the client without evaluating the client. Therapists should not accept clients when they exhibit certain undesirable behaviors or disapprove when clients behave in other dysfunctional ways.

A primary goal of AT group-based experiences is to create a physically and emotionally safe environment. This is done through the establishment of norms and values for the group, often referred to as a full value contract that is literally signed and agreed upon by the group. As Gass (1993a, p. 9) stated, "While still maintaining clear and appropriate boundaries, therapists become more approachable and achieve greater interaction with clients." Because therapists in AT settings are not as restricted in the time spent with clients, they often are provided with opportunities to be more patient and wait for the client to address certain issues in treatment. This makes the therapist-client relationship different from previous experiences most clients have encountered in counseling or therapy. Because of the unique factors associated with AT, therapists and leaders are able to deeply observe behavior and interpersonal interactions, and understand the contexts associated with these behaviors and feelings. This helps to facilitate the development of an unconditional positive regard in working with clients because assumptions do not need to be made in order to address certain therapeutic issues. One staff member at an AT program described the process this way: "It's not as though there's this removed sort of person who sits in a chair an hour at a time, it's also that those people providing you guidance and giving you suggestions and giving you clear feedback are also living through the same experience with you" (Russell, 1999, p. 243).

Empathy occurs when the therapist is accurately sensing the feelings and personal meanings the client is experiencing in each moment and can successfully communicate that understanding to the client (Rogers, 1961). This condition is very different from "I understand what is wrong with you" or "I, too, have experienced this, but reacted very differently." True empathic understanding occurs when someone communicates the understanding of what it is to be that person, without wanting to analyze or judge. The therapist must grasp the moment-to-moment experience occurring in the inner world of the client as the client sees it and feels it, but without losing the separateness of his or her own identity in this empathic process. When conditions of empathy are met, change is most likely to occur.

Empathy for the disposition of the client in AT is also enhanced by the availability and presence of the therapists and leaders through AT experiences. Therapeutic moments can occur at any given time. When those moments are experienced by the client, the treatment team must be available to be with the client, as well as work through the pertinent issues in an empathetic and caring manner.

The final therapeutic condition necessary to promote change is that of concreteness, which is especially critical for adolescents due to their physical, life stage, neurological, and psychosocial development. Therapeutic experiences for any client must be concrete enough so the therapeutic learning can relate to their daily lives. The therapist must be direct and specific and the lessons real and clear. Therapists who are nondirective, laid back, or highly conceptual often receive accommodating responses from clients who may not relate to the Piagetian approach. This is certainly true for adolescents in therapy, who are in the concrete operations stage of cognitive development and typically communicate in black-and-white, either/or terms. Adventure and wilderness experiences are ideal environments to facilitate this notion of concreteness. In one of the first studies on Outward Bound and why the experiences are concrete and real, Golins (1978, p. 27) noted:

> The outdoors always presents itself in a very physical, straightforward way. There are mountains to climb, rivers to run, bogs to wade through. As an adolescent delinquent whose principal mode of expression is an action-oriented one and whose thinking process is mostly concrete, the possible activities in the outdoors are limitless to fulfill his developmental capability. He just stands a better chance of excelling here.

Because these experiences are real and concrete and make sense to clients, the therapist/leader has an opportunity to relate these experiences to daily life. This allows the therapist to be concrete and link the physical, cognitive, and emotional development occurring in the experience to treatment and the client's individual needs.

Therapeutic Relationship

The therapeutic alliance is widely known in research on process factors in psychotherapy as one of the most significant predictors of treatment outcomes (Norcross, 2011). Because of the factors at work when establishing core conditions for change reasoned to be inherent in AT, the therapeutic relationship between clients and leaders/therapists is unique and has the potential to be developed more quickly and, in many cases, more powerfully. The therapeutic relationship has been shown through substantial research efforts to be the strongest predictor of outcome regardless of the model (Karver, Handelsman, Fields, & Bickman, 2006). Although often referenced in AT texts (Gass, 1993a), the dynamic has not been studied in AT settings until recently. In one of the few studies conducted in AT on the role of therapeutic relationship and its effect on outcome, Russell (2008) found that therapeutic or working alliance, assessed at midpoint as well as termination of treatment, was perceived by adolescent clients engaged in a wilderness therapy experience as very high, based on strong feelings of trust and competence in the therapists/leaders of that experience.

The reasoning why the therapeutic relationship is unique in AT settings begins with contact time. Because leaders and therapists are engaging in the day-to-day living of the experience, therapy is not confined to 1-hour sessions in an office but instead occurs on walks, around the campfire, or in evening discussions after dinner. Depending on the intervention, this contact time can be considerable. If one considers a 2-week pack trip during which a therapist/leader is with the clients on a day-to-day-basis, this would account for 168 hours of therapeutic contact (12 hours × 14 days = 168 hours). If a therapist was part of a 3-day family retreat, that would equate to over 36 hours of contact time with the family. It is important to also consider that it is not just the *amount* of contact time, but the *type* of contact time. By observing client behavior in real living situations that are specifically designed to evoke certain behavioral patterns and emotional responses, the therapist/leader is able to observe these patterns in real time, discuss strategies based on these observations, and address them with the client immediately.

The client also has an opportunity to see the therapist/leader in a different light. The therapist/leader also struggles with challenges, becomes frustrated, and is required to communicate with others in real ways, modeling appropriate (and sometimes not so appropriate, but recoverable) ways of relating to others. In this way, therapists/leaders are seen as real people, which for many clients may be a unique experience that helps break down preconceived notions and misperceptions of therapists in particular. This dynamic helps to build trust and mutual respect, which are key foundations of a strong therapeutic relationship. Newes and Bandoroff (2004) suggested this alliance process may provide greater opportunities for corrective emotional experiences to occur, as well as provide an example of how a trusting relationship established with a therapist may help to address abandonment issues that an adolescent client may have with a parent. This relationship is dynamic, fluid, and constantly evolving, requiring the therapists and leaders in AT experiences to be adept at observation and assessment of the client's needs. As Walsh and Golins (1976, p. 11) stated in their discussion of the many roles of the instructor, "Part of [his] skill is in making moves towards resolution; his decisions are based on the learner's experience and what the client's short and long term growth needs are."

MASTERY AND THE BENEFITS OF USING ADVENTURE AND EXPERIENTIAL ACTIVITIES IN THERAPY

This section is not meant to serve as a review of research on the benefits of AT, as that is done elsewhere in this text (see Chapter 13). The intent here is to focus on the benefits of the AT process, rather than just describe a variety of therapeutic outcomes. The discussion relates to the final variable discussed in the Walsh and Golins (1976) model. The participant, after engaging in the Outward Bound process and through interaction with peers, leaders, and therapists, is said to experience mastery. Simply put, mastery "reorganizes the meaning and direction of a person's experience" (Walsh & Golins, p. 12). This obviously has a strong and striking resemblance to the goals of therapy in general. The Outward Bound process does this—and parallels what occurs in AT—because the client or student finds it *inherently* "rewarding to solve the reasonable, concrete, manageable, and consequential problems holistically within a supportive peer group and in a novel and stimulating environment" (Walsh & Golins, p. 12). Most clients in AT experiences have not been provided with the opportunity to accomplish these types of tasks, especially in relation to other experiences in therapy they may have experienced. This is a critical point because most clients in AT have tried other forms of counseling or treatment approaches. In fact, Russell (2003b) found that 75% of a large sample of adolescents had tried other treatment options prior to engaging in a wilderness therapy experience. Elaborating on the uniqueness of AT compared to other treatments, one clinical director stated

> We have students in our program from most of the major metropolitan areas of the United States. I am quite certain each of these cities have an adequate

number of competent clinicians. Yet, time and again, we receive students whose parents indicate they have been in traditional individual therapy to no avail. While our program has wonderful, competent therapists, I doubt they are any more brilliant than their counterparts across the country. What makes our therapists effective is their ability to tap into this resource (the peer group) and enlist responsible young people to help each other practice new habits, challenge old beliefs, and daily develop skills that have been suggested in their traditional, hourly therapeutic sessions. (Russell and Gillis, 2010, p. 61)

By accomplishing these challenging tasks, Walsh and Golins (1976, p. 13) stated that "it makes one feel good about oneself and those who have assisted," a claim that is certainly supported by research. AT professionals repeatedly referenced the way in which the AT process kinesthetically impacts learners. The therapeutic outcomes emerging from this process are both refined psychosocial and motor skills, a unique and critical outcome from the AT process. These types of benefits are seen as integral to the full development of the client, especially given the adolescent stage of their lives. Walsh and Golins elaborated on this in discussing the cognitive, affective, and psychomotor development inherent in the Outward Bound experience. The link between self-concept and motor development through physical activity is well documented and is a current research focus for the National Institute of Health (Volkow, 2011). One does not have to look far into the media to know rising obesity rates in the United States are a significant health concern and represent a very real and serious threat to the health of an entire generation of young people.

Experiential activities also produce immediate and tangible learning opportunities and direct feedback. Linked to this idea is that the AT process helps clients develop a clear understanding of the cause and effect of their actions and emotional energy on people and place. Walsh and Golins (1976) referred to this dynamic as a reorganization of the meaning of experience, which literally develops new attitudes, values, and skills that help clients to be more equipped to address intra- and interpersonal problems in the future. This is sometimes referred to in the literature as resiliency.

It is important to note that each AT experience will differ for each individual, and that AT should not be seen as a panacea for all issues (although some practitioners sell it as such). It is also important to note that many of the factors discussed in this section are not unique to AT, but are reasoned to be uniquely experienced by clients in an AT experience. As Newes and Bandoroff (2004, p. 3) stated:

The theory of AT builds on the foundations of well-established premises of accepted psychological theory, including cognitive and cognitive behavioral theory, humanistic theory, and interpersonal aspects of object relations theory.

SUMMARY

This chapter explored the question: How does AT work? Key theoretical and practical foundations relevant to the AT process were reviewed and presented. A conceptual foundation of AT was presented, which included the integration of the Walsh and Golins (1976) Outward Bound process model within an AT context to illustrate how AT works in therapeutic settings. As discussed by Hogue (2002), AT is an interaction of participants, groups, leaders, and activities, which is designed to promote change. The complex interaction of these ingredients creates a process that in many ways is unique in psychotherapy. It is also similar to many traditional forms of psychotherapy, suggesting that therapists working in more traditional milieus can use some of these ingredients to augment their practice.

The AT process provides an autonomy-supportive atmosphere conducive to participants finding an internal source of motivation to begin thinking about change, and establishes the framework in which three basic psychological needs of participants in therapy can be met by the subsequent social milieu and through adventure-based activities that occur in this environment. The three psychological needs being met through these experiences are *autonomy* (through nondirective inquiry and reflection), *competence* (through provision of activity, demonstrated skill acquisition, and other factors) and *relatedness* (through a relationship with self, peers, therapists, and leaders characterized by relationships that are facilitated in the environment by genuineness, unconditional positive regard, empathy, and concreteness).

The AT milieu is unique in that it is continuous, is evolving, and relies heavily on strong relationships built between peer members of a group and their leaders and therapists. This facilitates the development of a therapeutic relationship that is reasoned to be stronger than in traditional approaches and is centered on activity. Adventure and experiential activities provide skill development, self-development, insight into intra- and interpersonal issues, and enhanced motivation to be involved in treatment. These experiences can also provide a frame to serve as kinesthetic metaphors for real-life situations. The centrality of activity sets this form of experientially based psychotherapy apart from other approaches in its ability to access clients with various learning styles and its de-emphasis on verbal aspects so paramount in traditional approaches.

Key questions that future research could address include:

- Are all elements of the milieu necessary?
- If a student or client is impacted by activity in only one of the ways mentioned, is this sufficient for AT to be successful?
- How might this approach build a strong evidence base?
- If students were previously involved in residential treatment that included AT methods, which elements of their experience provided "triggers" for change in their behavior?

- What if these responses began to cluster among the same (or different) aspects of this process?

These and other forms of effectiveness inquiry may shed light on the experience and potentially lead to a more informed discussion of how practitioners utilize adventure experiences, often conducted in natural settings to kinesthetically engage clients on cognitive, affective, and behavioral levels.

CLIMBING FOR CHANGE

Kim Wasserburger

Adventure therapy, therapeutic adventure, experiential education, and adventure education all took on new definitions for me in a moment of understanding and celebration of repentance. My adventure began when months of planning came to fruition. Seven adjudicated Native American boys, my friend (the guide), and I crossed state lines on a rock climbing trip. At the onset, crossing state lines with my boys, who wore ankle bracelet monitors, was phase one of our adventure: to climb for 7 days, with enough food for 3 weeks, not knowing the first thing about where we were climbing in an effort to create a life change. My thinking was to get them into a natural environment, hang them by a harness and rope 100 feet above Lake Superior at a known Ojibwa power spot, and somehow create a moment of epiphany for them to change their life paths. I had convinced them that the path they were on was leading to their destruction, and that was enough to have them buy into coming on the trip.

The first few days of the trip were glorious. We climbed, we ate, we climbed, we ate, and then did more of both. As we climbed, we cried on unnamed rock faces on our own made-up routes due to lack of a guidebook. We took our best guess, threw our ropes, lowered to the lake and climbed up with no option but success. On the third or fourth day, one of the boys complained about the lack of American cheese in the choices of five cheeses for the half-pound sirloin burgers. Something inside of me snapped and I decided what we needed was a minimal provision 50-mile hike into the Boundary Waters.

Upon return from the ranger station to obtain a backcountry permit, the boys had packed up camp and were sitting with sweatshirt hoods over their heads with headphones on. After considerable prodding as to what was going on, I noticed a puddle on the pavement beneath Walker's knees. He said through his tears, "These have been the best days of my life, and my life has changed, but I know that if I do what you say we are going to do, I will change even more, so much that I will never be able to go home." My moment of understanding came and the rain began to fall. We spent the day in the rain smudging ourselves in a cloud of cedar smoke and tears. Our circle began with me repenting for my arrogance—that somehow I determined that I knew what was best for them without truly understanding what each day of life held for them. We talked, we cried, we sang, we danced. We ate the remaining 4 days of food, then drove in the van instead of walking the miles. When passing by Smokey the Bear, who was boldly holding a sign stating that the fire danger was extremely high despite a drenching rain, Walker exclaimed, "Looks like Smokey F'd up again." We all laughed hysterically. Then we went home, nine changed men.

A big part of the intentionality with this group of boys was the alcohol and other drug abuse (AODA) issues involved, with 7 days high and dry away from the law (although one of the boys found out that there was a warrant out for his arrest 3 days into the trip—an intervening variable). We also used adventure tools off the charts (climbing, hiking, canoeing) to guide personal change toward desired therapeutic change.

The change was fast and dramatic. The problem came when further and more dramatic change was proposed. There was internalization on the part of the participants that transference was going to be impossible (with the change that had already been realized) based upon the context of "home" and not being able to fit once the change was fully realized. The central concept of this for me was my arrogance in providing what I determined was the remedy, without fully understanding how difficult generalizing the newfound behavior would be for the participant. In fact, their newfound self would be rebuked, beaten on, ridiculed, and perceived as weak.

Chapter 5

Nature's Role in Adventure Therapy

The tendency to wander in wilderness is delightful to see. Thousands of tired, nerve-shaken, over-civilized people are beginning to find out that going to the mountains is going home; that wilderness is a necessity; and that mountain parks and reservations are useful not only as fountains of timber and irrigating rivers, but as fountains of life.

John Muir
Our National Parks, 1901

Adventure therapy and education has been criticized for not recognizing and discussing the value and role that nature and wilderness play in therapeutic contexts. In fact, many researchers (Bacon, 1983; Gibson, 1979; Greenway, 1995; Johnson and Frederickson, 2000; Kimball, 1983) have made the case that nature is actually the main therapeutic power in adventure therapy interventions that take place in the outdoors, and that the therapy that is directed by leaders simply supplements the power of nature to heal. This chapter directly addresses this issue and explores the philosophical, theoretical, and practical dimensions of nature's role in adventure therapy.

By better understanding the philosophical, theoretical, and practical implications of nature's role in adventure therapy, practitioners and researchers can begin to develop a common language around a very powerful factor at work in this therapeutic milieu. In this chapter, an argument is made that our growing separation from the natural world in which people have evolved can cause a variety of psychological symptoms that include depression, anxiety, and stress. A growing body of literature suggests that this cannot be due solely to intrapsychic or intrafamilial dynamics (Chalquist, 2009). By spending time in the natural world and reconnecting with its processes, people are in essence also reconnecting to themselves and each other. This is a powerful therapeutic medium that has been shown to enhance physical health, self-concept, and interpersonal relations, as well as bring a sense of relief and happiness. This process is not specific to adventure therapy, but works across a variety of treatment modalities and has become the focus of other researchers in the broader psychotherapeutic community. In doing so, much can be learned from this research. Adventure therapy also has a unique opportunity to engage in the conversation and the research about the restorative effects of nature and its role in promoting change in individuals.

The therapeutic value of nature has been espoused at length by philosophers, nature writers, and contemporary researchers for hundreds of years. As the chapter-opening quotation by John Muir attests, nature is seen as restorative for people who are suffering from mental fatigue due to demands on their attention required by day-to-day living in a fast-paced and increasingly technology-driven society. When delving deeper into nature's restorative role, fundamental questions arise that form the foundation for this chapter and frame the discussions about why spending time in nature is inherently therapeutic for individuals. This chapter takes the perspective of a citizen of a Western industrialized nation, although other cultures, in place and time, held and still hold the view that nature and humans are not separate from one another.

Intricately linked with this line of inquiry is the increasingly relevant matter of examining the psychological and emotional effects of humans' current relationship with nature. The paradox is striking in that the very reason why nature is restorative and therapeutic is because of people's growing separation from nature and its natural processes. Few people know or understand from where their food originates. Many people do not know the source of the water that flows through their taps. Youth today, as discussed in Richard Louv's (2006) seminal book *The Last Child in the Woods*, rarely engage in free play outside anymore because parents are scared, there are too many things to do indoors, or they simply can't find a place to play. Although Louv's book has certainly struck a chord with parents, teachers, and mental health professionals, the central message in the book has been at the forefront of the camping movement, outdoor and environmental education, and adventure education and therapy practices for more than 100 years in industrialized nations. The very fact that his message has struck such a chord and spawned educational and political discussions to address the issue of nature-based play and education says something about the state of people's growing separation from natural systems.

Much attention has been paid to the restorative aspects of nature, with scant attention paid to the psychological, emotional, and developmental effects of people's growing separation from nature. Coupled with this is a collective unconscious of mounting environmental concerns, and the general fear and anxiety that are associated with these concerns as people are bombarded by the science and media that portrays the environment as being in great peril. In fact, Rust (2004) has said that the psychotherapy profession's response to recognizing and addressing the psychological and emotional effects of these concerns has been lacking.

This chapter explores these issues and asks some fundamental questions about the role that nature plays in a therapeutic process by first exploring the ramifications of people's growing separation from the natural world. The reasoned effects of this separation are discussed to present a philosophical and theoretical rationale for the use of nature in therapeutic processes. Referencing Kaplan and Kaplan (1989) and contemporary research on ecopsychology and ecotherapy, the chapter concludes with examples of how adventure therapy intentionally uses the restorative effects of nature in hopes of reconnecting the self, the self to others, and all people to the natural world.

EXPLORING THE FOUNDATIONS OF THE THERAPEUTIC VALUE OF NATURE

Though modern humans have existed for millions of years, it was not until relatively recently, triggered by the agricultural revolution some 14,000 years ago, that humans began to dramatically transform the natural environment around them in order to better meet their needs. Hunter-gatherer societies dependent on plant and animal species for their survival didn't have a term for wilderness. In fact, *wild-eor-ness,* or the place of the beast, was a term that emerged only as we became increasingly agrarian (Nash, 1982). With the advent of an agrarian society came cultural control over our relationship with nature, and the widespread creation of seminatural agro-ecosystems. In the groundbreaking text *Ecopsychology,* Theodore Roszak (1995) claimed that contemporary technological and industrial society has severed people's deep connection to nature and they need to strive to repair this relationship. A growing understanding exists that humans cannot continue to destroy rainforests, lose topsoil, and sacrifice plant and animal species to continual urbanization without the global ecosystem eventually collapsing under the weight of an advancing civilization.

Several fundamental questions are asked in this book about the ramifications of being a part of something that seems to be beyond people's control, yet at the same time affects them emotionally and psychologically at a deep and profound level. Why do humans continue to proceed down this path of least resistance to the eventual destruction of biota with the seemingly inevitable eradication of their own species? This is an important question that directly relates to the role that nature can play in any therapeutic process, especially in a process that occurs in and through nature like AT.

In response to the malevolent attitude towards nature exhibited by anthropocentric Western views of philosophy and religion, a new environmental ethic has emerged. The deep ecology (Naess, 1989) movement grew out of the environmental concerns voiced through the writings of Rachel Carson and

Aldo Leopold, which directly challenged claims that humans are superior to and should be separate from nature. Like a subconscious voice from the past, the emergence of deep ecology and its critique of anthropocentrism has challenged Western society to rethink its role and place in the natural world. Deep ecologists posit that to reconnect with nature would bring forward people's *true sense of self*. Deep ecology rests on the premise that this true sense of self is from, of, and part of nature, and therefore any actions that harm the environment would be construed as actions that in essence harm ourselves. Therefore, behavior that harms the natural world can only be viewed as irrational, immoral, and therefore wrong. Deep ecologists believe that all people unconsciously want to adopt a more biocentric worldview and begin to act in accordance to its values. However, Roszak (1995) and other ecopsychologists believe that the implications of a biocentric worldview are too disturbing to consider because of the impacts it would have on daily life. People simply do not know where to begin because the challenge is daunting. They therefore simply dismiss the worldview and carry on with their daily lives. By dismissing the biocentric ontology as radical and extreme, people are free to go about their business as usual, repressing this internal conflict.

Authors such as Paul Shepard (1995) reflect on this internal struggle. Shepard has suggested that people as a society are acting abnormally because they cannot reconcile this internal struggle. Sigmund Freud, in developing the psychodynamic model of psychotherapy, believed that abnormal behavior is a result of anxiety produced by conflicts and forces of which a person may be unaware. Wilson (1984) also suggests that there is a lost or forgotten aspect of self-identity that strives to reconnect with nature. The more isolated humans become from the natural world, the more difficult it becomes for them to grasp or understand the struggle with which they are engaged. This causes anxiety, which results in abnormal or irrational behavior and a desire to reconcile the internal conflict. What once was a self-identity derived from a deep and profound relationship to the natural world is now shaped by a highly industrialized technological society driven by consumption. As Paul Wachtel (1989, p. 71) wrote, "The idea of more, of ever increasing wealth, has become the center of our identity, and our security, and we are caught by it as the addict is caught by his drugs."

Ecopsychologists and authors like Shepard (1995) believe that as people struggle as individuals to define themselves in a technological and consumer-driven world, an inner voice from which people evolved tells them to respect their place in the beautiful, powerful, and mysterious processes of the natural world. The voice begs people to change their consumptive habits and the way they live, providing hundreds of examples of the social, economic, and environmental effects of this dysfunctional behavior. Yet, they cannot help but purchase a bottle of water, a sport utility vehicle, the latest smartphone, or a laptop computer to satisfy what they perceive as needs. As an addict struggles to control his or her desire to consume a drug, humans struggle to control their desires to consume products that make them feel better. Purchasing consumer goods fills an "empty self" by producing immediate pleasure and achievement, while often conferring status and recognition. Psychologist Philip Cushman (1990) described the empty self as seeking the experience of being continually filled up by consumer goods, calories, experiences, and romantic partners in an attempt to combat the growing alienation and fragmentation of its era. This response has been implicitly prescribed by a post-World War II economy that is dependent on the continual consumption of nonessential and quickly obsolete items and experiences. In order to thrive, society requires individuals who experience a strong need for consumer products—and in fact demands them (Cushman, p. 600).

It is therefore the central premise of this discussion and a key foundational aspect of why nature is inherently therapeutic. The dualism displayed in the way humans relate to nature is a projection of their suppressed unconscious needs and desires to reconnect with nature. The result of this irrational struggle of the human conscience represents "a kind of failure in some fundamental dimension of human existence, an irrationality beyond mistakenness, a kind of madness" (Shepard, 1995, p. 24). What are the ramifications of this struggle?

THE IMPACTS OF SUPPRESSING OUR ECOLOGICAL SELVES

In exploring the psychological and emotional effects of people's growing separation from nature, three metaphors are presented here that broadly examine behavior manifest in Western society reflecting these effects. This discussion is philosophical in nature and reflects broad trends in contemporary issues in psychotherapy and human development. This discussion is grounded in the work of Edward O. Wilson (1984), who suggests that because humans have adapted and survived in the natural environment for some 3 million years, they have therefore inherited the natural environment as much as they have inherited their genes. Wilson used the term *biophilia* to mean the inherent human need to affiliate deeply and closely with the natural environment, particularly its living organisms. He believes that biophilia is part of people's mental and emotional hard wiring, and is as much a part of our genetic human history as is the need for love, interpersonal bonding, and family. This longing for a connection with nature can be seen in people's establishment and love of national parks and wilderness, their fascination with nature films and wildlife, and the fact that gardening is the most popular recreational activity in the United States.

In exploring how nature-based evolution has affected the human mind, James Ashbrook (2003), a neuropsychologist, believes that humankind's whole mind comes out of nature and does not function apart from nature. The whole brain includes functions of both hemispheres of the "new brain," but is also influenced by the symbolic and subconscious activity of the "old brain" with its somatic and environmental roots. The old mammalian brain contains the biological root of human bonding with nature, a bonding that enabled the human species to survive for 3 million years. As the human brain and a sense of kinship evolved together, empathic caring marks the most striking change in evolutionary adaptation. This need for empathic caring is evidenced in people's need and desire for love and emotional bonding—with humans as well as nature.

The desired emotional bond with nature that the human consciousness yearns for and needs is left unfulfilled. Roszak (1995, p. 7) believed that humans have an inner desire to care for the planet:

> Granted the need for a "perfect environment," we might let it be the real environment of all living things: the planetary biosphere, which is everyone's "primary care giver"... let us imagine parenting that is responsible for making that environment as perfect as possible. What, after all, do parents owe their young that is more important than a warm and trusting connection to the Earth that accounts for our evolutionary history?

Expanding on this notion of the parent-child metaphor presented by Roszak, Paul Shepard was perhaps the first theorist to articulate a psychopathological metaphor for our destructive and exploitative treatment of the natural world. In his book *Nature and Madness,* Shepard (1995) shows how cultural pathology displayed in the historical development of Western Judeo-Christian civilization was caused by arrested human development, or what he termed "ontogenetic crippling" (p. 293). He sees two critical stages where Western civilization may have suppressed normal development of individuals: the infant/caregiver relationship and adolescent transition rites. He bases his analysis on the strong interplay between the extended period of immaturity and dependency of the human child and the ontogenetic support provided by society and culture. Developmental practices by hunter-gatherer societies, which had functioned properly for hundreds of thousands of years, were suddenly severed by agricultural domestication causing devastating consequences to human development. Shepard (p. 85) states that

> By aggravating the tensions of separation from the mother and at the same time spatially isolating the individual from the natural world, agriculture made it difficult for the developing person to approach the issues around which the crucial passages into fully mature adult life had been structured in the course of human existence.

During the infant/caregiver stage, the child's developing sense of self is comprised of basic issues of trust versus mistrust. If this stage is interrupted and development stunted, Erikson believes that the child may experience chronic insecurity. As Shepard (1995, p. 40) stated, "The social skills of the newborn and the mother's equally indigenous reciprocity create not only the primary

social tie but the paradigm for existential attitudes." The problems seen in adolescents today reflect the traits presented by Erikson of an interrupted infant/
caregiver relationship. Adolescents who experienced maternal rejection at a
young age report impaired self-confidence, a higher rate of depression, and
negative cognitions about the self and their ability to relate to others.

In Erikson's developmental model, adolescence is the time when the child
is struggling with an internal conflict between identity and role confusion.
Guided in the past by traditional rites of passage to celebrate and recognize
this difficult transition into adulthood, youth of today are left on their own as
parents struggle to deal with intense social stresses. Institutions that provide
the foundations of community are falling apart, leaving the community safety
net in tatters. Parents, exhausted by long hours required to make ends meet or
demoralized by their inability to cope with hardships of juggling careers and
family, are distancing themselves from children. Kids are left on their own in
essentially adultless communities.

Traditional rites of passage into adulthood have been replaced with inadequate Western traditions, such as bootcamp initiations of the military, fra-
ternity hazing, or the violence of street gang initiations. This has produced a
generation of adults who portray characteristics of a struggling teenager stuck
in the developmental stage of early adolescence. Erikson (1980, p. 98) wrote
that adolescents who have difficulty in this stage become "remarkably clan-
nish, intolerant and cruel in their exclusion of others who are 'different' in
skin color or cultural background." This description fits with the brash pursuit
of self-interest that typifies the consumerist, exploitative model of economic
growth in which the dominant value under consideration seems to be the
short-term profit of entrepreneurs and corporate shareholders.

Another related metaphor put forward by Thomas Berry (1988) is that the
human species has become "autistic" in the way they relate to the natural world.
The origin of this autism is reasoned to be associated with Descartes' notion of
mechanism. Derived from Cartesian dualism, in which the mind and body are
perceived of as clearly distinct from each other, mechanism is the doctrine that
all living things are in essence just machines. Once the mind and body were reasoned to be distinct and separate, the absolute independence of the material realm
from the spiritual secured the freedom of scientists to rely exclusively on observations for their development of mechanistic explanations of physical events.

This separation left no possibility for humans to enter into communal
relationship with nature. Nature was viewed as a machine with working parts
that could be dissected, explained, and understood. Through this separation,
Berry (1988) suggests that we have become autistic in our interactions with
the natural world. People have become deaf to its voices, stories, and sources
that nourished their ancestors in primitive societies. David Abrams (1996,
p. 7) spent years studying the ancient practice of shamanism in Nepal and
came to realize that "traditional shamans and magicians the world over act as
intermediaries between the human collective and the larger ecological field."

Through their rituals, trances, ecstasies, and journeys, magicians ensure that the relationship between human society and the larger society of nonhumans is balanced and reciprocal, making sure that the village never takes more from the living land than it can return. He suggests a link, illuminating the metaphor of autistic humans, deaf to the voices of the natural world with traditional magicians, interpreting those voices in order to clarify that which people have lost the capacity to know.

The American Psychological Association (1994) defines autism as characterized by qualitative impairment in social interaction, verbal and nonverbal communication, and in imaginative activity with a markedly restricted repertoire of activities and interests. Children with autism typically display stereotyped movements and behavior, restricted range of interests, obsessive routines, preoccupation with parts and objects, absence of imaginative play, and lack of awareness of the feelings of others. These traits are seemingly everywhere in Western society, as people are forced by the dictum of earning a living to drive cars to jobs and perform the same tasks week in and week out. The economy has been based on the fabrication of parts and objects since the invention of the assembly line. The violence people display towards each other reflects a lack of awareness and feeling for others. If Western culture is autistic, as the metaphor put forth by Berry (1988) suggests, the implications are daunting.

A final metaphor that illuminates the effects of the human-nature separation is that of addiction. Modern industrial society has become addicted to technology, complete with the ironic twist that improved technology will actually be people's savior from their own destructive behavior. There are even electronic pets for children who yearn to care for a living and breathing thing, yet are offered a lifeless electronic box to satisfy these desires. Chellis Glendinning (1990) conducted a psychological study of people who had become medically ill from exposure to health-threatening technology, such as Love Canal residents, war veterans, asbestos workers, and Dalkon Shield users. She equates the public's acceptance of these ills to the acceptance of alcoholism and smoking in the 1950s. Everyone drank and smoked because it was socially accepted. Since that time, a public awareness has grown to the potential hazards of alcohol and tobacco, leading one to believe that it may be time to rethink the addiction to technology and begin to ask the hard questions about its impact on physical, psychological, and emotional health, especially with children.

People are addicted to a human-constructed, technology-centered social system built on principles of standardization, compartmentalization, and efficiency. Again, behavior entrenched in the mechanistic world born of Cartesian dualism was espoused by Renee Descartes more than 350 years ago. As Morris Berman stated (1988, p. 243):

> Addiction in one form or another, characterizes every aspect of industrial society.... Dependence on alcohol, food, drugs, tobacco is not formally different

from dependence on prestige, career achievement, world influence, wealth, more ingenious weaponry, or the need to exercise control over everything.

People's failure to see the health hazards of the addictive actions of carbon dioxide gas emissions and radioactive waste burial are symptoms of this fragmented thinking that emerges from such mechanistic order. A blatant denial of widespread illnesses caused by technology by the insurance industry, justice system, medical establishment, government, and media strengthens the adage that mind and body are disconnected to health and disease. This reinforces, as Roszak (1995), Wilson (1984), and others argued, the belief that humans are disconnected to nature and restoring this balance is critical to the psychological and emotional health of contemporary humans.

RESTORING THE BALANCE BETWEEN NATURE AND THE SELF

Advancing industrialized civilization has brought with it a belief that human beings are separate from and superior to nature—a sentiment that has disassociated people from reality. It is becoming increasingly difficult to distinguish what is right or wrong when it comes to actions affecting the environment. The limitations of science to deal with the complexities of ecological problems on a global scale have shifted decision making into the ethical realm. Normative ethics has for 2,400 years tried to construct moral systems that provide a comprehensive account of the nature of moral judgment and moral truth. Many believe that a biocentric environmental ethic has been gathering force since medieval times (Naess, 1989). Throughout people's historical march away from nature, there has always been a segment of social thought, captured in the mythological and ethical treatise *Ishmael* by Quinn (1992), like an internal voice of reason that has begged people to remember where they came from and what they really are. As people pause and reflect on their past actions and turn to face the uncertainty of the future, they are realizing that the time has come to listen to that voice, begin to reconcile the struggle for self-identity, and recognize that they are not separate and superior to nature—rather, people are *of* nature.

In viewing the transformation of North America that started in the early 17th century, the human nature relationship was based on fear of the mysterious unknown and hostile environment of what is known today as wilderness. The wilderness was a foreboding and mysterious place, captured here in a quote by William Bradford, the first Governor of Massachusetts, commenting on the state of the first settlers to Massachusetts Bay colony in 1604 (cited in Merchant, 1993, p. 68):

But here I pause and stand half amazed at this poor people's present condition.... They had no friends to welcome them, no inns... no houses.... And

for the season, it was winter, and for those that know the winters of that country, know them to be sharp and violent and subject to cruel and fierce storms,
dangerous to travel to known places, much more to search an unknown coast.
Besides, what could they see but a hideous and desolate wilderness full of wild
beasts and wild men?

In this dark and dangerous setting lived the Native American cultures,
who were viewed by these settlers as creatures in need of the European man's
religion and civilization. The wilderness and its habitants were viewed as an
enemy that needed to be conquered and vanquished. The transformation of
wild nature to a cultivated and civilized nature to be used for human benefit
continued in North America, as it had previously in Europe, as the settlers
moved further and further into the heart of the Wild West.

As agriculture and civilization began to establish their roots, the quiet and
creative voices of writers, poets, and painters began to tell a different story
of the wilderness—a story that continues to be told today thousands of years
later. Throughout history, the natural world has always been valued for its aes-
thetic quality and may be the most ancient subject of artistic endeavors. Cave
paintings of bison found in Europe predate writing by thousands of years and
suggest a fascination with the natural world. Writers, philosophers, painters,
and poets began to convey a respect and understanding for the natural world,
which brought people closer to its mysterious processes. The Celts provided
descriptive metaphors to suggest that the natural and human worlds were intimately linked. The herbalists and botanists of the Enlightenment era of the
17th century tirelessly surveyed flora and fauna with the belief that a comprehensive survey might unlock the mysteries of natural evolution. The Romantic
era heightened people's sense of self and with it an enhanced sympathy with
the "otherness" of the natural world. During the Victorian era, natural history
became a public obsession, evidenced by plant hunters who would search the
globe for rare and valuable plants to return to England for display. As people
continued to control and subdue the natural world for human benefit, they
became more and more fascinated with its mysterious ways.

The Transcendentalists infused a spiritual understanding of people's relationship with nature through the writings of Emerson (1936), Thoreau (1971), and
later Muir (1901). The vast expanses of wilderness in North America gave Muir
and others writers of this epoch a freedom of language and expression which
brought readers closer to an understanding of their relationship with nature. For
perhaps the first time since the agricultural revolution began, Europeans began to
question humans' historic march away from nature. These ideas came to a head
during the classic fight for Hetch Hetchy, in which human progress was challenged
by the intrinsic value of wilderness, suggesting that the value of a mountain in its
pristine condition might outweigh the benefits derived from the efficient use of its
resources for human consumption (Nash, 1967). The seed had been planted and
a dichotomy firmly entrenched in people's consciousness. The development of
wilderness resources would never be viewed in the same way again.

As technology and growth ushered in the 21st century, the economic lens with which people view most natural areas has paradoxically helped define wilderness while pushing it to near extinction. Scarcity and crisis have worked to make the remaining wilderness areas highly valuable resources. The official definition of wilderness can be found in the Wilderness Act of 1964 (P.L. 88–577), which described wilderness as

> … an area where the earth and its community of life are untrammeled by [humans], where humans themselves are visitors who do not remain… (1) wilderness appears to have been affected primarily by the forces of nature, with the imprint of humans' work substantially unnoticeable; (2) has outstanding opportunities for solitude or a primitive and unconfined type of recreation; (3)… is of sufficient size…; and (4) may also contain ecological, geological or other features of scientific, educational scenic or historical value.

It is in this wilderness environment, in juxtaposition to the modernized and increasingly urban culture, that the restorative aspects of wilderness work in tandem with a therapeutic modality. In order to understand this process, it is first important to define and delineate factors that are inherently therapeutic about spending time in nature away from industrialized civilization. Although many aspects of our conception of wilderness have changed over time, one component has remained unchanged—the healing and restorative quality of nature.

THERAPEUTIC FACTORS OF NATURE

The seminal work researching the psychological benefits of experiencing nature was first posited by Kaplan (1989), who introduced the idea that nature—in all its complexity and beauty—elicits deep-seated and automatic responses by individuals in the absence of extensive information processing. Kaplan believes that restoration derives from the reduction of stimulus and arousal due to nature's calming effect, which elicits positively toned emotional states and blocks out negatively toned feelings. Nature removes individuals from their accustomed culture and surrounds them with a natural world that is very calming and nurturing. The impact this has on emotional states and thought processes can be very positive and indeed restorative.

The initial research on this topic was conducted on the Outdoor Challenge Program in the Upper Peninsula of Michigan (Kaplan & Kaplan, 1989). The program consisted of 2-week courses in the wilderness for adolescents and adults. One of the major findings was their discussion of the qualities that characterize a restorative environment. When speaking of restorative environments, a presupposition is made that there is something to be restored. Kaplan and Kaplan termed this *mental fatigue*, which asks the question: What are the common consequences that result from long hours of study, too many late nights at the office, or long hard days filled with worry and concern? The answer is from mental inertia, or the challenges of focusing in an increasingly technological world that is characteristic of mental fatigue.

William James (1892) identified two types of attention, distinguished by the effort involved in their use: involuntary and direct attention. Involuntary attention requires no effort at all, such as when something exciting or interesting happens and you are interested in discovering exactly what is going on, such as strange things, moving things, wild animals, and bright objects. Direct attention requires a person to pay attention to something that is not particularly interesting; it takes a great deal of effort and is not tied to specific stimulus patterns. Examples include lectures in school, reading difficult material, or listening to someone tell a rather uninteresting story. Direct attention requires the use of what James refers to as inhibiters. The way that people focus on a particular thought is not by strengthening that particular mental activity, but by inhibiting or blocking out everything else. The greatest threat to focusing with direct attention is competition from other stimuli. The frequency that inhibitors are called upon can lead an individual to mental fatigue. For example, youth today spend their days tied to some form of technology during their waking hours. (see http://www.pewinternet.org).

A decline in inhibitory control required by direct attention makes it impossible to focus in the face of distraction and human errors are committed. Another effect of lack of inhibitory control from too much direct attention is seen with people who cannot control their personal feelings and behaviors, which are required for socially responsible behavior. These people may appear rash, uncooperative, irritable, less likely to help someone in need, and less tolerant to socially important cues. How does the wilderness environment address this mental fatigue, when people are worn out and ready for a break from an overworked capacity for direct attention?

The first factor discussed by Kaplan and Kaplan (1989) and supported by wilderness researchers is the construct of *being away*, or leaving civilization and the normal routine of daily life. Early wilderness-based researchers, who examined this construct in relation to wilderness characteristics, found that the motivations and benefits of visitors to natural areas was to feel a sense of escape (Driver & Tocher, 1970), as well as to reduce tension by escaping the noise of the city (Lucas, 1963), a sense of crowding (Lime & Cushwa, 1969), the predictability of daily life (Catton, 1969), role overload associated with daily life (Knopf, 1972), and a feeling of social restriction (Etzkorn, 1965). In a therapeutic context, getting away from the personal and social situations that perpetuate and cause the tumult and having an opportunity to examine those situations from an objective perspective can be very important to reducing stress.

Another therapeutic factor associated with spending time in nature is the notion of *soft fascination*. Soft fascination occurs when involuntary attention is engaged and demands on a depleted direct attention are diminished, thus making restoration possible. A key aspect of restorative settings is their potential for eliciting soft fascination. Clouds, sunsets, and moving river water capture attention because they are visually and auditorily fascinating, but in a way that does not require direct attention. In this way, cognitive reflection can occur as one is engaged in something fascinating and stimulating. Hartig and Evans (1991) have tested Kaplan's theories and offered strong support for the claim that natural settings are restorative in part because they facilitate recovery from mental fatigue. Moreover, they concluded that being away is not sufficient to produce restorative effects. They did this by comparing two groups: one group had taken a "wilderness vacation" that involved a car tour and sightseeing, whereas the other group took a "wilderness backpacking trip." The group that spent the majority of their time on the backpacking trip returned to their lives more restored.

EMPIRICAL SUPPORT FOR NATURE'S ROLE IN ADVENTURE THERAPY

In addition to Kaplan and Kaplan (1989), a solid body of literature supports the notion that nature is restorative and promotes healthy physical, psychological, and emotional development, especially for youth. For example, Taylor, Kuo, and Sullivan (2001) asked the question: Is contact with everyday nature also related to the attentional functioning of children? They addressed the question by studying children diagnosed with Attention Deficit Disorder (ADD) and their interactions and exposure to nature. Parents were surveyed regarding their child's attentional functioning after activities in several settings. Their responses indicated that their children functioned better than usual after activities in green settings and that the "greener" a child's play area, the less severe his or her attention deficit symptoms. Thus, contact with nature may support attentional functioning in a population of children who desperately need attentional support. Kahn and Kellert (2002) reviewed the literature on nature and child development and concluded that cognitive, affective, and moral development is significantly impacted by contact with nature. In making this claim, the authors differentiate between *direct contact* (contact with wild nature unmediated by significant human manipulation), *indirect contact* (contact with nature in the form of parks and zoos), and *vicarious contact* (contact through television nature shows or books). In a review of literature in the journal *Ecopsychology*, Chalquist (2009) suggested a growing interest and empirical basis in understanding nature's role in therapeutic settings. In defining the focus of therapeutic practice in nature as *ecotherapy*, the author reviewed hundreds of studies on the role of nature reducing symptoms of depression, anxiety, and stress and promoting positive health outcomes in healthcare settings, the growing animal-assisted therapy movement, the outcomes of horticultural therapy, and outdoors restoration. In concluding this literature review, Chalquist stated that the evidence suggests that our "reconnection to the natural world—whether through gardens, animals, nature walks outside, or nature brought indoors—not only alleviates these symptoms, but also brings a larger capacity for health, self-esteem, self-relatedness, social connection, and joy" (p. 70).

Finally, Kaplan and Berman (2010) examined the evidence on the restorative role that nature plays in restoring executive functioning, which is a high-level cognitive mechanism, and promoting self-regulation, which is a mechanism involving the capacity to behave oneself and resist temptation. The authors believe that there is a growing recognition of resource depletion, a term used to describe the necessary cognitive resources to effectively engage executive functioning and self-regulation. They attributed this to the increased demands on people's attention that are required by present-day society. After reviewing the literature, Kaplan and Berman concluded that "research and theory in environmental psychology point to certain kinds of environments that have the capacity to play this role. For pragmatic and theoretical reasons, natural environments have been the most frequently studied restorative interventions, with a relatively high success rate" (p. 54).

Greenway (1995), in his classic chapter "The Wilderness Effect and Ecopsychology," stated that the movement of ecopsychology was centered on a search for language. It is hoped that this chapter adds to this endeavor in exploring the fundamental role that nature plays in AT practice. In the chapter by Greenway, he offers a quote from his journal, written during one of the many wilderness experiences he led with college student while a faculty member at Sonoma State University. He writes: "After a time we gravitated toward a large flat space on top of one of the rocks next to the pool and formed a circle, our habit over the past weeks. And then, without quite knowing how it happened, distance disappeared, and there was openness into ourselves that was an openness to each other, that embraced the pool, the river, and farther out into the wilderness, the 'other world,' the whole earth, the universe" (pp. 126-127). The power of nature to restore, heal, and erase the barriers that disconnect us from ourselves, each other, and nature, will always remain somewhat of a mystery. It is hoped that continued dialogue, research, and innovative practice will continue to explore how nature helps facilitate processes, described by Greenway and experienced by many of us who are involved in AT research and practice.

ACTION, ASSESSMENT, AWARENESS

Sean Hoyer

Carlos, Jose, and Ivan were midway through the third day of a 9-day backpacking trip. All three claimed allegiance to the same street gang. Carlos and Jose were brothers and it was evident on this trip that Jose would again follow Carlos in whatever his older brother decided to do. Carlos was a "veteran" of treatment. Three different long-term residential substance abuse programs were under his belt as he neared the end of his current 9-month "tour" of outpatient counseling. This backpacking trip was to be where he would demonstrate that he had achieved his treatment goals.

But on this day, the three were aligned by more than blood or gang ties. They were making their stand against the group process that had been called by staff to address the theft of food. Each in turn had denied involvement, then claimed responsibility to cut the process short, then returned to their denials of culpability once their pleas did not result in getting the group to start hiking again. So now they were doing what they had done in life and in treatment so many times before: leaving. They hoisted their packs and started off down the trail—gone for more than 90 minutes before returning empty handed.

Over the next several days, each related a different experience of their time apart from the group. Carlos stated his awareness of his pattern of fleeing during emotionally trying times was rooted in his emotionally codependent family system and proceeded to make significant behavioral, attitudinal, and clinical strides. Jose revealed that he was lost. He did not know what to do without the leadership of his brother, whose erratic swings from delinquency to responsibility confused him. He acknowledged that he had done nothing in treatment for the last 9 months. He felt he was living life without direction and wanted to change. For Ivan, his realization was that his delinquent thinking and gang lifestyle was not a good match for the woods, for his family, or for probation. He now knew the mismatch between his worldview and the way things really were.

A therapist who is always present in wilderness therapy had served these youth: wilderness. Whether through the milieu, the activity of hiking, the solitude of nature, or the parallels of the experience to their own lives, each youth came to their own level of understanding through a process that was not directed by a therapist. Their conclusions drawn from their experience will resonate within them more than statements made by a counselor in the office or even a peer in a group. These three youth shared a common life story, a common fear of emotional rejection, a common situation, and a common response. They also shared the development of a greater level of internal locus of control and honest self-assessment. The wilderness as the therapist was patient and persistent and eventually effected change upon the stories of these three young men. This is an example of what I call adventure therapy.

My journey as an adventure therapist involved several paths that converged the moment I met my first employer. During a summer of high school, I took a 10-day canoe trip to Quetico Provincial Park with classmates and my biology teacher. It was during that trip that I came to appreciate the demands and rewards of wilderness travel, group dynamics, and the interdependence of the two. I also recognized that I was drawn to the challenge of helping people solve problems.

Over the next 8 years, I developed my clinical and technical skills despite the ever-present feedback from both worlds that my interests would never work together, much less materialize into a career. I was a camp counselor, a resident assistant, and a social work major in college. I soaked up opportunities for small group leadership. I explored technical training in wilderness skills and outdoor living. I read what little I could find in the literature that related to the use of the outdoors with individuals and groups seeking change. In graduate school, I continued my pursuit of understanding human and organizational systems. I took a course at a local teachers' college on adventure in the classroom. Although I was the only noneducator in the class, I quickly saw the opportunities to apply the concepts of Dewey to the group dynamic present in so many adolescent counseling settings. As my professional destiny seemed to come into focus, I found many more examples that reinforced my internal compass—that I was on the right path toward something, even though it still had no name. I stumbled across the master's thesis written by Richard "Rocky" Kimball and soon thereafter read the work of Bacon, Wurdinger, and Davis-Berman and Berman.

Destiny was a word I used to describe a chance encounter with my first employer at a job fair where they were seeking an individual with my exact skill set. Others have clarified that I had established my resume as an adventure therapist through disparate means. And although I didn't know what to call myself, I knew what I wanted to do. Since that meeting, I have continued to strive to develop myself as an effective adventure therapist: interpersonal, technical activities, clinical, medical, and wilderness travel skills. I have engaged in research, presented internationally, and authored a chapter in a conference proceedings. But most importantly, I have engaged my professional peers in an ongoing discussion of how we as a profession can mature and improve our work with the individuals we serve.

Chapter 6

Adventure Therapy Models

This chapter provides examples of current and past adventure therapy programs that have been implemented with various clients. Adventure therapy addresses issues of prevention (e.g., adolescent substance abuse prevention, high school dropout prevention, underachieving adolescents, reintegration program for soldiers returning from combat situations) and treatment (e.g., adjudicated populations, adolescent sex offenders, alternative public schools).

Clients are often identified or labeled by the dysfunctional behavior they exhibit or face (e.g., adjudicated youth, school dropouts, reintegration of soldiers) or by actual diagnoses assigned by mental health professionals (e.g., depression, substance abuse, posttraumatic stress disorder). Classifications created on the basis of dysfunctional behavior are generally made by entities outside of the mental health professions in order to label the person with the dysfunction in an attempt to find a means to address this behavior. Although this approach may clarify some problematic issues and resolve certain symptoms, it often does little to reduce or eliminate the problematic behavior. From a therapeutic perspective, the use of actual diagnoses (while still possessing some limitations) often serves as a means to reduce or eliminate not only the associated symptoms or outcomes but also the root of the problematic behavior. How each of these program models address this issue is sometimes evident in their approaches to working with clients through such structures as logic models.

LOGIC MODELS

Alice: Would you tell me, please, which way I ought to go from here?
The Cat: That depends a good deal on where you want to get to.
Alice: I don't much care where.
The Cat: Then it doesn't much matter which way you go.

Alice: … so long as I get somewhere.
The Cat: Oh, you're sure to do that, if only you walk long enough. (Carroll, 1865)

Just like Alice in this scenario from *Alice in Wonderland,* some programs often wander through various parts of treatment not knowing where they want to go, what resources are available to them, and what short- and long-term success will look like in their clients' lives if it happens. To address this issue, many programs have begun to use logic models to provide a clearer picture of their clients' needs; the resources and treatment experiences to address these needs; and the immediate, intermediate, and long-term indicators of treatment success. The Kellogg Foundation (2004, p. 3) defines a logic model as

> … a picture of how your organization does its work—the theory and assumptions underlying the program. A program logic model links outcomes (both short-term and long-term) with program activities/processes and the theoretical assumptions/principles of the program.

Logic models are typically constructed along a linear continuum, as shown in Figure 6.1. Programmers start to create these models by either identifying the resources professionals use in the treatment of clients (also sometimes referred to as inputs), the clients' needs, or both. These needs/resources are used to intentionally design adventure activities/experiences for client treatment and interventions. When properly conducted, client treatment should produce positive outputs/outcomes that result in immediate, intermediate, and long-term productive changes. Logic models are presented for several program models in this chapter to illustrate the intentional program design process of adventure therapy.

The following adventure therapy program models include examples of

- Prevention programs for adolescent substance abuse, individuals at risk of dropping out of high school, and posttraumatic stress disorder/depression prevention for returning combat soldiers
- Treatment programs for adjudicated youth, struggling youth, and students enrolled in an alternative high school

After an overview of the presenting problem, a logic model is presented for each program illustrating the need and input of the program, strategies and activities used to address this need, and immediate/intermediate/final

FIGURE 6.1 Logic model structure. A linear continuum design of program planning beginning with client needs, which are used to design specific adventure experiences to achieve immediate, intermediate, and long-term outcomes.

outcomes measuring the success of the program intervention for this particular population.

Adventure Therapy Prevention Programs

Substance Abuse Prevention

Adolescent substance abuse remains a persistent and serious problem in the United States. In 2006, the Substance Abuse and Mental Health Services Administration reported illicit drug use for 9.2% of U.S. adolescents ages 12–17. According to the Monitoring for the Future Study (NIDA, 2006), 50% of 12th graders tried an illicit drug by the time they finished high school. Of particular concern was that nearly one third of eighth graders had tried inhaling drugs, and there was a notable increase in prescription drug abuse and binge drinking rates. These indicators and others point to the fact that substance use among adolescents still remains as a persistent and costly problem in the United States—and this problem continues despite a number of existing evidence-based prevention programs.

Probably some of the most influential concepts related to substance abuse prevention with young adolescents have been the theories associated with resiliency. While psychologists continue to refine the definition of resilience, Masten and Reed (2002, p. 75) described it as "positive adaptation in the context of significant adversity or risk." As resilience theories have evolved, researchers have begun to focus on which strategies are most effective for enhancing resilience in individuals. While a number of models have been presented, Constantine, Benard, and Diaz (1999) explained that many programs are attempting to promote resilience traits or internal assets (e.g., empathy, problem solving, self-efficacy) in youth through the intentional fostering of external assets (caring adult and peer relationships, high expectations, meaningful participation).

The Santa Fe Mountain Center offers a well-developed substance abuse prevention and antibullying resiliency program called Adventures in a Caring Community (ACC). ACC is an experiential learning program focusing on violence and substance abuse prevention through the use of experiential activities to increase students' resiliency as well as promote life skills. In this program, ACC does not promote new substance abuse prevention concepts, but seeks to enhance students' acquisition of these concepts through experiential methods.

Didactic programs sometimes have difficulty instituting these concepts, whereas experiential adventure programming offered by the Santa Fe Mountain Center's ACC program is optimized through a progression of therapeutic adventure programming techniques. These techniques have been formalized in the model shown in Figure 6.2. In this model, the concepts of resiliency are paired with adventure programming elements to optimize the

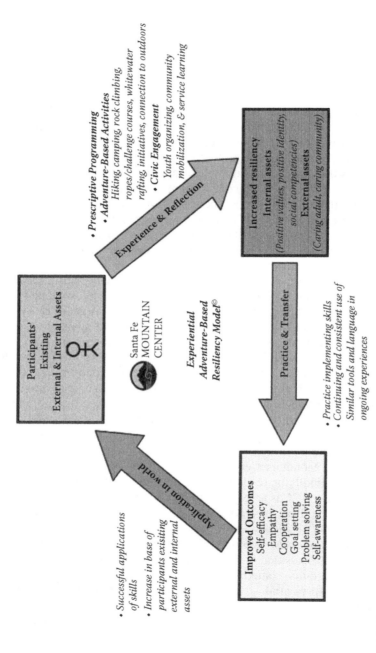

FIGURE 6.2 Resilience cycle for the ACC program.

gains in adolescent substance abuse. The program begins with connecting participating adolescents with external assets of the AAC program (e.g., establishment of physical and emotional safety guidelines, consistent definition of resilience) through adventure activities centered on an experience/reflection model. From these enriched experiences, the internal assets of participating adolescents are increased and applied to real-life situations in school through consistency and continuity in the school setting. With improved outcomes, opportunities for increased responsibilities and further enhancement of external assets are also implemented (e.g., peer mentorship opportunities, assistant facilitator on future adventure experiences with younger peers). If done correctly, the cyclical nature of the model is self-perpetuating, leading adolescents to further enhance their resilience in drug prevention. Key features or "elemental kernels" to remember about this model are that students begin with adventure experiences providing a set of success-oriented tools and common language focusing on resiliency against using abusive substances. These tools and verbal behaviors are practiced in adventure experiences with the focus on enhancing internal assets of resiliency in each child, peer group, and school setting.

In between each adventure experience during which this building of internal assets of resiliency occurs, school administrators and teachers provide consistency and continuity of the adventure program by practicing similar behaviors in this same process mechanisms (e.g., full value contracts; Schoel, Prouty, & Radcliffe, 1988) to assist in the transfer of lessons from the adventure experience into real life situations and in the community. This integrated model between adventure experiences and school implementation practices leads toward improved outcomes and greater levels of resiliency that students can use in other environments. Students choose to involve themselves in environments that build external assets of resiliency and self-efficacy, as well as recognize environments promoting substance abuse they should avoid. This cycle is reinforced further by students participating in the program as mentors for younger children as these children begin their own cycle of resiliency.

The program works with the entire fifth-grade level within an elementary or middle school. Students participate in nine 2-hour experiential school-based sessions and three full-day ropes course programs at Santa Fe Mountain Center site locations working on life skills training, violence prevention, and substance use prevention. These sessions focus on practicing the skills necessary to support healthy peer relationships, creating a caring community, and increasing resiliency skills.

The ACC curriculum has been designed by combining components of the Santa Fe Mountain Center's Experiential Adventure-Based Resiliency Model along with Botvin's life skills and alcohol, tobacco, and other drug research (Tuttle, et al., 2006). This strengths-based resiliency curriculum focuses on the internal assets of positive values, social competencies, and positive identity development as core components.

In addition to the guiding concepts and philosophies, there are four key components of the ACC curriculum:

1. Five-finger full value commitment
2. Challenge by choice/comfort zones
3. Positive peer support
4. Reflection/processing

Outcome findings of the ACC program, as portrayed in the logic model in Figure 6.3, aim to achieve the following objectives:

1. Increase levels of resiliency and self-efficacy
2. Decrease intention of self-prediction of future use of substances
3. Delay the first experience of substance use
4. Create more caring communities and classrooms for students

Input/ Need	Strategies/Activities	Immediate Outcomes	Intermediate Outcomes	Final Outcomes
Decrease intention and "self fulfillment/ prediction" of future drug use	Create a more positive, caring, and safe learning environment for students.	Building of internal assets of resiliency traits (tools, transfer, continuation)	Improved Social Competencies Students form friendships with peers less likely to result in substance use behaviors	Significant changes in resisting drug scale (IBD) (i.e., actual reduced *perceptions* and *intentions* about using tobacco, alcohol, and marijuana)
Delay first use of substance abuse	5th grade students participate in 12 experiential program sessions for each participating classroom centered on goals and aspirations, problem solving, empathy, and self-efficacy	Development of external assets like: teachers, peers, older students, caring adults	Improved Positive Identity Increased self-efficacy Stronger goal setting skills	Significant abstinence from actual reduced use of tobacco, alcohol, and marijuana Positive changes in perceived self-efficacy scale
Develop school culture supporting resiliency and drug-free behavior				
Develop school culture promoting a caring community and peer-supported interventions	Community, parents, school staff receive a Community Forum to discuss issues and support positive culture outside of school	Change in classroom and school culture School staff reinforce program norms	Healthy decision-making and resistance skills Students resist peer pressure to use	Positive changes in resiliency Increases in school attendance
	School Staff receive experiential education and facilitation training to promote caring community culture	School staff model and provide practice time for program norms	Students understand the consequences of using drugs and the benefits of staying drug-free Students gain a more accurate view of healthy peer acceptance and substance abuse Students are more likely to say that drug use is wrong Students improve ability to recognize, manage, and appropriately express their own emotions and respond to others	Increases in school performance Decreases in incidences of school violence Examination of ethnic and gender differences

FIGURE 6.3 Substance abuse prevention logic model.

Dropout Prevention

According to the U.S. Department of Education (Alliance for Excellent Education, 2007), about 1.3 million American students did not graduate high school in 2004, costing more than $325 billion in lost wages, taxes, and productivity. More than 12 million students will drop out over the next decade, and this will will cost the nation about $3 trillion (City Year, 2011). Key factors for predicting dropout risk are poor grades in core subjects, low attendance, failure to be promoted to the next grade, and disengagement in the classroom, such as behavioral problems (Kennedy & Monrad, 2007). However, there appears to be a window of opportunity in reaching middle grade students who show such signs of poor behavior, but are not yet failing academic subjects prior to the start of ninth grade.

One prevention method designed to address dropout issues are adventure dropout prevention programs (Dobkin & Gass, 2010). The center of these successful programs focus on taking traditional methods for dropout prevention and enriching them through adventure experiences and other forms of experiential learning. Methods needing conversion should center on the following concepts with the added adventure elements of change (U.S. Department of Education, 2010):

- Attendance and behavior monitors connected with both the standard school and adventure programs
- Tutoring and counseling with the establishment of small learning communities for greater personalization
- Experiential catch-up courses taught as part of a summer enrichment academy that is connected to the adventure program
- The establishment of ninth-grade academies (e.g., schools within a school where ninth-grade groups share classrooms and teachers)
- Block scheduling to provide enriched and extended time and focus to help students catch up in areas of math and reading to acquire grade level competence, often accomplished through experiential learning methodologies
- Focus on rigorous coursework and high expectations with established social expectations and support through the creation of supportive cultures
- Community engagement and service activities as part of the summer academy for eighth- to ninth-grade transition programs
- Specifically designed eighth-grade classes preparing students for the transition to high school

One critical key to the development of such a program is the planning prior to its actual implementation. Table 6.1 presents a timeline for program development. Figure 6.4 presents the program's logic model.

TABLE 6.1 Denver Adventure Dropout Prevention Program Timeline

One year prior to implementation

September

1. Curriculum development staff members attend school as ninth graders for the month. Identify problems, resources, strengths/opportunities, and places where afterschool programs serve students the best.
2. Receive consensus buy-in from all contributing working party members.
3. Establish initial contact with all potential participating members.
4. Obtain initial buy-in for all working parties.
5. Receive signed contract for the funding of the project from the financially supporting program.
6. Review literature and other similar research on similar adventure dropout prevention programs.

October to December

1. Hold focus groups to identify issues and helpful solutions to specific dropout needs, including focus groups of current dropouts, high-risk dropout youth that remained in school, families of appropriate youth, ninth-grade teachers, school administrators, supportive community members (e.g., spiritual leaders, vocational employers, significant and successful adult figures, potential adventure staff).
2. Obtain ninth-grade curriculum and examine possibilities of experiential learning models and outcomes that would enhance learning and capabilities of participants in the dropout program. Begin writing a curriculum manual identifying these components and share with participating ninth-grade teachers. Examine ninth-grade curriculum and ways it can be enhanced, enriched, and made less "boring."

   Develop after-school adjunctive curriculum defined and illustrated through experiential methods.

   Create adjunctive aids provided for interested teachers.
3. Hold multiple meetings with school administrators and other individuals of significant political importance to conduct a feasibility study of operating the program in the school with these particular youth.
4. Meet with coordinators of research in the Denver public school system to discuss the research objectives and outcomes. Begin process and receive initial permission from this governing body.
5. Select participating schools into experimental and comparison groups. Determine selection process of participating students and appropriate comparison groups.
6. Begin to create a "skeleton structure" of operations for the entire program for the ninth-grade academic year.
7. Conduct needs assessment of all participating programs, matching intended program design with student needs.
8. Conduct first feasibility study to examine likelihood of program's success.

TABLE 6.1 Denver Adventure Dropout Prevention Program Timeline (Continued)

9. Create cost-benefit analysis structure for program implementation in the intended research project.
10. Test logistical procedures of process and outcome evaluation with all research groups.
11. Select, pilot test, and finalize all research instruments.

January to May
1. Pilot test elements of curriculum with current ninth-grade students at participating schools.
2. Provide training around areas of mentorship, including mentorship themes with family mentors, teacher mentors, adventure program mentors, and community mentors.
3. Establish institutional research board protocols, research protocols, and reporting structures.
4. Write and evaluate all curriculum elements. Conduct staff trainings in these areas.
5. Conduct second feasibility study of program.
6. Clarify and finalize job responsibilities of all participating members in the program. Select and train project staff.
7. Hold staff trainings for all participating project members. Finalize job responsibilities for each participating project member.
8. Retest logistical procedures of process and outcome evaluations.
9. Conduct initial treatment fidelity research on program implementation.
10. Finalize all program logistical procedures.

Reintegration Programs for Combat Soldiers (Contributed by Matt Chisholm)

The U.S. military has been engaged in combat since October 2001 with Operation Enduring Freedom and Operation Iraqi Freedom. The number of U.S. soldiers deployed in these two military operations has been estimated at 1.64 million troops (Burnam, 2009). One of the key factors in soldiers' lives is their reintegration back to military settings in the United States or to American society as productive and contributing civilians. For most soldiers, this reintegration process is satisfactorily negotiated.

However, for some soldiers this reintegration process is not successful. It is estimated that 300,000 Gulf war soldiers, or 18.5%, suffer from post-traumatic stress disorder (PTSD) or major depression (Burnam, et al., 2009). The financial expense of treating soldiers suffering from these two issues has already cost the United States more than $6.2 billion in the first 2 years following deployments. Note that these figures do not account for additional soldiers with traumatic brain injury.

The U.S. Army has also begun to explore the use of several forms of adventure programming to assist the reintegration process. The model most

Input/Need	Strategies/Activities	Immediate Outcomes	Intermediate Outcomes	Final Outcomes
Target population identified 8th graders before the beginning of the 9th-grade year Close dropout gap Promote successful completion of high school	Adventure program summer preparation institute for identified youth and staff. Focus includes resilience training as well as 8th- to 9th-grade transition program, establishing group norms, social and emotional learning, and mentor presentations	Attendance rate in first 30 days of 9th grade Attendance rates for first semester of 9th grade	Benchmark measures on attendance, grades, and program involvement in 10th and 11th grade	Higher student graduation rate
		First-quarter freshman grades, particularly English and math	Number of credits earned in 10th grade and 11th grade	
	In-school support including: attendance and behavior monitors, benchmarking, progress monitoring, high expectations, and rigorous coursework	First semester grades in 9th grade	Greater development of student responsibility measured through: • Increase in attendance rates • Decrease in suspension rates • Decrease in disciplinary referrals	
	• After-school and summer supplement programs, including: after-school tutoring and counseling, experiential learning, external mentors and role models	• End of year grades for 9th grade • Attendance rate for entire 9th grade • Number of credits earned in 9th grade Promotion to 10th grade		

FIGURE 6.4 Dropout prevention logic model.

commonly used is the Warrior Adventure Quest program. This program is between 1 and 3 days in length and aims at addressing reintegration issues with adrenaline refocusing activities (U.S. Department of Defense, 2008, 2010). While the U.S. Army has spent an excess of $7 million on the creation and piloting of this program (Bell, 2009), no formal research has been published on the effectiveness of this program and there are concerns that it may not use the strongest principles of adventure programming.

Another adventure program, the Outward Bound for Veterans Program, uses backcountry programming for soldiers still on active duty as well as those who have been discharged. This program has been found to increase feelings of confidence, physical safety, emotional safety, and success as defined by the Outward Bound Outcomes Instrument (Ewert, Frankel, Van Puymbroeck, &

Luo, 2010). Ragsdale, Cox, Finn, and Eisler (1996, p. 278) also explored a 26-day inpatient treatment for PTSD that utilized a 2-day trust building adventure curriculum, finding the program reduced "feelings of hopelessness, guilt, shame, loneliness, and emotional isolation." Although both of these programs showed positive results, the connection between these results and the central issues facing soldiers returning from combat has yet to be made.

Another adventure program, Operation Reintegration, was designed around three targeted objectives: focused adjustment to civilian life, increased feelings of value from the civilian community, and the provision of positive outlets for stress. The program developers believed these objectives would decrease negative behaviors, mitigate PTSD, increase unit support, and include mental health professionals in a positive way. One key difference between the Operation Reintegration program and other efforts is when the soldiers participate in the program. To achieve maximum effectiveness in this program's reintegration process, soldiers stay in their military units during the therapeutic adventure experience. Another key feature of the program is the integration of military structures, external facilitation, and the integration of mental health professionals. These are seen as key elements for enhancing of treatment.

The first stage of the program consisted of 3 days of adventure programming, including 1 day of rafting, 1 day of hiking, and a mixed day of high ropes activities and an adventure race. Debriefing sessions were strategically placed throughout the activities and focused on reintegration issues raised by soldiers. Many of these sessions centered on individual metaphor building, in which soldiers were asked to explain how the activities in the program were related to traditional reintegration themes.

The second stage of the program consisted of soldiers involved in a selected adventure activity 1 day a week for 8 weeks. Groups were organized and led by soldiers in the company in adventure experiences like mountain biking, motorcross, horseback riding, climbing, and shooting. The activities started with safety briefings and beginner lessons, and assisted participants in proficiency, culminating in an overnight event. This stage started shortly after the soldiers returned from the first stage of the program.

The use of metaphors and solution-focused facilitation were key features of the program. Using the Gass (1995) seven step metaphor model as a guide, early activities were developed to increase comfort around personal disclosure. The use of personal stories describing irritation caused by family or civilian interaction helped to open the door to later disclosure. Experiences were designed using the seven-step process in order to maximize impact. Solution-focused facilitation also assumes that each participant is an expert on their own lives (Priest, Gass, & Gillis, 1999). By using this technique, facilitators assist soldiers in creating greater personal meaning, all while decreasing the distrust that is common in soldier–civilian interaction. Both of these techniques have origins in Milton Erickson's utilization principles. Erickson asserted that effective therapy could be achieved by using: "Whatever the behavior offered by the subjects[,] it should be accepted and utilized to develop further responsive behavior" (1952, p. 155).

Figure 6.5 shows a logic model of Operation Reintegration. Chisholm and Gass (2011) reported statistically significant positive outcomes from Operation Reintegration around issues of unit support, stress management, views of the Army, and views of the civilian community immediately following programming as well as 6 months following the conclusion of programming. Qualitative analysis of soldier participants resulted in the emergence of five themes from the program that were critical factors in outdoor soldier reintegration: civilian transition, reintegration issues, importance of group in the therapeutic process, changing routine, and developing constructive use of time.

AT Treatment Programs

The Office of Juvenile Justice and Delinquency Prevention (2009) reported that 2.11 juveniles were arrested in the United States in 2008. In addition,

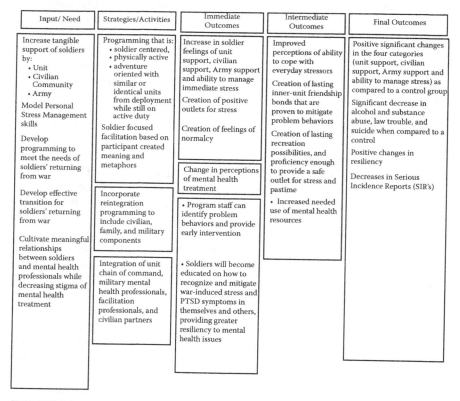

Input/ Need	Strategies/Activities	Immediate Outcomes	Intermediate Outcomes	Final Outcomes
Increase tangible support of soldiers by: • Unit • Civilian Community • Army Model Personal Stress Management skills Develop programming to meet the needs of soldiers' returning from war Develop effective transition for soldiers' returning from war Cultivate meaningful relationships between soldiers and mental health professionals while decreasing stigma of mental health treatment	Programming that is: • soldier centered, • physically active • adventure oriented with similar or identical units from deployment while still on active duty Soldier focused facilitation based on participant created meaning and metaphors Incorporate reintegration programming to include civilian, family, and military components Integration of unit chain of command, military mental health professionals, facilitation professionals, and civilian partners	Increase in soldier feelings of unit support, civilian support, Army support and ability to manage immediate stress Creation of positive outlets for stress Creation of feelings of normalcy Change in perceptions of mental health treatment • Program staff can identify problem behaviors and provide early intervention • Soldiers will become educated on how to recognize and mitigate war-induced stress and PTSD symptoms in themselves and others, providing greater resiliency to mental health issues	Improved perceptions of ability to cope with everyday stressors Creation of lasting inner-unit friendship bonds that are proven to mitigate problem behaviors Creation of lasting recreation possibilities, and proficiency enough to provide a safe outlet for stress and pastime • Increased needed use of mental health resources	Positive significant changes in the four categories (unit support, civilian support, Army support and ability to manage stress) as compared to a control group Significant decrease in alcohol and substance abuse, law trouble, and suicide when compared to a control Positive changes in resiliency Decreases in Serious Incidence Reports (SIR's)

FIGURE 6.5 Operation Reintegration logic model.

juvenile crimes account for 1 out of 8 violent crimes, 1 out of 10 arrests for murder, and 1 out of 4 arrests for robbery, burglary, larceny–theft, and vehicle theft. Such figures create issues not only for the arrested youth, but for their family, community, and the nation as a whole. Addressing the problem of adjudicated juveniles involves both treatment issues as well as cost concerns. States spend anywhere from $4 million (in smaller states like Hawaii) to $450 million in larger states such as California on their annual juvenile corrections budget (Cadue, 2010). Locked confinement in a state juvenile correction institution can run in excess of $60,000 annually (Tyler, Ziedenberg, & Lotke, 2006).

Several different models of adventure therapy programming have been implemented to try to assist with this expansive and endemic issue. Most of these programs were created with the belief that such experiences would produce beneficial changes more effectively than time spent within a locked treatment facility (Association for Experiential Education [AEE], 2011). Adventure therapy programs for juvenile delinquents date back to the beginning of the 1960s, yet often are quite different when they are actually implemented and conducted: "Because of the variance in these factors, confusion around program models has emerged and led to difficulties in the examination and generalization of the effectiveness of adventure therapy programs with juvenile offenders" (AEE, 2011, p. 1).

The next two examples presented in this Chapter are for adjudicated youth. One is the Wendigo Lakes Expedition program that primarily uses wilderness programming for youth. The other is the Behavior Management through Adventure program from Project Adventure that primarily uses adventure activities for therapeutic programming. A logic model (see Figure 6.6) for Wendigo Lakes Expedition program follows after these programs' descriptions.

Wendigo Lake Expeditions (Contributed by Steve Glass, Executive Director)

Wendigo Lake's Project DARE (Development through Adventure, Responsibility, and Education) program for adjudicated youth has been in continuous operation since 1971. It is the longest running and best-known adventure therapy program in Canada. The program is licensed and funded by the provincial government, and all students must be serving an open custody disposition and be referred by their probation officer based on a case management plan. The average length of stay is approximately 10 weeks based on the participants' court-ordered custody disposition. Project DARE was directly operated by the Government of Ontario until 2000 and continues to be fully funded by the Province.

Wendigo Lake Expeditions is a hybrid wilderness therapy and residential boarding school program using a base-camp model where student groups

Input/ Need	Strategies/Activities	Immediate Outcomes	Intermediate Outcomes	Final Outcomes
Decrease recidivism rates of juvenile offenders	Base-camp model of adventure therapy with wilderness expeditions and open campus concept	Gains in self-efficacy	Individualized program matching goals to needs	Lowered recidivism rates
Reduce number of youth "growing" into adult offenders	Adventure therapy program focused on developing:	Progress in hope that change is possible	Assignment of caseworker works with parents and community-based services for continued rehabilitation in community	Reduced number of youth entering adult prisons
Reduce tax rate costs on public for incarceration expenses	-Responsibility -Participation -Problem solving	Continuation of therapeutic goals matched to identified needs	Healthy integration into community with positive choices	Reduced tax rate costs for public to cover incarceration expenses
	Develop appropriate case management plan			
	Average length of stay 10 weeks	Success in program activities combined with positive engagement equals success in therapeutic goals	Maintenance of expectation and hope for continued healthy change	
	Match therapeutic goals to client's identified needs			
	Pro-social skill development			

FIGURE 6.6 Adventure Therapy for adjudicated youth logic model.

continuously alternate between engaging in wilderness expeditions of 5- to 14-days duration with similar periods living on a campus in open concept dormitories. The program serves male youth ages 14–18 years of age organized into groups of 9 or 10 students.

All students in the Project DARE program are interviewed by Wendigo Lake staff prior to admission. Students have extensive protection of their rights related to consent, nutrition, harsh or degrading treatment, and physical restraint (unless they pose a serious risk of harm to self or others), and are allowed private contact upon their request with family and independent external advocacy staff. Wendigo Lake is tightly regulated and licensed by the government and voluntarily participates in accreditation through the Association for Experiential Education and is a member of the Outdoor Behavioral Healthcare Industry Council. Wendigo Lake employs approximately 50 full-time-equivalent staff to serve a total of 28 residential students.

Almost since its inception, the Project DARE program has been widely viewed as an exceptionally successful program, primarily based on anecdotal reports from past students, parents, and probation officers. Although some core features of the program have remained remarkably consistent over its 40-year history, the program has undergone substantial evolution, particularly since 2000, with the most significant changes in 2008. The most important changes include increased individualization and matching of therapeutic goals to the identified needs of the young person, greater focus on prosocial skill development and practice, introduction of a prime worker model and master's level therapist, development of a program manual to guide staff, a reframing of therapeutic stance to embrace a stages of change orientation, "rolling with resistance," and introduction of motivational interviewing as a core program practice. The overall context of a group-oriented wilderness expedition and adventure-based experiential education program with an integrated school component remains the constant core of the program as it was initially conceived.

Based on the importance of the client's perception of his self-efficacy as the precursor to creating an expectation/hope that change is possible, and the highly defensive stance of young people to attempting change, the Wendigo Lake program uses games, initiatives, challenge activities, and wilderness expeditions to help the young person develop the experience of meeting and solving challenges. This is done through basic transferable change skills such as participating, problem solving, practicing, asking for help, and perseverance. A positive correlation is typically seen between the student's experience of success in program activities and the degree of engagement and success in the more overt therapeutic goals of the program.

Project DARE now operates on a significantly more individualized program, which matches program goals directly to the risk need assessment and goals established through the case manager and case management reintegration plan. Each student is assigned a prime worker. The custody students and staff have dedicated access to a master's-level therapist who works with the parents and community-based services to support the student's continued rehabilitation in the community. A program manual and enhanced staff training has been implemented to support greater intentionality and consistency of program content addressing the identified risks and needs of each student. The governmental ministry advocates ongoing monitoring and evaluation processes. In addition, Wendigo Lake engages in annual licensing, accreditation, and high-level participation in the Outdoor Behavioral Healthcare Research Cooperative, the AEE Therapeutic Adventure Professional Group, International Adventure Therapy Conference, Youth Justice Ontario, Probation Officers Association of Ontario, and National Association for Therapeutic Schools and Programs. Project DARE has also engaged in direct consultation and staff training with numerous leaders in the field of adventure therapy for youth.

Soltreks Wilderness Therapy Program (Contributed by Lorri Hanna)

Soltreks is a therapeutic wilderness program for adolescents, young adults, and older adults seeking awareness and change in their lives, their relationships with others, and their relationships to life. Soltreks accomplishes this by conducting small group and custom individual treks as a way to provide guided journeys into self-discovery (see Figure 6.7). Founded in 1997 by Lorri Hanna and Doug Sabo and located in northern Minnesota, Soltreks integrates principles of wilderness therapy with family systems perspectives. These principles are grounded in evidence-based clinical practices promoting personal growth, promoting change, and restoring healthy families. These strength-based approaches teach and model solution-focused processing skills as clients understand the power of their choices and the impact they have on their lives.

Soltreks views wilderness therapy as an opportunity for personal growth in which individuals are presented with natural and logical consequences, as well as challenges designed to be therapeutic in nature. Soltreks uses the wilderness environment or remote outdoor setting to offer the following components for the development of personal growth, awareness of self-defeating behaviors, and opportunity for change:

- Limited distractions
- Separation from negative influences or a familiar environment
- Structured daily activities with consistency and accountability
- Skills or tools for effective relationships
- Individual and group counseling/therapy
- Small group environment
- Progression of phases
- Unique staff/student relationship
- Focus on relationships with self and family

Need	Strategies/Activities	Immediate Outcomes	Intermediate Outcomes	Final Outcomes
Adolescents, ages 13–17 that have difficulty coping with the challenges of life (e.g, depression, learning challenges, low self-esteem, anxiety, underachieving)	Specially designed trips of appropriate trek length: 4–7 days (specialty) or 6–8 weeks (small group or one-on-one)	Independence, patience, assertiveness, self-reliance, and maturity	Improve stress management skills	Positive significant changes in school performance, leisure activities, accountability, respect of boundaries
Supported by their parents and siblings (as appropriate)	Emotionally safe settings based on structure, consistency, and accountability through group norms, daily routine, mindfulness practices, experiential education, ceremony, and rituals	Experience emotional and physical safety, healthy habits, intentionality, and reflection, validation, and empathy	Willingness to take emotional and physical risks (e.g. speak their truth)	Increased communication with family members
Individualized experiences	Individual therapist with each student to create individual Personal Development Plan	Goal-setting skills (e.g., Personal Development Plan)	Address negative and limiting thought processes	Positive results from Youth Outcome Questionnaire (Y-OQ)
Restore family relationships (family involvement required)	Develop and practice strategies for effective communication and problem solving	Demonstrate outdoor living skills	Increase emotional regulation (e.g, waiting until group to share emotions; appropriate expression of emotions)	Obtain academic credit
Need for emotional regulation, Increased self-awareness, responsibility and accountability of behavior	Use appropriate curriculum activities, including: art therapy, initiatives, leader of the day, letter writing with parents	Support peers in skill development	Identification of unhealthy behaviors and coping skills	Improved parent-child communication and relationship
Reclaim or develop personal power and true potential	Identify thinking and behavior patterns, limiting and empowering personal characteristics	Practice sharing, cooperation, language of power	Develop healthy boundaries	Increased motivation
Rites of passage opportunity	Identify role in family and social settings	Improve coping and social skills base	Increased self-efficacy (e.g, socially, academically)	Desire to do new leisure activities
Intervention to determine level of care/transition (e.g., boarding school, therapeutic environment, home)	Individual and group therapy	Value of healthy nutrition and personal care	Ability to receive and give appropriate feedback	Decrease in family conflict
	Academic work		Demonstrate responsibility and accountability	Less social isolation
	Adventure experiences		Improve motivation	Demonstration of new, healthy habits
	Parent and sibling participation in assignments			Healthy structure developed in home
	Transition Planning: goals and action steps, home agreement, continuity of care			Increased self-assurance and confidence

FIGURE 6.7 Soltreks wilderness therapy program logic model.

During Soltreks programming, students are provided with nutritious food, adequate water, and appropriate shelter and clothing. Soltreks staff believes that meeting basic needs is vital to creating emotional and physical safety.

Soltreks is a strength-based program whose focus is on nurturing the spirit of the individual through self-examination, learning, cooperation, and contribution. The program is designed to assist clients with a variety of challenges including depression/anxiety, learning differences, grief and loss, school issues, family conflict, adjustment, and relationship issues through diverse therapeutic modalities. To address these issues, clients move through a series of phases grounded in ritual and ceremony with the intention to tailor opportunities to derive meaning from each experience.

While Soltreks offers several types of programs (e.g., young adult programs, women's treks, family retreats and treks, parent weekend retreats), its central program is the wilderness therapy program offered in the summer for adolescents ages 13–17. This program offers closed as well as open enrollment groups with a structured therapeutic intervention and assessment for clients who need to evaluate an appropriate academic setting, a transitional bridge prior to or following residential placement, or out-of-home support. The summer program's open enrollment groups allow for rolling admissions and flexible trek length. Average length of stay is 6–8 weeks.

Each trek balances physical and emotional challenges with support and encouragement. During the initial phase of the trek, students learn low-impact camping and self-care skills and begin to develop an awareness of their roles in their families. Emphasis is placed on creating a supportive environment with appropriate boundaries, challenges, feedback, therapeutic assignments, and relationships. Lessons taught foster the development of trust and confidence as students identify their core issues and beliefs. Relationships are nurtured with integrity and care, while students are supported in moving toward a place of authenticity, personal power, and self-love.

Like many effective wilderness therapy programs, family involvement is vital to each client's success. Soltreks works particularly well with families whose children were overlooked in larger settings and need a more individualized approach toward health and healing. Experience shows that when a family is engaged in a positive way in their child's healing, the child's chance of a positive outcome and long-term success is greatly magnified.

To assist in each client's progress, Soltreks provides weekly progress reports by way of e-mail and telephone conference calls. These reports keep parents informed and involved in their child's progress and the lines of communication open between staff and parents. Parents are expected to participate in weekly conferencing with field therapists; write letters and timely focused assignments; take part in parent workshops; seek counseling support at home; and participate in onsite family sessions, experiential activities with their child, and the graduation ceremony. Siblings are encouraged to participate as appropriate.

Regarding follow-up and aftercare, Soltreks helps students and parents carefully create contingency plans for decisions relating to peer influence, family relationships, employment, school, activities, personal growth opportunities, and preplanned strategies for anticipated mistakes. Soltreks collaborates with educational consultants and other professionals to assist parents in making the best choice for their child's educational and personal growth transition. Whether the student returns home or continues his or her progress away from home, Soltreks staff members continue to support the child and family through phone calls, e-mail communications, and aftercare programs (e.g., home visits, family workshops). Student alumni may also return as student leaders or interns, and some return for a customized trek. Families are encouraged to participate in a family trek once their child has graduated to enhance specific family goals.

Primary therapeutic staff members possess master's degrees in therapeutic recreation, counseling, psychology, social work, or education. Bachelor's and master's level field instructors possess diverse educational and experiential backgrounds and are certified as Wilderness First Responders or Emergency Medical Technicians, with extended experience as outdoor leaders. The primary qualification Soltreks seeks in staff is their ability to engage children and develop relationships. Soltreks has several professional advisors providing additional support with therapeutic, medical, nutritional, and program needs. Consultation is available by a licensed clinical psychologist and medical advisor (M.D. degree).

Omni's Journey Wilderness Therapy Program
(Contributed by John Conway)

Journey is a wilderness therapy program offered by OMNI Youth Services. Based out of Buffalo Grove, Illinois, the Journey program looks to use the wilderness to lead youth and families to the natural consequences of their good and bad decisions in adventure experiences. On these wilderness therapy experiences, youth learn to work with others, improve team leadership skills, develop trust, take appropriate risks, increase their self-esteem, and have appropriate fun. The Journey program also seeks to empower youth to test their limits as well as encourage them to set productive personal goals. At the end of the trip, adolescents typically experience a sense of accomplishment and achievement. Youth also have the chance to interact with the outdoors in ways they have not previously experienced.

Wilderness settings separate our youth from negative influences they face in their everyday routine and remove them from their comfort zone. By doing so, staff focus on breaking barriers that sometimes hinder typical one-on-one counseling sessions. Once removed from their normal surroundings, youth recognize the value of the counselors' expertise. Adolescents are naturally resistant to authority figures. In fact, for some struggling adolescents, being oppositional can be a large part of their identity and treatment resistance can become a source of pride. However, in the wilderness, counselors bring knowledge and expertise in navigating terrain, avoiding bugs and sunburn, and rationing food and water supplies. This earns the respect of participants because the therapists on the trail have the tools that they need to successfully complete the experience in a comfortable fashion.

Trips are easily accessible and vary from day-long rock-climbing trips to 10-day whitewater rafting trips. Journey trip locations occur throughout North America and feature activities such as ice climbing, backpacking, rock climbing, coastal kayaking, and whitewater rafting. Staff members possess training and certifications in counseling, wilderness travel and activities, first responder medicine, and the use of experiential counseling within a wilderness setting.

Under the guidance of licensed professional clinicians, adolescents are challenged in outdoor settings. Treatment goals addressed on Journey trips closely parallel treatment issues at home. Tailored to the individual circumstances of each youth, trip goals are established in a cooperative effort between the youth, family, referring counselor, and Journey trip staff.

While the Journey experience can be valuable by itself, it works best as part of a complete treatment plan to address the needs of the youth and the entire family. Journey serves as a catalyst for treatment and aids in solidifying the successes gained in counseling. The experience helps young people remember the lessons they learned in treatment for a longer time. In many cases, youth and families who participate in Journey complete treatment in a much shorter time than those who do not.

The Journey program centers its therapeutic approaches around brief, solution-focused treatment, striving to make every experience meaningful and intentional. The program's comprehensive experiential philosophy pursues a vision of providing youth with skills for life. The program has found that experiential learning, coupled with traditional talk therapy, is the most effective method to date. Such a process becomes more real and meaningful as it is applied over an extended period of time to a variety of situations. Consequently, clients develop the ability to adapt these learned skills to real life situations that arise throughout life.

Unlike some wilderness therapy programs, clinicians lead every Journey trip. Clinicians talk with youth as they walk on a trail, set up their tents, and during numerous other quiet moments. This allows clinicians more time to get to know the youth, understand their thought processes, and change negative behaviors and beliefs. With constant attention to treatment goals, clinicians can use any small occasion to illustrate a life lesson without the youth feeling that they are being counseled.

Trip staff members collaborate with the ongoing counselor to assist youth and families in making important connections between things learned through a trip experience and situations at home, school, or in the community. This consistent attention to individual growth offers participants the opportunity to make considerable gains in therapy in a brief period of time. In essence, a weeklong Journey trip provides more than 80 hours of clinical contact, equal to several months if not a year of traditional outpatient counseling.

Trip staff members are also clinicians in the office, providing an array of individual, family, group, and multifamily group counseling services. Participants often have close contact with trip staff members before and after a trip, seeing them around the office, having them as a group therapist, or even seeing them in individual and family sessions. This familiarity provides a basis of trust that eases anxiety and accelerates growth from the trip experience.

Adventure-Based Alternative High School
(Contributed by Jessalyn Hobson)

Longview School is an alternative, adventure-based high school located in Raymond, New Hampshire, serving youth from 14–21 years old with behavioral, emotional, and educational disabilities. These students have a history of unsuccessful experiences in previous traditional educational settings. Longview is a state-approved alternative high school, allowing students to acquire a traditional education while also receiving services supporting their emotional and behavioral development.

Most students are referred to Longview School from guidance counselors at their traditional school settings and their tuitions are funded through their referring school's special education budget. Longview students and staff maintain contact with referring schools to update them on the student's progress, as well as collaborate on individualized education plan goals and progress data. Longview's ultimate goal is for students to either return to their referring schools or graduate with a high school diploma and transition to postsecondary education (e.g., vocational schools, college, military schools) or work. To reach this goal, Longview supports students in their academic and emotional development in order for them to achieve appropriate levels of academic, social, and emotional growth. All of the efforts center on students becoming functional and contributing members of their communities.

Longview addresses the specific needs of students through four key program elements: academic support, behavior management and counseling, adventure-based counseling programming, and transition services. Through these program elements, Longview focuses on the following objectives:

1. Provide students with a supportive educational community that promotes academic success
2. Administer behavioral management support for students and their families through professional counseling, feedback, reflection, and meetings with Longview staff

3. Assist students in developing better intrapersonal (e.g., self-efficacy, self-awareness) and interpersonal (e.g., social skills, cooperative behavior) skills
4. Facilitate student development of positive behaviors and provide appropriate outlets for harmful and destructive behaviors
5. Support students in their transition to traditional schooling or postgraduation placement

A typical week at Longview consists of an integration of these services and program goals into a student's school day in various ways. From Monday through Thursday, Longview students attend classes at Longview's school building. These classes include traditional math, English, social studies, science, art, woodshop, bike mechanics, computer science, and other similar courses. Longview's school consists of a structured school day, and small class sizes, as well as personable, academically certified, and effective teachers. These elements help create a supportive and close academic environment. Longview's teachers assess each student's specific and individual academic needs as well as their academic goals, which are incorporated into each student's individualized education plan during their enrollment at Longview. A logic model for Longview School can be found in Figure 6.8.

A critical component of Longview School's curriculum is the adventure-based counseling (ABC; Schoel, Prouty, & Radcliff, 1988) days on Fridays. The school is divided up into ABC teams and two teachers are assigned to lead each team. Every Friday these teams meet, check in, and partake in adventure therapeutic activities. ABC days are used to help students develop better intrapersonal (e.g., self-efficacy, self-awareness) and interpersonal skills (e.g., social skills, cooperative behavior, leadership skills), help students develop positive and appropriate outlets for harmful and destructive behaviors, and also strengthen the school community by creating relationships among peers and Longview staff.

During ABC days, teachers incorporate therapeutic tools and adventure activities to provide learning and development opportunities for students. Adventure activities include hiking, canoeing, skiing, snowshoeing, sledding, biking, fishing, challenge courses, and rock climbing. During these activities, students are challenged to overcome physical and emotional challenges. By overcoming these obstacles, students develop new coping skills, interpersonal skills, and a better awareness of themselves and the world around them. Longview staff members also use therapeutic tools to enhance and transfer the development and learning from ABC days. These therapeutic tools include therapeutic and natural art projects, use of rituals, expressive therapy tools, warmup activities and icebreakers, service learning projects, and group discussions or debriefing tools.

The therapeutic tools used on ABC days vary depending on the style and strengths of the Longview staff members running the team. For example, with an art project debriefing strategy, each student would select a stick they think

Input/Need	Strategies/Activities	Immediate Outcomes	Intermediate Outcomes	Final Outcomes
Supportive educational community to help students succeed academically	**Academics** Provide supportive learning environments with effective staff, small class sizes, and individualization of student academic needs Create IEP's outlining academic goals and monitoring progress Use certified teachers and public school curriculum for student to work on high school diplomas	Develop positive relationships with staff and peers	Improve social competencies	Develop into functional community members
Behavior management		Increase self-efficacy and accurate self-image	Develop ability to ask for help	Successfully transition to independent living settings
Improved self-concept and self-awareness of others	**Behavior Management** Provide academic and emotional guidance	Develop realistic self-expectations	Develop academic, vocational, and social coping skills	Access appropriate community systems and resources
Successful transition back to sending schools, community or post-graduation	Include student behavioral goals in IEP's measured and monitored for student progress	Develop positive coping strategies	Improve academic performance	Increased social awareness and adaptability for social and professional settings
Development of positive and appropriate outlets for behaviors.	"Time-outs" for students to de-escalate, reflect, and address inappropriate behaviors	Gain higher academic achievement levels	Effectively communicate emotional needs and deficiencies	Obtain a high school diploma or equivalent
	Monitor behavioral progress family and staff meetings	Develop oral and written communication skills	Avoid unhealthy & harmful behaviors	Develop employment capabilities
	Use real-life consequences for level system		Increase self-efficacy and accurate self-image	Develop appropriate relationship building skills
	Adventure-Based Counseling Develop teamwork and positive peer community through outdoors therapeutic activities		Create accurate self-appraisal skills	Reduced levels of substance abuse
	Promote self-awareness through behavioral reflection in adventure environments		Develop the ability to take ownership for one's actions	Successful transition to post-secondary educations (college, vocational schools, military)
	Promote physical activity and environmental appreciation			Lower recidivism rates for students involved with the law
	Teach social skills through adventure activities focused on interpersonal situations			
	Transitional Services Develop vocational and maturity skills through role-playing and real-life situations			
	Create post-secondary goals			
	Implement future plans			

FIGURE 6.8 Longview alternative high school logic model.

represents themselves during an ABC day hike. As a group, they would discuss why they chose this stick and what it represents. The team could then create a team sculpture that incorporates the sticks that they chose. From this project, students are able to express themselves through art, working together, and group discussions allow for self-reflection, social interaction, and teamwork. These projects also provide a tool for counselors to assess what is occurring with individual team members or the group (e.g., who chose the biggest stick and why, who chose the smallest stick and why, what student took a leadership role in creating this sculpture, were there any conflicts while creating the sculpture, what students strongly participated in the project, why certain students did not participate). Through this assessment, counselors are able to understand each student and the group better and meet their needs more effectively.

ABC days also allow staff members to assess students and their behaviors. Through adventure, staff members are able to see the strengths of students as well as how students are learning to engage others in real life situations (e.g., how they cope with challenge, how they react to frustration, how they behave with peers and social situations, what triggers anger and outbursts in the student). ABC days also provide students with opportunities to practice the tools and strategies they develop during counseling with the support of peers and staff.

SUMMARY

This chapter provides a wide variety of adventure programs conducted with therapeutic populations in a continuum of programming. And seen in Chapter 10, adventure programming can occur in recreational, educational, enrichment, adjunctive therapy, and primary therapy purposes. These purposes can also address issues of prevention (e.g., adolescent substance abuse prevention, high school dropout invention, underachieving adolescents, reintegration programming for soldiers returning from combat situations) and treatment (e.g., educated populations, adolescent sex offenders, alternative public schools).

The models in this chapter do a wonderful job of illustrating adventure programming along this continuum. For educational examples, the Denver drop out prevention program shows how adventure programming can be used as a preventative tool in educational settings. The Longview school program shows how adventure programming can be used in educational settings for youth having difficulty in traditional school settings. For an adjunctive adventure therapy program, Operation Reintegration illustrates how adventure programming can be used to provide an adjunctive therapy for combat soldiers already in programming designed for therapeutic purposes. And the Wendigo Lakes/Project DARE illustrates an example of a primary treatment program using adventure programming for therapy. The ramifications of these program differences will be illuminated even more in later chapters of this book, particularly Chapter 10.

Program models to address client issues are sometimes expressed through such structures as logic models. A logic model is typically a linear continuum design program, beginning with client needs that are used to design specific picture experiences to achieve immediate, intermediate, and long-term outcomes.

THE POWER OF COLLABORATION

Bobbi Beale

I regularly work with kids with behavior disorders, including attention deficit and oppositional defiant disorders. I love working with these kids, ages 8–16, at our therapeutic resident camp in large and small groups. When they first get to camp, they are excited to be outdoors and away from home, but also anxious about what is expected, who will be their friend, and how they should negotiate daily living tasks. This anxiety extends from meal procedures to group living challenges for the next week.

Our camp staff is well versed in lots of cooperative games and icebreakers. We quickly get the campers involved in fast-paced, interactive tasks that are intentionally designed to orient participants to the new environment, introduce them to daily routines, and help them learn everyone's names. The mood quickly shifts from anxious apprehension to happy engagement.

Every day, the campers participate in a small group challenge session, typically 8–12 kids per group. One day, I was concerned that my group kids were having power struggles with each other, not unlike the relationship troubles they experience at home or in school. I decided that we needed a challenge with a wide diversity of roles, so everyone would be needed to accomplish the task but no one could do it all themselves. I took them into the woods where we have a tension traverse installed, which is a cable suspended between two poles about 18 inches off the ground. One pole has a long rope attached to it. We established safety zones made from hula-hoops at the base of each pole, divided the group in half, and sent them to opposite poles. The challenge was to move simultaneously across the traverse until they were at the opposite pole from where they started.

In typical fashion, the more assertive kids insisted on going first—and quickly fell off the cable without support. A quieter 10-year-old girl pondered the possible uses of the rope aloud, inspiring others to brainstorm other suggestions as well. Taller kids offered to assist smaller ones, stretching out from the safety zones as far as they could. In a flash of insight, someone suggested that the two teams could help support each other, rather than try to race past each other and beat the other team. Everyone began to look for ways to help each other, lots of encouragement was shared, and when the last kid made it to the end they all cheered, happily high-fiving and grinning. They quickly asked if they could do it again, explaining that they were sure they could do it even better this time. How could I say no to an opportunity to rehearse new skills?

The intentional use of interactive games and challenges to engage kids, reduce symptoms, increase skills, and improve self-concept is what I call adventure therapy.

Chapter 7

Assessment in Adventure Therapy

> In the process of assessment, wilderness adventure experiences can be viewed as similar to projective psychological tests.... Clients reveal a composite picture of their global personality in the ways in which they respond to tasks, demands, and stimuli.... Like the well known Rorschach ink blots, wilderness challenges are high in ambiguity. Clients must interpret or structure the task demands as well as their own responses to it.
>
> *Kimball*
> 1983, p. 154

Rocky Kimball's description of adventure activities as a projective test may not be familiar to all readers. In psychological assessments, the use of projective tests, such as the well-known inkblot or Thematic Apperception Test, allows clients to tell what they see in the picture or image. Some therapists actually use Chiji cards (Cavert & Simpson, 2010), which are a set of images clients can use to tell stories, about their goal for the day or their current situation, and to project what they are thinking on to the image of the card. By using these cards, adventure therapists are able to hear how clients tell their stories using pictures. In much the same way, therapists can also use adventure activities to see, hear, or feel/intuit how the client is functioning by observing their experiences.

In Chapter 3 on the theory of adventure therapy, several assessment approaches were briefly mentioned on how to use the ABC≈R model of adventure therapy for assessment. This chapter will delve deeper into how assessment is used in adventure therapy. A macro view of assessment with models like CHANGES (Gass & Gillis, 1995) will first be presented, along with a mention of the experiential wave model of Alvarez and Schaeffer (2001). Next, the original GRABBS model (Schoel, Prouty, and Radcliffe, 1988) acronym will be covered as a microassessment of the moment-to-moment assessment(s) the adventure therapist can conduct in order to adjust the experiences to further generate and evaluate information for accuracy. An example is presented in the following section.

ASSESSMENT EXAMPLE

I (H.L. "Lee" Gillis) worked at Project Adventure's residential treatment facility in Covington, Georgia for many years with the same group each week. These were not young men who desired to speak about their issues with one another, even with prompting. They were in many psychoeducational groups every week where they used workbooks, listened to lectures, or watched videos containing information that was for their benefit in living healthier lives and making healthier decisions. When first began with this group of eight young men, they had no idea what to expect from me, I knew they were in this particular program due to their issues with substance use, most of the clients were previously involved with social services, and more specifically, they had numerous unsuccessful placements in foster care. This was further informed by my colleague and I completing a brief diagnostic interview with each young man. Each client also completed a recent brief psychological evaluation.

Previous experience with similar young men led me to believe they would test any boundaries set forth in group in an effort to see if I could be trusted. I also knew many of the young men put up a façade that they did not want to participate in any "games," but if presented with some sense of cooperative competition they would most likely become engaged with the activity. So based on my previous experience I initially chose an activity that I believed would have a high rate of success, as well as one that would give me information about their level of engagement, energy, willingness to participate, and reaction time—all in one activity (and I could get to know their names quickly). I picked the activity Wampum (Rohnke, 1994, p. 10) as it had been a never-fail activity. The activity involves one person sitting in the middle of the group using a pool noodle to try to hit the sole of someone's foot when their name was called before that person could call another name.

These young men liked hitting one another; the pool noodle on the bottom of the feet made a loud noise, but caused no harm. The young men had never participated in this activity—it was novel to them—but most caught on quickly. For me, the activity generated a tremendous amount of information as the group members projected their behaviors on the rules and regulations required to be successful in the activity. We observed the taunting of group members who could not "catch on to the game" by other members. I witnessed some very slow and very quick reaction times among the group members. I quickly learned who in the group knew the names of their peers and who did not. I also learned the names of the group members quickly and was able to be humbled into the middle of the group myself when I did not react quickly by calling another's name. Group members could laugh with and at me—and we could laugh together—which are all key elements of building a relationship and the critical element of therapeutic alliance.

Using this activity as a warm-up for the 1-hour weekly group allowed me to learn key elements of therapeutic consistency with them (e.g., building trust, same startup each week), and we would vary from first names to using animal or vegetable names to assess their ability to change a cognitive set from the familiar to the unfamiliar. In this way, the familiar activity could be made unfamiliar and allow for additional assessment opportunities. The use of this activity was part of a larger CHANGES plan, as described in the next section.

MACROASSESSMENT: CHANGES

We have found the CHANGES model (Gass & Gillis, 1995b) to be a helpful way to organize interactive steps to acquire information and reflect upon it to enable the development of functional client change. The seven steps that make up the acronym CHANGES are: Context, Hypotheses, Action, Novelty, Generating, Evaluation, and Solutions. This model possesses the three elements of adventure therapy assessment—Diagnosis and Design, Delivery, and Debrief—as discussed in the following sections.

Diagnosis and Design

Context

In preparing for the group experience, adventure therapists gather as much information about the client group as they can. Why has the client group entered into this experience? How long will they be involved? What are their stated goals as a group and as individuals? In the example above, having previously led many experiences with drug-involved youth before, the therapist had some ideas of how the youth might behave in an initial group session within a residential treatment facility.

Questions adventure therapists might ask in this part of the model include:

- Where am I working and with whom?
- Am I competent, and am I able to be competent, with this group given the parameters of the situation (e.g., do these factors set me up for success or failure)?

Hypotheses

After gathering this assessment information, adventure therapists establish tentative hypotheses about what behavior(s) might be expected from the group.

These hypotheses are tested through engagement in carefully designed adventure experiences. The Wampum experience was used to see if the group could maintain their composure with an activity that involved hitting one another. The fact that the activity was chosen inside the controlled environment of a residential treatment facility was intentional, as there was an assumed level of physical safety due to the proximity of other staff.

Questions adventure therapists might ask themselves in this part of the model include:

- What information about this client group from my past experiences do I bring to the client situation that I want to test out?
- What information about the client group am I provided with to formulate initial questions I wish to test out?

Delivery

Action

Much of the material used for constructing change is obtained from the actions of group members as they involve themselves in adventure experiences. As noted earlier, group members project a representation of their behavior patterns, personalities, structure, and interpretation onto the adventure activities because they are typically unfamiliar with what is being asked of them in the experience. The adventure therapist in the previous example was able to observe a group in action with an experience that had the potential to physically get out of hand as well as contained an inherent, high frustration level due to the confusion created as members rapidly called out names of other members. Note that the idea of a "never-fail" activity was used. As one develops a repertoire or database of activities, experience leads one to find that some activities seem to always work. Activities such as Moon Ball (Rohnke, 1984, p. 31), and Group Juggle (Rohnke (1984) p 112), often work well as assessment activities in the authors' experience.

Questions adventure therapists might ask themselves in this part of the model include:

- Are clients' actions congruent or incongruent with your hypotheses?
- Do initial hypotheses confirm, adapt, revise, or reject your thoughts?
- Can you engage clients in their motivational areas, not your own?

Novelty

As described in detail in Chapter 4, actions that are unfamiliar or new to the group can result in group members struggling with the spontaneity of an adventure experience. As a result, group members do not always know how they are expected to act, which prevents them from hiding behind a false or "social" self. This further leads them to show their true behaviors and provides additional information to the adventure therapist. Karl Rohnke (personal communication, 1988) has often commented that when you bring out a basketball or soccer ball, most youth have expectations of what might follow. These expectations can be positive or negative, depending on past experience. However, bringing out a pool noodle or a rubber chicken usually does not engender assumptions of what might happen next. The result can be a heightened sense of projection.

Adventure therapists might consider, in this part of the model include:

- The strong use of spontaneity, which allows therapists to see the real/core issues of the client group instead of the "socially proper" ones because of the spontaneous manner the clients use to respond
- The strong use of projection, as people typically do not come to the experience with preconceived ideas of success or failure (e.g., how they are supposed to act because they have no previous knowledge base to determine socially accepted roles)

Generating

By careful observation of group members' responses to a multitude of actions, adventure therapists can identify functional and dysfunctional behaviors; concrete, abstract, distorted, or critical thinking patterns; as well as appropriate or inappropriate affect. These patterns are most accurately perceived when there is a functional relationship (therapeutic alliance) with an adventure therapist and the client or client group.

Questions adventure therapists might ask themselves in this part of the model include:

- What is the language of the clients (e.g., are there words that possess isomorphic connections, homonyms)?
- What are the clients' value systems and beliefs?
- Can you track behavior patterns (e.g., what happens in what order)?
- What are the cyclical patterns of behavior?
- How can the therapist understand why, and at what level, this behavior makes sense?
- Is there a congruency between actions and spoken words?
- What is the interplay of intimacy, closeness, distance, boundaries, etc.?
- Are group member roles assumed alliances, or are they "at odds" over particular issues?
- What are the communication techniques being used (e.g., nonverbal/verbal, speaking through another person)?
- What do the therapist's intuitions say about what is going on?

Debrief

Evaluation

When information has been generated from observations of the group's behaviors, it can be compared with the working hypotheses once again. Do group actions fit the working hypotheses? Are these hypotheses supported or refuted? What new knowledge now exists to revisit action, novelty, and generating in the next experience? In the case mentioned earlier, the adventure therapist was able to confirm the hypothesis that not all group members could easily recall all the names of other group members. Thus the need for further name games is warranted until all group members become comfortable with others names. The therapist also observed that some group members possessed legitimized power within the group to set a norm to prevent other members from getting too carried away with the hitting involved in Wampum. Therefore, the adventure therapist further hypothesized/tested whether these same "power" members would also be able to lead the way in more in-depth debriefing.

Questions adventure therapists might ask themselves in this part of the model include:

- What are the therapists' interpretations of the information generated by the client group?
- What type of general, specific, and circular feedback is occurring?
- What hypotheses are being confirmed or rejected?
- Which hypotheses seem to be validated by client behavior?

Solutions

Finally, and most importantly, when the evaluation provides a clear picture of the group's issues, it can lead toward solutions of those issues. Integrating and interpreting information gathered in previous steps helps in making decisions about how to construct potential solutions to the group's concerns. Although these solutions can be reached within one session, it is more likely that (over the history of this particular group) the activities and actions that worked well would be increased, thus potentially pushing out negative actions to lead to a healthier group.

Questions adventure therapists might ask themselves in this part of the model include:

- What would be potential solutions to the issues?
- If problems are noted, are there exceptions when they do not exist?
- How can clients do more of what is working in order to resolve their issues?

CHANGES is model that feeds on itself, constantly moving in the mind of the therapist as more and more information is received. Different aspects of CHANGES may become more relevant at different times during the experience, as illustrated in Figure 7.1.

It is critical, to note the interactive and nonlinear nature of the CHANGES model. All seven steps are related to one another and do not just influence one another in a sequential fashion. Every step feeds into the systemic understanding of the client issue to contribute to a more accurate assessment.

The CHANGES model is one way to acquire and organize information to systemically structure a change experience. Alvarez and Stauffer (2001) (also described in Lung, Stauffer & Alvarez [2008]) have formulated an experiential wave placing similar emphasis on assessment (which they call Point A for previous life experiences). They advocate that as Point A may not be the same for each member of the group, that adventure therapists must be careful not to assume that two individuals who come from the same "place" have the same Point A. It is the responsibility of the adventure therapist to explore the unique Point A for each individual using experiential methods. Point B in their wave model indicates the desired therapeutic goals of the experience that are mutually agreed upon between the client and the therapist. The authors clearly state that their model is a macroassessment involving

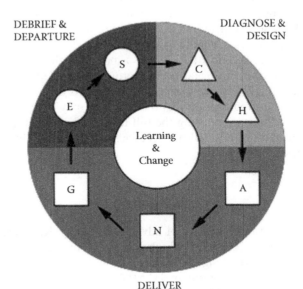

FIGURE 7.1 One method of viewing the steps of the CHANGES model is in a time sequence. For the most part, the first two steps (i.e., Context and Hypothesizing) are accomplished prior to the assessment activity. The next two steps (i.e., Action that is novel and Generating information) are accomplished during the activity. The final two steps (i.e., Evaluating and Solutions) occur after the assessment activity.

the environmental conditions, the "here-and-now" corrective experience of the adventure, and the clients' response to the activity. Alvarez and Stauffer stated, "While understanding the meaning of behavior within an experiential context provides the big picture overview, it does not provide much direction in how to intervene in a specific session" (p. 89). By attending to the group's experience in the here and now while being mindful of the each individual's Point A and Point B, the therapist can provide the corrective experience needed at that time for that group.

Models that can also help guide the moment-to-moment decisions of the therapeutic assessment process are also useful. One such helpful model is GRABBS.

MICROASSESSMENT: GRABBS

As noted in Chapter 3, the original GRABBS model (Schoel, Prouty, & Radcliffe, 1988) was developed by Project Adventure as a scanning device for helping facilitators remember important domains when holistically assessing their groups in the moment—Goals, Readiness, Affect, Behavior, Body, and Stage. The GRABBS scanning device has proven invaluable to many adventure therapists. Although the model has been updated (Schoel & Maizell, 2002) to include an additional S for Setting, the original scanning device seems more applicable for adventure therapy as a microassessment.

The multiple levels that GRABBS operates on should not be overlooked. As noted above, this is a helpful way to assess the individual client and the client group in the moment-to-moment aspects of the adventure therapy experience. This aspect is explained in more detail in the following sections. However, each of these aspects can also be applied to the adventure therapist, the agency or organization that the therapist may work with or for, and the person or organization paying the bill for the adventure therapy. How do each of the elements of GRABBS affect each layer involved in the adventure therapy process?

Goals

Goal setting is a critical practice of adventure therapy. Knowing the client's goals, and ideally co-creating goals that both the therapist and client agree to, are important in knowing how progress toward these outcomes is being achieved. The well-proven acronym SMART—for designing therapeutic goals that are Specific, Measurable, Attainable, Realistic, and Trackable—is critical in this aspect of the GRABBS assessment. In addition, a cliché is equally valid: If you do not know where you're going, you're not going to get there. Keep in mind that the person or organization paying the bill may have their own goals for the adventure therapy experience that need to be monitored as the experience unfolds. If the adventure therapy experience does not move toward these "paid for" expectations, then future funding is threatened.

Readiness

What is the client group able to do at this point in their experience? Here the ABC≈R triangle should be used as a guide for determining where the clients are in the treatment plan. For example, how invested are the clients in the therapeutic relationship with the adventure therapist to be able to take some of the physical and psychological risks required by some adventure activities?

Affect

How is the group feeling right now? Are they in a good mood? A foul mood? Do they exhibit flat affect? Are energizer activities with a high success probability needed for the group to gain some positive feelings about their ability to work together? How might a read of the group's emotions in the moment affect the next activity chosen?

Behavior

Similar to the Affect scan, how is the group treating one another? Is bullying going on in the group? Backstabbing? Or are the members of this group supporting and encouraging one another when trying new activities or self-disclosing past/current transgressions?

Body

This scan generally involves the level of physical shape the group is in with regards to the level required of the adventure activity. Can they lift one another if that physical skill is required? Are they able to climb the route you would like to climb? How have you assessed their physical condition?

Stage

Finally, the authors of the original GRABBS felt it was important to be mindful of where the group was developmentally. Were they just starting as a group, in the middle, or toward the end of their time together? Was this an open group in which new members were entering and exiting as they began or ended the program? Or was this a closed group that began together as a cohort and went through a prescribed program together from start to finish?

Each of the elements of GRABBS is important in the microassessment process with clients. Some elements may rise to the top of awareness—especially in retrospect should an error in therapeutic judgment occur. The therapist should be mindful of each of the six elements because they are critical to a safe and effective adventure therapy experience.

THE PRESCRIPTIVE USE OF EXPERIENCES IN ADVENTURE THERAPY

Recall the definition of adventure therapy presented in Chapter 1:

> AT is the prescriptive use of adventure experiences provided by mental health professionals, often conducted in natural settings that kinesthetically engage clients on cognitive, affective, and behavioral levels.

Note the intentional use of the word *prescriptive* in this definition. Adventure therapy looks at, and properly uses, models like CHANGES and GRABBS which make adventure therapy an incredibly informative assessment process for *prescribing* pathways of change for clients. Figure 7.2 is one format an adventure therapist may use based on information from these assessment processes. An informed adventure therapist (through the use of the CHANGES and GRABBS models) could write or draw an activity in the middle of this prescription as the appropriate intervention experience for a particular client based on information acquired from the assessment experience. This prescription should not only include the particular intervention experience, but also how it would be framed, delivered, adapted, and tailored for this particular client or client group.

CASE STUDY

The following is a case example of a young adolescent male who participated in a wilderness therapy program. As you read through the case study, notice how the GRABBS and CHANGES models interact to guide the therapist to support the therapeutic process. When appropriate, stages of the GRABBS model are indicated in the text describing the CHANGES model.

Context

"Bobby" is 15 years old and a junior in a public high school. He was adopted when he was 5 years old and lives at home with his adopted father, his adopted

R$_x$

H.L. "Lee" Gillis

FIGURE 7.2 A prescription for change.

father's second wife, three brothers, and a sister. He entered wilderness therapy because of problems with his attitude, experimentation with drugs, explosive anger, signs of depression, and low self-esteem. DSM-IV diagnoses for Bobby included alcohol dependence (303.90), and oppositional defiant disorder (313.81).

Bobby's primary treatment goals were:

1. Improving his relationship with his father
2. Developing a positive attitude and managing his anger
3. Improving his personal image and peer relations
4. Managing his issues of drugs, alcohol use, and cigarettes

Hypothesis

Bobby's social history profile included being kicked out of two structured military schools, his gang appearance, and negative behavior. These factors, as well as the manner in which Bobby presented himself, informed the wilderness therapist that he needed to approach the therapeutic relationship with this client very cautiously. Using a nonconfrontational approach, the adventure therapist was able to relate to Bobby in a positive way and lessen further walls of resistance. The adventure therapist hypothesized this approach would help the client come to a better understanding of his behavior, as well as the effects his behavior was having on several aspects of his life (i.e., **Readiness**).

Action That Was Novel

Bobby's anger toward his father persisted until the third week, when he made the following statement that was noticed by the leaders, "I have a place in my heart for my dad." In his session with the wilderness therapist, Bobby received mail from his family (including his father) and made the statement that "this place is changing me." During this week, he wrote a letter to his father, further opening up the walls of resistance he had built up throughout several years. These incidents marked a positive shift in the third week of the client's feelings (**Affect**) toward his father, and the beginning of a realization that he wanted to improve this relationship. Because Bobby was away from his family and father for 3 weeks, the anger and pain had an opportunity to subside and the healing and forgiving could begin.

The wilderness therapist helped Bobby write a constructive letter (**Behavior**) to his father, explaining that he would like to be accepted for the person he is. Bobby stated that wilderness leaders were not negative and forceful, accepting him for who he was no matter what his behavior. These factors helped advance the therapeutic progress noted by the adventure treatment team, suggesting a fresh start for Bobby and his father to begin to put the past behind them and move forward on a path of personal growth (**Stage**). In another Behavior example, Bobby smuggled cigarettes on the trail and smoked them during the first week. He quickly established a **Goal** to quit smoking the second week and stated throughout the process that he was done smoking cigarettes.

Generating Information

In the fourth week, Bobby stated he "did not like his dad" and posed questions to the adventure therapist in their weekly session why he and his father could not get along. These comments referenced Bobby trying to work through his emotions and he began to construct ways to communicate with and accept his father. In the seventh week, he restated he wanted a better relationship with his father, and worked with the adventure therapist on how to forgive his father for the things he has done and to move forward. This was accomplished through reading assignments and discussions of what it meant to forgive someone you love. Bobby had moved from anger and hatred for his father to forgiving him and wanting a better relationship.

Evaluating

By finding an outlet for his anger and learning new ways to control his emotions, Bobby made progress on defusing his explosive anger and quelling his suicidal thoughts. Comments made throughout the process by Bobby included that he was going to "look at the future in a new way," "think about the consequences of his actions," and "change how I look at life." By changing his outlook on life, Bobby had made steps in the right direction.

Bobby stated that as a result of the adventure therapy process, he now had set some Goals and he was happier (**Affect**) with the present. In these self-reported effects, he reflected how he viewed himself after the experience (**Readiness**). Bobby stated, "I want to be a better person. I care about myself more and I want to look at people and respect them for who they are no matter what. I want to look at life more importantly, go to school." The wilderness therapist reinforced these ideas indicating that he increased his sense of self-worth from the accomplishment of the wilderness therapy experience.

Analysis of responses made during the clinical debrief with the adventure therapist who worked with Bobby throughout the adventure therapy process demonstrated that the client gained a sense of self-worth from feelings of accomplishment. Bobby also began to show a gentleness about him with a more caring attitude, breaking through the "tough guy" image that he previously perpetuated. The adventure therapist stated Bobby became more appreciative of the things he had in life and was more accepting of himself, his father, and others. Bobby stated he was invested in improving his relationship with his father and felt good about the changes they could make. The adventure therapist believed that Bobby would have to continue to focus on the relationship with his father, as there was an opportunity to continue the lines of communication that were opened as a result of adventure therapy. He also had to recognize his self-worth, which was an important source of strength to help deal with negative influences in his life.

Solution

Four months after completing the adventure therapy program, a phone call prompted the parents and the client to discuss how the client was making the transition and implementing the changes proposed. Bobby stated to his father that the most important thing he learned from the experience was to talk to his father and share his feelings, and since then their communication had improved. His father offered a good example of how things have improved when referring to trouble Bobby had encountered since returning home from the program. Bobby received a violation as a minor possessing alcohol and had to appear in court to answer to the charge. He talked about the issue with his father openly and they both agreed that Bobby would have to deal with the consequences of his actions. Bobby's father felt good about their discussion and said that things would have been handled poorly prior to adventure therapy. Bobby's father felt good about the progress he and his son had made in strengthening their relationship.

Bobby believed adventure therapy gave him a fresh start to begin building his relationship with his father. He also stated they were communicating better. He felt good about the progress he had made and wanted to spend more time with his father "just doing stuff." He did note that he was frustrated with his father because he felt he was trying hard to change and be more open, but said his dad was not responding with the same effort. He felt like his father could expend more effort, so he was not the "only one wanting to change and grow." His main concern was to maintain the lines of communication established with his father and have his father learn to accept him for who he was. Bobby said that he still thinks about the program all the time, about the hiking and the scenery, and was glad he went through the process.

As one can see throughout this case study, information prior to the wilderness therapy experience, during the experience, and after the experience provided important guiding principles for the therapist to follow. Information prior to the wilderness experience in the program design stage—content about the client as well as initial hypotheses that needed to be tested and confirmed—guided the therapist in a congruent and "joining" manner that opened up Bobby not only to the therapist for assistance, but also to himself for introspective self-reflection. Once Bobby saw himself in this new light, he was able to involve himself in novel experiences offered by the adventure program, to not only see changes he wished to make from his past behavior, but also to try out new behaviors that might prove to be more functional for him. In the attempts of these behaviors, Bobby and his therapist are offered new revisions of Bobby's story that they are free to evaluate and test as possible solutions to the issues facing Bobby. This pathway illustrates the intent of the CHANGES model: to provide therapists with a global roadmap to empower clients to functional change.

Undergirding the CHANGES global roadmap is a heightened sense of what is occurring throughout the therapeutic experience with the GRABBS model. Regardless of the step of the process, therapists remain vigilant for potential meaning of experiences for client goals, the state of readiness of the client for change, what indications client affect/emotions signified to the therapist, what the client's body and behavior told the therapist about the readiness of change of the client as well as their acceptance of certain therapeutic concepts, and how certain stages in the therapeutic process interacted with the client's perceptions and behaviors. As with any elements of the assessment process, many of these processes seem quite intuitive to most therapists. However, having the security of these two models as a framework for therapists can help guide therapeutic process, particularly when things seem to be unproductive or unchanging.

SUMMARY

This chapter began with a quotation from one of the earliest adventure therapists on his reflection of using the wilderness. In comparing the wilderness to a Rorschach inkblot test, Kimball was partly correct. What we have learned since that time is that adventure therapy assessment is not a one-time snapshot projective experience, but a fluid cycle that continually feeds information to the joint therapeutic relationship of client and therapist. The CHANGES model (from a macro level) and GRABBS model (from a micro level) seek to inform the client and therapist on which pathway functional behavior seems to reside.

The seven steps that make up the CHANGES model are Context, Hypotheses, Action, Novelty, Generating, Evaluation, and Solutions. This model possesses the three elements of adventure therapy assessment: Diagnosis and Design, Delivery, and Debrief. As a scanning device, the GRABBS model—Goals, Readiness, Affect, Behavior, Body, and Stage—has proven invaluable to many leaders in the moment-to-moment microassessment of their groups, the individuals within their groups, themselves, and their clients. When used together, both of these models seek to inform and enrich the client–therapist relationship and effort toward achieving functional change.

SETTING TRAPS

Tiffany Wynn

A coed group of adolescents, ages 14–16 years, were referred to adjunctive therapy because of behavioral/emotional issues interfering with school participation. Five of the youth are deaf and one is hearing impaired. Four youth were fluent in American Sign Language (ASL), one signed English, and one predominately communicated verbally. During the initial session, it became clear that these youth were not accustomed to working with other youth. As a hearing therapist with no sign language training, the situation felt complicated, even though there was an interpreter and school personnel in attendance. After several 3-hour sessions, the group was communicating better and even taught the therapist to communicate with only moderate interpreter support. Group activities included low/no-prop initiatives, zip line, climbing wall, bouldering, hiking, creeking, and low constructed elements. (Note that when working with participants who are deaf, sign language typically requires uncovered hands. Environment/temperature conditions that can create communication barriers should be considered.)

At this point in treatment, the goal was to help the group address underlying issues of trust and to take responsibility for creating a safe environment. For the next session, I met the group indoors. First, I asked them to identify a superpower they would have if they could have any power. Then we discussed the benefits these powers have to help (or not) create safe places for people. At this point, I placed unset mousetraps on the table, which produced an immediate anxiety response from the group, along with, "I am not doing anything with those. I am not doing that with this group. F' this!"

After demonstrating how to safely set and release mousetraps, the group practiced this skill. Then with a set mousetrap in my hand, I invited the group to pass it along in their open palms without setting it off. After one mousetrap was passed successfully, I added more in opposite directions until we had five moving around our group. Then, in dyads, one person was invited to hold a set mousetrap in each palm while his or her partner released them with his or her hands (safely). The youth struggled to identify who they would trust, stating, "I can't trust this group to be nice to me. Why would I let someone set mousetraps off in my hands?"

We discussed how their behavior in previous sessions had not been safe enough to take risks now. They stated that disrespect, put downs, and overall meanness lead to feelings of uncertainty, fear, and anxiety. As an example, they said that they isolated youth who did not sign, and compared this to setting off a mousetrap because the isolated participant became explosive. The group decided to take responsibility not to "set off traps" in session. Referring back to our check-in, I asked, "What about your superpower could help you to not set off traps?" This ultimately became the connection between sessions, with youth sharing the power they brought to group that day to help reduce setting off traps. This became a metaphor for self-awareness and control, and mousetraps a metaphor for emotion and maintaining safety in the group. Using activity to intervene with the intention of supporting healthy change is what I consider adventure therapy.

How did I become an adventure therapist? I participated in my first initiative activity when I was 12 and it changed how I saw myself working with others and how people respond to activities versus talking to one another. Later I graduated from the University of Maine and finished a contract working at a conservation camp attending to the needs of underserved youth. I left Maine to train in a wilderness therapy program in Utah. I had no idea what I was doing; I had never been backpacking before. All of my wilderness experience was composed of canoeing in relatively slow water in Maine; I had never slept outside without a tent or a car nearby. After 8 days of training, hypothermia, a lesson in backcountry gear, and how to navigate in the desert and mountains, I took a field staff position. I worked in the backcountry guiding 45- to 60-day trips with male adolescents for the next year. At the end of that year, I had seen multiple restraints, behavior interpreted as "difficult" instead of related to a diagnosis or treatment plan, very little clinical oversight, and young men who struggled in all areas of their lives. I noticed that most of us working in the field were trained with a bachelor's degree and few had degrees in fields related to social service or mental health. After watching a suicidal young man not receive the appropriate treatment in the field and be forced to remain in the field with no psychological evaluation, I left the job and decided to return to graduate school.

In graduate school, I studied counseling psychology and concentrated in adventure-based psychotherapy. During the program, I worked in logistics and risk management for a wilderness therapy program and then shifted to intake and assessment for the same program. Working as part of the clinical team, I was exposed to how wilderness can be used as a treatment tool. Four years and multiple internships later, I found myself working in residential and outpatient treatment settings trying to use experiential practices with little support from the agency. Later that year, I found a program that worked with underserved youth, using all aspects of adventure tools and techniques with families, individuals, couples, and groups. Now I have opened a private practice focusing on the use of experiential practices and adventure in an urban setting with adults dealing with chronic pain and long-term injury.

Chapter 8

Practicing Adventure Therapy

A single word can possess multiple meanings;
Yet as the common saying goes, one picture can be worth 1000 words.
And if one picture can be worth 1000 words, then one experience can be worth 1000 pictures.
And if an experience can be worth 1000 pictures, then one metaphor can be worth 1000 experiences.
But in the end, a metaphore can only possess value when it is able to interpret the experience in a manner:
  -that provides the picture
  -that produces the words
  -that have meaning for
  -that particular client.

Michael Gass
Book of Metaphors, Vol. 2, 1995

In the passage above, Gass (1995) stressed the importance of metaphor and its potentially powerful impact on a client. Metaphors are part of people's lives. Lakoff and Johnston (1980) pointed to the fact that people's frequent use of spatial concepts such as up/down, front/back, in/out, and near/far are relevant to daily life—indicating how people literally and figuratively move about. As such, these concepts have "priority over other ways we refer to space" (Lakoff & Johnston, p. 57). Concepts that emerge from people's consistent and repeated use of metaphors end up constituting how and what they live by in the most fundamental ways.

In adventure therapy, these statements and concepts can indicate physical, kinesthetic movements, or they may be fundamentally metaphoric to what people feel, do, and think. When adventure therapists co-create a metaphors with clients, layering it with context created by clients and nuancing the adventure experience with rich connective language, they can make it feel like a personal gift especially tailored for those clients at that moment (Itin, 2002; Zeig, 1992). When clients are placed in these situations, they have the potential to tap into the affective, behavioral, and cognitive resources that promote healthy change. The challenge for adventure therapists is co-creating kinesthetic metaphors that speak to the client in their own words.

This chapter applies the CHANGES model to the practice of adventure therapy using kinesthetic metaphors from the seven-step kinesthetic metaphor process (which we refer to as 7KMP; Gass, 1991). The chapter explains how CHANGES and 7KMP are intertwined to produce a method of "doing" adventure therapy. We give examples that relate to several of the common diagnostic categories of the *Diagnostic and Statistical Manual of Mental Disorders, Fourth Edition* (DSM-IV, American Psychiatric Association, 1994) seen in adventure therapy settings. This method is presented as our way of conducting adventure therapy; we recognize and encourage other ways of doing adventure therapy, but we have found that this method worked best for our clients. The method is based on the power of the prescriptive metaphor in adventure therapy.

We begin the chapter with a case study using the CHANGES model to actually *do* adventure therapy.

CASE STUDY

Five couples elected to participate in an adventure enrichment program consisting of five 2.5-hour sessions facilitated by two co-therapists. All of the couples were also participating in traditional therapy for different issues, with the adventure enrichment program serving to augment their traditional therapy. This adjunctive intervention occurred during the fourth session of the five-session program.

One of the couples in the program, "Juan" and "Maria," were owners of a family-run business. The business was placing a tremendous strain on the couple's relationship, so they were seeing a couples' therapist for issues of communication, trust, support, and how to work through this difficult time in their lives.

Juan professed at least once during each session that their time would be better spent back at work and that he really didn't see the value of doing this enrichment program. Juan also was quite resistant, concrete, linear, and nonmetaphorical in his thinking about adventure experiences, even after having heard a number of examples of metaphorical interpretations of adventure experiences from other clients. Maria often retreated nonverbally during these discussions, often being quite sullen and depressed during activities or emotional around the idea that there was little that could be done to save their marriage let alone their family business. During most of the time in the enrichment program, the couple would either argue about how to accomplish a particular task or choose to work separately from one another as individuals.

One critical issue in many of the previous adjunctive adventure therapy experiences was that the couple seemed to have problems with providing beneficial levels of support for one another. They described supporting one another as difficult. At certain times, not enough support was being given to each other (even though a great effort was being made). At other times, so much support was being offered that it was difficult to maintain a sense of positive individual autonomy.

When observing and hearing these perspectives from Juan and Maria using the CHANGES stages, the **Context** of their issues became enriched for the therapists. Several informed **Hypotheses** emerged in the minds of the therapists based on past work with couples similar to this couple, combined with the validation of recurring themes of what they had been saying during the sessions. These hypotheses were assessed through the **Novel Action** of the adventure and began to center around the following:

1. Engaging the couple in doing more solution-focused behaviors that worked for them, so they could learn some different behaviors when the current ones did not work for them
2. Making tangible connections from adventure experiences to their relationship that could make a difference in their business and marital relationships

The novel adventure experience selected for this particular day was the Inclined Log (more is said on how this selection took place later in the chapter; Rohnke, 1977 p. 50). One major adaptation of the experience included changing the language used with the rope commands when climbing. Instead of saying "up rope" or "tension" when the belay rope was being held too loosely by their partner and the dangers associated with falling off of the log were increased, the commands "support" or "I need more support" were used. The command "slack" was used when the partner was supporting them too much, so much that is was prohibiting them from completing their task, literally pulling them off the path they needed to travel to be successful.

During their experience (the **Generating** information aspect of CHANGES), Maria went first. As she progressed up the log, she started asking, in progressively firmer tones, for more support. Juan tried his best to provide more support by pulling up the rope in the system, but Maria's gyrations and movement back and forth on the log made it difficult to take up the rope in the belay system to provide the level of support she wanted. Maria would ask for more support, and Juan would say he could not give any support when she was out of balance. The therapist asked Juan what he could do to help Maria get to a position where he could support her. He asked Juan if Maria could stop, center herself, take a breath, or even take a step back to help him support her. After Juan asked her to consider these choices, Maria was able stay centered in balance and Juan could easily take up the excess rope in the system and provide the support Maria was looking for from him. In that moment, the therapist asked Juan what it was like to support Maria when she was balanced and what he did to help her get in balance. The therapist also asked Maria to talk about what it felt like to receive this level of support from Juan and what she did to make it easier for Juan to support her. The therapist asked each to consider what happened during the experience and practice what was working in the continuation of the experience. They did so, switched roles, and implemented these strategies.

For the **Evaluation** part of CHANGES, the discussion after the experience centered on highlighting what the couple learned, which is explained later in this chapter as *analogous metaphoric transfer.* The couple mainly expressed how important their interconnectedness was to their ability to support one another. Juan referred to how helping Maria balance herself made it easier for him to support her (and how when they were out of balance as a couple, it was impossible for either of them to support one another, no matter how hard they were trying). Strategies of being in balance, taking a step back, and communicating were all related to issues currently facing the couple. Also of note was the tremendous change of affect in both Juan and Maria—laughing, closer connectiveness physically and verbally, and enjoyment of each other's company. Future traditional therapy sessions centered on the Solutions that took place in the adjunctive enrichment experience to create analogies of creating strategies similar to what happened on the log.

THE POWER OF LANGUAGE

The words residing in a client's language and their interpretations of meaning can also become more than just "figures of speech"—they become actual "figures of being" or "metaphors we live by" (Hovelynck, 1998; Lakoff & Johnson, 1980). When this occurs, client interpretations become more than just cognitive thoughts. They also become interpretations affecting personal emotions and kinesthetic actions. The following example illustrates this concept.

Example: "Be Laying"

Craig Dobkin and I (Mike) were working with some adolescents identified as "inner city gang/tough kids." They were scheduled to work with us on issues of inappropriate behavior at an adventure challenge course over a series of days, and we were told to be ready for some of the worst kids imaginable. On this particular day, they arrived about 15 minutes late to the program because a fight had broken out on the bus.

As they stepped off the bus, we adjusted the day's schedule to try and get us back on schedule. After several marginally successful icebreaker activities, we moved on to some high-challenge course experiences. Craig asked if any of these young men knew what *belaying* was in an effort to join with the reluctant group. Expecting a series of oppositional responses and maybe even some "who cares" attitudes, Craig received quite the opposite. One young man turned to him with all seriousness and stated, "I'm not quite sure, but all I know is that I need to hold on tight to this end of the rope, 'cause if I don't the person in the air is going to fall off, come crashing down, hit and 'be laying' flat out on the ground and is not going to get up. Then you'll come over with wood chips from that pile and cover him up."

We really didn't get the true meaning of what this young man was saying until we turned around and looked over our shoulders. The grounds crew for the facility had placed three piles of wood chips behind us to spread over the challenge course during the following day. We finally became aware of the full interpretation of what was going on in this young man's mind: The wood chip pile was large enough that he felt there must be three people laying in there from yesterday's challenge course failures, so if he and his peers were not careful, some of them were going to "be laying" underneath piles next to them!

Releasing himself from the traditional contextual interpretation of belaying, Craig told the young man his definition was the best one ever expressed for the concept and it was the definition we were going to use today. Throughout the experience, the concept of not getting "laid out" out on the streets at home through mistakes or violence became a recurring theme of a very successful day.

In this particular learning experience, the term *belaying* (which possesses a pretty clear meaning in the field of challenge/ropes courses or rock climbing) served as a powerful reality context for the entire experience of a day that potentially was headed for disaster. The context of not wanting to "be laying" on the ground was accessed by Craig through client language and led to several rich interpretations and connections for the therapeutic process. Key to this type of processing are adventure therapists who possess the ability to recognize and use client interpretations, even when they are quite different from standard presentations.

THE USE OF THERAPEUTIC METAPHOR IN ADVENTURE THERAPY

Bacon and Kimball (1989) identified three ways that adventure therapy uses metaphors: spontaneous, analogous, and structured. With spontaneous metaphoric transfer, clients make instinctive and relevant connections between the adventure experience and their lives in the therapeutic process. Spontaneous metaphoric transfer is sometimes referred to as "letting the mountains speak for themselves" (Baillie, 1979). The idea behind this form of metaphoric transfer is that the implicit messages of the natural environment and challenging experiences will lead the client toward more healthy and productive behaviors. In some cases, such transfer occurs, but in other cases positive change is short lived or even nonexistent.

For example, a group of sons and mothers was working on conflicts from home. In an adaptation of "on belay, gotcha" (Rohnke, 1989), both son and mother had a rope around them. Standing about 8 feet apart in a standard belay stance, they were instructed to cause the other to fall off balance. After being "jerked around" by her son several times, one mother threw the rope to the ground in utter frustration saying, "This is exactly what goes on at my home every afternoon." Her experience with the rope and her son demonstrated spontaneous metaphoric transfer. The young man in Craig and Mike's story also generated spontaneous metaphoric transfer when he verbalized he did not want to "be laying" on (or under) the ground.

With analogous metaphoric transfer, adventure therapists use discussions, structured reflective activities, or debriefing techniques following the adventure experience. This is done to assist clients in centering their interpretation of the parallel processes/metaphoric connections between the adventure therapy experience and their clinical issues. This is probably the most basic way in which metaphors and analogies are drawn from the experience, and it is how many therapists began to see the power of the adventure experience. It is also how the experience with Juan and Maria was debriefed. The therapist may finish the activity and ask, "What happened?" After a description of the task by one or more members of the experience, the therapist may then ask, "So what does that mean?" Clients may then speak about the connections (often metaphoric) that they make with the activity and their lives. The therapist may also ask, "So how does this experience relate to your treatment?" The insights that clients have about therapy, the task at hand, or the process of the adventure experience are often remarkable. All of these insights fuel the therapist's further understanding of the **Context** of the client or the client group due to the information **Generated** from the experience. Finally, many therapists proceed to the question, "Now what are you going to do?" The implication of this question is that the client will make some affective, behavioral, or cognitive change by evaluating the insights generated from experience.

As noted, a three-question process is probably the most common questioning process used in the field of adventure therapy, as adapted from the experientially based Gestalt therapy (Borton, 1970; Priest & Gass, 2005) and parallel to S-O-A-P or D-A-P notes used in clinical settings (Cameron & turtle-song, 2002):

- **What?** = What happened?
- **So what?** = So what did you learn about changing?
- **Now what?** = So how will you now integrate this change into your life?

One of the advantages of this three-question format is that it mirrors the last three stages of the CHANGES cycle. That is, the *what* questions target client responses to the generating part of the model, the *so what* questions focus client responses on the evaluation part of the model, and the *now what* questions center the attention of the clients on the solution part of the model.

With structured metaphoric transfer, the adventure therapist works with the client to co-create a framework of interpretation about the adventure experience *before* the experience actually begins. This can be accomplished through a number of techniques, but it is tied critically to the **Context** and **Hypothesis** stages of the CHANGES model. If implemented, well the briefing of the experience is inviting, engaging, and meaningful to the client. The language for such a briefing emanates from what the therapist knows and has learned about similar client groups, as well as what the therapist co-creates with this particular client or client group to strengthen the isomorphic connection. This type of briefing or metaphoric introduction of the activity increases the likelihood of the client (or client group) focusing their clinical interpretation of the adventure experience on their therapeutic issue. In the **Action** and **Novelty** stages of CHANGES, the therapist looks at two methods of structured metaphor transfer: isomorphically framing client perspective prior to the adventure experience and indirectly framing the experience through paradox and double bind techniques.

Isomorphically Framing the Experience

The term *isomorphism*, which literally means "same structures," is a key principle in the use of structured metaphoric transfer. Highlighted by a number of professionals in the field (Bacon, 1983, 1987; Gass, 1985, 1991, 1993; Mack, 1996; Nadler & Luckner, 1992; Priest & Gass, 2005) as well as outside the field (Bateson, 1972; de Shazer, 1982; Minuchin, 1981), isomorphism explains how metaphors create current relevance as well as future importance for clients in adventure experiences. Once again, an isomorph is an idea, object, or description that is identical in form or structure—but not necessarily composition or function—to another idea, object, or description. As noted previously, using spatial concepts (e.g., up/down, front/back, in/out, near/far, over/under, around/through) is one of the ways people access metaphors in their everyday lives.

One of the most effective and ethical ways advocated in this text for conducting adventure therapy is to honor the clients' experience with prescribed therapeutic actions that enhance their abilities to engage in their own change process. Gass (1991) provided seven steps for co-creating metaphors that honor clients' context. The remaining pages of this chapter discuss the use

TABLE 8.1 Aligning the Seven-Step Process for Creating Kinesthetic Metaphors (7KMP; Gass, 1991, 1995, 2005) with CHANGES (Gass & Gillis, 1995a)

7KMP	CHANGES
1. Assess, identify, and rank client goals, thinking in terms of creating a "storyline" introduction of the adventure experience for the client	**C**ontext **H**ypothesis
2. Select a metaphoric adventure experience that just naturally "matches" the client's issue and potential solutions to this issue	Matching the client's issue(s) also incorporates the therapist's awareness of how the client is processing **A**ffect,
3. Examine potential successful resolutions to the therapeutic issue	**B**ehavior, and Cognition in the context of the current **R**elationship of the
4. Strengthen the isomorphic framework by creating revisions and changes in the adventure experience	client's issues/diagnosis/current situation **A**ction that is **N**ovel
5. Review client motivation, working to appropriately adjust any particular issues to achieve appropriate levels of stress and reflection opportunities	
6. Conduct the experience, making appropriate revisions during the experience	
7. Debrief the experience, focused on punctuating the isomorphic connections between the adventure experience and the clients' therapeutic issues	**G**enerating information **E**valuating Further understanding the context of the client's **S**ystem and developing **S**olutions that can deepen the therapeutic experience

of 7KMP for creating kinesthetic metaphors with the CHANGES stages and the ABC≈R theoretical foundation. Table 8.1 aligns the seven steps with the stages of CHANGES.

Although adventure therapy possesses many unique features, most therapeutic processes and techniques used in traditional settings work well in adventure therapy settings (e.g., a four-sided, walled-off room holds little advantage over reflective natural settings). There are, however, several advantages to processing therapeutic issues in natural settings that adventure therapists should strive to use to benefit clients. Note the intent in this chapter is not asking therapists to abandon effective therapeutic techniques they may use in nonadventure therapy settings, but to adapt and integrate them with adventure therapy processing techniques to strengthen both immediate and lasting client change.

Verbal and Kinesthetic Double Entendres

Joining the realities of clients' lives and their change experience through the vehicle of isomorphism is the key to making metaphors work in therapy. The purpose of this joining of parallel content and process is to create situations where successful resolution of the adventure experience mirrors and provides guidance and meaning to successful resolution of the client's issue. In other words, if the client acts in their familiar, dysfunctional way, they will not have success in the activity. However, success in the isomorphic activity ideally provides knowledge, insight, and realization in terms of therapeutic content and process such that success (i.e., positive change) with the issue is possible. The ability to create such isomorphic connections can occur in several ways, two of which are through the use of verbal and kinesthetic structured double entendres. Seeking isomorphic structures by fostering the metacommunication between clients' lives and experiential activities is crucial to the ability to use metaphors in the adventure therapy process.

When being mindful of these concepts, adventure therapists often are aware that metacommunication occurs through double entendres offered to them by their clients. Common verbal double entendres naturally reside in a number of change experiences, providing metacommunication pathways between the two realities. In the previous example, Craig was able to access a client's interpretation of the experience through this young man's language ("be laying") and connect it to the reality of the challenge course experience with this language. One of the best uses of metacommunication occurs when therapists are able to proactively access double entendres from clients' lives and match them with a parallel structure (i.e., isomorphic structure) from an appropriate adventure experience before the experience begins. The adventure therapist uses this information to join intervening experiences and clients' lives. Within CHANGES, this process would occur in the Context and Hypothesis stages; within the 7KMP, it would occur during the first five steps. The goal is to provide a parallel kinesthetic structure where successful resolution of the intervening experience mirrors and provides guidance and meaning to successful resolution of the clients' issue (Gass, 1993, 1995).

Metacommunication (e.g., turning client words into gerands; "role confusion" is transformed into "confusing roles") is a method to strengthen the parallel process with the client when they select a novel isomorphic activity. In Step 2 of the 7KMP, the therapist selects a metaphoric adventure experience that naturally matches the client's issue and potential solutions to this issue. In Step 4 of the 7KMP, the therapist strengthens the isomorphic framework. By listening to the client's language, the therapist may accomplish this strengthening process by transforming the verbs used by the clients into actual activities that have inherent isomorphic structures. Using the same language as a parallel process, often in the form of a double entendre in the briefing of the activity, strengthens the isomorphic connection. Table 8.2 shows some

TABLE 8.2 Some Common Verbs and Their
Associated Gerunds and Nominalizations

Verb	Gerund	Nominalization
Trust	Trusting	Trusted colleague
Cooperate	Cooperating	Cooperator
Problem solve	Problem solving	Problem solver
Initiate	Initiating	Initiator
Decide	Deciding	Decision maker

common verbs and their associated gerunds and nominalizations. This is certainly not the only list of metacommunicating verbal double entendres. It is critical to seek understanding on how the clients and their various life contexts (including culture) possess their own language. This is an important concept to understand when therapists are seeking richness in isomorphic words.

Kinesthetic double entendres are physical metaphoric structures that join the realities of change experiences to clients' lives, just as verbal double entendres do through cognitive metaphoric structures in language. Although clients vary in their needs and corresponding life stories, the physical structures and patterns in certain particular change experiences tend to be naturally rich in their ability to provide isomorphic experiences, regardless of the facilitation techniques used.

Kinesthetic metaphors are intentional actions (movements) with isomorphic links that focus on the ABC (Affect, Behavior, Cognitive) pathways in the transfer of learning. This occurs because of a client's conscious or unconscious perception of the parallel connections made by the client between the adventure experience and the therapeutic issue. Just like the verbal aspects of metacommunication, the relationship (~R) of the adventure therapist and the client group is essential in integrating the kinesthetic metaphor into the client group's reality. As noted above, ideally these kinesthetic metaphors mirror clients' issues up to the point where choices in the adventure experience lead to new learning and/or breaks in dysfunctional behavior patterns.

For example, one of the authors (Mike) was building a challenge course with the help of Bob Ryan, a master in the field of challenge course construction and risk management systems for adventure programs. In constructing one particular element, Mike wanted to create a physical structure where the client would leave the safety and security of the stable position to make progress in the journey across the particular element; by letting go and taking appropriate risks, it would serve as a physical reality in the element. Under Bob's guidance and mastery with construction, the pair created a high element multivine walk that fit such as description. It literally required a participant to let go of a particularly secure tree. Participants needed to trust themselves and their support system to let go of this tree, and move forward 3–4 feet to a hanging vine that represented something specific for the client (e.g., new security, the next step in the client's life, a particular goal requiring risk and strong self-belief). In using this element with multiple clients over the past 20 years, the effectiveness of the physical double entendres created by the physical structure of this high-challenge course element has been undeniably rich in many client stories. In many ways, the archetypical structure of literally and figuratively letting go served to provide multiple and varied physical metaphoric structures that joined the realities of change experiences.

All of these concepts come together when the therapist puts CHANGES into practice, fueled with the 7KMP and with attention paid to the ABC≈R. This next section is an attempt to operationalize the process within the context of the DSM. There are numerous difficulties with using only text without the client–therapist interaction to demonstrate how one would practice what we are advocating as adventure therapy. However, the intent is to demonstrate the thinking of the therapist when presented with clients from common diagnostic categories seen in adventure therapy.

OPERATIONALIZING KINESTHETIC METAPHORS WITHIN THE DSM

Guidelines from the DSM provide a list of behavioral criteria that must be present in order for a psychiatric diagnosis to be given. For all of its benefits as well as criticisms, this manual provides a common language and set of standard behavioral criteria for the classification of symptoms of mental disorders. We are not here to argue the usefulness of the DSM, although we do recognize it is critical to the culture of mental health practice in the United States and is part of the context in which adventure therapists operate.

In order to show how DSM behavioral criteria can be used as one pathway in assessment and treatment of clients using CHANGES and the 7KMP of creating kinesthetic metaphors in adventure therapy, the following three common diagnostic categories will be presented to illustrate the process: attention deficit/hyperactivity disorder (ADHD), oppositional defiant disorder (ODD), and substance disorders.

Attention Deficit/Hyperactivity Disorder

ADHD is a persistent pattern of impulsivity or hyperactivity. It occurs in about 3–7% of the population and is more likely to occur in boys than girls, with a ratio of 3:1. It is a highly prevalent diagnosis among those referred to adventure therapy (Gass & Zelov, 2010). The DSM-IV assigns six behaviors in categories in order for a client to be diagnosed with ADHD. Some of these behaviors include *difficulty finishing* schoolwork or paperwork or performing tasks that require concentration; *frequent shifts* from one *uncompleted activity* to another; *forgetfulness* in daily activities (e.g., missing appointments, forgetting to bring lunch); and frequent shifts in conversation, *not listening* to others, not keeping one's mind on conversations, and *not following details or rules* of activities in social situations. When examining these symptoms, notice the italicized terms in these four behavioral criteria. In one context (e.g., a traditional classroom), such criteria can provide difficulty in learning and problems with disruptive behavior. Adventure therapists actually look for such behavioral criteria in the italicized terms to use at a metacommunication level as described earlier. The adventure therapist does this to acquire key information to create isomorphic connections between these terms in clients' language (thinking/cognitions), behavior, and emotions and the selection of kinesthetic metaphor experiences. This metacommunication process is part of gathering the information used in the context stage of CHANGES and helps in the development of hypotheses that can be tested in the novel action (see Table 8.3).

The following two such attention-focusing activities also can be seen at http://kinestheticmetaphors.com. The first is a patterned clap-clap, snap-snap activity, which sets up a sequence of claps and snaps that must be followed in a call-and-response fashion in order to stay in the game. In this activity, one individual is selected to begin a patterned, four-beat sequence of a particular series of body movements. Members of the group look to replicate this movement in the same manner as it is being produced (e.g., to the beat of slapping hands followed by the beat of snapping fingers). However, group members must also be aware of a new pattern emerging from someone else in the group and match that new patterned behavior as quickly as possible. The information generated from this experience allows the therapist to focus on:

1. How the client can maintain concentration when idiosyncratic changes in the activity require a large degree of attention-focusing behaviors
2. Simultaneous thought processes
3. Resilience to "stick with it" and get the patterns correct

These switches must be accomplished while numerous additional behaviors from other individuals in the group are occurring as they try to match the behavior themselves. Mistakes in this activity are common, and when they occur emotions often need to be negotiated between individuals and within the group. Therefore, the therapist in Step 7 of the 7KMP and in the Evaluating stage of CHANGES is observing how the individuals in the group can tolerate the mistakes made in the activity. When major "mistakes" are made, they can be positively negotiated immediately with laughter and a return to persistent efforts in a functional and healthy manner. Such a productive and engaging resolution to this occurrence in the activity is vastly different than the client with ADHD who simply throws up their hands, gives up, and socially withdraws from the group.

TABLE 8.3 Seven (7) Kinesthetic Metaphor Process (7KMP) and CHANGES Models

7KMP	CHANGES	ADD with Hyperactivity
1. Assess, identify, and rank client goals, thinking in terms of creating a "storyline" introduction of the adventure experience for the client	**C**ontext **H**ypothesis	• *Difficulty* performing tasks that require concentration • *Frequent shifts* from one *uncompleted activity* to another • Frequent shifts in conversation • *Not listening* to others • *Not following details or rules* of activities
2. Select a metaphoric adventure experience that just naturally "matches" the client's issue and potential solutions to this issue	**A**ction that is **N**ovel	• A kinesthetic experience that centers on focused attention, detailed remembering, and attentive listening to be successfully completed
3. Examine potential successful resolutions to the therapeutic issue		• Being successful in the adventure experience, the client and therapist are provided with clues/ pathways/processes to be successful in other arenas, even the classroom
4. Strengthen the isomorphic framework by creating revisions and changes in the way the adventure experience is offered and conducted		• See text for examples
5. Review client motivation, working to appropriately adjust any particular issues to achieve appropriate levels of stress and reflection opportunities		
6. Conduct the experience, making appropriate revisions during the experience		
7. Debrief the experience, focused on punctuating the isomorphic connections between the adventure experience and the clients' therapeutic issues	**G**enerating information **E**valuating Further under-standing the context of the client's **S**ystem and developing **S**olutions that can deepen the therapeutic experience	See text for examples

This table outlines the Seven (7) Kinesthetic Metaphor Process and the CHANGES model on how they might be used to inform an adventure therapist when working with an adolescent with ADHD issues.

Similarly, concentration can be assessed through a circular hand slap activity (a variation of knee slap in Rohnke & Butler, 1995, p. 246) that focuses attention on a pattern of slapping the floor with one's hands intertwined with the person on either side. Group members are arranged in a circle lying on their stomachs with their heads and hands placed inward in a circular fashion. While on their stomachs, group members rest their upper body weight on their elbows in this "hands forward, palms down" design. To further create an intertwined effect, group members place their hands between the hands of the person next to them. In such a design, the hands immediately in front of the vision of each individual are actually the hands of their neighbors. Once this intertwined pattern is established, one person begins by slapping one of their hands downward once, indicating that the person whose hand is toward the immediate right/clockwise must slap their hand down within the next 3 seconds. Once that person slaps her or his hand down once, the next person's hand on the right/clockwise must slap their hand within 3 seconds. However, if a person slaps their hand twice, this reverses the direction of the pattern to move in the opposite direction. After appropriately practicing the activity, a person who makes a mistake should remove her or his hand from the circle. As the group becomes more proficient with the activity, additional hand signals can be added to the repertoire of choices to make.

As one can see in these activities, the focus required by ADHD treatment is made kinesthetic in the activity. Such kinesthetic behavior acts as a vivid representation of productive as well as modeled behavior. One, but certainly not the only, metaphoric introduction to either activity that would accompany the activity rules and safety guidelines is presented in the following example.

Therapist: You know, as I have been watching and listening to you as a group I have been really curious—and sometimes even fascinated—by how some of you sometimes are able to do incredibly well at one particular task but not at others. Some of you are so focused on a particular task your awareness to other things going on around you just doesn't happen! Like I could walk through the middle of this room in a green monkey suit while you are doing a task and some of you wouldn't notice me!

And you are not all the same. Some of you never really are able to get to the first task, some of you forget, and others of you remember everything. But you all really are sort of experts on yourself on how you go about accomplishing things. I have this activity that I think might be interesting to see how each of you go about finishing tasks, changing to other tasks, and being aware of what is changing around you. If we can, I'd like to go around the circle and have each of you predict how you think you would do with an activity that asks you to complete a task while still being aware of changes around you, aware enough that you could change and match a new pattern that someone introduces. And I promise, the activity we will do will be fun!

So starting with the person immediately on my right and going counter-clockwise around the circle, tell me on a scale of 0–10 how you think you are going to do in this activity, what you predict you will do well, and where you may have difficulty. Remember, the activity is going to ask you to focus on doing a fun task, notice when change happens in the circle, and adapt to that change. And if it's okay with everyone in the group, I'll just jot down a brief phrase or two so I can remember what we predicted at the beginning of the group. We'll see who comes the closest to predicting their behavior after the activity is over. Any questions?

In this introduction by the adventure therapist, the clients are being invited to view the adventure therapy experience in a particular manner to increase treatment effectiveness. Using the strength of the existing therapeutic alliance with the clients, along with the Context and Hypotheses of these particular clients, the adventure therapist presents a frame focused around the concepts of task completion, focusing, resilience, multitasking, listening to others, and transitional skills. All of these concepts are solution-oriented skills and processes for clients presenting ADHD behaviors. Note that not only are the verbal presentation and kinesthetic actions of the activity metaphors for the client, but so is the actual structure of the process of having the clients respond to the activity. This responding framing structure asks the clients to:

1. Plan the various tasks they will do in the activity to be successful
2. Predict how they will do on the task
3. Evaluate themselves on task completion
4. Notice when change happens and adapt to change in the activity
5. Watch and observe how others accomplish the task and assimilate this information into their own set of problem-solving skills

This type of responding structure adds redundancy, depth, and strength to the already existing verbal and kinesthetic double entendres of the isomorphic framework, further tailoring a particular experience for a particular group at a particular time of a particular stage in their development. Being able to implement structures within the isomorphic framework has a rich, enhancing effect on implementing isomorphic adventure therapy experiences.

How do adventure therapists find these types of clues to create metaphor introductions with this type of depth? One of the best places to find such sources of information is within the clients themselves. Three rich sources of this information can be found in the CHANGES model by

1. Generating clearer and more applicable information from the particular client's stories (e.g., observing cyclical patterns of client behavior, using the clients' own language in metaphorical introductions, tracking behavioral patterns)
2. Evaluating previous interventions and metaphors with the client (e.g., using what has worked in the past, using hypotheses validated by previous client behaviors, examining what types of general, specific, and circular feedback exist in the client system)

3. Gaining further understanding of the Context of the client's System by developing and including Solutions that can deepen the therapeutic experience (e.g., examining what potential solutions to the issues might be, further hypothesizing what would be effective in working towards solving the therapeutic issues)

Oppositional Defiant Disorder

ODD is one of the two disruptive externalizing behavior disorders described in DSM-IV. It is a disorder that is often overdiagnosed by parents but has a lower prevalence when evaluated by teachers, parents, and clinicians. It has been found in 10.2% of the population over their lifetime, with more cases occurring in males than females (Nock, Kazdin, Hiripi, & Kessler, 2007). It is also a common disorder with many participants in adventure therapy programs. ODD typically presents an ongoing pattern of disobedient, hostile, and defiant behavior toward authority that goes beyond the bounds of normal childhood behavior. Behaviors associated with ODD include a pattern of negativistic, hostile, and defiant behavior. A client with ODD often *loses temper, argues* with adults, actively defies or *refuses to comply* with adults' requests or rules, deliberately annoys people, *blames others* for his or her mistakes or misbehavior, is touchy or *easily annoyed* by others, and is *angry* and resentful or spiteful or *vindictive*. When examining these symptoms, notice again the terms that are italicized. These behavioral symptoms often become the metacommunication pathways for creating isomorphic connections.

Therapeutic interventions for ODD include building trust and rapport between the therapist and the client. Remember this therapeutic alliance and relationship is highly predictive for success in treatment, and it is why the R is at the center of the ABC triangle model. Beyond this relationship, building a connection between the client's actions and consequences of the actions, as well as having the client take responsibility for their actions, are key dynamics to foster in this therapeutic relationship. Kinesthetic metaphors for ODD promote *managing anger, taking responsibility,* and *empathizing with and respecting the rights of others*. Activities that have clear consequences have been found to be critical aspects of these therapeutic experiences.

One activity that can address ODD symptoms with these dynamics in mind is a circular name game (similar to the Wampum activity in Rohnke, 1994, p. 10). The activity begins with the group standing in a circle with one member placed in the middle of the circle. Group members in the circle stand shoulder to shoulder, facing inward, with their palms extended at waist level and turned upward. The experience begins by one member in the circle saying the name of another member in the circle. The person, located in the middle, attempts to slap the hands of the person whose name is called before that person can successfully call the name of another individual in the circle. When the person in the middle successfully slaps the hands of the individual who is called before they can say another individual's name, these two individuals (i.e., the person in the middle of the circle and the person whose hands have been successfully slapped) exchange positions. The game can be made a bit more complex by having group members in the circle not be able to repeat the name of an individual whose name has already been called. One, but certainly not the only, metaphoric introduction to the activity that would accompany the activity rules and guidelines is presented in the following example.

> *Therapist:* Okay, before we get started I just want to ask if everybody understands the rules of the game. I want to quickly check in because with this activity things can get fast and furious and I want to make sure everyone understands. Okay?
> Before we get started, I just want to share with you one quick observation I have learned over time when working with groups doing this activity. It is watching people's reaction when they are in the spotlight by being the person in the middle of the circle. Being the center of attention can sometimes be enjoyable, but at other times can make us feel quite vulnerable and can put us on the spot. The question becomes how people negotiate, or deal with, the choices in what they personally do to make it more enjoyable and less vulnerable and reactive. I don't know how each of you will respond when given this choice, but it will be interesting to see how you handle this. Some past folks I have worked with doing this activity have ended up losing their temper, arguing, or blaming others. Other people have coped with this vulnerability by laughing things off, joined the game for what it is—a game!—and had a great time. I don't know what will happen with each of you, but it will be interesting to see how you go through this process. I probably will end up asking each of you what worked for you and maybe even what didn't work.

Individuals caught up in the dynamics of the experience, and their associated issues, must cope with the anxiety and resulting defiance by using executive management skills of their anger. Again, those abilities and competencies used by the client in the middle of the circle often provide clues and guidance for the ABC≈R pathways to resolve issues confronted by the clients in their lives.

INDIRECT FRONTLOADING—MOST USEFUL FOR OPPOSITIONAL CLIENTS

When introducing activities to clients, inviting and supportive metaphoric introductions often attract and engage clients toward functional behavior. Much of this attraction is often fueled by the excitement of the upcoming adventure experiences. There are some instances (e.g., some clients with ODD who for a variety of reasons disrupt, defy, or reject) in which clients are unwilling to accept supportive and attracting frameworks for metaphorical introductions to adventure experiences. In these situations, the harder the therapist tries to engage clients in functional behavior, the more they resist and rebel against the therapist and their efforts. The adventure therapist and client are literally in a lose-lose situation. The therapist loses if he or she forces the client to try and comply with direct treatment efforts, possibly even resorting to negative consequences. In some programs, this is where a power struggle can lead to attempts at physical restraints that turn injurious for both client and therapist. If the client does comply with the verbal directive of the treatment team, the therapeutic objective typically only remains effective as long as the treatment team members who applied the directive are with the adolescent. The other side of the "lose situation" occurs if the therapist discontinues or forgets the treatment directive, and rewards the client's oppositional defiant disorder as a method for problem resolution by letting the client opt out completely. It is also likely the therapeutic alliance becomes diminished between the adventure therapist and the client.

When this form of oppositional behavior occurs, the therapeutic issue for adventure therapists becomes how to turn a lose-lose situation into a win-win situation while still retaining the advantage of metaphor framing. In these particular situations, indirect frontloading of metaphors is used to create a win-win situation and avoid power struggles.

When should adventure therapists implement indirect approaches? The first step is to exhaust the attempts at direct approaches; indirect or paradoxical techniques should be used when direct interventions have failed. Second, much of the implementation of this therapeutic technique depends upon the therapist's comfort level with and the proper use of the indirect technique. Third, such techniques should never be based on trickery, manipulation, or power struggles. The use of indirect techniques should be centered on legitimacy, clients' best interests, and sincere reasons for using these therapeutic techniques in adventure therapy. Many therapists believe the best win-win strategies for therapy are when the therapist really does not care which portion of the win-win situation occurs. The therapist is equally invested in either outcome. Being in this type of state reduces conscious and unconscious resistance from the client when the indirect frame is delivered and progressed through. This also places more responsibility, investment, and the choice of outcome with the client.

Building off of the work of Gregory Bateson and Milton Erickson (widely considered to be the creative minds behind paradoxical and double bind therapeutic techniques), Bacon (1993) identified several strategies for using indirect approaches with adventure therapy clients, including interventions for adolescents who act out, persons with anxiety issues, clients with substance abuse issues, and alcoholics in a relapse prevention program.

When properly prepared with appropriate therapeutic conditions, a scenario for indirect framing might be used with a student who wishes to run away. Probably one of the most common forms of resistance and oppositional behavior in adventure therapy programs is when clients wish to run away from the group in the wilderness experience. As seen in Chapter 9 this form of resistance has potentially negative consequences for programs as well as for clients. Note that runaway behavior therapeutic clients are not limited just to wilderness settings. Runaway behavior is a classic acting out behavior offering an opportunity for indirect frameworks to be used for success. Direct frameworks, such as telling the client not to run away or trying to stop the client from running away, can produce probably the most obvious example of a therapist distancer–client pursuer relationship, as known in the field of adventure therapy. Often, the more a therapist tries to stop a client from running away, the more the client becomes convinced to actually run away, often less prepared and in a more secretive, covert, and undefined manner, which causes even more problems for the outdoor program.

With an adventure therapy program that is adequately prepared with appropriate levels of staffing and risk management plans to support this therapeutic contingency, when the client begins to run away from a group, the adventure therapist should not attempt to stop the client. Instead the therapist should state that there probably are good reasons why the client might want to run away. As a follow-up, the client should be told this statement: "If you wish to run away, you need to be prepared to handle and situations in the wilderness, so also you will probably need to take an adventure therapist with you when you run away." The client does not need to talk or walk with the adventure therapist, but the therapist needs to go with the runaway client for risk management procedures. Two general outcomes may occur from this indirect frontloading presentation:

1. Having an adventure therapist go with the client takes away the power and oppositional utility of the act of running away, maybe so much that the client loses interest in running away.
2. If the client actually does follow through with the act of running away, the action of running away with an adventure therapist creates a rich atmosphere for a one-on-one counseling session "somewhere down the road." In many ways, this could be a turning point in the wilderness experience for the client.

In both these scenarios, four steps for indirect frontloading outlined by Bacon (1989) are apparent. A situation arose where direct interventions were attempted but did not produce enough therapeutic change to the point where a client is turning opposition to current therapeutic approaches and wishes to run away (Step 1). Rather than being opposed or consequenced, the act of running away is accepted and reframed in terms of "there are probably good reasons to run away" (Step 2). In being accepted, beneficial results begin to emerge (e.g., opportunities to engage in one-on-one counseling regardless of the decision) and the power of the dysfunctional or oppositional behavior is diminished (Step 3). The dysfunctional behavior is abandoned and opportunities for greater therapeutic alliance emerge (Step 4).

Substance Use Disorders

The term substance *use,* instead of *abuse* or dependence, is how mental health professionals now approach alcohol and other drug use; drugs can be used appropriately or misused, or one can develop a dependence on a drug. The key to appropriate diagnosis is assessing patterns of substance use leading to distress: recurrent substance use resulting in a failure to fulfill major role obligations at work, school, or home; or recurrent substance use in situations in which it is physically hazardous (e.g., driving an automobile or operating a machine when impaired by substance use, continued substance use despite having persistent or recurrent social or interpersonal problems caused or exacerbated by the effects of the substance). Russell (2008) reported that substance use diagnoses accounted for 26% of students admitted to Outdoor Behavioral Health Programs; almost 50% were dually diagnosed, which means that a mental health diagnosis was combined with a substance use diagnosis.

Experiential options for treating substance abuse include a focus on activities that help bring out *thinking errors* and *promote success, decision-making, and interpersonal communication skills.* Two such thinking error activities promoting appropriate and successful decision making and interpersonal communication skills are described in this section.

In the helium stick activity (Gass, 1999), the group stands in two lines facing one another. Once in their lines, they place their hands out in front of them, with their elbows bent and their palms facing down to the floor. Their hands should alternate with the hands of the person from the line across from them, similar to the zip-like stance people often use with the trust fall experience. They then close their hands except for their forefinger (i.e., their pointer finger), which should point forward away from them.

Once in this position, it is critical that the participants clearly understand the rules of the activity before they begin because the dynamics of the experience occur so quickly. Clients are told that the goal of the exercise is to lower the stick to the ground as a group without their pointer fingers leaving contact with the stick. Every member of the group must maintain contact with the stick with their forefingers at all times. If a person's fingers come off the stick, the group must begin from the starting position again. Once the group understands the rules, ask everyone to zipper up into the "forefinger, palms down" position. Once the group is in this position, the adventure therapist places the stick on the top of the zipper-patterned fingers and releases the stick.

What typically occurs is that the group members, in their effort to maintain contact with the stick with their forefinger, overcompensate so that the stick actually rises like it is filled with helium rather than achieving the objective of being lowered to the ground. The group, plus each individual, needs to come up with a system that changes their errors in judgment through proper decision making and constructive interpersonal communication. It is only through such adaptive behaviors that the group is able to achieve the objective of lowering the stick to the ground.

Another-longstanding adventure therapy experience for substance use is the minefield (Gass & Gillis, 1995b; Rohnke & Butler, 1995, p. 148). Note that most adventure therapists rename and refocus the activity, not only to have the clients come into contact with symbols of drugs and alcohol, but to add positive elements into the "field" that the clients could be directed to in order to use for navigating their path to success. The reality testing allowed in these kinesthetic activities and others described in Gillis & Simpson (1994) can help bring the substance use and behavior into focus in order to highlight the cognitive thinking errors.

One, but certainly not the only, direct metaphoric introduction to the activity that would accompany the "field of drugs" activity is presented in the following example for a group consisting of parents and an adolescent dealing with issues of substance abuse.

Therapist: So we've been talking about the various issues of drug use and sobriety that your adolescent daughter Cheryl is faced with. And the reality is that no matter what we do here, she is going to be constantly faced with dealing with a world full of drugs and the temptation to start reusing again. She has faced these issues in the past, and we know the consequences that has led to, but most certainly she will face these again and there is probably no better time than now to start practicing for these very situations.

This is what this next activity is all about. As you can see in front of you in the enclosed area, we have done our best to try and represent what Cheryl will be facing once she leaves treatment. You can see that we've filled this area with items such as white bags, empty beer bottles, baggies filled with oregano, used plastic syringes, and mousetraps to represent what the world outside of this facility will be like for Cheryl—the area is saturated with the very things to tempt her to relapse and started using again.

Although it's really easy to focus on all these problems, we'd like for you and your daughter to notice, if you can, the treatment tools interspersed among all of these threats to your daughter's sobriety. Among all of these dangers and temptations, you may be able to recognize things that actually will help Cheryl on the path to sobriety. Just so I make sure you understand, do you think you and your daughter could point out what I'm talking about? [Clients identify a treatment book, telephone, list of support meetings, and the phone number for the sponsor.]

As Cheryl has told you, and you have probably already figured out, individuals in recovery possess a very important decision to make. They have the ability to seek out and acquire the very resources that will equip them to negotiate their way through their lives in a substance-free reality, or acquire the very things that will lead them back toward their substance-filled lifestyle that led them to this very point. Basically, it comes down to this: it is your daughter's choice, combined with how you support her as her parents. What are you going to center your attention on when you leave here? How will this focus affect Cheryl's efforts toward a lifestyle where she avoids risk that can lead to unhealthy choices?

To represent the times when Cheryl cannot see the various issues that will either help or hinder her progress, we have a blindfold for her to wear in the activity. We also have a set of boundaries that Cheryl must stay in throughout her recovery path indicated by the old climbing ropes on the floor. While it is Cheryl's role in this activity to literally walk the talk in her efforts to reach the other side of this activity, it is your role as her parents to offer the best guidance that you can for your daughter in making this journey. You obviously have several choices here: try and guide her away from problems, toward resources to help her, tell her to do a better job in working on her new lifestyle, etc. If there are any ideas you have right now to help her stay sober, please use them in this next activity.

I guess there is only one more thing that I want to share with you. With all of the groups that I have done this experience with, I'm never quite sure how parents will choose to guide their child. What I do know is that the groups that find out what works for them and center more of their attention on what works rather and what doesn't work seem to do the best. And after the activity is over, it will be interesting for us to see what has worked for your family and what may not have worked.

Anyway, enough with my own personal perspective. If you have no other questions, have your daughter place her blindfold on and let's begin!"

As with other introductions presented earlier in this chapter, the adventure therapist in this scenario invites the clients to view the adventure therapy experience in a particular manner to increase treatment effectiveness. Once again, by accessing the strength of the existing therapeutic alliance with clients—combined with the knowledge of this particular client's background, current hypotheses, behaviors, and verbal clues—this therapeutic intervention is centered around the needs and resulting therapeutic objectives for adolescents and their supporting parental structures in their efforts to maintain a substance-free lifestyle.

Based on this client's context and existing hypotheses, the adventure therapist begins the CHANGES process (Action and Novelty) and Steps 2–5 of the 7KMP model by selecting a novel adventure experience with kinesthetic double entendre connections to the client's therapeutic goals. Note that this process not only includes a physical isomorphic structure but also a verbal double entendre structure to create a richer intervention. The creation of this verbal structure not only includes the introduction of the experience (like the one presented here), but the tailoring of language surrounding the experience.

For example, the following kinesthetic metaphor was developed for a relapse prevention group in Singapore. The activity was designed to be used during the last 45 minutes of a 3-hour relapse group meeting. The relapse group consisted of 12–15 clients (ages 20–35) with past histories of drug misuse. They were in various stages of the recovery process trying to maintain a drug-free lifestyle, often under difficult conditions. A common theme in their lives was the temptation to return to a drug-using lifestyle (often from friends and family members), even though they possess a sincere desire to stay drug-free and strong knowledge of the consequences that returning to using will have on their lives.

Presented in this manner, this adventure therapy experience hypothesized that the foci in relapse prevention for this particular group were the following:

1. Maintaining a drug-free lifestyle
2. Identifying, staying connected to, and having a strong focus on the elements for maintaining abstinence
3. Strengthening clients' resistance to the social temptations that often lead them to begin using again

The adventure experience chosen for these treatment objectives was the Stepping Stones activity (e.g., see Rohnke & Butler, 1995, pp. 186–188). The equipment used included two ropes to mark the beginning and finish lines; a flat, unobstructed distance of anywhere from 20 to 50 meters; and one prop per person that could be written on (or a piece of tape to place on the prop on which to write 1–3).

The goal of the activity is to get from one end line to the other without touching the ground in between. People were positioned behind the beginning line and provided with approximately 25 minutes to get over the finish line. Anyone touching the ground between the lines returned back to the beginning. If at any time during the experience anyone lost physical contact with any prop, the group lost that prop for the duration of the activity (this is a key rule). The following introduction was presented to the group.

Therapist: It's been good to be together for the last couple of hours and share your triumphs as well as your concerns about recovery. And even though we've addressed some hard topics, it actually is almost too comfortable here in this room! I say this because while it's tough looking at the things we've addressed today, it is almost certainly going to be tougher for all of you when you step through the door of this room at the end of our group meeting. You know it is not a matter of if you will be tempted to use drugs again, but when you will face this decision. And this decision will not come from strangers, but a lot more likely from people you know best and who may be close to you.

One of the great things we have gone over in here are the qualities, commitments, and elements you feel will help you refrain from drug use. And in our discussions, it seems the more committed and connected you stay to these elements or qualities, the more likely you are to make it back into this room next week having avoided temptation.

And this is what the final activity of our time here today is all about: (1) how to make it back here to this meeting next week drug-free, (2) how to stay connected to those things helping you maintain your abstinence, and (3) how to strengthen your resistance to the temptations that will occur, trying to get you to use drugs again.

But before we begin, I want you to each take a plate and write on the back of it 1–3 words describing a quality or element you think will help you over the next week—particularly one that if you stay connected to and focused on, it will specifically help you to stay drug-free. After you've done this, let's go around the circle and have each person share what they've written and briefly describe the reason why they feel staying connected to and focused on this quality is so important. [Clients share their qualities.]

Okay, please join me over here on this flat stretch of ground behind this line. Here's the way I see it and you might see it this way too. Behind this line represents us right now in this room. The thing is, we can't stay in this room forever! In 45 minutes or so we are all going to walk out that door and be in places over the next week that are going to challenge our abilities to stay drug-free. And there is probably no better time than now to start practicing for those times. After explaining the rules to the activity, I am going to give you 5–7 minutes to plan and talk as a group on how you might want to consider going about this process.

Here's the deal. You need to get from this beginning line over across the line 30 meters away, just like you need to get from where you are here today once you leave this meeting next week. As you go between the lines, you must not touch the ground. If you do, you need to return to the beginning of this line. The only way you can do this is by using your qualities—on your plates—as protection to step on to get across to the other line. As long as your foot remains on your plate (resources) and no other part of your body touches the ground (such as your arm), you're fine.

You also must stay in constant contact with your resources. If at any time you lose connection with your plate—even for a split second—I (representing addiction) will get to take it from you. I may even tempt or trick you into to giving it to me, so just as you need to be on constant vigil throughout this coming week, you also need to have that level of attention to these qualities during the activity.

You have 25 minutes to get over the end line. Again, if anyone touches the ground between the ropes, they must return back to the beginning. At any time or instant a person loses physical contact with any resource, the group loses that prop/quality. If there are no questions, your 5 minutes of planning begins. Good luck.

Specific considerations taken by the adventure therapist in this particular intervention experience included careful consideration to clarify rules, punctuate isomorphic connections of the activity to clients' recovery processes, and watch for people losing contact with their plates/resources.

Losing contact often happens at very innocent times. People may just lift up a foot, go to place a plate down, or just simply not pay attention. These actions may have some strong relationship to issues that are going to arise over the coming week. If clients decide to go back to try and help others, punctuating the consequences of their decisions may provide rich insight to dynamics such as enabling, boundary issues, and enmeshment.

Debriefing should focus on the three therapeutic objectives of the activity and how they relate to the clients' coming week. As participants leave, the therapist may anchor some of the individual learning for each participant with selected words and appropriate physical connection (e.g., handshake, squeeze on the shoulder, hug).

SUMMARY

This chapter outlined how adventure therapists connect positive and functional changes in adventure experiences with positive and functional changes in clients' lives using kinesthetic metaphors. Through the use of double entendres occurring in language as well as behavior, facilitators are able to proactively use double entendre structures from clients' lives with guidance from clients, match them with a parallel structure (i.e., isomorphic structure) from an appropriate experience before the experience begins, and use this information to join intervening experiences and clients' lives. The goal becomes to provide a parallel kinesthetic structure where successful resolution of the intervening experience mirrors and provides guidance and meaning to successful resolution of the clients' issues.

A website has been established where readers can augment the reading found in this book with case demonstrations (see http://www.kinesthetic metaphors.com). Three client symptom areas were discussed in this chapter as well as on the website: ADHD, ODD, and substance abuse disorder. In some instances, clients are unwilling to accept supportive and attracting frameworks for metaphorical introductions to adventure experiences. When appropriate, indirect frontloading often serves as the best intervention for addressing this issue.

GOING IN CIRCLES...

Maurie Lung

Grace is a 49-year-old white female raised in Georgia. Her husband, Juan, is a 52-year-old Puerto Rican male. They were referred to therapy through their employee assistance program after Juan's productivity at work had declined significantly due to excessive absences. Both Grace and Juan work outside of the home in professional occupations. They have been married 22 years and have two children, ages 15 and 19 years. The older child is attending college out of state. Grace called to set up the initial appointment, although Juan stated at the first session that he was willing to participate in therapy. Both Grace and Juan are bilingual in Spanish and English. As emotions escalate, they lean toward expressing themselves in Spanish.

At their first session, Grace reported she had found evidence of an affair, including hotel receipts and phone texts. Juan claimed that it was not a physical affair, but only an emotional affair. Both stated they love each other and want to salvage their marriage, but felt they had lost direction and the "ability to steer the ship" together. After providing and gathering the rest of the intake information, I leapt on their metaphor of steering the ship and asked if they might be interested in meeting at the canoe launch for the next session. Both of them laughed and seemed to breathe a sigh of relief; in unison, they said "Si!" (Note that there were other cultural considerations addressed in therapy, including language preference, religion, and role expectations in marriage.)

Paddling a canoe requires an almost meditative ability to sit for long periods of time as well as repetitive physical movements. My hope for Grace and Juan was that learning to paddle simultaneously would become so natural that there would be a shift in attention to connecting with each other. The following week we met at the canoe launch. After reviewing safety precautions and basic canoe strokes, we set off into the warm waters of the bay. Juan was in the rear of the boat and Grace at the front. Not 5 minutes out, I heard a flurry of Spanish and I turned to find them, literally, paddling in circles. Slowly approaching, I heard Grace say, "I am trying to navigate where we are going so that we don't get in trouble and you just go wherever you want despite what I say or think is best for us." She then burst into tears. Slightly stunned, Juan responded by saying, "I was just trying to head over there because I thought I saw something and wanted to get a closer look." Grace then responded, "All we are doing is going in circles." By that point, I had reached their canoe and was able to guide the conversation into what they were not able to be express at our first session. Suddenly there was the desired direction of treatment and their relationship. Canoeing became our metaphor for working together, in different roles, to guide the relationship in the direction that both of them wanted to travel. This is an example of what I call adventure therapy.

I suppose I became an adventure therapist long before I had even recognized that is what I was. From age 8, after a camp experience too complicated to describe here, I had wanted to embrace the outdoors and experience it as a way to provide opportunities for connection and change for others. After studying outdoor recreation and environmental education in college, I still found my experiences lacking and I wanted more. I directed a camp and conference center and readily saw how participants were learning more knowledge and skills, but

I wanted to increase the opportunity to learn more about oneself and others in relation to self. So I went back to school to obtain my master's in counseling psychology, focusing on experiential treatment. I did not intend to be a therapist; however, I found that working with people who were in the process of change was incredibly inspiring. I was honored to witness their diverse life stories. Striving to be able to better provide services to my clientele, I continued my education in clinical psychology, focusing on the use of nature in multicultural therapeutic populations. I wake up every day grateful to find myself "going to work" in the way that I do.

Chapter 9

Risk Management of Adventure Therapy Programs

I was facilitating a rock climbing experience with a group of adolescent "at risk" males. After a slightly unsettled beginning, things progressed quite well where the young men began to choose to participate in the challenges and risks they were taking with positive group support. At midday we decided to take a break for lunch and a couple of the young men asked me why I would spend my day taking them rock climbing and what were some of the thoughts behind our endeavors. One of the things I mentioned was that there was a psychologist by the name of Maslow who thought such experiences were very important for your belief in yourself. He also mentioned that when everything "came together" for a person he often would call that a "peak experience." I also said some of Maslow's followers believed that the average person would have about six or seven such peak experiences in their life. One young man from the group who had been particularly quiet up until now quickly sat up and stated, "Well if you are only supposed to have six or seven of these type of experiences in your life I have to slow down! I've already had three or four and I don't want to use them all up."

Michael Gass
From client conversation in therapy, 1998

The concept of risk is incredibly important for the adventure therapy field. As stated in Chapter 1, actual risks taken by clients through adventure experiences are often a critical and key factor in the process of functional change. In fact, many adventure therapists would argue that not incorporating some form of risk in adventure therapy undermines some of the most critical elements (e.g., eustress, contrast, structured challenges) of this psychotherapeutic approach.

It is also important to remember that the types of risks in adventure therapy are not only physical ones. Certainly social and emotional risks, when applied appropriately, provide an important milieu for functional change with the right client. Conversely, when applied inappropriately, they can be quite damaging. In many ways, the concept of risk is the ultimate paradox in the adventure therapy field. Too much risk or inappropriate risk places clients in unnecessary positions of danger as well as overwhelms clients to a point where functional change fails to become an outcome. With too little risk, clients remain in a state of homeostasis, failing to be motivated to change dysfunctional behaviors and gather new perspectives. Just as adventure therapy interventions need to be tailored to specific individual/group needs, so do levels of risk. So in many ways, managing risk at physical, psychological, emotional, and social levels is one of the most important abilities of an adventure therapist.

To learn how to appropriately manage risks as an adventure therapist for constructive client change, this chapter examines categories of physical, psychological, and medication risks. The appropriate use of risk—not its elimination, even if this was humanly possible—is the goal of risk management as an adventure therapist.

PHYSICAL RISKS: HOW MUCH ACTUAL RISK IS THERE?

One factor influencing risk management is the perception of risk compared to the actual level of risk with a particular activity. With adventure experiences, particularly given internal mechanisms like contrast and unfamiliarity, most individuals perceive adventure experiences as possessing more risk than there actually is when participating.

How much actual risk is there in adventure experiences? To see if you know, try to rank the following activities from the most risky activity (i.e., 1) to the least risky activity (i.e., 9):

_____ Driving a car
_____ Riding a horse
_____ Women's gymnastics
_____ Football
_____ Basketball
_____ Downhill skiing
_____ Backpacking
_____ Adventure therapy programs
_____ Challenge/ropes courses

If you ranked these activities in the order they are listed, you are correct! You have properly presented the actual amount of risk involved in participation of these experiences. Driving a car is ranked first as the activity with the greatest amount of comparative actual risk; adventure therapy and challenge/ropes courses are last on the list.

Cooley (2000) used a more formal method for comparing the accident/ incident rates of four Outdoor Behavioral Healthcare Industry Research Consortium (OBHRC) wilderness therapy programs to other more typical activities for 15- to 19-year-old adolescents—the most common ages for participants in wilderness therapy programs. Although his analysis was somewhat compromised by the necessity of collapsing data through different methods to make comparisons, his conclusions are similar to the ones shared above. He found that wilderness therapy programming possessed similar incident rates to cross-country skiing and was a little safer than canoeing, summer adventure camps, and general backpacking. He also found wilderness therapy programs to be more than twice as safe as downhill skiing and teenage driving, as well as being about 18 times safer than high school football practices and cheerleading.

A more recent comprehensive and longitudinal analysis of risk and adventure programming was completed by Leemon (2008), with support from the National Outdoor Leadership School (NOLS), Wilderness Risk Managers Committee (WRMC), and the Association for Experiential Education (AEE) (Shankar, 2007). The programs involved in this analysis represented some of the very best and professional adventure programs in North America, if not the world. Of the 43 organizations submitting data, 32 were accredited by the AEE, which is the most comprehensive adventure program accreditation process in current existence. Note the OBHRC injury rate has dropped by more than half over the past decade, from 1.12 injuries per 1,000 client days in 1998 (Cooley, 1998) to 0.52 in 2010 (OBHRC, 2011). Table 9.1 presents incident rate data for adolescents in the general population (i.e., 0.37 injuries per 1,000 days) and several specific activities for comparison.

Leemon's (2008) findings are very similar to OBHRC's analyses: professional, state-of-the-art adventure therapy programs possess incident rates a little lower than cross-country skiing and flat-water canoeing, about 10 times as safe as downhill skiing, about 30 times safer than high school football practices, and more than 138 times safer than high school football games (2007). As discussed later on in this chapter, given the conservative structural design for over-reporting by OBHRC programs for incidents, the figures for adventure therapy programs may actually be lower than the statistic used here (i.e., the actual incident rate for OBHRC programs is probably less than 0.52).

Based on Web-based Injury Statistics Query and Reporting System figures obtained from the U.S. Centers for Disease Control and Prevention for all adolescents in America, the national estimates of injuries treated in U.S. hospital emergency departments for adolescents age 14–19 from 2001–2009 was 0.37 injuries for every 1,000 days. Participating on current wilderness therapy programs only increases the actual risk to an adolescent by 0.15 incidents for every 1,000 days, or one additional accident every 6,667 participant days. Given that most individuals entering wilderness therapy programs are generally involved in behaviors with higher risks than the general population (e.g., self-abusive

TABLE 9.1 Injury Rates per 1,000 Days of Specific Activity

Activity	Injury per 1,000 participant days
Manufactured climbing wall activity (Leemon, 2008)	.04
Initiatives (Leemon, 2008)	.09
Low/high element challenge courses (Leemon, 2008)	.11
Accident rates for 14- to 19-year-olds in 2001–2009 (CDC, 2011)	.37
OBHRC programs, 2001–2010 (OBHRC, 2011)	.52
WRMC/AEE Incident Data Reporting Project, 1998–2007 (Leemon, 2008)	.52
Backpacking (Leemon, 2008)	.77
Cross-country ski touring (Leemon, 2008)	1.08
OBHRC wilderness therapy programs (Cooley, 1998)	1.12
Cycling, road (Leemon, 2008)	1.18
Swim/dip (Leemon, 2008)	1.50
Flat water canoeing, portaging included (Leemon, 2008)	1.68
Climbing, snow/ice (Leemon, 2008)	2.91
Cycling, mountain (Leemon, 2008)	2.92
Winter camping (Leemon, 2008)	3.88
Downhill skiing (ski area) (Leemon, 2008)	5.15
Snowboarding (Leemon, 2008)	16.77
High school football practice (AJSM, 2007)	15.36
High school football games (AJSM, 2007)	72.24

behaviors, high-risk behaviors, drug use, reckless behaviors in automobiles), it is quite plausible to state that given the high-risk behaviors of these clients, the relative overreporting practices of OBHRC, and the evolved practices of adventure therapy practices, there is less actual risk for these youth to be on adventure therapy programs than it is not to be on these programs.

MINIMIZING ACTUAL RISKS IN ADVENTURE THERAPY EXPERIENCES AND RETAINING THERAPEUTIC AFFECT

How are such decreased rates of adventure therapy programming achieved? Once you understand the difference between actual and perceived risks, how do you go about minimizing clients' exposure to the actual risks of adventure experiences while still retaining their vital and essential qualities for fostering change? The first step is to understand how accidents occur based on past accidents in the field. The most recognized model explaining factors associated with accidents in adventure therapy settings is the one first created by Williamson and Meyer (1979). This model has been refined over 30 years of annual analyses of accidents in adventure experiences by Jed Williamson. It is based on the central premise that most accidents tend to occur because of an interaction of three connected sources (see Figure 9.1): inappropriate conditions in the environment, unsafe acts performed by participating clients, and errors in judgment made by adventure therapists (Priest & Gass, 2005; see Table 9.2).

The greater the intensity of any of these items, in terms of both strength and quantity of items, the more each particular circle moves toward the middle and creates a larger intersection and greater likelihood for an accident to occur. Obviously one factor/circle can be strong enough to produce an accident, but generally speaking it is the interaction of two or three areas/circles that lead to the greater likelihood of an accident.

Using transportation as an example, one can see how these intersecting factors work together (Priest & Gass, 2005):

> Inappropriate conditions could include an icy road at night with a 15-passenger van fully loaded with a roof rack and trailer of equipment and no tire chains. Unsafe acts by clients could be not wearing safety belts and distracting the driver. Judgment errors include driving with minimal van driving experience, driving too fast, driving while tired, and driving on a dirt road with no previous experience. You can see how each of these factors alone could create an accident, but the chance of an accident is obviously increased when these factors combined together (p. 93).

Just as certain factors can increase the likelihood of accidents and injuries, if adventure therapy professionals are properly informed of the contributing factors to accidents, these can be proactively addressed. Doing these risk management procedures "moves" each factor/circle out so the intersecting

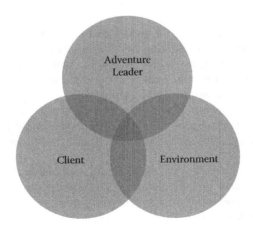

FIGURE 9.1 Examples of causes of accidents in adventure experiences (Priest & Gass, 2005; Meyer, 1979).

TABLE 9.2 Examples of the Interacting Factors that Increase the Probability of Accidents in Adventure Activities.

Inappropriate conditions (environment)	Unsafe acts (client)	Judgment errors (adventure therapist)
Falling rocks/objects	Inadequate protection	Desire to please others
Weather	Inadequate instruction	Following a schedule
Swift/cold water	Inadequate supervision	Misperception
Inadequate area security	Unsafe speed	Disregarding instincts
Inadequate equipment/clothing	Inadequate food/drink	Fatigue
Animals/plants	Poor position	Distraction
Psychological/physiological profile	Unauthorized procedure	Miscommunication

possibility of an accident becomes reduced. For example, reloading the van to create a lower center of gravity, removing the trailer and using two minivans, and putting on tire chains reduce the influence of the environment on the possibility of an accident occurring. Putting on safety belts and not distracting the driver reduce unsafe actions by clients. Properly trained staff, reducing speed for the conditions, limiting the length of driving time by rotating competent drivers, and having previous and current experience with the road and its conditions pulls the judgment error circle further away from the middle of the accident intersection.

Examine the following example of a program conducted in wilderness settings under the pretense of therapy. Inappropriate environmental conditions could be overextended forced marched hiking, high temperatures, an exposed environment, and carrying a backpack of 40% of body weight. Unsafe client acts could be a past history of prescription drugs contraindicated by the environment, excessive loss of weight during the program, inadequate water and food intake, and physical presentations of nausea, vomiting, repeated exhaustion, and severe sunburn. Instructor judgment errors could include behavior control techniques of physical beatings, withholding food/sleeping bags for punishment, emotional abuse, and inappropriate training for staff handling client issues they are encountering. Obviously none of these factors has a place in adventure therapy programs, let alone how each of these factors negatively influences their respective circles in the Williamson/Meyer model presented in Figure 9.1.

In addition to addressing the issues in the accident model, adventure therapy programs can also proactively create cultural expectations that can even further reduce the possibility of accidents and injuries. As seen in Figure 9.2, involving staff and programs in professional reviews, professional training, and networking with other programs can further reduce accidents and associated injuries. Opposite from the Williamson and Meyer model in Figure 9.1,

FIGURE 9.2 Proactive development model for reducing accident potential (Corteo, Vallee, & Gass, 2010).

these professional development activities move each factor/circle in so the intersecting possibility of an accident becomes reduced due to a more professionally supported and educated adventure therapist.

In this model, program staff members look to use various professional activities to reduce accidents. Sources used to reduce accident exposure include professional reviews, trainings, and networking (see Table 9.3). Note that as with the interactive model identifying sources of accident potential by Williamson and Meyer, this Venn diagram model also recognizes the value of interaction between each of the three sources of support.

DRUG RISK MANAGEMENT

In the beginnings of adventure therapy programs (prior to 1970), the interaction between environmental conditions and adventure program participants created very few contraindications. However, with the increase of prescription medications and intensive drugs used by abusers, a heightened level of

TABLE 9.3 Interacting Professional Development Activities Lessening Accident Probability

Professional reviews	Professional training	Networking
AEE accreditation	Maintain certifications	Professional exchange
Peer reviews	Maintain licenses	OBHRC membership
External consultants	Continuing Education Units (CEUs)	AEE TAPG/REAP
Individual/group supervision	Staff trainings	NATSAP research database
Accident simulations	Conferences	Staff exchanges

inappropriate risk began to occur. Such heightened levels of risk have resulted in serious injuries, complications, and even death for adventure program participants.

As these contraindications began to occur, so did the awareness of the negative interactions certain drugs had with adventure programming elements. Stitch and Gaylor (1984) were probably the first adventure therapy professionals to write about this dangerous interaction in the areas of climactic considerations and the side effects of medications. Climatic considerations should include consideration of the interactions of drugs with heat, cold, and altitude factors of the outdoor environment. Side effects of medications may include orthostatic hypertension (i.e., rapid changes in blood pressure) and extrapyramidal symptoms (e.g., involuntary disorders of movement, sun/light sensitivity, dry mouth).

Drawing on more than 35 years of experience in the adventure therapy field (as a licensed drug counselor and from personal experience in the field), Wells (2008) organized the identification of medical contraindications into four categories for adventure therapists:

1. Client prescription drug use interaction
2. Effects of nonprescription/illegal drugs on outdoor adventure experiences
3. Medications and exposure to sun
4. Drug detoxification in the field

These four categories help to present the current issues of risk with medical contraindications for adventure therapists. However, these issues change rapidly, so adventure therapists need to work closely with medical advisory personnel as new findings emerge.

Prescription Drug Use and Environmental Interaction

A large number, if not the majority, of clients participating in adventure therapy programs are diagnosed with mental health issues requiring drug prescription as a form of treatment (Russell, 2008). Many of these clients are not removed from their prescription medications during their involvement in adventure therapy treatment, and many of these medications can have negative side effects in common conditions occurring in adventure therapy settings. Wells (2008, p. 127) identified the most common compromising conditions created by medications in the outdoors:

1. The body's ability to stay hydrated
2. The body's ability to maintain an appropriate core temperature
3. The body's ability to perform appropriate sweating and cooling
4. The body's propensity to develop a fever

Probably the most dangerous of all of these is drug-induced hyperthermia, which can occur very quickly, possesses few warning signs or symptoms, and is difficult to treat in wilderness field situations.

Nonprescribed (Street) Drug Use and Environmental Interaction

Many clients may begin wilderness therapy programs with remnants of non-prescribed medications still in their system. This obviously can present serious contraindications with environmental conditions if appropriate measures of monitoring and analysis of toxicity are not followed. This especially includes clients with a history of extended use of methamphetamine, crystal methamphetamine, cocaine, crack cocaine, speed, and misuses of prescription drugs for bipolar conditions. Consider the example presented by Wells (2006, p. 130):

> A 17-year-old male experienced a heart attack in the first 36 hours of admittance to a program. At about 2:00 AM staff were notified and began to monitor the client because of feelings of nausea, severe chest pains, sweating, and pain in the left shoulder. The symptoms continued off and on throughout the night. Although it seems illogical that a 17-year-old would be having a heart attack, the symptoms were clear and he appeared very ill. At a local medical clinic, the clinic personnel ran five EKGs because the medical staff (including the doctor) could not believe that a healthy 17-year-old would be having a heart attack. Doctors monitored his progress in a local hospital for 24 hours, with the cardiologist at the Hospital in Salt Lake City also monitoring the status. The next morning, a decision was made to life-flight him to the hospital. He returned to the program six weeks later and he completed the program.

Medication and Sun Exposure

Another drug-related contraindication is the interaction between medications and exposure to the sun. As pointed out by Wells (2006), there is an increase in medications that heighten sensitivity of clients to the sun and also cause the skin to be more sensitive to sunlight. Note that clients may remain more sensitive to sunlight for 2 weeks to several months or more after stopping these medications. Wells identified knowledge of two occasions in wilderness therapy programs where individuals sunburned their fingernails as a result of doxycycline use (an antibiotic) in the field.

Drug Detoxification in the Environment

As one can ascertain from the three previous categories of drug interactions and outdoor settings, clients should be screened appropriately before beginning wilderness therapy programming. Drug screening processes should cover what clients are currently using, but also issues addressing the amount of drugs taken, for how long, and the last time used (Wells, 2006). Wilderness therapy programs often require detoxification procedures for appropriate clients, medical clearance from physicians to clear clients for participation, and close observation (when appropriate) for certain clients in the first 72 hours of programming. It is also important to note that certain drugs used in medical detoxification with clients must be monitored and cleared from physicians before wilderness therapy programming should begin.

Each particular drug will have its own withdrawal symptoms and environmental interactions. As identified by Wells (2006), adventure therapy programs need to be sensitive to opiate withdrawal symptoms, amphetamine/cocaine withdrawal symptoms, barbiturate withdrawal symptoms, and alcohol withdrawal symptoms. Adventure therapy program staff need to work closely with their medical director when admitting clients with drug detoxification issues.

Wells (2006) identified the following specific considerations for program staff to include in all coordination efforts when working with clients and medication issues:

1. Have proper training and awareness of withdrawal symptoms and associated risks of withdrawal
2. Receive training in researching and permitting client medications before beginning programming (e.g., medications affecting heat regulation, hydration, or conditions difficult to handle in the field be discontinued before programming)
3. Have all medications reviewed by medical personnel for final approval
4. Be aware of symptoms and risks of street drugs
5. Develop a system of assigning staff to monitor clients for a minimum of 72 hours in the field
6. Have appropriate policies and procedures for the potential need for evacuation due to drug issues
7. Have appropriate communication procedures in place to notify support personnel of drug-related signs and symptoms
8. Adjust programming appropriately (e.g., layover days) to accurately address high-risk clients and their symptoms
9. Understand how withdrawal symptoms such as nausea, weakness, fatigue, vomiting, and diarrhea negatively affect appropriate water and food intake
10. Understand the specific effects of certain drugs and their interaction with environmental conditions, especially hyperthermia

PSYCHOLOGICAL RISK MANAGEMENT

There are various levels of psychological depth with adventure therapy programming. With these levels of application comes the responsibility for adventure therapists to help clients attain and maintain an appropriate psychological depth of treatment focus.

Therapists cannot always predict which clients will respond in what specific ways. There are, however, patterns of response to topics of conversation that can alert adventure therapists to when the psychological depth is appropriate for the intended level or if it becomes inappropriate. Obviously, adventure therapists have an ethical and professional responsibility to keep clients at appropriate levels for the type of learning/therapy that is designed for the specific client group. The adventure therapist's language and behavior are vital to maintaining or steering the level of psychological depth for the client.

To provide guidelines for adventure therapists to assess the level of psychological depth of their clients, Ringer and Gillis (1995) identified seven levels of depth commonly occurring in adventure therapy experiences. Table 9.4 summarizes these levels and their specific attributes.

Obviously some of the questions in Table 9.4 accurately address the intended depth sought for psychological change, whereas others are wholly inappropriate in other certain situations. As one can see, adventure therapists need to proactively appraise, as well as reactively address, the psychological depth for targeted interventions. Equipped with this awareness of various levels of psychological depth, adventure therapists use four criteria to appropriately assess clients' depth of responses and focus.

The four criteria for assessing psychological depth identified by Gillis and Ringer (1995) are:

1. Determine how the client is involved in the topic under discussion. Noninvolvement indicates minimal psychological depth, whereas involvement at the level of archetypical issues indicates a psychological depth even beyond the level of normal therapy.
2. Determine the level of emotional arousal experienced by the participant. No emotional involvement may indicate shallow psychological levels with stronger emotional arousal indicating increasing depth.
3. Pay attention to the nature of the relationships that are embedded in the structure of the client's conversation. Relationships with insignificant persons indicate shallow psychological depth and memories of relationships with primary caregivers and significant others indicate deeper therapeutic depth.
4. Analyze the "normal boundaries" of confidentiality and privacy with the subject under discussion. Granted, some people will sometimes tell a perfect stranger sitting next to them on an airplane some of their deepest dark secrets. Adventure therapists need to monitor the level of disclosure by the client and ascertain if it is appropriate for the situation.

When a client makes a statement that is deeper than the negotiated psychological level, there are generally three steps adventure therapists should

TABLE 9.4 Seven Levels of Psychological Depth, Emotion, Appropriate Discussion Group, and Examples of Statements at Each Level

	How is the client involved in this?	How much emotion is presented?	Who is discussed?	Who would find this "normal" discussion?	Sample question at this level
Surface level	Very little	Very little	Other insignificant people	Anyone, public information	"Did people like what we had for lunch?"
Personal experience level	Involved in a social or professional role	Very little	Friends and colleagues	Anyone in their social setting	"Turn to your partner and share three things they have contributed to the group."
Current task level	Only as a member of this group right now	Usually very little	Group members only	Current group members	"Share with the group how you think we are communicating with one another"
Encounter level	Only as a member of this group right now	May involve a high level (e.g., anger, sad, joy, excitement)	Group members only	Current group members	"Frank, could you please share with the group why you chose not to participate at the end of the activity."
Contextual level	As a member of their particular social group	Often a high level (e.g., rage, love, depression)	Family, friends, colleagues	Family, friends, colleagues	"Identify and share aspects of your behavior in the last activity that will help you in your future."
Identity formation level	Very involved	Typically a high level	Family and childhood memories	Trusted companions and therapists	"The last activity reminded me of the time I was a small child and my Dad needed to rescue me."
Historical/cultural level	Completely involved	Deep loyalty	Cultural heroes	Facts discussed in public; true feelings discussed with close and trusted individuals	"Share with the group the 3 most important guiding principles from your culture."
Universal level	Fully immersed	Powerful feelings about self or life's purpose	Spiritual entities (God)	Facts discussed in public; feelings are kept private	"When we die, what do you think happens to us?

take to guide the client back to the appropriate level. The first step is for the adventure therapist to fully acknowledge and validate the client's statement. The second step is to empathize with the client's feeling at that level. The third step is to redirect the client back to the appropriate level of psychological work that is part of the implicit contract with the client group. Generally, the therapist will move the client back to the current task or encounter level by using present tense language. As an illustrative example, here is how these three consecutive steps work:

Step One: The adventure therapist responds at the presented psychological level by naming or describing what key statements she or he heard without interpreting or placing meaning on the client's statements.

Step Two: The adventure therapist empathizes with the feeling associated with the statements being made by the client.

Step Three: Following this, the adventure therapist redirects the client back to the desired psychological level.

For example, say an adventure therapist was having a therapeutic discussion with a group after a particularly eventful day of backpacking. One client shares with the group how they faced certain challenges during the day and flashes back to a particular situation where challenges did not go so well for them in a traumatic and abusive situation in the past. Although this issue may need to be addressed by the adventure therapist at another place and time, the intent of group described in this example does not match the psychological depth intended by this particular process. In addressing this situation, the adventure therapist should (1) acknowledge and validate what was stated without placing a meaning or interpretation on the client's statements; (2) empathize with the feeling associated with the client about their past traumatic situation; and (3) ask the client to focus on what specifically happened "here and now" in handling such challenges on this particular day on this particular hike. Such a process maintains respect for the client's statements while appropriately guiding the group discussion back to the desired and appropriate psychological level.

PHYSICAL RESTRAINT AND THERAPEUTIC HOLDS IN ADVENTURE THERAPY PROGRAMS

Probably the most comprehensive, valid, clear, and accessible presentation of risk management in the adventure therapy field is the ongoing work done by the OBHRC, the research arm of the Outdoor Behavioral Healthcare Industry Council (OBHIC). OBHIC is made up of organizations that are "competitors" in one sense of being, but have voluntarily chosen to collaborate not only to raise the standards of their own programs but also the standards of all programs in the industry. The work accomplished by this Council certainly sets the current standards for reporting, analyzing, sharing, and making revisions based on actual risk management procedures with a system designed by Russell beginning in 1999. In a true comprehensive procedure, the OBHRC risk management program analyzes the following elements of the leading wilderness therapy programs in North America: incidents, therapeutic holds, therapeutic restraints, runaways, client injuries, client illnesses, guide illnesses, and guide injuries. At 13 years of operation, this program may be the longest ongoing, multiple program risk management database in the adventure programming field that is currently operational, let alone the adventure therapy field. In a true trend analysis fashion, these elements of adventure therapy risk management have been tracked over the past 13 years. While a brief summary of these figures are discussed here in this text as programmatic examples, further up-to-date resources on all of these risk management elements can be found on the OBHRC website (http://www.obhrc.org).

The use of physical restraints is an all too frequent intervention in inpatient mental health settings (Prinsen & van Delden, 2009). A review of the literature prior to 2000 reports physical restraint prevalence rates of 28–60% in psychiatric facilities serving children and youth (De Hert, Dirix, Demunter, & Correll, 2011). Although there is some evidence that physical restraint is an acceptable practice with children and adolescents when they are in danger of causing harm to themselves and others (Dean, Duke, George, & Scott, 2007; Delaney, 2006), the majority of evidence supports the contrary, showing restraints to be physically and emotionally harmful to both staff and clients (De Hert et al., 2011; Masters et al., 2002; Miller, Hunt, & Georges, 2006). Nunno, Holden, and Tollar (2006) reported 45 fatalities related to restraints in child and adolescent mental health facilities between 1993 and 2003, and there is significant ethical concern from the national and international community about the practice (Steinert et al., 2010). The Joint Commission on the Accreditation of Healthcare Organizations reported 124 deaths between the years of 1995 and 2004 due to restraints alone (Russell & Harper, 2006). The most recent proposed edition of HR Bill 1381, sponsored by Representative George Miller, focuses on the prevention if not reduction of physical restraint and seclusion in schools and for other purposes (112th Congress, April 6, 2011).

In 2003, the Substance Abuse and Mental Health Services Administration published a National Action Plan for reducing the use of restraints in mental health services. The plan suggests changes in policy to empower staff to use treatment approaches that discourage the need for restraints and called for improved monitoring of restraint interventions in the mental health industry. Several programs have been developed to address these goals, and evidence shows significant decreases in restraint rates in child and adolescent mental health facilities following their implementation (LeBel et al., 2004; Martin, Krieg, Esposito, Stubbe, & Cardona, 2008; McCue,

Urcuyo, Lilu, Tobias, & Chambers, 2004; Miller et al., 2006). Despite significant reductions in restraint rates following such programs, the National Association of State Mental Health Program Directors Research Institute (NASMHPDRI, 2010) reported the national restraint rate for youth ages 13-17 in inpatient mental health care was 8.4 restraints per 1,000 client days as of December 2009.

OBHRC (2011) has maintained a database tracking incident rates on restraint frequency in member programs since 2001. To add even further clarity and definition to the analysis, OBHRC has further broken down restraints into the following categories:

1. **Restraints**: Any action that restricts a client's freedom of movement against their will for 30 minutes or longer, even in the absence of physical or chemical restraint devices
2. **Level II therapeutic holds:** Similar interventions that are 15–30 minutes in duration in which the client actively resists and is propelled or held still against that resistance
3. **Level I therapeutic holds**: Similar interventions that are less than 15 minutes in duration where the client actively resists and is propelled or held still against that resistance
4. **Physical assists**: A client's freedom of movement is not physically restricted. A client is led along the trail or moved to his or her campsite by a hand pulling gently on a backpack strap or guiding her or him by the elbow. In such a case, the client may not want to go in the direction encouraged, but is willing to go when urged along and any resistance is passive.

OBHRC restraint and therapeutic hold data include all incidents meeting the definition of restraint, regardless of time. This formula is more inclusive than that of NASMHPDRI, which requires a physical restraint to last longer than 5 minutes. OBHRC restraint rate trends for 2001 through 2010 represent over 16,063 clients, or 733,818 client field days. As seen in Figure 9.3, the 2009 restraint rates decreased again slightly from previous years to 0.22 per thousand days or one every 87 clients. Restraint rates decreased even further in 2010 to 0.16 per thousand field days, or 1 every 6,383 client days, or one every 129 clients. As seen in Figure 9.4, in 2007 the number and rate for therapeutic holds fell to below 2 per thousand field days (1.95), was similar in 2008 (1.93) and 2009 (1.82), and dropped to 1.67 in 2010, 1 every 597 client days, or one every 12 clients.

Analysis of OBHRC incident data shows 2.1 restraints and therapeutic holds occurred for every 1,000 client field days. The restraint rates for children and adolescents in inpatient mental health facilities alone was *four* times the amount used in OBHRC programs (NASMHPDRI, 2010). This

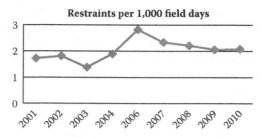

FIGURE 9.3 Restraints on OBHRC programs per every 1,000 field days.

difference is even greater when the complexity and multiple issues facing clients in OBHRC programs are considered. Zelov and Gass (2011) found 60% of clients in OBHRC programs possessed more than three presenting clinical issues when first admitted into programs (e.g., a combination of substance abuse issues, depression or mood disorders, attention deficit disorders, attachment disorders).

How are OBHRC programs able to achieve decreased restraining rates with more problematic clients than traditional inpatient mental health facilities with clients with less problematic presenting symptoms? While further research needs to be done on this topic area, some of the factors in these wilderness therapy programs that may be contributing to substantially lower rates of restraint include:

1. The potential contribution of adventure and wilderness experiences working to reduce the need for restraining procedures
2. Lower staff to client ratios (i.e., more staff involved with smaller groups of clients)
3. The type of unique therapeutic relationship and alliance created in these adventure therapy programs
4. The effect of nature on positive client behavior

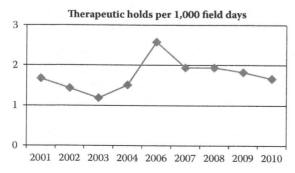

FIGURE 9.4 Restraint and therapeutic hold rates of OBHRC programs from 2001–2010.

INJURY AND ILLNESS INCIDENTS

Earlier in this chapter, the actual rates of incident were discussed, particularly in light of the perception that exists concerning the danger of adventure experiences. Thanks to the work of Cooley (2000), Leemon (2008), and others—regardless of what the perception might be—the actual incident rates of professional, state-of-the-art adventure therapy programs possess incident rates a little lower than cross-country skiing and flat water canoeing, about 10 times as safe as downhill skiing, about 30 times safer than high school football practices, and more than 138 times safer than high school football games. (Shankar et al., 2007).

How have OBHRC programs incident rates fluctuated over the past 10 years? In order to receive even more information on incident rates, OBHRC programs, guidelines include:

1. Separate incident data into two forms of injury incidents and illness incidents
2. In addition to using the "12 hours" criterion used by NOLS in order to report data, OBHRC programs report any illness or injury serious enough to cause the equivalent of a missed day of school as an incident. Note that following this procedure has probably caused OBHRC programs to actually overreport in comparison to programs like NOLS and others just using the 12-hour standard for reporting.
3. Add further definition and resulting interpretation on the severity of incidences, coding Level I incidences as those meeting the "12-hour/missed day of school" requirement but not requiring an overnight hospitalization, and Level II incidences as requiring an overnight hospitalization or the equivalent.

As seen in Figure 9.5, from 2008 to 2009, client injuries decreased to 1 for every 1,801 days, or 1 injury for every 35 clients in treatment. Injury rates continued to drop in 2010 to 0.48 per 1,000 client field days, or 1 every 2,075 client field days, or 1 injury for every 42 clients. As seen in Figure 9.6, with

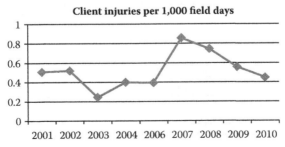

FIGURE 9.5 Client injury and illness rates of OBHRC programs from 2001–2010.

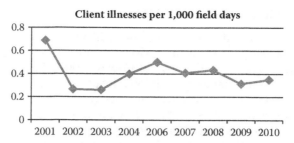

FIGURE 9.6 Injury and illness rates of OBHRC programs from 2001–2010.

client illnesses, for 2009 one illness occurred for every 63 clients; in 2010, there was a decrease to 0.35 per 1,000 client field days, or 1 every 2,862 client field days, or 1 illness for every 58 clients.

Figure 9.6 presents the data on program-caused illnesses, which are different than injuries during program activities. Note all illnesses are reported 72 hours after program admission. This is due to the fact that some participants may enter programs already infected with an illness, and these 72 hours provides an agreed-upon incubation period.

RUNAWAYS

One form of client resistance in adventure therapy programs is running away. The definition OBHRC uses for classifying a runaway is a client who is away from program area and staff oversight without permission for more than 60 minutes. For 2009, the rate decreased slightly from 2008 to 1 for every 2,083 client field days. The 2010 overall rate increased to 1.54 attempted runaways per 1,000 client field days, 1 every 648 client field days, or 1 for every 13 students who entered treatment (see Figure 9.7). Note that

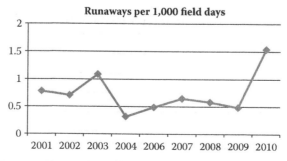

FIGURE 9.7 Runaways from OBHRC programs per every 1,000 field days.

in order to receive as much information as possible on runways, three categories exist:

1. A Level II runaway is away from staff oversight for *more* than 24 hours without permission
2. A Level I runaway is away from staff oversight for *less* than 24 hours without permission
3. If a client walks away from camp and is followed by staff who keep him or her under observation or continue to engage a client in conversation, the incident is not considered a runaway.

Note that all of the runaways in 2010 were Level I runaways. There were 130 Level I runaways and no Level II runaways in OBHRC programs.

GUIDE ILLNESSES AND INJURIES

Note that, as with injuries and illnesses with clients, to add further definition and resulting interpretation on the severity of incidents guide injuries and illnesses were further divided into Level I incidents (i.e., those meeting the "12-hour/missed day of school" requirement but not requiring an overnight hospitalization) and Level II incidents (i.e., those requiring an overnight hospitalization or the equivalent). In 2009, a guide experienced an injury every 1,675 days and an illness every 2,513 days. Both these rates have continued a decreasing trend since 2008. In 2010, guides experienced a decrease of 0.42 for every 1,000 field days of an injury every 2,380 days (see Figure 9.8. and Figure 9.9.).

As far as illnesses for guides, they experienced a decrease to 0.16 every 1,000 field days or an illness every 6,348 days. Note no guides reported any Level II injuries or illnesses due to programming.

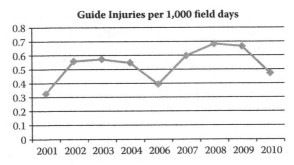

FIGURE 9.8 Guide injuries on OBHRC programs per every 1,000 field days.

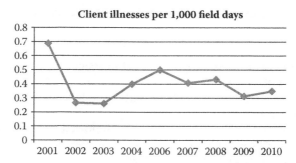

FIGURE 9.9 Guide illnesses on OBHRC programs per every 1,000 field days.

Using the five following report criteria established by Russell and Harper (2006) to report on incident monitoring for OBHRC, the following five statements can be made about OBHRC programs:

1. In 2010, and since at least 2001, over 90% of all OBHRC program clients complete treatment.
2. In 2010, and since 2001, OBHRC programs relatively low rates of restraints and therapeutic holds, typically at least four times less than the rates seen in inpatient mental health facilities.
3. In 2010, injuries occurred at a rate of 0.48 per 1,000 client field days, or 1 every 2,075 client field days, or 2 injuries for every 42 clients.
4. In 2010, illnesses occurred at a rate of 0.35 per 1,000 client field days, or 1 every 2,862 client field days, or 1 illness for every 58 clients.
5. The death rates in all adventure programs continue to be difficult to compare by both internal and external comparison factors. While no deaths occurred on any OBHRC programs in 2010, any death occurring in any mental health program needs to undergo appropriate scrutiny and review to analyzing contributing factors, make appropriate changes, and implement alternative methods.

A final step for consideration in the risk management of adventure therapy programming is the establishment of sound and systemic programmatic guidelines. Even the very best of individual adventure therapists are exposed to unnecessary risks with poor program risk management. One of the most beneficial, systemic, and comprehensive efforts for reviewing programs made by the adventure programming field has been the development of the accreditation program by the Association for Experiential Education. Established over 20 years ago, the accreditation program by AEE possesses targeted guidelines for adventure therapy programs. Elements of the work of AEE can be found in other review processes of accrediting bodies (e.g., Council on Accreditation).

To better serve members who are in adventure therapy programs, the accreditation program of AEE has produced eight specific standards for adventure therapy programs seeking accreditation. In summary, these eight standards focus on:

1. The use of appropriate therapeutic methods
2. With mandated or involuntary programs, organizations still strive to involve clients in the therapeutic process as much as possible
3. Written policies and procedures exist for conducting adventure therapy programming
4. Policies and procedures exist that address the management medications for participants
5. Policies and procedures exist that address adverse psychological reactions of participants
6. Policies and procedures exist that promote the use of interventions that are least invasive, stricter, and less physical and include seclusion methods
7. The provision of clinical supervision for staff
8. The inclusion of appropriate and effective verbal reflection experiences to augment adventure/experiential therapy

For a broader and more comprehensive review process, Gass (2003) presented 25 guidelines for adventure therapy programs to use in the analysis and review of their organizational policies and practices at the 2003 International Adventure Therapy Conference. Based on similar principles to AEE's accreditation program, these 25 items are offered in Appendix A as an overview to assist in the construction, or verification, of an adventure therapy program risk management system.

CONCLUSION

The concept of risk is an incredibly important one for the adventure therapy field. Types of risks in adventure therapy are not only physical ones, but also social and emotional risks. One factor influencing risk management is the *perception* of risk compared to the *actual* level of risk with a particular activity. Professional, state-of-the-art adventure therapy programs possess actual incident rates a little lower than cross-country skiing and flat-water canoeing, about 10 times as safe as downhill skiing, about 30 times safer than high school football practices, and more than 138 times safer than high school football games (Shankar et al., 2007). Given that most individuals entering wilderness therapy programs are generally involved in behaviors with higher risks than the general population (e.g., self-abusive behaviors, high-risk behaviors, drug use, reckless behaviors in automobiles), it is quite plausible to state that given these high-risk behaviors of these clients, the relative overreporting practices of OBHRC, and the evolved practices of adventure therapy practices, there is less actual risk for these youth to be on adventure therapy programs than to not be on these programs.

The first step is to understand how accidents occur based on past accidents in the field. The most recognized model explaining factors associated with accidents in adventure therapy settings is the one first created by Williamson and Meyer (1979). It is based on the central premise that most accidents tend to occur because of an interaction of three connected sources: inappropriate conditions in the environment, unsafe acts performed by participating clients, and errors in judgment made by adventure therapists. In addition to addressing the issues in this model, adventure therapy programs can proactively create cultural expectations that can further reduce the possibility of accidents and injuries by involving staff and programs in professional reviews, professional training, and networking with other programs.

With the increase of prescription medications and intensive drugs used by clients, heightened levels of risk need to be addressed. Four categories for adventure therapists to focus on include client prescription drug use inter-action, effects of nonprescription/illegal drugs on outdoor adventure experi-ences, medications and exposure to sun, and drug detoxification in the field. Specific considerations need to be considered for program staff to include in all coordination efforts when working with clients and medication issues, especially around issues with hyperthermia.

It also is the responsibility of adventure therapists to help clients attain and maintain an appropriate psychological depth of treatment focus. Adventure therapists cannot always predict exactly which clients will respond in what specific ways. There are, however, patterns of response to topics of conver-sation that can alert adventure therapists to when the psychological depth is appropriate for the intended level or becoming inappropriate. Obviously adventure therapists have an ethical and moral responsibility to keep clients at appropriate levels for the type of learning/therapy that is designed for the specific client group. Adventure therapists use four criteria for assessing psy-chological depth: how the client is involved, the level of emotional arousal, the nature of the relationships that are embedded in the structure of the client's conversation, and the normal boundaries of confidentiality and privacy.

When a client makes a statement that is deeper than the appropriate psy-chological level, there are generally two steps that adventure therapists should take to guide the client back to the appropriate level. The first step is for the adventure therapist to fully acknowledge the client's statement and the second step is guide the client back to the appropriate level of psychological work.

Probably the most comprehensive, valid, clear, and accessible presenta-tion of risk management in the adventure therapy field is the ongoing work done by the OBHRC, the research arm of the OBHIC. OBHIC organizations have voluntarily chosen to collaborate not only to raise the standards of their own programs but also the standards of all programs in the industry. The work by this Council certainly sets the current standards for reporting, analyzing, sharing, and making revisions based on actual risk management procedures. In a true comprehensive procedure, the OBHRC risk management program analyzes the following elements of the leading wilderness therapy programs in North America: incidents, therapeutic holds, therapeutic restraints, runaways, client injuries, client illnesses, guide illnesses, and guide injuries. At 10 years of operation, this program may be the longest ongoing, multiple program risk management database in the adventure programming field that is currently operational, let alone the adventure therapy field. In a true trend analysis fashion, these elements of adventure therapy risk management have been tracked over the past 10 years. While a brief summary of these figures is discussed here in this text as programmatic examples, further up-to-date resources on all of these risk management elements can be found on the OBHRC website (http://www.obhrc.org).

A final step in the risk management of adventure therapy programming is the establishment of sound and systemic programmatic guidelines. Even the very best of individual adventure therapists are exposed to unnecessary risks with poor program risk management. Twenty-five items were identified as a beginning overview to assist in the construction, or use as a verification checklist, of an adventure therapy program risk management system.

THROWING OUT STUFF

Gary Stauffer

John, 45 years old, was initially sent to counseling by his wife who complained that he was distant, moody, and such a perfectionist that regular things, like eating dinner with their two children, was difficult. He fit the diagnostic category for obsessive-compulsive disorder.

True to his wife's description, it was difficult to engage with John in our initial sessions. He described himself as a man of few words and a "duck out of water" whenever emotions came near the surface. We agreed to try individual therapy sessions. The first two proved his wife to be prophetic. John talked in short phrases and seemed to retreat inside himself whenever we approached anything that looked like conflict or emotion.

As John entered his third individual therapy session, he sighed deeply when he sat. Looking to engage with any action from the client, I also sighed and said, "Wow, I wonder what's in that sigh?"

John: What do you mean?
Therapist: That was a deep, genuine sigh, like you were getting rid of something.
John: Well, there's a lot of stuff I'd throw out if I could.
Therapist: You would throw stuff out, huh?
John: Yes sir! Wouldn't you?
Therapist: I suppose you're right. We all have that stuff. What stuff is it for you?
John: Just stuff.

At this point, the session entered familiar territory. The progress toward elaboration on the material just stopped. It was a characteristic response to emotion and personal connection that impacted his functioning in all areas of his life and kept him isolated and alone. In an attempt to keep the momentum of the session moving forward, I introduced an adventure activity:

Therapist: I have some "stuff" [purposely using his language] in this cup that I'd like to throw out. Problem is, it's really difficult, sometimes dangerous, to actually touch it. So, we need to keep a distance from it. [Therapist puts a rope tied into a circle about 24 inches in diameter around the cup] We can't get closer to the cup than this rope, and our task it to pick it up and dump the stuff (poker chips, water, other objects) in this other cup. [Therapist puts a second cup across the room surrounded by a similar rope.] The task, if you are willing to take it on, is to get rid of the stuff in this cup by dumping it in the second cup over there. Are you willing to give it a try?
John: How can I move it if I can't get any closer than this?
Therapist: I will give you this one tool [a rubber band with six 18-inch strings attached].
John: Hmm. [Saying nothing, he spends close to 5 minutes evaluating the tool and the overall problem. He silently begins to approach the problem by pulling the strings, using both hands and feet, and experimenting generally with the tool.]

Therapist: [After waiting silently for at least 5 minutes] John, I noticed that you have been absorbed in thought about solving this problem, but you haven't asked me a single question or requested my help in any way.

John: No, I like to figure things out for myself.

In my work as an adventure therapist, I am always looking for a parallel process between the client's functioning in my office and the referring problems. In this case, John's life pattern of remaining distant and isolated even in his intimate relationships seemed to parallel his desire to figure this problem out by himself without any help. At this point in the therapy, I am working with a "here and now" situation with the issue of distancing himself.

John: You told me this was my only tool.

Therapist: It is the only inanimate object you can use, but I've done this activity dozens of times and I probably have information and maybe other ways of helping you out.

John: Hmmm ... [continues to study the problem silently]

Therapist: [After another long period of silence] John, I'm getting the picture here again that when there is a problem in your life, like this one, that you like to figure it out for yourself.

John: I do. Other people add to the commotion.

Therapist: So you try to keep down all the commotion by doing things yourself without involving others in the process?

John: Exactly.

Therapist: I'm sure that strategy has worked for you a lot of the time. But in this situation, you are missing out on my valuable experience and assistance. We have talked about other times you shut people out who might be able to help.

John: Yeah, Jane [his wife] wants me to talk more.

Therapist: And she might like to help you out, to be involved in your struggles.

John: I know she does, and it is what I want but I've never had anybody really want to do that.

This session went on to provide extremely rich material for weeks. We had entered John's inner experience using an experiential activity. We had arrived at a treatment contract to "get rid of the stuff that prevents him from engaging more intimately with his wife" which was vividly illustrated by our experience together in this activity. These results are what I call adventure therapy.

My career as a master's level social worker focusing on children and youth began in 1976. I spent the first 10 years in community mental health settings doing individual, family, and group counseling with latency age and adolescent children. It was exciting for me to bring these clinical skills into a school social work setting where I have spent the last 25 years.

My first year as a school social worker rocked my professional and clinical world to the core. I became involved in a substance abuse prevention program for middle school students that aimed to build community and interpersonal connections through the use of adventure. I was fortunate to also find a mentor who worked at the local YMCA camp that partnered with us, who introduced me to the wonders of experiential education and adventure activities for reaching youth at-risk with various problems.

This beginning foundation was enhanced by another job transition that took me to a clinically based day-treatment program. My clients were students who had failed in traditional treatment, students who joked about the incompetence of counseling in general, and students who had experienced more emotional and physical trauma than I had previously even imagined. This time mentoring came from an unexpected source. A gifted child psychiatrist who knew nothing of adventure therapy guided my work. He identified basic concepts like using shared experience to enhance relationship development and how discussion of the experience in the moment reduces resistance tenfold. It was an exciting time of professional growth. A time when I can say without hesitation that I became not just a therapist, but that I understood once and for all that I was an adventure therapist.

Chapter 10

Adventure Therapy Competencies

Many professionals are drawn to the practice of adventure therapy for a variety of reasons: its solution-oriented approach, the richness of the assessment process, and the ability to reach clients with this therapeutic approach where other approaches may have failed. However, using adventure therapy appropriately means individual professionals (or treatment teams) must be competent in both the adventure and clinical treatment aspects of the field.

What would a person who is competent as an adventure therapist look like? What qualities would they possess? What type of training would they receive? How would they be different from or similar to other mental health therapists? In seeking answers to these questions, four sources will be used to inform the development of adventure therapy competencies: adventure programming competencies, mental health therapist competencies, specific therapeutic population competencies, and past explorations into the development of adventure therapy competencies. This chapter presents an overview of each of these four sources, presents a current model for assessing levels of competency in appropriate areas, and offers an additional model inviting adventure therapists to achieve new levels of excellence beyond basic competency levels.

Before this discussion begins, it is important to note the distinction between *competencies* and *skills*. As pointed out by Sperry (2010), skills development primarily pertains to attaining areas of competency acquired for training aspects, but not the background knowledge, theory, or value components associated with the learning of skills. Competency refers to the "knowledge, skills, and attitude components which are necessary for professional practice" (Sperry, p. 6). Other supporting differentiations regarding the term *competencies* include:

1. Competence includes the capacity to appropriately evaluate and modify professional decisions with reflective practice, as well as possess "integrative knowledge of concepts and procedures, skills and abilities, behaviors and strategies, attitudes/beliefs/values, dispositions and personal characteristics, self-perceptions and motivations that enable a person to fully perform that task on a wide range of outcomes" (Kaslow, 2009, p. 2).
2. Competence means that the professional possesses sufficient capabilities to reach the expected outcomes necessary through appropriate professional practices (Falender & Shafranske, 2004).
3. Competence aligns itself with current evidence-based practices paradigms.
4. Competencies "are reflected in the quality of clinical performance, can be evaluated against professional standards, and can be developed or enhanced through professional training and personal growth" (Kaslow, 2004, p. 2).

The following examples epitomize the difference between competencies and skills in the field of adventure therapy. Consider the long-debated statement of adventure professionals: "Is the purpose of teaching rock climbing to teach people to be better rock climbers, or to teach people to be better people?"

The first purpose represented in this statement of teaching people to be better rock climbers requires the teaching of requisite skills to appropriately manage risks. The second purpose represented in the statement, using rock climbing to teach people to be better people, not only requires these requisite skills but also the necessary focus on knowledge, frameworks, ethics, additional intersecting professional standards, and reflective practices to make rock climbing more than just the teaching of the skill. In another example, think of the rationale of using the teaching of bow-drill fire starting skills on a wilderness therapy course. Typically speaking, the ultimate reasons for teaching bow-drill skills on a wilderness therapy course are for the associated processes, competency building objectives, and lessons of persistence—typically not solely for teaching adolescents how to start fires.

A second example would be the teaching of self-concept through adventure experiences. The singular goal of self-concept itself has very little to do with the lasting positive development for most clients. In fact, there is little to no correlation between gains in self-concept and positive growth in social practices, behavioral health, or client well-being (Baumeister, Campbell, Kreuger, & Vohs, 2003; Marsh & Craven, 2006; Swann, Chang-Schneider, & Larsen McClarty, 2007). As discussed in greater detail in Chapter 13 of this book, using adventure experiences just to increase self-concept has very little to do with improving functional social conditions for clients (e.g., reduction in recidivism rates). However, when placed in the context of such things as social skill development, ethical behavior, and positive transfer to functional behaviors, self-concept can become a competency jointly correlated with positive growth opportunities for clients. To implement self-concept in such frameworks requires the focus on necessary competencies, and not just the teaching of technical skills.

ADVENTURE PROGRAMMING COMPETENCIES

Primarily constructed from the master's and doctoral projects of Green (1981), Swiderski (1981), Buell (1981), Priest (1984), Raiola (1986), and the international doctoral study by Priest (1986), Priest & Gass (2005) wrote a chapter in the textbook *Effective Leadership in Adventure Programming* on the training competencies for leaders of adventure experiences. In this competency schema, a metaphor of a wall was used as a description, with the following components:

1. Bricks of hard skills including *technical skills* (e.g., competencies in adventure activities for outdoor pursuits being used with clients), safety skills (e.g., competencies required for appropriate risk management), and environmental skills (e.g., competencies related to protecting the natural environment, often including leave no trace practices)
2. Bricks of soft skills including *facilitation skills* (e.g., competencies fostering productive group dynamics, task completion with appropriate interpersonal dynamics), instructional skills (e.g., competencies necessary to teach clients skills related to the adventure experience), and organizational skills (e.g., competencies enabling leaders to carry out particular adventure experiences for particular client groups)
3. Mortar of *meta-skills* (holding the wall together) including effective communication (e.g., competencies enabling leaders to use empowering methods of information exchange between two or more people), flexible leadership style (e.g., competencies enabling leaders to utilize varying leadership styles to reach client objectives), professional ethics (e.g., competencies in the moral standards and value systems related to the facilitation of adventure experiences), problem-solving skills (e.g., competencies enabling adventure leaders to solve issues that arise with adequate professional knowledge), decision-making skills (e.g., competencies enabling leaders to select best decisions and practices), and experience-based judgment (e.g., competencies where adventure leaders are able to use periods, knowledge, and skills to make appropriate choices)

In another text focused on facilitation, Priest, Gass, and Gillis (1999, 2009) further identified and clarified elements that are key to successfully facilitating adventure practices. Although certainly not all of the competencies are discussed, 10 of the competencies most related to adventure therapists discussed in this text included effective listening, feedback, debriefing/reflection skills, group development stages, transfer of learning, client assessment, dealing with difficult clients, experiential learning, processing skills, integration strategies, and solution-oriented processing. As with other competencies, those that are identified and listed for adventure programming certainly overlap with those for many mental health professionals.

MENTAL HEALTH THERAPY COMPETENCIES

Certainly there are at least as many paradigms for mental health therapy competency frameworks as there are differing approaches to mental health. The ones selected here to serve as sources for input for this discussion are from the fields of psychotherapy, social work, and marriage and family therapy.

Psychotherapy Competencies

Probably the broadest of these three fields is the discipline of psychotherapy. In an effort to describe core competencies in psychotherapeutic practices, Sperry (2010) devised a model possessing six general core competencies with discrete elements. To show the interrelationship between these competencies in this model, Sperry (2010) uses a metaphor of a journey to convey the relationship of the core competencies of a psychotherapist. These six core competencies (with the metaphor in parentheses) and list of components include:

1. Conceptual foundations (the vehicle for the journey): the foundations, forms, and approaches involved in psychotherapy (e.g., psychotherapeutic process, cognitive behavioral therapies, elements of systemic approaches)
2. Therapeutic relationship (the traveling companion for the journey): building and maintaining effective therapeutic relationships, strong therapeutic alliances, beginning assessments, intervention strategies and tactics
3. Intervention planning (taking into consideration all that is needed on the trip, and what should be avoided, as well as obtaining a map of the territory): conceptualizing therapeutic case, comprehensive assessment, treatment planning
4. Intervention implementation (obtaining necessary supplies for the trip): therapeutic strategies and interventions, recognizing and resolving therapy-interfering factors, handling treatment failure
5. Evaluation and termination (tracking the progress of the journey and the arrival at the destination): outcome assessment, treatment monitoring,

maintaining treatment gains, preparing for conducting termination strategies

6. Cultural and ethical sensitivity (travel with regard to respect, integrity, and the care for others): cultural assessment and formulations, ethically sound decisions, providing ethically sensitive treatment

Social Work Competencies

Although not always focused on therapeutic settings, the competencies informing the certain concepts behind AT competencies are important to consider. In the most recent version of the *Educational Policy and Accreditation Standards* (2008), the Council on Social Work Education identified 10 core social work competencies. In the competency areas most related to therapeutic practices, the following competencies were identified:

1. Apply social work ethical principles to guide professional practice
2. Engage diversity and difference in practice
3. Engage in research-informed practice and practice-informed research
4. Engage, assess, intervene, and evaluate with individuals, families, groups, organizations, and communities

Marriage and Family Therapy Competencies

In 2004, the American Association for Marriage and Family Therapists (AAMFT) established core competencies for marriage and family therapists. These competencies are organized into domains, with six primary domains identifying the content marriage and family therapists must know to be considered competent and five subdomains identifying processes used to learn and ultimately use the six primary domains.

The six primary content area domains are:

1. Admission to treatment
2. Clinical assessment and diagnosis
3. Treatment planning and case management
4. Therapeutic interventions
5. Legal issues, ethics, and standards
6. Research and program evaluation

The five process subdomains (AAMFT, 2011) are:

1. Conceptual (factual knowledge)
2. Perceptual (accurately observe what is occurring)

3. Executive (apply appropriate therapy skills)
4. Evaluative (assess effectiveness)
5. Professional (follow ethical/professional standards)

The resulting model produces 128 individual competencies meant to "encompass behaviors, skills, attitudes, and policies that promote awareness, acceptance, and respect for differences, enhance services that meet the needs of diverse populations, and promote resiliency and recovery" (AAMFT, 2011, p. 1).

SPECIFIC THERAPEUTIC POPULATION COMPETENCIES

Not surprisingly, the core competencies required for working with specific therapeutic populations are strikingly similar to those for therapists from various disciplines. Probably in the best representative sample, a therapist wishing to receive certification as an addictions counselor must show confidence in the following areas: treatment admission (screening, intake, and orientation); clinical assessment; ongoing treatment planning; counseling services (individual, group, family, crisis intervention, and client education); documentation; case management; discharge and continuing care; and legal, ethical, and professional growth issues. The major focus and benefit behind all eight of these areas is the increased sensitivity, knowledge, and ability to address the specific needs of these particular clients.

To show competency in these areas, professionals take written examinations covering areas of counseling practice and theory, pharmacology of psychoactive substances, and professional issues related to alcoholism and drug abuse treatment. Although certain elements exist for treating every specific therapeutic population and how they are approached, there are large degrees of similarity occurring throughout most all other treatment paradigms. For example, similarities to the substance abuse competency areas listed above exist when comparing competency with treatment issues for eating disorders (Academy for Eating Disorders, International Association of Eating Disorders Professionals), posttraumatic stress disorders (e.g., Frueh et al., 2007), autism (Statewide Autism Council, 2004), and depression (e.g., Trepka, Rees, Shapiro, Hardy, & Barkham, 2004).

Figure 10.1 inventories the various areas covered by psychotherapy, social work, marriage and family therapy, and specialized areas of mental health treatment training competencies. As one can see from the figure, categories such as assessments, interventions, and ethics are the most common themes in determining competencies.

	Content/ Conceptual Knowledge	Treatment Admission Issues	Client Relationship Building Therapeutic Alliance	Assessment/ Intervention Planning for Treatment	Documentation/ Ongoing Case Management	Intervention Implementation	Resource Planning	Evaluation/ Termination	Ethical/ Cultural/Legal Competencies	Feedback/ Evaluation
Psychotherapy	√		√	√		√		√	√	
Social work			√	√	√	√	√	√	√	√
Marriage and family therapy		√		√	√	√			√	√
Specific therapeutic population training		√		√	√	√		√	√	
	1	2	2	4	3	4	1	3	4	2

FIGURE 10.1 An inventory of the various areas covered by psychotherapy, social work, marriage and family therapy, and specialized areas of mental health treatment training competencies.

COMPETENCY DEVELOPMENT FROM ADVENTURE THERAPY LITERATURE

The development of competencies from the adventure therapy field can be traced to the early 1990s. Based on the work of Gillis et al. (1992), Gass (1993) presented a model that focused on the level of intervention provided by adventure therapists, and accordingly the level of training necessary to deliver these different levels of adventure therapy. As seen in Figure 10.2, these five levels increase in depth, complexity, and need for training for purposes, ranging from recreation to primary therapy.

Recreation deals with the use of adventure experiences to provide the "recreation" of supportive and enjoyable structures into clients' lives. Gass (1993) described this as working with clients who, due to their therapeutic issues, are lacking opportunities to enjoy their lives individually or with one another. In this case, recreation is used with clients and therapeutic situations to give them respite, enjoyment, and fun to provide a break from their therapeutic situation. Although this form of adventure programming is on the left side of the continuum, recreation can serve as a potent source of healing for therapeutic clients. There is a lot to be said for a small community of individuals enjoying themselves in the immensity and awe of the natural environment. Many therapeutic recreation programs using adventure experiences for recreation would find themselves in this category of programming for therapeutic populations.

Education is the use of adventure experiences to provide modeling and social development in key yet critical global areas. Gass often refers to working with clients not on issues of rehabilitation but the actual "habilitation" (i.e., the teaching of new skills) of certain valuable individual and social characteristics relevant to the clients' growth. The modeling and exemplification of positive social skill development in after school settings through the use of adventure experiences and associated facilitation technique (e.g., full value contracting) is one example of using adventure therapy at the level of education application. Examples of such programs also include psychoeducational programs and special education programs using adventure therapy programming.

Enrichment is the category that fosters beneficial growth on global therapeutic issues through adventure experiences. Cooperation, self-efficacy, communication, and problem-solving can provide beneficial growth for clients in therapeutic situations when these issues are positively introduced/

FIGURE 10.2 Depth of intervention continuum with adventure therapy. This continuum illustrates the different forms of adventure programming and their increasing complexity from recreational focuses to primary therapy. Adventure therapy would fall in the boxed area of adventure programming.

reintroduced into clients' lives through the unique avenues provided by adventure experiences.

Adjunctive therapy refers to the addition of adventure therapy experiences in alliance with other therapeutic approaches. Gass (1993) refers to the implementation of adventure therapy experiences with clients and other therapeutic situations, where adventure is conducted for a focused and targeted short period of time to "jump start" or augment the pre-existing therapeutic modality being used with the client. An example presented by Gass of using a contracted six-session adventure therapy program with clients also in traditional couples' therapy represents one format of this model. Another model is provided by Webb (1993), who used a three-day therapeutic wilderness adjunct program by a Colorado Outward Bound school with survivors of violence.

Primary therapy refers to adventure therapy as the central form of treatment for a particular therapeutic issue or psychological dysfunction. Here adventure therapy replaces other therapeutic approaches as the primary medium for therapeutic change.

To determine which form of adventure programming with therapeutic populations would be best for a particular client, Gass (1993) identified eight factors:

1. The specific needs of the client
2. The complexity of the clients' therapeutic issue(s)
3. The background training and therapeutic expertise of the adventure therapist
4. The length of time the adventure therapist has to work with the client
5. The context the client comes from and will return to after the adventure experience
6. The presence of aftercare or follow-up treatment following the adventure experience
7. The availability of adventure experience(s)
8. The therapists' abilities and limitations in using adventure experiences in her or his treatment approaches

Ringer (1995) used this continuum to center on the types of professionals who would be using or delivering these forms of programming. Figure 10.3 illustrates the level and types of professionals involved with clients at these five particular levels. As one can see in the figure, Ringer inferred that with higher levels of client intervention, greater responsibilities, training, and competence are required for the adventure therapist.

Representing another perspective, Davis-Berman & Berman (1994) believed that training adventure professionals engaged in therapeutic situations involved three conceptual dimensions: client population, risk of the activity, and goals of the adventure activity or program. Using the structure of a three-dimensional pyramid, the authors noted that as an adventure therapist moves

Types of adventure programming with therapeutic populations	Types of professionals using adventure with therapeutic populations
Primary therapy Adjunctive therapy Enrichment Education Recreation	Clinician Human behavior expert Expert communicator Group facilitator Instructor/coach Enthusiastic adventurer Limits setter/safety supervisor Skilled outdoor practitioner

FIGURE 10.3 Ringer's (1994) continuum on the types of professionals using adventure for therapeutic purposes.

from lower levels in each of these pyramid sides to higher levels, the risk in each of these three conceptual dimensions increased. With this increase, the skill level required by the therapist also increased, requiring the professional to possess more knowledge and skill to assist clients at this level. The authors further noted that there are a few adventure therapists with the required education and skill levels necessary to appropriately work with high-risk populations at the top of the pyramid (i.e., adventure therapists who have been trained to work with high-risk populations, the knowledge and experience to properly engage in high-risk activities, combined with the knowledge to provide and use appropriate therapeutic techniques successfully).

Itin (1997) further clarified the expectations of what a therapist using adventure experiences with clients would need to know to appropriately work with these clients. Recognizing that different forms of adventure therapy would require different areas of competence, he summarized the main issues in the training of adventure therapists to be:

1. Technical components of adventure work
2. Apprenticeships or mentorships
3. Appropriate understanding of therapeutic client populations
4. Skills and training in areas of conflict resolution, group process, crisis management, feedback, facilitation, leadership, and related areas necessary for working with clients
5. Self-understanding of old processes and the ability to consciously use themselves and their own experiences through critical self-reflection
6. Comprehension of self-change and growth processes and be able to use this understanding to assist others
7. Understanding of group processes, including knowledge of experiential education philosophy and the ability to put this understanding into action
8. Familiarity with a range of therapeutic approaches and the ability to develop a holistic approach to working with clients

Crisp (2002) in Australia developed an individual certification curriculum called the Australian Wilderness Adventure Therapy Accreditation Scheme. This program is designed to take individuals with previous training and orient these professionals through a series of three courses, two seminars on psychological first responder issues and risk management, and three practicum/field placements totaling 100 days in the field. The first course is 5 days in length and covers an introduction to wilderness adventure therapy, theory, clinical procedures, and therapeutic methods used in Australia. Following a practicum of 20 days, another 5-day course called the wilderness adventure therapy intermediate course is offered, covering topical areas such as client presentation and psychological disorder, assessment and advanced assessment for wilderness adventure therapy, writing individualized treatment plans, developing wilderness adventure therapy psychological risk management, and addressing special client issues such as homelessness, sex abuse, violence, substance abuse, and body image issues.

After another 40-day practicum occurs, interested professionals are encouraged to complete their training by attending an advanced wilderness adventure therapy course. Following this course, participants complete the certification process by taking a test in their particular area of training.

Building on the work of all of these authors, Papadopoulos (2000) used a research technique called the Developing a Curriculum (DACUM) process to identify many of these concepts in a model. Through this process, a series of 38 competencies were recognized as necessary for entry-level adventure therapists. These 38 competencies were divided into five component areas of programming, adventure, therapy, operational, and personal. These competencies were further operationalized by placing them in a sequential graph where the five components build on each other, with one component placed next to another depending upon highest to lowest level of importance. The related 38 competencies were then organized into this same sequential and continuum structure. Figure 10.4 illustrates this organizational structure and the ranking of the 38 competencies.

By using elements of the development of competencies in the four areas of adventure programming, mental health therapies, specific therapeutic populations, and previous adventure therapy work, a strong platform is established to take a next step in identifying the current adventure therapy competencies for professionals. What is interesting to note is that separate from this analysis, Priest and Gillis (1999) used a Venn diagram structure to portray a graphic representation of how to build skills and knowledge toward becoming an adventure therapist (see Figure 10.5). This structure is similar to the approach used in this chapter to identify the competencies of an adventure therapist by assessing competency analysis work that has been done in the fields of adventure programming, mental health therapy, and specific therapeutic populations. In Figure 10.5, there are three intersecting circles. Each of these circles represents the basic idea of the knowledge and experience of

	1	2	3	4	5	6	7	8	9
A. Personal component	Adaptable and flexible	Understands importance of and is able to communicate effectively	Has an awareness of personal strengths and challenges	Has good interpersonal skills	Understands decision-making processes	Demonstrates first aid competency as it relates to adventure programs provided	Understands theories of leadership and is aware of personal leadership style	Is committed to lifelong learning	
B. Adventure component	Understands and adheres to environmental ethics	Demonstrates competency in at least two adventure fields (e.g., canoeing and rock climbing)	Understands and applies concepts of risk management and assessment in context of adventure programs	Understands foundational theories and principles of experiential learning	Can identify and assess adventure opportunities and options	Understands and demonstrates expedition planning and management as it relates to any adventure program			
C. Programming component	Can facilitate group process	Can establish and monitor goals with clients and self	Understands and applies reflective processes and transfer of learning	Can integrate therapeutic interventions and adventure-based activities	Can assess client needs	Understands theories, principles, and practices of programming	Understands different client populations	Can prepare and deliver adventure therapy programs	Can conduct program evaluation
D. Therapy component	Understands counseling/therapy theories and their applications	Understands context and structures/systems within which clients may be involved	Understands and applies best practices of intervention related to adventure activities	Understands application of various styles, techniques, and protocols related to therapeutic interventions	Understands full range of client populations, their behavior, and abilities	Understands the release, principles, and foundations of social psychology and their applications	Understands theories and principles of good pedagogical practices and their applications		
E. Operational component	Understands and adheres to professional and community standards & ethics	Can develop and understands application of emergency procedures	Can write clear and concise reports, logs, proposals, protocols, and treatment plans	Understands operational contexts of adventures therapy	Understands legal implications of working in the adventure therapy field	Understands principles of management and marketing in the field of adventure therapy	Understands issues and concerns of staff hiring, training, and supervision	Understands basic budget preparation and management	

FIGURE 10.4 Thirty-eight competencies necessary for entry-level adventure therapists (Papadopoulos, 2000). Note there is a value system inherent in the chart, with the competencies closest to the upper left-hand corner of the chart being the most important and those in the lower right-hand corner being judged as less important. For example, with the row of personal component qualities, Adaptable and flexible is the highest ranking quality for personal components, with the second being Understands importance of and is able to communicate effectively, and so forth until the eighth-ranked quality for personal components of Is committed to lifelong learning. This ranking system is also present with the columns of the graph. For example, personal components are rated the highest of the five components, with operational components being the lowest.

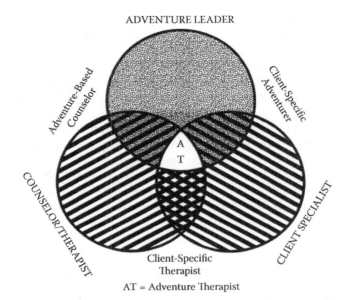

FIGURE 10.5 How to build skills and knowledge toward becoming an adventure therapist.

the adventure leader, the counselor/therapist, and the client specialist (similar to a therapist with specific knowledge on a particular treatment population or with specific therapeutic knowledge about an area of mental health). For instance, a substance abuse therapist would be an example of a client-specific therapist—that is, an individual possessing training as a therapist and in the area of substance abuse populations, but not in the area of adventure programming. Correspondingly, a client-specific adventurer would possess integrated training in adventure skills and in techniques for working with youth with substance abuse issues, but not necessarily in training as a therapist.

As one can see from these two examples, categories of differing professionals are used to label what occurs when competencies overlap. There are two main purposes for the diagram in Figure 10.5:

1. For individuals to call themselves adventure therapists, they need to possess competencies from all three circles as well as the knowledge and skill sets these circles represent.
2. When such a single comprehensive individual is not available, most adventure/wilderness therapy programs solve this issue by creating an effective treatment team by combining two or three professionals together to deliver the combination of necessary competencies and expertise to offer adventure/wilderness therapy. This Venn diagram shows what type of individual is needed based on existing members of the treatment team.

The white intersection of the diagram in Figure 10.5 represents when the central features of adventure therapy programming come together to provide the best treatment possible through one or more professionals. Conversely, when professionals are not able to achieve and provide this form of integrated adventure therapy, the diagram also represents what can happen when certain areas of expertise are not covered. One thing is for sure: Gaps in terms of areas covered are sure to exist and possibly negatively affect the full potential of treatment. In a team approach to adventure therapy, if professionals with different training backgrounds come together with respect to what the other brings to understanding of the client and how to work with the client, then the process is enlightened. Conversely, when there is little respect for one another's professional judgments or there is competition for who is right and who knows best, then the process loses its value and potency for treatment effectiveness.

ADVENTURE THERAPY COMPETENCY CHECKLIST

Based on the four sources used to trace the formation of adventure therapist competencies earlier in this chapter, a comprehensive schema outlining 10 competencies for adventure therapists was constructed. As seen in Figure 10.6, each competency is comprised of a rubric with suggested elements to attain intended levels of the identified performance. Rubrics are evaluative tools that are often used to identify levels of quality, particularly surrounding behavioral expectations associated with a particular level of performance. They typically include a set of criteria, an evaluative narrative to explain the criteria, and a point value or ranking system based on the criteria. One advantage of using rubrics is that the quality of the performance is spelled out in advance for participating individuals. Another advantage of a rubric is that as the field evolves and becomes more defined, rubrics can be adjusted for increased clarity and definition.

At one end of this continuum are identified professional behaviors associated with *emerging-level* adventure therapists, in the middle are behaviors associated with *competent* adventure therapists, and at the other end of the rubric are behaviors associated with *exemplary* adventure therapists. Adapting performance assessment structures from several related psychotherapy, counseling, and mental health organizations (e.g., Oregon Office of Alcohol and Drug Abuse Programs, 2011), rubrics for each of 10 identified categories were developed for determining the level of competence for adventure therapists (see Appendix B for the entire comprehensive schema outlining adventure therapy competencies). *Emerging-level* adventure therapists have a basic knowledge of the procedures, models, and practices of adventure therapy. In their evolving growth, they have not reached a level to practice independently, and they require regular supervision. *Competent* adventure therapists

Emerging adventure therapist	Proficient adventure therapist	Exemplary adventure therapist
- Follows established written assessment procedures - Makes structured and basic professional interpretations and hypotheses of assessment material - Develops 1–2 possible insights into potential treatment interventions - Uses assessment primarily prior to treatment and interventions (e.g., diagnosis, delivery) - Documents necessary information - Assists in crisis situations - Relies on supervision to formulate comprehensive and accurate client assessment	- Considers both a macro and micro perspective in assessment planning - Understands how to use adventure therapy models for therapeutic assessment (e.g., CHANGES, GRABBSS) - Understands how to diagnosis and design particular assessments using adventure therapy - Interprets client behaviors in adventure therapy experiences and link them to specific client needs - Views assessment not only as a procedure done prior to treatment, but also as a process done throughout client treatment - Identifies more than one hypothesis as a rationale for client behavior - Accesses more than one source of information for corroborating certain behaviors (e.g., affect, behavior, cognition, relationships) - Manages crisis situations - Uses assessment to join with clients, build therapeutic alliance, and design treatment - Seeks out supervision and feedback when necessary for alternative perspectives on assessment and interpretation	- Utilizes assessment as part of building a therapeutic alliance as well as integrating interventions and planning for positive transfer of learning once adventure experiences completed - Analyzes and interprets data to build multiple tenable hypotheses of client behavior in meetings - Collaborates with supporting professionals to confirm hypotheses and assessment - Documents assessment findings and treatment reports and appropriate manner - Inventories all sources of information on clients' behavior (e.g., affect, behavior, cognition, relationships)

Rating scale: Circle all statements above that best describe the proficiency level of the adventure therapist regarding client assessment. Check one box below indicating the adventure therapist's overall level of proficiency related to client assessment:

☐ Emerging   ☐ 2   ☐ Proficient   ☐ 4   ☐ Exemplary

FIGURE 10.6 The examination of clients in mental health settings through adventure experiences and supportive documentation for screening and creating potential interventions.

demonstrate and apply procedures, models, and best practices expected of adventure therapy as the particular "standard" of current field practices. In a variety of situations, these adventure therapists typify proficient levels of expected practices that are acceptable, and these individuals also possess the necessary training to operate using the common practices and principles associated with adventure therapy. *Exemplary* adventure therapists use the very best elements of the field with consistency, clarity, and the best expressions of effectiveness for clients. They strategically conceptualize their practices and therapeutic procedures around understanding the background context of their clients, implement interventions based on insightful assessment, and integrate lasting change based on the systemic influences related to lasting change of each clients' particular environment where they will return. Their practices are ones that you would want all adventure therapists to emulate, and they serve as role models for other professionals. Exemplary adventure therapists are highly encouraged when possible to share their work and new techniques with other professionals through presentations, case studies, and publications for advancing the field.

The 10 areas of professional practice for adventure therapists are:

1. Technical competencies
2. Facilitation/processing competencies
3. Organizational/administrative competencies
4. Content/conceptual knowledge competencies
5. Therapeutic alliance building competencies
6. Assessment and intervention planning competencies
7. Intervention competencies
8. Therapeutic monitoring/maintenance and integration/termination competencies
9. Documentation competencies
10. Professionalism competencies

Assessment competencies include:

- Knowledge of adventure therapy assessment procedures (e.g., CHANGES, GRABBS)
- Collect important information on the context of the client
- Develop multiple hypotheses regarding client response during adventure experiences for intervention recommendations
- Appropriately document client responses and behaviors
- Screen for potential client contraindications to adventure experiences, including physical abilities, injuries, and contraindications with medications
- Identify and determine integration strategies for client when adventure experience is completed

BEYOND BASIC COMPETENCE AND PROFICENCY: ONE PATH TO ACHIEVING AND ENCOURAGING EXCELLENCE IN ADVENTURE THERAPY

Once therapists are licensed, pass their state certification exams, acquire their required clinical and supervision hours, and are sent their certificates indicating their licensure, they hopefully do not stop evolving into even better therapists. To describe such an evolving process of professional development and not just one that stops once basic competence is achieved, Gass and Gillis (2000) created a five-step evolutionary process that they believe many of the very best adventure therapists go through to achieve even further levels of competency in their therapeutic practice. To describe this process, they use a metaphor of an evolving mathematical paradigm. Linked to the CHANGES model discussed earlier in this book, these are the five levels of development in a progressive sequence:

1. **Emerging professional**: When professionals begin to explore the connection between clients' presenting issues and adventure experiences, they tend to see the elements of adventure therapy as summative (e.g., "I've got a lot of information, but I don't really understand how it all connects together!")

$$(c + h) + (a + n) = g$$

   "I know the context/background (c) of the client and I have some hypotheses/ideas (h) about what has worked with clients with this presenting problem in the past. I also see that there are these adventure experiences (a + n) and some of them seem to work better than others. But while I have all of this information, I'm having a hard time seeing how it all fits together or tells me anything about what I could do to help my client." (g)

2. **Adventure professional**: The next formula represents a person well versed in adventure experiences (hence the capital A) but not yet trained in therapeutic issues and the interaction of adventure experiences in therapeutic settings. Selecting adventure experiences to conduct with clients centers on those favorite adventure experiences this professional does with most clients because they like these experiences better than others. But there still remains a lack of richer connections (e.g., isomorphic or similar linking structures) that might be present if the professional had a greater understanding of therapeutic issues and interaction between these issues and adventure experiences.

$$(c + h) + (A + n) = g$$

"I know the context/background (c) of the client and I have some hypotheses/ideas (h) about what has worked with clients with this presenting problem in the past, but I don't have the training/knowledge about these issues to understand the interaction of these variables and therapeutic situations. I know a number of great adventure experiences (A) that clients just love to do, and we tend to do those favorite/all-time best activities (n). Clients get wrapped up in the moment of these activities, but sometimes I wonder deep down how they are going to make a difference in their lives." (g)

3. **Therapeutic professional**: This formula represents a person well versed in therapeutic practices (hence the capital C and H) but not yet trained in the range of adventure experiences in the interaction of these experiences in therapeutic settings. Selecting adventure experiences is limited to the ones the therapist understands out of a book or the 3-day training he or she attended. But there still remains a lack of richer connections (e.g., isomorphic structures) that would be present if the professional had a greater understanding of the paradigm/archetypical structures of adventure experiences in the interaction and adaptation that can occur between therapeutic issues and adventure experiences.

$$(C + H) + (a + n) = g$$

"I have depth of knowledge in the background and therapeutic issues of the clients (C + H). However, I don't see how there is a deeper connection between adventure experiences and these issues for my clients. We usually do adventure experiences (a + n) and therapeutically debrief them in a reactive manner, which provides rich dialogue for us to talk about in therapy after the experience." (g)

4. **Isomorphic adventure therapy professional**: The next formula represents when therapists start to select adventure experiences on the basis of how they match client issues, background, presenting problems, and their clinical hypotheses. When this occurs, a synergy that was lacking at previous levels evolves (hence the use of capitals for the letters presenting a greater understanding and clinical effectiveness). When these components are added together, each element informs one another and the therapist grows in understanding the client's story, as well as how it informs which adventure experience should be used in a particular manner to assist clients toward resolving their therapeutic objective.

$$(C + H) + (A + N) = G$$

"I have a depth of knowledge in the background and therapeutic issues of the clients (C), and when I have this information (H), it informs me on which adventure experience to conduct with my clients.

I proactively select and sequence adventure experiences for their thera-
peutic richness (A + N), and doing this brings clients issues to life dur-
ing the adventure experience in the therapeutic session." (G)

5. **Exponentially enlightened (E2) adventure therapy professional**: This
   formula represents when therapists select and adapt adventure experiences on the basis of how they interact with client issues, background,
   presenting problem, and associated clinical hypotheses. Therapists tailor
   and adapt adventure experiences specifically for a client at a particular
   time in the treatment. A deeper synergy that was not present at previous
   levels occurs (hence capitals for all of these letters presenting a greater
   understanding and clinical effectiveness), plus dialogue of informing
   or a richer understanding occurs between the therapeutic paradigms
   and the nuances in experiential practice (e.g., the therapist changes the
   rules of the adventure experience appropriately, creating a new initiative
   designed specifically for the client's issues). These components are truly
   interactive, in which each element exponentially informs one another.
   Because of this, the therapist receives the deeper understanding of the
   client's story and how it informs which adventure experience is used in
   a particular manner to assist clients toward their therapeutic objective
   (hence the exponentially larger G).

$$(C \times H) \times (A \times N) = G^2$$

"Having the knowledge base in therapy informs me how to select and
adapt adventure experiences and tailor them to clients' needs (C × H).
Adventure experiences literally changed the manner in which I conduct
therapy (A × N). I don't ignore therapeutic approaches; I just bring them
to life and have clients "walk their talk" in our therapy sessions." (G²)

SUMMARY

This chapter explored the competencies an adventure therapist should possess.
Several individuals have previously explored this question to one degree or
another. Gass (1993) focused on the level of intervention provided by adventure
therapists. These authors identified five levels of adventure therapy practices
increasing in levels of depth, complexity, and need for training: recreation,
education, enrichment, adjunctive therapy, and primary therapy. Ringer (1994)
built on this model as it related to the competencies necessary for adventure
therapists delivering these forms of programming, illustrating the level and
type of competencies necessary for adventure therapists involved with clients
at these five particular levels. Berman and Davis-Berman (1993) believed that
training adventure professionals engaged in therapeutic situations involved
three conceptual dimensions: client population, risk of the activity, and goals

of the adventure activity/program, creating a three-dimensional pyramid to help guide the training of adventure therapists. Itin (1997) further clarified the expectations of what a therapist using adventure experiences with clients would need to know to appropriately work with these clients. Building on the work of all of these authors, Papadopoulos (2000) used a research technique called the DACUM process to identify 38 competencies that were recognized as necessary for entry-level adventure therapists.

Other sources were also used to inform this answer, including the allied fields of psychotherapy, social work, marriage and family therapy, and specific therapeutic fields such as addiction counseling and substance abuse treatment. Based on these sources, a comprehensive schema outlining 10 competencies for adventure therapists was constructed. These competencies are technical competencies, facilitation/processing competencies, organizational/administrative competencies, content/conceptual knowledge competencies, therapeutic alliance building competencies, assessment and intervention planning competencies, intervention competencies, therapeutic monitoring/maintenance and integration/termination competencies, documentation competencies, and professionalism competencies. As seen in Figure 10.6, each competency is comprised of a rubric with suggested elements to attain intended levels of the identified performance.

Once competencies are achieved, adventure therapists need to continue their professional development. Gass and Gillis (2000) presented a model for adventure therapists to continue to evolve through a mathematical metaphor following the CHANGES model.

TURNING OFF THE FAUCET OF ANGER MANAGEMENT

Antonio G. Alvarez

Todd is a 14-year-old eighth grader who comes to see me regularly because he gets in trouble with teachers and peers for his impulsive and aggressive nature. His bravado and aggressive presentation was learned from many years of living with a pretty angry father and an older brother who took his anger out on Todd. He came in today after yet another disciplinary referral from yet another teacher, which read: "Foul language, aggressive actions toward peers and me."

I gave Todd a balloon and told him we are going to the bathroom for a minute. In the bathroom, I asked him to connect the balloon to the faucet and turn the water on. The balloon started to fill with water. I told Todd, "The activity ends when you can tell me three ways to make sure the balloon doesn't pop!" He was intrigued. "Turn the water off," he said, "Pull the stupid thing off the faucet." As the balloon kept filling with water, he held it up with his hands and asked if pinching the top would count. I told him to try, as the top part of the balloon started filling with water. He started laughing and said, "This is gonna pop!" I said, "Just one more solution." He asked for my help to hold the balloon up, but the balloon popped and we both got wet and laughed. Then I pulled another balloon from my pocket and asked, "Are you ready to try again?" Todd responded, "Not yet, not until I can come up with another thing to do." I gave him three additional balloons and told him to see if he can figure it out while he is on his 1-day suspension. Then we headed off to get dried up, amidst the curious looks from others in the building.

When I next saw him, Todd had his balloon for me, ready with a pinhole that he put at the bottom of the balloon. We had a long talk about anger management following his discovery. This is an example of what I call adventure therapy.

I have been an experiential creative human being for a long time. Growing up in the Philippines with eight siblings, who were my friends and playmates, we spent many summer months creating games and activities and facilitating large experiences for each other. Bamboo sticks became swords, banana leaves were our horses, and papaya stems were our underwater breathing hoses.

As a new school social worker, in 1975, I became acquainted with the Pfeiffer and Jones collection of experiential activities for team building (e.g., The Lifeboat, The Cave-in) that I adapted for use with my second- and third-grade group of boys and girls. "My room is an abandoned mine that we are going to visit today. Here are flashlights for each of us. When the door opens, we need to crawl into it (i.e., table and chairs in a pile in the center of the office covered by a blanket or two). While there, alas, we experienced a cave in. Now we must figure out who we should send to tell the principal of our dilemma before we run out of oxygen...." It was also then that I started going on field trips with the students on my caseload and learned what they found of value. We missed our appointment at the science museum because the students had never been to a four-story parking building where they could see "the whole city" and experience snow falling on them!

In 1987, a graduate student from the University of Michigan School of Social Work who was assigned to work with me all year informed me, "The way you work is called adventure by these folks I got training in down in North Carolina—people from a place called PA." It was then that I realized I didn't need to invent all these activities and that I now had a name for what I was doing. My first training in adventure came from PA in 1987 and the rest is history.

Chapter 11

Supervision in Adventure Therapy

Supervision of therapeutic practice is one of the cornerstones of the mental health professions (Brown & Lent, 2007; Falender & Shafranske, 2004). In fact, most mental health professions require a certain number of hours of supervision before beginning therapists can become licensed. Seasoned adventure therapists seek out supervision to improve their skills by receiving feedback from peers. Supervision is intended to provide professional growth for therapists, more effective therapy for clients, and some measure of protection for the welfare of clients and the public (Freitas, 2002). Probably the main purpose of supervision is to provide a source of information on the content, processes, and insights into situations that have become difficult, if not problematic, for therapists and their clients.

One active experiential supervision model that has emerged to address these issues is the ENHANCES model (Gass & Gillis, 2010). The ENHANCES model was designed to use unique sources of cognitive, affective, and kinesthetic insights to create structurally relevant experiential events that enhance the effectiveness of the supervision and feedback process. The model has been refined through presentations of the model with case studies at the Association for Experiential Education (AEE) annual international conferences, as well as through pilot testing and feedback from other professionals from their use of the model.

The ENHANCES supervision model takes advantage of the parallel processes existing between the supervisor–supervisee relationship and the therapist–client relationship. Note that such parallel processes already exist whether or not the supervisor–supervisee or therapist–client choose to acknowledge or use them. These processes can produce positive or negative benefits for these relationships. When properly used, the parallel processes between these two relationships can provide insights for both the supervisor and the therapist to make therapeutic interventions more effective. This is particularly useful when the supervisor and therapist find themselves "stuck" or hindered in addressing issues in this process.

The key to the ENHANCES model is to structure the supervision process in an active, engaging, and informing manner that will aid the therapist in the process of therapeutic improvement. The ENHANCES model is not designed to provide just one particular answer or insight that occurs in a specific way; its purpose is to offer a structural methodology with several pathways toward a more successful therapeutic relationship and associated content. It is from this structural methodology that the supervisor in the ENHANCES model selects appropriate experiential activities for the active elements of the supervision process.

There are three main stages of the ENHANCES process. The supervisor typically begins this process because some of the elements of the current hypotheses, therapeutic processes, and resulting behavioral outcomes are not producing expected levels of healthy and productive behavior. In the first stage, the supervisor **E**ngages with the therapist to promote the exploration of **N**ew **H**ypotheses for client behaviors. In the second stage, the supervisor uses the context the therapist brings to the supervision session, along with the new hypotheses co-created by the supervisor and therapist, to conduct an **A**ction that is **N**ovel and will **C**o-create insights into content and processes for the therapist. In the third stage following the experiential and novel action, the supervisor and therapist **E**valuate the **S**olutions from the experience and possible applications for new or revised hypotheses, therapeutic processes, and behavioral outcomes.

STAGE 1: ENGAGING WITH CLIENTS TO CREATE NEW HYPOTHESES IN THE SUPERVISION EXPERIENCE

This section presents examples for actual presentations of three cases of supervision to explore the first stage of the ENHANCES model.

Case 1: Who's In Control?

Supervisee Joanne is a child and adolescent clinician. She is conducting therapy in an office setting for 16-year-old Sara (all names are changed in these scenarios) and her family for issues associated with anorexia. Sara was recently discharged from an eating disorder hospital to address what was seen as more pressing family issues. Sara is noncommunicative in therapy.

Pressing issues in therapy are issues of control with Sara's mother Mary, especially evident in Joanne's monitoring of Sara's caloric intake. In order to achieve proper nutritional needs, Sara drinks 10 cans of Boost Plus daily (a nutrient-rich weight gain supplement). Mary needs to remind Sara to drink the Boost and stands over her when she drinks it. Mary becomes very overwhelmed at these times, becoming emotional and breaking down into tears.

As the therapist, Joanne finds herself becoming very impatient with Mary, wanting to rush in and address control issues. This impatience further overwhelms Mary in therapy. Joanne sees Mary and Sara more successfully on an individual basis than together; when seen jointly Sara rarely speaks, and when she does Mary becomes easily overwhelmed. Joanne has seen the family for four sessions so far.

Joanne wants to further explore control issues and increase her ability to meet Mary where she is at. Mary has become resistant to receiving input or feedback on how to control Sara. It is hard for Mary to talk with Joanne about anorexia; Mary often becomes overwhelmed and tearful in these discussions. Joanne's supervisor Mike presented the metaphor of Mary having a full emotional bucket. Joanne joined, agreed, and confirmed this, stating that Mary's bucket is already full when she arrives for therapy, and entering her office adds the extra drops necessary to overfill/overwhelm her into tears.

Case 2: Restructuring the Family

Supervisee Tiffany is a clinician for a secondary intervention unit supporting a primary care treatment organization providing wraparound/stepdown services for adolescents and their families. She runs three to four groups a week and also works with families. She has seen this particular family for 10 sessions, with each session running 2 hours in length with mixed results.

The client, Andres, is a 16-year-old adolescent who has been suspended from school due to unrestrained/acting-out behavior, violence, and some drug use. As part of his treatment plan, Tiffany has been seeing the family as adjunctive support to address these behaviors and assist them in parenting efforts. The family consists of a single mom and four children. The older son, who is 17 years old, is academically and athletically successful and is embarrassed by his brother and family when problems occur. In incidents when the mother Wendy focuses her attention on Andres and is somewhat successful, his siblings become reactionary and often sabotage Wendy's efforts to support and guide Andres. Wendy is much more caretaking and supportive with the two girls in the family.

The family has done several experiential activities during the 10 sessions with mixed results. During a trust task activity (i.e., the Mohawk/Tomahawk walk; Rohnke & Butler, 1995), the family as a whole did quite well demonstrating great help and support of one another. Other positive behaviors that were demonstrated included honesty, authentic communication, and sensitivity to what everyone in the family needed (especially Andres). Some negative issues were some challenging of mom's directions and struggling and sub-sequent sabotage by Andres' older brother.

Case 3: Whose Rules Are These?

Rob is an adventure therapist who oversees weekend enrichment programs for families in crisis or need of supervision. One of the groups participating in his program consists of a mother named Sarah and her 15-year-old daughter Amber, who are in the middle of a family reunification process. A stepfa-ther is also a part of this family, but does not generally come to the weekend enrichment program.

The most pressing issue for Rob and his staff with this family is that Sarah has become notorious for not following the rules of the experiences as well as the program. This behavior seems congruent to the staff in the way Sarah raises her daughter. It appears to the staff that Sarah is much more interested in being best friends with Amber than supervising her in her deci-sions as an adolescent. For example, Sarah will buy cigarettes and alcohol for Amber to help maintain a close friendship, which is just one example of the blurred nature of parental rules and parent-child boundaries that are prevalent in this mother–daughter relationship.

These issues were probably best exemplified in a previous adventure enrichment activity for families 2 weeks prior to this supervision session. During this activity, the adventure programming staff had constructed a carpet path activity (Aubry, 2009, pp. 52–53) for participating families to complete. In constructing a relevant framework for the activity, the adventure program-ming staff had written family roles, rules, and responsibilities on the bottom side of each carpet square for families to consider as they made their pathway from one carpet to another. As part of their consideration, families were to decide if the roles, rules, and responsibilities were for parents or adolescents. When family members answered the questions on the bottom of the carpet squares correctly, they were able to advance. If family members answered the questions incorrectly, they had to return back to the beginning. Rob reported that in this activity Sarah and Amber were not only failing, but also often sabotaging the experience for other families by saying, "Whose f-ing rule is this anyhow?" Sarah would begin with this behavior and comments, and Amber would pick up on her modeling and repeat her mother's inappropriate behavior and statements.

Discussion of the First Stage

All of these cases present various levels of perplexing issues for their thera-pists. Certainly therapy is not addressing some issues for these clients as the therapists would like. As stated earlier, the goal of the first step of the ENHANCES model is to join with therapists and engage in the exploration of new hypotheses that will lead toward more productive therapeutic outcomes.

The engagement process focuses on three distinct areas: developing specific therapeutic skills, personal growth, and the promotion of courage to be imperfect (Gass & Gillis, 2010). Table 11.1 shows examples of different types of therapeutic skills addressed by this engagement process.

Perceptual skills allow therapists to see specific patterns and external interactions occurring in therapy that they may not have noticed. Growth in this area assists therapists in tracking specific interactions and enhancing knowledge of client behavior. *Conceptual skills* allow the therapist to access various therapeutic models to benefit the client. Increased knowledge in this area helps therapists implement effective therapeutic techniques they may not have used with this client. *Intervention skills* include the capability of therapists to actually design and implement beneficial therapeutic processes. Supervision focuses on this area, assisting the therapist and their execution of intervention processes and therapeutic technique. *Relationship skills* involve the critical ability of the therapist to join with the client and create an effective and functional therapeutic alliance, which is one of the most beneficial elements of supervision a supervisor can provide.

None of these therapeutic skills can be realized if the therapist lacks the confidence in being able to be effective with their clients. Building confidence in a supervisee is one of the main objectives of supervision. Helping therapists grow in confidence is often accomplished through the modeling of appropriate behaviors, the validation of what the therapist is doing well, and the encouragement to take appropriate risks in therapy with clients to improve confidence.

The supervisor should also support the therapist's personal growth by promoting the creation of a supportive environment where "therapists have the courage to be imperfect and are encouraged to try new and novel

TABLE 11.1 Therapeutic Skills Often Sought and Received by Supervisee in the Supervision Process

Therapeutic Skills for Supervisee Received in the Supervision Process	Benefits of Therapeutic Skill in the Supervision Process
Perceptual skills	Observe specific patterns and external interactions
Conceptual skills	Access various therapeutic models
Intervention skills	Improve in the design and delivery of therapy
Relationship skills	Increase client connection

approaches with their clients" (Gass & Gillis, 2010, p. 78). The validation that "nobody's perfect" and the encouragement of appropriate risks with therapy not only increase therapist confidence as stated above, but also promote the growth of the therapist in the delivery of effective therapeutic techniques and practices. All three of these areas in the engagement process are critical for therapists' growth.

When looking back at the three case studies presented earlier in the chapter, hypotheses can already start to be generated around what might prove to be helpful for the therapist, and consequentially, their clients. In Case 1, issues of overwhelming behaviors and accurate appraisals seem to be areas where perceptual and conceptual skill development may assist the therapist. In Case 2, addressing inappropriate structures and sabotaging behaviors seems to be where the implementation of new conceptual and intervention skills may prove helpful. In Case 3, ideas and thoughts around additional intervention, conceptual, and relationship skills would seem to assist the therapist in his efforts. Table 11.2 outlines examples of issues in each particular case and those skills that might be sources of assistance for the therapist.

Certainly many therapists would benefit from appropriate modeling from the supervisor, as well as the encouragement to take a risk or "fail forward" in their thinking regarding the use of a new and novel experiential therapy activity to inform and intervene with the clients' issues.

Using a Reflecting Team

Although the previous information may be sufficient to assist the therapist, the ENHANCES model generally includes the use of a reflecting team to add depth and multiple perspectives to the supervision process. This is particularly useful in the early part of the supervision process. The following steps are used to implement the ENHANCE model with this reflecting team-enhanced process as described in Gass and Gillis (2010):

TABLE 11.2 Summary of Specific Problematic Issues for Individual Cases and Supporting Skill Areas

Case	Sample Issues	Supporting Skill Areas
Case 1	Overwhelming behaviors, inaccurate appraisals	Perceptual and conceptual skills
Case 2	Inappropriate structures, sabotaging behaviors	Conceptual and intervention skills
Case 3	Need for additional intervention ideas matching client reality	Relationship, intervention, and conceptual skills

1. The supervisor and therapist dialogue occurs in the center of a circle, with four reflecting team members observing from an outer circle distance of 5–10 feet (see Figure 11.1). During this time, reflecting team members cannot talk with the supervisor and therapist or any other reflecting team member.
2. After an appropriate amount of time of the interview (i.e., somewhere between 25–75% of the supervision period, at a time where the supervisor believes receiving input to the dialogue between supervisor and therapist would be beneficial), the supervisor and therapist move out of the circle and just listen to the conversation of the reflecting team. The reflecting team moves into the center of the circle to discuss any pertinent observations they may have seen or heard, centering primarily around what additional information they desire from the supervisee (e.g., more context for creating activities) and what activities come to mind that have isomorphic connections to what is being discussed.
3. The reflecting team and the supervisor/therapist trade places (again) and discuss what they have heard from the reflecting team.
4. Based on input from the supervisee and the reflecting team, the supervisor assists in the co-creation of a novel action (Stage 2).

Let us look back at the three case examples to see what types of information and questions about processes the reflecting teams thought were particularly relevant for each case, as well as what the supervisor and therapist thought about the reflecting teams' comments. Figure 11.2 shows a summary of information and questions from the reflecting teams in each case study,

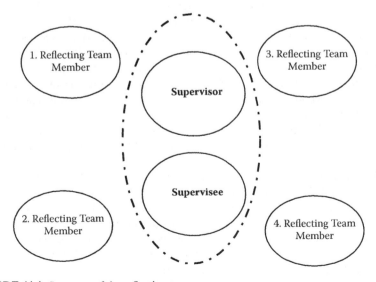

FIGURE 11.1 Structure of the reflecting team.

followed by the thoughts from the supervisor and therapist about the reflecting teams' comments.

Case 1 Reflecting Team

In the first case study, the four reflecting team members said they would like to hear more about other family members and their roles in the family, family dynamics, why the daughter was released out of the hospital to address critical family issues, family strengths, getting the family to imagine things that would lead to a better transition, and why Sara and Mary were so often seen separately during therapy. Potential experiential activities that were suggested would be ones involving increased communication between Sara and Mary, metaphors involving a small stream running next to the clinic, control issues, and mirroring/connection activities between Mary and Sara.

In thinking about the reflective team's comments, Joanne (the therapist and supervisee) reported that no father was present in the family and an older brother was in the family but possessed a very conflicted/dysfunctional relationship with the mother. The current treatment at a local hospital was viewed as not nearly as important for Sara as was her need to work on family issues. Family engagement activities were seen by Joanne as a possible way to restructure the dyadic relationship in a healthier manner.

Case 2 Reflecting Team

In the second case study, the four reflecting team members said they would like to hear more about Andres's problems and why Tiffany was having such a difficult time in her role as the therapist. They also wished to explore issues surrounding what Andres does outside of the home to be successful, the struggles between Andres and his brother and the potential symbolic meaning of Andres's language with Wendy that activates her in a negative manner (e.g., "chillin'"). The team saw Andres as often running the family with his behavior and Wendy being stuck in a sort of survivalist mode when having to parent for kids. They wondered if Wendy could change Andres's behavior from wanting to run the family to a role where he would want to support it. They also wondered if Andres's sensitivity could be used in a more positive manner.

As far as potential future experiential activities Tiffany might wish to offer to the family, they offered the following possibilities: having the brothers do something together where they both needed each other in order to be successful; a family "whale watch"/balance beam (Rohnke & Butlller, 1995), where family members would need to clearly communicate and work together to achieve the activity's common objective; the All-Aboard activity (Rohnke, 1977) that would bring everyone together in a cooperative manner; "win-win" activities; and activities to connect the boys in a more positive manner.

Case	Reflecting Team Comments and Suggestions	Therapist Response
Case #1: Who's in control?	• Hear more on family roles and dynamics, family strengths, family thoughts on transition • Potential experiential activities involving increased communication, control issues, and family connection activities	• No father was present in the family, older brother possessed conflicted/dysfunctional relationship with Mary (mom) • Need for Sara to work on family issues and restructure family relationships
Case #2: Restructuring the family	• Hear more about Andres's problems, therapist difficulties, struggles between Andres and his brother, the potential symbolic meaning of Andres's language, Andres—Wendy dynamics, access Andres's strengths • Potential experiential activities: Have the brothers do something together where they both need each other, family "whale watch" activity with clear communication and cooperation, cooperative "all aboard" activity, "win-win" activities	• Collaborative activities have already been attempted, Andres's self-directed compulsive behavior, Tiffany enjoys working with Andres and the family, solution-focus difficulties when problems become "saturated," Wendy quit her job to help Andres, Wendy describes situation as "hopeless," Andres's future goal of being away from home, Andres's struggles when asked to be supportive and asking for guidance
Case #3: Whose rules are these anyway?	• Role and boundary confusion, parallel process between therapist and mother, the mother lacking information, "safety" and "frontloading" issues, parallel process around anxiety, need to use different ideas to develop mother's subjective responses	• Limited contact and knowledge affect efforts to assist mother, valued concept of "frontloading information," need to justify answers and actions, need for empathy and knowledge-building exercises from supervisor

FIGURE 11.2 Summary of reflecting team comments and therapist responses.

In responding to the reflecting team's comments and suggestions, Tiffany said that a number of the suggested collaborative activities had already been done. As far as impulsivity, Andres chooses when to be compulsive and when not to—he's very intelligent. Tiffany enjoys working with Andres and the family, has been quite solution-focused with their work, and has run into difficulties when problems have become saturated. For now, Wendy has quit her job to help Andres during these difficult times. Wendy described the current situation as hopeless: "I don't know where to go, what to do, or how to make things better."

Wendy was asked if Andres had any dreams of thoughts for the future. Wendy replied that Andres wanted to be away from home and spend time with his girlfriend. Wendy was asked to clarify Andres's ability to be supportive. Wendy said that her son struggles when asked to be supportive and asks for guidance in a more demanding tone.

Case 3 Reflecting Team

In Case 3, the reflecting team commented in depth on the confusion of roles and boundaries that existed in the family. They also commented on the parallel process that existed between the therapist in his role and the mother in her role, primarily on how the lack of providing appropriate information led to confusion and the inability to do particular roles in an adequate manner (i.e., the therapist not having enough information on the mother led to an inability to design appropriate interventions, the mother not having enough information on how to address certain issues with her daughter led to an inability to conduct parenting skills).

Several reflecting team members thought that receiving greater specificity from the mother would help the therapist create a "personalized learning curve" that would enable the mother to access her strengths and become a better parent. One reflecting team member summarized what she saw in terms of safety and frontloading as key issues. Safety referred to the ability to create a therapeutic environment in which the mother feels secure enough to bring forward her efforts to be successful. Frontloading referred to providing enough information ahead of time for the mother to feel secure and not anxious in her behaviors and responding, particularly in front of other participating parents in the program. This same reflecting team member saw a parallel process around this supervisor–supervisee relationship and the therapist–client relationship regarding anxiety. Final comments from the reflecting team centered around the need to use different ideas to bring out the subjective responses from the mother that may not fit objective standards but may work for the mother in her environment.

In responding to the reflecting team members, Rob agreed that limited contact and knowledge certainly affected his team's ability to know how to assist the mother in her efforts. He thought the reflecting team member who keyed in on the role of anxiety within him as well as within the mother, as well as the concept of frontloading information, was quite accurate in her appraisal of the situation. What is interesting to note during this reflective process was the feeling of the supervisee to justify his answers and actions to the supervisor. Although this had some value in terms of content to share with the supervisor, the process was parallel to the mother justifying her parenting style during therapy. This parallel process spoke volumes in terms of information for the supervisor, which he incorporated in the next section of the ENHANCES model. In fact, as one can observe on the video clip, the supervisor led Rob through a series of mini-experiential activities to heighten his empathy, understanding, and knowledge about their relationship (i.e., the supervisor–supervisee relationship) in an effort to assist Rob in his empathy, understanding, and knowledge about the adventure therapy programming structure for this family. One pivotal example of such an activity was a lose-lose double-bind coin flip (i.e., "heads I win, tails you lose"), parallel in process to the lose-lose double bind the mother was placed in during the adventure enrichment experience that caused her to swear and stomp out of the experience and the room. Sarah loses if she volunteers her response because she does not know the "correct terms," but if she does not respond she also loses by validating the belief of others that she does not know the answers to parenting so she is not a good parent.

STAGE 2: CO-CREATING AN ACTION THAT IS NOVEL IN THE SUPERVISION EXPERIENCE

Once the supervisor and therapist have heard the feedback from the reflecting team and had the chance to discuss their observations, the second stage of the model begins. In this second stage, supervisors of the ENHANCES model collect all of the information provided thus far from the therapist and reflecting team, as well as the expertise from their own background, and reengage in a dialogue process with the therapist. However, instead of using divergent dialogue to engage with the therapist and look for new hypotheses, the supervisor and client use more converging and confirming dialogue to co-create these new hypotheses by using actions that are novel. As seen in Figure 11.3, the middle stages of the CHANGES and ENHANCES models are the same. The central purpose of both models is to create a novel action to produce new parallel pathways and unexplored venues to solving the problematic issue.

In many ways, just as a therapist would use this part of the CHANGES model to provide a novel action for generating information, the supervisor uses this part of the ENHANCES model to create a novel action to co-create an appropriate supervision experience for the therapist. From the converging and confirming dialogue process mentioned above, combined with the processes

C-H-A-N-G-E-S	E-N-H-A-N-C-E-S
• Context • Hypotheses • Action (which is) • Novel • Generating (Information) • Evaluating • Solutions	• Engage • New • Hypotheses • Action (which is) • Novel • Co-create • Evaluate • for Solutions

FIGURE 11.3 Comparing the CHANGES and ENHANCES models. Note the same structure in the "AN" portion of both models.

outlined in Chapter 8 (e.g., verbal and physical double entendres), the supervisor is drawn to certain activities and supporting verbal frameworks to offer to the therapist as possibilities for exploration. As the supervisor is drawn to a particular framework, he or she can explore possibilities of potential novel activities with the therapist through continuation of confirming dialogue and metacommunication.

As this dialogue becomes more confirming, the supervisor using the ENHANCES model views this rich isomorphic metacommunication as an invitation to get out of the chair and do an experiential activity. The richer or stronger this metacommunication process, idea, or cognitive thought becomes, the more inviting the invitation should feel for the supervisor and the faster they should get out of their chair to begin the activity and its associated inductive verbal framework when presenting the experience for the therapist.

Let us return to our case studies to see how this process evolved for the therapists and their supervisors.

Case 1: Who's in Control?

Mike asked Joanne to take a blank piece of paper and write down an inventory of all of the ideas presented to her—her own, ones co-constructed with her dialogue with the supervisor, and ones offered from the reflecting team. While Joanne was doing this, Mike collected a water bottle, a pitcher full of water, and a plastic cup that was available in the conference seminar room.

Joanne wrote down a long and overwhelming list of more than eight ideas. Mike stated that with all of the things they had to do, and for every idea that she could handle, she needed to pour an appropriate amount of water from the water pitcher into the cup to represent each idea. Mike offered that Joanne had to determine how much emphasis she wanted to place on an idea by pouring a corresponding amount of water into the cup (i.e., how important each strategy is for this family at this time should match the amount of water Joanne pours into the cup).

Mike then informed Joanne that after she accomplished this task, they would jointly carry the cup perched on top of the paper (holding the four corners of the paper) and deposit the water into a large bucket in the corner of the seminar room that could hold the water. (See Gass [1998c] for further activity description related to family systems.) The supervisor–supervisee needed to handle and control this task without spilling any water ("becoming overwhelmed") or they had to begin the process again. Mike reminded Joanne that it was her judgment as to how much water/ideas they could handle and how they would successfully implement a plan to make it to the intended bucket. When Joanne asked who should do the pouring, Mike told her she does everything and he was there to facilitate her efforts.

Joanne then verbally identified the need to maintain a safe and equitable space as her most important task to implement with this family ("the only thing I really need to do") and filled the cup over halfway. She then added drops for focusing on control dynamics. She mentioned that other ideas were great ones, but they might contraindicate these current primary needs and adding more into the current treatment plans might make things too overwhelming to address at this time.

Joanne then guided Mike in assisting her to take the cup of water placed in the center of the paper to the large bucket. Mike asked Joanne how she thought she was doing and she said "very well." They successfully completed the task without spilling any water.

In this particular case, the supervisor Mike was drawn to several elements in Joanne's presentation, comments of the reflecting team, and his background experience with previous similar clients, including:

1. The overwhelming nature of many portions of this therapy, including emotions, tasks, and investment, as well as how all of these portions were closely monitored by the mother and daughter
2. How this monitoring process easily led to overwhelming emotions and spilling over into tears
3. How issues of control through reminding, monitoring, and standing over were already combined with control issues that often exist with eating disorder clients
4. The dynamics of being impatient as well as some forms of nonverbal communication

From these elements as well as other informing sources of information (e.g., emotions presented by the therapist in supervision), Mike offered a confirming verbal metaphor of an emotional bucket for Mary. This metaphor revolved around the idea that Mary's emotional bucket was already so full that when she arrived at therapy, it only took two or three drops of tears to overwhelm/overflow her bucket. When Joanne (the therapist) enthusiastically joined, agreed, and confirmed this metaphoric presentation, the supervisor moved out of his chair and presented a novel action.

The novel action offered by Mike was the system activity (Gass, 1998c) where the mother's emotional bucket was balanced/secured/unstable based on issues of inventory, control, patience, and connecting efforts. As with true parallel processes and metacommunication, this last statement was true for the mother–daughter relationship, the client–therapist relationship, and now the supervisor–supervisee relationship. Some of the kinesthetic processes of the novel action included:

- Taking an inventory of potentially overwhelming ideas
- Prioritizing these ideas
- Linking these ideas to amounts of liquid in the container with only so much emotional room to contain these ideas
- Handling and balancing these ideas
- Guiding these ideas toward an appropriate goal
- Developing a plan of supervision to monitor all of these ideas
- Supervising communication that would provide an appropriate structure and balance to maintain emotions, guide the process toward an appropriate goal, and monitor all elements of the situation

One way to further illustrate this process is to use methods presented in Chapter 8 to strengthen the parallel process with the therapist when presenting a novel isomorphic activity. Listening to the therapist's description, the supervisor enhances the process by transforming the verbs and nominalizations, as well as refraining negative connotations, used by the therapist into the actual novel activity. Using the same language as a parallel process, often in the form of a double entendre in the briefing of the activity, strengthens the isomorphic connection and relevance for the therapist. Figure 11.4 summarizes this connective process for Case 1.

Case 2: Restructuring the Family

Mike, the supervisor, asked Tiffany if she had done some previous trust activities with the family. Tiffany replied yes but that there could be more room to work with the family on these issues. Some blindfold activities went well but Wendy struggles in this role, primarily with issues of communication and being blindfolded in the context of the family. The supervisor asked Tiffany about situations in which Wendy was asked to work directly with Andres. Tiffany says that during this time the rest of the family members become shut off in their interactions with Wendy.

Verb	Gerund/Nominalization/ Reframe	Active, Experiential Activity with Appropriate Framework
• Overwhelm (emotion) • Take inventory • Control (remind, stand over) • Noncommunicative • Impatient	• Listing and ranking of appropriate tasks • Taking inventory • Judgment/decision making • Maintaining safe and appropriate control • Communicating constructive ideas • Being patient with the process	• Gass, M. A. (1998). The system. *Ziplines*, 36. 52–53 • Experiential actions of writing, ranking, judging, communicating, "pouring" and monitoring emotions, balancing, directing toward goal

FIGURE 11.4 The supervisor's process of linking verbs, gerunds, nominalizations, and reframing negative interpretations into active, experiential activities with appropriate frameworks in Case 1.

As Tiffany provided an example of this, the supervisor asked one of the training group members to serve as a daughter having a conversation with her mom. Tiffany described how when Wendy and Andres are interacting, the daughter becomes reactive. Based on this information, the supervisor sculpts the group into a trust lean formation, where the supervisor serves as Andres, leaning back and being directed by Tiffany, who is acting as the mother. The daughter is then directed to grab a belt loop and tug on Tiffany/mom when the daughter feels like she is not receiving appropriate attention from Tiffany/mom. The supervisor informed Tiffany that he will be working hard to "trip her up" and make things as difficult for her, in a similar manner that Andres makes things difficult for Wendy. The supervisor also asks Tiffany to describe what language Wendy uses with Mike that is successful when directing him, and further asks Tiffany to use this type of language when directly guiding him through the successful resolution of the activity (e.g., language that ties into the positive use of his sensitivity).

After this language pattern is established, the supervisor not only directs the team member serving as the daughter to pull on one belt loop for attention, but also enlists the aid of two more team members to serve as Andres's other brother and sister to act in a similar manner (i.e., pull on another belt loop when mom/Tiffany is interacting with Andres/Mike but not giving them the attention they need and want).

The supervisor increases the intensity of the activity by building on Tiffany's successes with the trust lean by moving farther away from Tiffany before beginning the trust lean process. In a critical moment of insight, Tiffany asks to restructure the family, particularly redirecting the siblings to move from a confrontational position (i.e., tugging at her to receive attention) to a more collaborative one (i.e., restructuring and redirecting the other children to get in line with her to make the family more functional). Tiffany also asks Andres to change his language to recognize the fact that the family will be

changing their behavior to be more functional. The family successfully nego-
tiates this process in the new structure and with new language (e.g., a trust
circle structure).

With this case, the supervisor Mike was drawn to several elements
based on his interview with Tiffany, the comments of the reflecting team,
and his background experience with previous similar clients. Several of these
elements included both negative as well as positive behaviors. The positive
behavior elements included the support family members offered, particularly
in their sensitivity toward one another and the needs of the family; the honesty
that existed in the interactions of family members; and the apparent strength
in communication between family members. The negatively connotative elements included acting-out behaviors, sabotaging of siblings and the related
overwhelming powerlessness the mother felt when this occurred, and the reactionary level of behavior in the children of the family, particularly in strength,
volatility, and quickness in response. Notice that in order to use negatively
connotative elements, the supervisor reframed these elements into strengths
when in an appropriate structure (e.g., instead of labeling the children in the
family as acting out, sabotaging, and quick to react, the supervisor adapted
his vision for the moment as a group of children who were sensitive and quick
to respond when someone needed them without even having to ask them to
help). To test and see how accurate his confirming hypotheses were, Mike
asked Tiffany background information on the context of trust, what occurred
when these issues arose, what happened when Wendy was asked to work with
Andres, and the associated behavior with the rest of family. Already having a
version of the trust activity for the family designed with issues of restructuring
in mind, the supervisor moved out of his chair and presented the novel action
for supervision.

Just as the necessity of restructuring the family was a critical therapeutic
goal to accomplish, the supervisor needed to restructure the activity to make
it more applicable for this particular client. This parallel process of appropriately involving the therapist in the restructuring of the novel adventure activity to fit the supervision case was a critical method of metacommunication for
the therapist to use with her client and Wendy to use with her children (i.e.,
this process was parallel across the mother–children relationship, the client–
therapist relationship, and the supervisor–supervisee relationship).

The evolutions and adjustments in the restructuring process successfully
negotiated by Tiffany throughout the progression of the novel adventure experience served as the key connecting factor of success. This was especially
true in evidence when Mike increased the intensity of the activity. As seen
in the case study above, at a critical moment of insight Tiffany restructured
the family in several functional and healthy ways for the activity and for the
family. This process exemplifies the very essence of why ENHANCES is used
as a supervision model to supplement verbal supervision processes. Figure

11.5 outlines the process of taking verbal double entendres and making them operational through processes of turning these verbs into gerunds, novelizations, and positively reframed behaviors. Based on these metacommunication concepts, an active novel experience providing a parallel process extending over three relationships (i.e., supervisor–supervisee, therapist–client, mother–children) is co-created with the supervisee. This restructuring process follows multiple isomorphic experiential interactions (e.g., mother directing and children following with supporting, trusting, communicating, unifying controlling behaviors appropriately in stressful situations, organizing and orchestrating attention, responding).

Case 3: Whose Rules Are These Anyway?

Building off of the comments from a reflecting team member, the supervisor Mike and Rob began to dialogue about how overwhelming such a parental testing system may actually feel to some parents. Rob stated that during the activities the staff thought they were clear that there was no one correct answer, but as they continued to talk Rob began to consider how maybe that perception did not come across to Sarah (the mother) and Amber (the daughter). Rob stated Sarah's engagement in the adventure program had always remained somewhat distant and disengaged.

To initially assess this concept with Rob, Mike had them return to the Jeopardy game. Building off of the easier $20 category of facilitation answers, Rob was asked to identify the third type of facilitation. When Rob gave his answer, rather than stating whether it was the correct or incorrect response according to Mike, Mike asked him if this particular answer worked for him. When Rob said it did and provided justified reasons for why it worked, Mike told him that he had provided the correct answer and asked him to expand even

Verb	Gerund/ Nominalization	Active, Experiential
(+) Support (+) Honesty (+) Communicating (+) Sensitivity (-) Acting-out behavior (-) Reactionary siblings (-) Sabotage support	• Supporting • Communicating • Sensing • Reacting in a healthy manner • Connecting • Trusting • Mother directing, children following	• Trust lean progression with specific structures in mind • Experiential actions of mother directing and children following with supporting, trusting, communicating, unifying controlling behaviors appropriately in stressful situations, organizing and orchestrating attention, responding

FIGURE 11.5 The supervisor's process of linking verbs, gerunds, nominalizations, and reframing negative interpretations into active, experiential activities with appropriate frameworks in Case 2.

further on why the answer was correct. Rob self-validated the accuracy and cor-
rectness of the answer for him, as well as impressed Mike with his answers.

Mike also shared his feeling with Rob that the gap for Sarah and Amber
in some of these therapeutic adventure experiences (and their lives) must
be almost as large as the gap between the $20 and $1,000 Jeopardy game
questions. In order to travel the distance to arrive at the intended goal on the
other side of the room, Mike suggested a novel activity often referred to as
Stepping Stones (Aubry, 2008). Confirming with Rob that he had never done
the activity before so it retained its novel status, Mike started the activity
with Rob after only explaining 50% of the rules to the activity. Obviously
within the first 30–60 seconds, Rob made some mistakes and lost several
resources because he was unaware of certain rules and guidelines and the
resulting consequences of the activity. This obviously held parallel processes
with the frustration and anxiety experienced by the therapist and Sarah in the
adventure therapy enrichment experiences, as well as parallel issues of parenting experience by Sarah when trying to parent Amber. As easily observed
on the video clip, as Rob became aware of the rules of the game (as well as
created some of his own rules that worked well for him, such as ripping one
of his pieces of paper in half), he became much more directive when guiding
Mike's movements in the activity to be appropriate and not consequenced. He
also increased his ownership by taking responsibility for making sure Mike
completed the Stepping Stones activity appropriately.

As seen in Table 11.1, the areas of therapeutic skill development that
Rob would benefit the most from were areas of relationship, intervention,
and conceptualization development. As more information was received from
the therapist, relationship development seemed to grow in importance for
therapy to progress in this family. As the therapist was sharing his frustration in searching for answers, empathy skills became a primary area for the
supervisor. Mike attempted to show appropriate joining and alliance skills in
dialogue, confirming experiential activities, and the novel supervision action
itself. As this alliance was created, content and process supervision focused
on confronting the seemingly double-bind, "lose-lose" scenarios of both the
therapist–client and mother–daughter relationships. As seen in Figure 11.6,
the supervisor structured the novel action to transform these dysfunctional
scenarios with qualities that could address these situations, such as modeling
the following behaviors:

- Advocating for self-belief systems while being open to listening to the
  thoughts of others
- Accepting input from others while leading these same individuals
- Explaining reasons for certain choices and behaviors while remaining
  open to feedback
- Directing others in some areas and following others in different areas

Verb	Gerund/Nominalization	Active, Experiential
(-) Follow (-) Act out (+/-) Control (-) Refuse to participate (-) Don't ask (-) Defend	• Advocating while listening • Accepting while leading • Explaining while being open to feedback • Directing and following • Asking while being confident • Justifying while being accepted	• Jeopardy game on facilitation styles, double-bind coin flip, stepping stones (Aubrey, 2009) • Experiential actions of mother in balance of "win-win" situations: following and leading, listening as well as sharing, etc.

FIGURE 11.6 The supervisor's process of linking verbs, gerunds, nominalizations, and reframing negative interpretations into active, experiential activities with appropriate frameworks in Case 3.

- Asking questions of others to learn while being confident in self-abilities
- Justifying reasons for actions while still being confident of being accepted

In dysfunctional structures, any one of these behaviors could be seen as oppositional instead of complementary. By building confidence and encouraging "falling forward" risk-taking behavior in Rob, the supervisor was instilling a parallel process that hopefully would extend to the therapist–mother and mother–daughter relationships.

STAGE 3: EVALUATING SOLUTIONS PRODUCED IN THE SUPERVISION EXPERIENCE

In the third stage following the experiential and novel action, the supervisor and therapist evaluate the solutions from the experience and possible applications for new or revised hypotheses, therapeutic processes, and behavioral outcomes. Knight (2006) and Lowe and Guy (1996) encourage at least some part of the evaluation to be based on some level of solution-focused goals, as well as the ability of the therapist and client to use the skills developed during the supervision process. This is accomplished by evaluating what is productive, implementing what produces functional behavior for the client, and using this in the therapeutic intervention.

Along with identifying new structures and information that arise from the novel action, particular attention is paid to what is working and how to do more of this, as well as to what is not working and how to do something else. You may ask the following questions based on what you have learned:

1. What did you do to give greater attention to your therapeutic issue in the novel experience when you were productive?
2. How can you do more of this?
3. What will you do differently in situations that are not working?

TABLE 11.3 Solution-Focused Goal-Setting Guidelines

Evaluation Criteria	Key Words	Sample Questions
In the positive	Instead	What will you be doing then instead of what you're doing now?
In process form	Howing	How will you go about doing that?
In the here and now	On track	When you leave today, and you are on track, what will you be doing differently or saying differently to yourself? How about others?
As specific as possible	Specifically	How specifically will you be doing this?
	Saw you	If I saw you tomorrow behaving in the appropriate way we have discussed, what would I see you doing? How would your actions tell me that you are being successful?
Interactions with others	Interacting with others	If I saw you successfully interacting with other individuals, what would I see you doing? How would I see behaving with them?
Within the client's control	You	What will you be doing when that happens?
In the client's language	(Use the client's words)	

Expanded from the work of Walter and Peller (1992, p. 60), the eight guidelines in Table 11.3 can be used to further implement solutions produced by the ENHANCES supervision experience into goal-setting structures.

SUMMARY

Supervision of therapeutic practice is one of the cornerstones of mental health professions (Brown & Lent, 2007; Falender & Shafranske, 2004). Supervision is intended to provide professional growth for therapists, more effective therapy for clients, and some measure of protection for the welfare of clients and the public (Freitas, 2002). Probably the main purpose of supervision is to provide a source of information on the content, processes, and insights into situations that have become difficult, if not problematic, for therapists and their clients.

An active, experiential supervision model that has emerged to address these issues is the ENHANCES model (Gass & Gillis, 2010). The ENHANCES model was designed to assist with these situations by using unique sources of cognitive, affective, and kinesthetic insights to create structurally relevant experiential events that enhance the effectiveness of the supervision/feedback process. The model has been refined over the past 10 years through presentations of the model with case studies at the AEE annual international conferences, as well as pilot testing and feedback from other professionals from their use of the model. Three of the case studies from the AEE conferences are included in this chapter, as well as on video clips at http://www.kinesthetic metaphors.com.

The ENHANCES supervision model takes advantage of the parallel processes existing between the supervisor–supervisee relationship and the therapist–client relationship. When properly used, the parallel processes between these two relationships can provide insights for both the supervisor and the therapist to make therapeutic interventions more effective. This is particularly useful when the supervisor and therapist find themselves stuck or hindered in addressing issues in this process.

The key to the ENHANCES model is to structure the supervision process in an active, engaging, and informing manner that will aid the therapist in the process of therapeutic improvement. There are three main stages in the ENHANCES process. In the first stage, the supervisor engages with the therapist to promote the exploration of new hypotheses for client behaviors. In the second stage, the supervisor uses the context the therapist brings to the supervision session, along with the new hypotheses co-created by the supervisor and therapist, to conduct an action that is novel that will co-create insights into content and processes for the therapist. In the third stage following the experiential and novel action, the supervisor and therapist evaluate the solutions from the experience and possible applications for new or revised hypotheses, therapeutic processes, and behavioral outcomes.

BUILDING SOMETHING WITH THAT...

Christine Lynn Norton

I was working with a therapeutic wilderness program that led 28-day wilderness canoe trips for groups of struggling teens. I was serving as the field supervisor for a group that consisted of seven adolescent boys who had been referred to the program either by their families and/or various professionals from around the country. They were there for problems such as anger management, school failure, family problems, and substance abuse. The group consisted of five Caucasian males, one Hispanic male, and one African American male, all between the ages of 14 and 17 years. As the supervisor for this group, I was scheduled to meet them in the field partway through their expedition and lead them in several days of rock climbing, as well as check in with the field instructors to see how things were going.

My colleague and I woke early one morning and set up the climbing site in anticipation of a great day with the boys. However, when the group paddled up to our site with their field instructors, we could see that the group was storming and vying for power and control. Unknown to us until that point, the environment had become very emotionally and physically unsafe due to racial slurs and threats of physical violence. The field instructors were overwhelmed and needed support and supervision. My colleague and I immediately knew that rock climbing would not be an appropriate activity for a group at this stage due to safety concerns and the need for a higher level of trust. So we let the group know that before any climbing could occur, we would need to examine the harm that had been done in the group and revisit the group norms in order to reestablish physical and emotional safety.

The group was obviously disappointed and one young man, the African American client, felt even angrier since he had already been the target of many of the slurs and now he was also going to lose one of his climbing days. In order to help him manage his anger, we asked if he needed a time out from the group to decompress. He agreed that this was a good idea and proceeded to sit down in the dirt, huffing and cursing. I walked over to him quietly and noticed a pile of sticks nearby. "Why don't you build something with those?" I gently suggested, simply hoping to take his mind off his anger through a benign distraction. He looked at me kind of funny, but then proceeded to spend the next hour in deep focus taking those little sticks and building a type of shelter. When he was done, he was noticeably more relaxed and asked if he could show the group what he had built.

We had spent that same hour working with the other young men about how to restore the harm that had been done in the group, but they were having a hard time understanding what was such a big deal. Upon the young man's request, however, the rest of the group walked over reluctantly to where he was sitting. "See this," he shouted emphatically, pointing to his little house of sticks. "It took me an hour to build—but LOOK!" Then, he kicked with anger at the house and it collapsed, "It don't take but one second to destroy it! That's how our group is. At first, we worked so hard to get along and make it this far, but then people started talking shit and fronting, and now everything's jacked up. But we've got to rebuild it. What are we gonna do to rebuild it?!?"

This young man was now shouting and clearly had the attention of the entire group in a way that we had not. From this demonstrative outburst, we were able to sit back down with the group as a whole and talk about the problems the group was having. We sat *all day* with that group, sometimes meeting with the boys one-to-one and sometimes sitting all together. At the end of the day, everyone had recommitted to the group norms and had taken responsibility for their part in the group conflict. Just before the sun was setting, I had to run back down the trail to take down the climbing site for the night, only to have to put it up early the next day for the group to climb. But that time, they were ready— although they wouldn't have been without our assessment that the activity we had planned was no longer appropriate for where the group was at, as well as without the magical surprise of one young man's anger channeled into a little stick house. This is an example of what I call adventure therapy.

I have always loved being in nature, and I have gravitated naturally to risk and adventure. However, it wasn't until I was 19 and I completed an Outward Bound course with Hurricane Island that I realized I could lead others in transformational wilderness experiences. This course changed the trajectory of my life and after college I decided to live and work outdoors at the Salesmanship Club Youth camp with young people who were dealing with emotional problems. This year-round therapeutic camping work inspired me to pursue an advanced degree in social work so I could be more informed about the complex interrelationship between human beings in the social environment. But I never gave up my belief that human beings' relationship with the natural environment was also crucial. Since completing my master's degree, I have had the privilege of practicing adventure therapy for several amazing organizations, including Outward Bound, OMNI Youth Services, and various schools and mentoring programs. Now, as an assistant professor, I work to train social work students in how to engage in adventure-based group work.

Chapter 12

Adventure Therapy Ethics

Above all else, do no harm.

Hippocrates
300 BC

In the mental health professions, many of the decisions made with clients are concerned with what is right, best, or appropriate at that time. Many of these decisions involve possible and differing choices in the selection of professional behaviors, and sometimes these choices conflict with one another. When these choices are made, they usually affect judgments leading to professional actions taken by adventure therapists. Examine the following common questions facing adventure therapists, often on a daily basis:

- How should I interact with this client?
- What should I do with this client with these specific issues as an adventure therapist?
- What would be the right technique to use with this client?
- Is this the most appropriate adventure therapy experience to use with this client?
- What is an example of good behavior in this adventure therapy experience?
- What would be the best way for me to care for my client given what they need?

For each of these questions a variety of answers could be provided. When one of these answers is selected as the best answer, fits most appropriately into the relative context of the client's life, and the resulting actions for the client are better than other choices, then we are concerned with ethics. Does this sound difficult and potentially contentious? It certainly can be, but some of the most important professional decisions made in adventure therapy deal with ethics.

The field of ethics covers a wide variety of issues and subjects. Whole cultures and countries make important ethical decisions every day based on their belief systems. This is also true for professional organizations intersecting with adventure therapy programs, such as the American Psychological Association, American Alliance of Marriage and Family Therapists, National Association of Social Workers, American Counseling Association, and Association for Specialists of Group Work. This chapter centers its attention on how adventure therapists might consider preparing themselves for ethical situations. Then, when adventure therapists find themselves in ethical dilemmas, what should they do, who might they be, and what actions should they take to care for their clients?

PREPARING TO BE AN ETHICAL ADVENTURE THERAPIST

Probably the first point to understand when preparing to strive toward ethical action is that, regardless of the amount of training, the process never ends! Changing factors in society, combined with advances in the field, are just two of the factors that require adventure therapists to continually prepare to address potential ethical dilemmas they may encounter. Although they are certainly not the only sources of preparation one can receive, several of the methods used to aid in such a preparation process include:

1. *Understand* your nonnegotiable values
2. *Recognize* your own value systems as well as those of your clients
3. *Know* the ethical standards of your profession and use them
4. *Practice* ethical decision-making by reviewing ethical cases related to your practice
5. Continually *advance* your professional practice through continuing education and receiving supervision and feedback while working with clients

Know and Understand Your Nonnegotiable Values

Adventure therapists work with a wide range of clients. Some of the clients' belief systems, preferred behaviors, and value systems are not only different than those of the therapists who work with them, but may involve situations where these differences cause some sort of conflict between client and therapist. Note that most therapists can effectively work with clients whose behaviors differ or even conflict with the belief systems of the therapist. However, sometimes these conflicting value systems can be so objectionable or oppositional that a therapist might find it too difficult to negotiate or effectively work on these issues with the client (e.g., it would hinder the therapist's ability to construct a positive therapeutic alliance). Priest, Gass, and Gillis (1999, 2009) labeled such values as *nonnegotiable values*—that is, values you are unable to negotiate or adapt to serve in a positive therapeutic manner for your potential client.

One way adventure therapists can address nonnegotiable values is to proactively identify those beliefs, behaviors, and values that they are unwilling to negotiate to be able to work with a client. For example, a client may possess violent behaviors and use extremely objectionable comments in a way that a therapist finds so unacceptable, objectionable, or offensive that the therapist does not believe he or she could use appropriate therapeutic techniques to work with this client. In such cases, the nonnegotiable value regarding these behaviors leads the adventure therapist to proactively eliminate ethical conflict by recognizing certain client behavior that is nonnegotiable, not enter into a therapeutic relationship with this particular client, and refer the client to an appropriate and qualified therapist.

Understand Your Values and Those of Your Clients

When you agree to work with a client, a critical preliminary step in adventure therapy is to understand how your values, as well as those of your clients, connect or conflict in terms of culture, worldview, and identity factors (Wilcoxon, Remley, Gladding, & Huber, 2007). Values develop through a compilation of various personal experiences, learned behaviors, and social interactions. Understanding how values affect and interact with an individual's culture, worldview, and identity factors is a critical first step in using appropriate ethical decision-making processes in adventure therapy. Failure to consider the value structures of clients by an adventure therapist can result in the following presumptions and errors (Hoare, 1991; Wilcoxon, Remley, Gladding, & Huber, 2007):

- Overemphasizing cultural similarities, leading to a "melting pot" mindset
- Overgeneralizing differences, leading to stereotyping
- Assuming the need to emphasize *either* similarities *or* differences, leading to devaluation of the uniqueness of each client's perspective and values
- Development of pseudospeciation, where a form of oppression develops around the idea that one set of culturally derived values and perspectives are superior to others

One model to help assess the way various cultural, worldview, and identity factors affect professional ethics in adventure therapy has been adapted from the work of Jones and McEwen (2000), Baruth and Manning (2003),

Carter and McGoldrick (2005), and Gass (2005). This model identifies 10 areas for adventure therapists to assess before making ethical decisions with clients in adventure therapy:

1. *Gender:* Biological differences, cultural and socialization processes, potential gender-based differences
2. *Race:* Stereotypical assumptions, institutionalized forms of oppression or privilege
3. *Ethnicity:* Commonality of heritage/nationality, shared political experiences, common values
4. *Social class:* Socioeconomic status, perceived power or powerlessness, risk or security, privilege or helplessness associated with social class
5. *Sexual orientation:* Levels of acceptance and support, discrimination and prejudice in social, work, and institutional circumstances
6. *Disability:* Struggle for awareness, sensitivity to bias, stereotyping, discrimination, and depression, personal identity associated with personal factors versus disability
7. *Religion:* Religious traditions and practices, codify set of beliefs and practices, socialization and distinct groups, specific rules, codes of conduct, ceremonies, traditions and values, privilege versus oppression
8. *Worldview:* A composite picture of one's association with a particular reference group, individual experiences of this reference group, and the frame of reference influencing perceptions and values
9. *Psychosocial identity:* Related elements of acculturation and socialization, contextual nature of one's identity, dynamic nature of one's identity
10. *Systemic fit of change:* The manner and level of congruence of fit on how behavioral change fits into the system of the individual involved in adventure therapy practices

These 10 items are to be used in a self-assessment. They can indicate areas of congruence and incongruence between an adventure therapist and her or his clients, as well as inform the adventure therapist regarding the selection and potential use of particular ethical decision-making processes. Just because there are different values between an adventure therapist and her or his clients does not necessarily mean the adventure therapist cannot deliver ethically sound treatment. But when differences occur, professional judgment needs to guide a decision as to whether these differences prevent the application of such treatment. Let us examine how three of these factors influence the type of decisions made with particular clients.

Potential Gender Differences

Throughout a series of articles, Mitten (1994, 1996, 2002) advocated for the ethical use of different adventure therapy program elements for women with a history of sexual abuse. Rather than use the original program elements designed primarily for men on standard Outward Bound courses, she used the concept of ethics to encourage and promote the focusing of treatment objectives and corresponding program activities and facilitation around the following:

1. Having women clients learn what risks to take
2. Focusing on the learning of trust with the support of other women
3. Relying on other program participants for emotional support
4. Using the environment for a source of restoration and mental recovery rather than strictly challenging experiences
5. Having women clients be in charge of who they can physically and emotionally trust and who they cannot trust
6. Encouraging female clients with a history of sexual abuse issues to say no to activities where they feel they are being pushed into participation

Beyond treatment differences for women, Mitten also advocated for changes in adventure therapy based on treatment differences for gender-specific perspectives. Although not completely finished, her work and others' work in this area have led the field to focus on more specific treatment objectives and the need to vary adventure therapy treatment practices not only for gender issues but also other particular client characteristics.

Potential Ethnic Differences

At a professional conference in 1991, Dan Garvey, executive director of the Association for Experiential Education AEE, was delivering a keynote address. Two members from a youth organization in India attended his presentation. During his keynote address, the concept of a solo was introduced, with several features highlighted, including the opportunity to select to not eat over a 24-hour period, sleep alone on the ground with only a tarp, and be alone for the 3-day solo period. After the keynote was completed, the two professionals from India came forward and asked Dan why he would consider using a solo as a growth experience. They politely explained that they were having a hard time seeing the value of the solo experience. They further stated that the conditions of the solo represented the conditions of most of their youth they were attempting to change—children who often were alienated and abandoned, youth who often went for 24 hours or longer without food to eat, and clients who had to sleep alone on the street with just a tarp or less for protection. They were wondering how the solo experience would be valuable for their program.

As highlighted in this story, different ethnic groups sometimes view certain elements of adventure experiences differently based on their ethnic culture and background. Ashley (1990) and Hall (1987) both examined the

issue of under-representation of ethnic minorities in the field of adventure programming. Their research found several reasons for this under-representation,
including an inability for certain ethnic minorities to relate to adventure experiences (particularly in wilderness settings); preconceived stereotypes that
certain ethnic groups do not participate in adventure experiences; perceptions
around wilderness areas as being an alien, white, Anglo cultural environment;
conflict with basic cultural values; and potential feelings of distrust by some
members of ethnic minorities (Ashley, p. 372).

Potential Systemic Conflicts

While centering attention on the individual needs of the client in an adventure
therapy experience, it is equally important to understand how the changed client integrates back into their social structures upon completion of the adventure therapy experience. As pointed out by Gass (1998a, 2005), it is important
to understand the interconnectedness between clients and the value systems
of their social structures. Although individual clients possess their own individual characteristics, they are part of a broader system of social structures
that have various degrees of systemic influence on the individual client. When
the clients' changes complement their broader social structures, these changes
are supported and not only maintain their gains but also evolve as the client
grows. However, when these broader systems are conflicted with the changes
undergone by the client, problems occur. To explain this alignment, Gass
(2005) used a metaphor of a kaleidoscope. As with client's objectives, the
goal of the kaleidoscope in achieving the "end result" is to orient the various
structures in an appropriate alignment that supports the client's goals. Figure
12.1 shows the variety of systems to consider in just one adolescent client's
process.

   Remember, the purpose of adventure therapists assessing their values in
these 10 areas is to prepare them for potential ethical decision-making processes they might use with clients. Proactively examining these concepts not
only prepares adventure therapists to handle potential conflicts with clients
in their value systems, but also guides therapists to select and use ethical
decision-making processes that make the most informed ethical decision.

Case Example of Conflicting Worldviews and Psychosocial Identities

I (Mike) was once asked to work with a client who possessed a history of
violence toward women. For a number of reasons based on incidents and
previous history, this young man had been caught by the police stalking
pregnant women with hostile intent to attack and beat them with a baseball
bat found in the trunk of his car. What made me examine my ability to effectively work with this young man even closer was that my spouse happened to
be pregnant with one of our children at the time. I found myself questioning

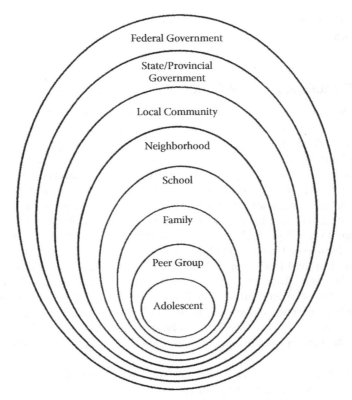

FIGURE 12.1 Systems surrounding an adolescent in treatment. A single adolescent in treatment is "nested" or surrounded by a variety of other influencing systemic elements affecting her or his behavior. For treatment to be sustained and lasting, therapists need to consider how these systemic elements can be aligned to support, or change to support, the individual adolescent after treatment.

my ability to work with this young man effectively given his behavior (current worldview) and my own personal family situation (psychosocial identity) at the time.

There obviously were a number of things I needed to consider in the ethics of working with this young man. For example, would elements of my psychosocial identity (e.g., my personal family situation) cause me to be ineffective in my therapeutic work with him? Would my worldview on the use of violence against women interfere with our therapeutic work? What would I do if he asked me in therapy if I was married and did my wife and I have children? Or was she pregnant? With the support of my clinical supervisor, I considered these issues and believed I could work with this young man to help eliminate his destructive violent behaviors despite my circumstances. We began therapy and were able to create an effective therapeutic alliance, much of it initially around our joint interest in following a local baseball team. Our work on several issues proved to be successful for him and his violence and other therapeutic needs were replaced with positive and constructive life tasks.

Know Established Ethical Codes of Conduct and Use Them

Along with determining appropriate clients to work with in adventure therapy, it is also important to be fully cognizant of what are considered ethical behaviors in the field. Fortunately for the field of adventure therapy, there has been the development of ethical guidelines with the support of allied disciplines. Probably one of the greatest advancements in ethical decision making for adventure therapy was the formulation of ethical guidelines by the Association of Experiential Education (AEE) Therapeutic Adventure Professional Group (AEE, 1992). These ethical guidelines were created with the support of the American Psychological Association, American Alliance of Marriage and Family Therapists, Council on Outdoor Education for the American Alliance of Health, Physical Education & Dance, Council of Accreditation of Services for Families and Children, and Worldwide Outfitters and Guides Association (WOGA). Twenty-seven professionals came together at a session prior to the 1991 AEE conference to produce these guidelines through a process of consensus. A copy of these guidelines can be found in Appendix B. These guidelines are broken into seven categories in the following areas and subareas:

1. **Competence** (e.g., not working beyond your capability): Boundaries of competence, continuing training
2. **Integrity** (e.g., using honesty, fairness, and respect in therapy with clients): Interaction with other professionals, supervision
3. **Responsibility** (e.g., caring for the clients' well-being as well as the environment): Basis for professional judgments, initiation and length of services, and concern for the environment
4. **Respect** (e.g., fundamental rights, dignity, worth of clients and peers): Policy against discrimination, ethic of empowerment, describing the nature and results of adventure therapy, informed consent, fees, advertisement, distortion of information by others, and public opinions and recommendations
5. **Concern** (e.g., clients' physiological and psychological needs and well-being): Professional relationships, dual relationships, sexual relationships, physical contact/nonsexual contact, behavior management, physical needs of clients, physical treatment of clients, appropriate use of risk, assisting clients in obtaining alternative services, confidentiality, use of case materials with teaching or professional presentations, and storage and disposal of client materials
6. **Recognition** (e.g., social responsibility toward the broader community needs)

7. **Objectivity** (e.g., limiting relationships with clients only to the roles of adventure therapist and client)

The establishment and implementation these guidelines has also positively affected other areas of the field and its practices. For example, the ethics section in the original *Manual of Program Accreditation Standards for Adventure Programs* (Williamson & Gass, 1993) presented all of these seven guidelines for accredited programs to follow. Major elements of these guidelines still exist in the fifth and current AEE program accreditation standards manual edition (Smith, 2009). Although these guidelines have not established a required ethical code in the field and have not been established as "rules" adventure therapists must follow or be censured from practice, they do show that the field is certainly on record as supporting these types of practices.

Since the time these guidelines were produced in 1991, the adventure therapy field has certainly evolved in ethical applications. As mentioned in Chapter 1, one area of additional focus receiving a great deal of attention and that needs to be included is the concept of social justice. One way to encapsulate additional guidelines is to incorporate the work and writings of Warren, Mitten, and Loeffler (2008), Flippo and Warren (2010), and others, along with the structure of aspirational ethics advanced by the National Association of Social Workers (NASW, 1999), to include:

8. **Service** (e.g., assist people in need by addressing client social issues): The ultimate goal of this ethical principle may be to serve clients in certain ways so they become servant leaders themselves within their own culture and society (Greenleaf, 1977). As pointed out by Warren (2008, p. 399), the idea of service "needs to be critically analyzed on how it is framed and carried out." For example, remember the potential conflicts of ethical differences presented earlier in this chapter with Dan Garvey and the two professionals from India.

9. **Social Justice** (e.g., challenge social injustices, particularly for those clients who are subject to society's greatest levels of unjust actions and perspectives): Adventure therapists, as well as other mental health professionals, often work with clients who may find themselves in extremely vulnerable and powerless situations. It should be the goal and focus of adventure therapists to advocate for and strongly support these individuals and groups of people. This could include individuals experiencing prejudice, poverty, discrimination, or other forms of social injustice. Active efforts should be made by adventure therapists to address social injustice at all levels, using the tools of awareness, comprehensive knowledge, dialogue, action, advocacy, and decision making to rectify unjust social imbalances.

10. **Dignity and Worth of the Person** (e.g., respecting the personal rights of each individual): Making sure to match the context of cultural and

ethnic diversity, empowering clients to create their own destiny and pathway to achieve their own goals, should be a key focus of adventure therapists. With socially responsible self-determination as the focus, adventure therapists should respect and empower the personal rights of each individual.

11. **Importance of Human Relationships** (e.g., recognizing the key value of relationships): As presented earlier in the section on systemic conflict, it is important for adventure therapists to understand the role of human relationships in changing behavior, as well as maintaining functional behavior once it is achieved. Clients just don't wake up one day and say, "Oh, I think I'm going to be dysfunctional or problematic today!" Quite often it is an orchestration of human relationships that greatly contributes to dysfunctional behavior. But these human relationships, when restructured, informed, or changed in some other manner, also can serve to promote or support functional change. Equipped with this knowledge, adventure therapists often look to strengthen relationships among people in "a purposeful effort to promote, restore, maintain, and enhance the well-being of individuals, families, social groups, organizations, and communities" (NASW, 2011, p. 1).

A second and emerging source of ethical guidelines for adventure therapy are located on the Best Practices site of the Therapeutic Adventure Professional Group (TAPG) of the AEE (http://tapg.aee.org/tapg/ethics/scope). These guidelines and their supportive references and readings represent an organic and emerging dialogue to inform professionals on emerging developments in the field.

Although all of these guidelines represent critical steps in advancing the adventure therapy profession, simply following such guidelines does not release or excuse professionals from the need to apply and use principles of ethical judgment. For example, such guidelines may conflict within certain cultures and require professionals to adapt them in such instances. Or situations can arise where conflicts exist among legal, organizational, and ethical guidelines. Conflict between ethical guidelines and their interpretation will likely arise and lead to ethical dilemmas to resolve. This is why just having and following ethical guidelines are not enough for professionals. To be fully prepared to handle ethical dilemmas, adventure therapists must not only follow ethical guidelines, but must also apply such guidelines in practical situations, often through the use of ethical case studies.

Practice with Case Studies for Ethical Preparation

The use of case studies can provide another vehicle in the ethical preparation of adventure therapists. Case studies are probably most valuable for professional and ethical development when therapists hear or read about a particular case from another therapist, and then adapt elements of the case to their own clients.

The following illustration is a case example of using an adventure experience as a medium for change with a couple. I used the framework of the activity "Boundary Setting" with "Push off/Take a Step/Collaborative Competition" and several extensions/variations to mirror the clients' issues and potential resolutions. The therapeutic objective was to assist this couple in rewriting their "script" for sexual intimacy with one another. "John" and "Bill" were a couple who had been committed to each other for 13 years and had two sons. Bill was a victim of sexual abuse as a young boy, and while this experience sometimes had negative effects on their ability to be sexually intimate with one another throughout their relationship, it is particularly problematic now when John initiates sexual intimacy with Bill, who experiences flashbacks and dissociative states. The power and prevalence of these experiences are also beginning to effect other areas of their relationship. Although the entire family did participate in therapy, this session was only John and Bill.

I introduced the activity in the following manner: "I'd like to do an exercise with the two of you to explore what may be currently occurring in your relationship. What I would like to do is have John stand on one side of the room and walk toward Bill with Bill directing how close John can walk toward him. Start facing one another from across the side of the room standing with your palms up at your side. Bill, the guideline for you to use is that John can walk toward you only as long as you feel comfortable. At the first sign that you feel uncomfortable, to the point where you do not feel you are able to handle your 'uncomfortableness,' tell John to stop. He must stop. In fact, ask him to back up to a point where you feel comfortable with his distance from you." (We did this exercise a number of times until John and Bill could stand together with their palms barely touching.) "Now that you have arrived in this comfortable position, I would like for you to work together in trying out 'cooperative touching, (Rohnke, 1977).' Standing toe to toe and palm to palm as you are, John, try and follow Bill's movements in slow motion—Bill guides while John does his best to follow your lead. There may be times where, John, you will be able to pick up Bill's cues and guidance. There may also be other times where you may have difficulty following Bill's cues and guidance. While both of these times may exist, I encourage the two of you to explore what works when John is able to follow Bill and what to do differently when John is unable to follow. Explore the different positions you can guide one another to without feeling uncomfortable and enjoying the presence and love of one another."

This activity took two sessions. During the first session, Bill was able to tolerate John within 3 feet. The remainder of the session explored what Bill did to enable John to come as close as he did and to also reinforce and punctuate John's ability to follow Bill's guidelines without becoming too frustrated.

The homework assignment was to do this exercise with the strict guidelines that the couple was to never exceed the "boundary" where Bill would feel uncomfortable. For this particular couple and issue, the couple was encouraged not to have sexual relations with one another between therapy sessions (Gass, 2009).

Lung (2009) included ideas from this case study to use with her clients, making several revisions to make it relevant for her clients. Examples of the adaptations she made were having "Martha" use a foam fun noodle as her bumper (Martha's idea) as "Chris" closed his eyes to focus on Martha's voice (the couple's idea). This type of appropriate sharing and professional adaptation is one of the major benefits of using case studies.

Note that using case studies is an ethical issue in itself. Primarily done to protect the confidentiality of the client, certain guidelines must be considered before using this informative teaching tool. While each discipline has particular guidelines regarding the sharing of information concerning clients, whether it be with preparing case studies, professional presentations, or written articles, the Human Givens Institute (2011) provides one set of guidelines that cover most disciplines' directives and concerns. The recommended steps for writing about and using case studies are:

1. Before using case studies, consider whether the use of some other alternative method may produce the same results (e.g., reporting the results of research studies).
2. If deciding to use case studies, in order to avoid issues of client privacy and consent, determine whether it is possible or not to present therapeutic principles and applications by not using an actual case example.
3. If still deciding to use case examples, understand the reasons for doing so. Generally speaking, case studies are used to illustrate actual examples of successful treatment strategies for the benefit of colleagues and their similar clients.
4. If the decision is made to use material from an actual case with clients, written permission must be obtained from the client to use this material for this specific purpose. Care is taken to carefully explain to clients the purpose of the case study and how their identity will be protected.
5. When the identity of a client is used or published, protecting that identity is of the utmost importance. This is typically accomplished by changing the name and other identifying factors of the client. These factors could include locations, gender, organizations, specialized occupations, or any other information that could identify the client.
6. Use your supervisor or more than one objective colleague to review this process.

Probably one of the most important ethical case studies for every adventure therapist to proactively consider is the area concerning the "risk–benefit analysis" of adventure experiences as treatment. Willi Unsoeld introduced the first form of this ethical issue in a series of speeches in the 1970s, and a similar case study was formalized by Hunt (1990) in a book that continues to be one of the best resources on ethical case studies in the field of adventure programming. The ethical issue facing Unsoeld occurred during a presentation in which he was inviting parents to send their children on an Outward Bound course. At the end of his presentation, a parent came up to Unsoeld and asked him, "If I let my child go on this Outward Bound course, can you guarantee for me that he will come back alive?" Unsoeld replied, "I can't guarantee his safety and that he can return back alive, but I can guarantee that if he doesn't go on this experience he will lose his soul" (Unsoeld, 1974).

While most professionals cannot match the flair of the dramatic possessed by Unsoeld, the question remains a critical one. Is it worth the risk of sending clients on adventure therapy programs knowing that it is impossible to guarantee their safety? Stated another way, are the risks of adventure therapy worth the benefits? The ethics behind such decision making become even more onerous and value laden for the program when many of the parents of children considering such programs are in compromised situations. That is, most parents have exhausted themselves attempting to find help and support for assisting their child with their therapeutic issues. Given they have literally and figuratively exhausted numerous options, they may be more susceptible to consider *any* choice, let alone a *good* choice. When working with parents in such vulnerable situations, the ethical responsibility of the program becomes greater. This ethical issue is debated later on in this chapter, but several other ethical decisions should be proactively considered first in case studies before they are ever encountered in the field:

- Ethical issues with clients "forced" to participate in an adventure therapy program
- Questions around the use of secrecy, deception, and withholding information as ethical approaches, or not, in adventure therapy programs (Hunt, 1990)
- Ethics around therapeutic contracts
- Issues of confidentiality, professional disclosure statements, privileged communication, and privacy on adventure therapy programs
- Sexual issues not only between staff and participants, but staff and staff, as well as between participants in voluntary adventure therapy programs with consenting clients
- Ethics around issues of client autonomy, welfare, financial arrangements, and informed consent
- Social justice ethics
- Ethics around contributions to the profession and community
- Ethics around adventure therapy competence, practice, and due care

- Ethics around dual relationships
- Ethics of if, how, and when escort services should be used to bring clients to adventure therapy courses
- Ethics of choice and other variables with individuals who are incarcerated

Certainly many other resources (e.g., Hunt, 1990, 2009; Johnson & Fredrickson, 2000; Mitten, 1994, 1996, 2002; Priest & Gass, 2005) spend more effort and time on analyzing and promoting various ethical models for use in the adventure therapy field. Interested readers are encouraged to investigate these as well as other resources.

Continuing Education and Supervision for Ethical Maintenance and Growth

Most other mental health therapies require licensed professionals to maintain if not enhance their professional development through continuing education experiences. Certainly ethical (and effective) professionals using adventure therapy experiences maintain as well as increase their professional development through continual learning and ongoing professional, up-to-date interaction with the field and other colleagues. Although not always limited to these factors, most professionals must complete the following within a specified period of time (e.g., 2 years) in order to remain in good standing or continue to possess a license to practice as a therapist:

1. Complete a renewal application verifying certain requirements as well as ascertaining whether there are any active complaints against the therapist or if they have violated any particular laws related to practicing therapy
2. Complete specified continuing education requirements in relevant professional areas for a specified length of time (e.g., 40–100 hours)
3. Have these documents notarized
4. Pay an established professional fee to maintain licensure

In addition to continuing education and maintaining a professional license, therapists also use supervision as a way to grow professionally, deliver more effective therapy, and receive objective feedback to protect the welfare of clients (Freitas, 2002; Gass & Gillis, 2010). While traditional supervision models certainly provide one source of professional development, given the experiential nature of adventure therapy, professionals are encouraged to explore integrated models of supervision, such as the one presented in Chapter 11.

ETHICAL DECISION-MAKING PRACTICES: WHAT SHOULD I DO? WHO SHOULD I BE? HOW SHOULD I TAKE CARE OF MY CLIENTS?

Regardless of how much preparation an adventure therapist completes, situations will arise that will require the implementation of an ethical decision-making process to determine the best ethical professional practice. This chapter highlights one ethical decision-making model that uses the intersecting perspectives of three sources of ethical decision making relevant to the adventure therapy field: principle ethics, virtue ethics, and feminist ethics.

Principle ethics are typically based on objective, predetermined, and impartial rules, which often are pre-established by a governing body or professional organization. They are based on the belief that the issues being examined are similar in context, and that these issues can be compared for relative merit (Priest & Gass, 2005). Principle ethics are independent of the situation, creating specific rules for all situations.

Virtue ethics are guided by the belief that ethical situations are independent of one another, with each situation possessing its own particular informing factors and influences. Contrary to principle ethics, virtue ethicists believe you *cannot* link any decisions made in one situation to another situation, and that ethical behavior must be determined independently for each specific situation. Virtue ethics are guided by the particular virtues associated with being a moral outdoor leader rather than the principles of being ethical. Virtue ethics are dependent on the situation, creating specific rules for each particular situation (Priest & Gass, 2005).

Feminist ethics seek to take into account the emotional, intuitive, and individual characteristics of the client in the ethical decision-making process. In fact, feminist ethical decision-making models seek to include the client in the resolution of the ethical dilemma whenever appropriate and possible (Hill, Glaser, & Harden, 1998). Feminist ethical principles consider the personal experiences and involvement of the therapist as part of the resolution of the ethical dilemma, potential power differences between the therapist and client, and the influence of possible cultural biases in making value-based decisions.

For comparison, the following three questions typify the central focuses of each of these three ethical perspectives:

1. Principle ethics look to answer "What shall I do?" and "Is this situation unethical?" (Jordan & Meara, 1990, p. 108).
2. Virtue ethics are concerned with professional character traits, focusing on "Who shall I be?" and "Am I doing the best for my client?" (Jordan & Meara, 1990, p. 108).
3. Feminist ethics look to answer "How does who I am affect the process?" (Hill, Glaser, & Harden, 1998, p. 111).

The model presented here consists of a series of five steps in a process of ethical decision making. It follows the stages of the models developed by Kitchner (1984) and Hill, Glaser, and Harden (1998), but incorporates the elements of all three forms of ethics in its series of five decision-making steps. In this model, if you cannot make a well-founded ethical decision at one step, you advance to the next one. The five specific steps of this model for making ethical decisions are intuition, option listing, ethical rules, ethical principles, and ethical theory. In order to illustrate how each of these five steps can be applied, the ethical dilemma introduced earlier in the chapter on the risk versus the benefits of adventure therapy will be used following each of the steps.

Step 1: Intuition

Ethical responses in the *intuition* level come from prereflective or gut reactions to the question, "What feels right?" The ethical beliefs associated with these decisions are so established that the answer is obtained through ordinary moral sense. There is little need to even consider that the decision exists since the ordinary moral sense process is predetermined, usually by your "individual experience, ethical knowledge, and level of ethical development" (Zygmond & Boorhem, 1989, p. 271). In their feminist model, Hill, Glaser, and Harden refer to a "feeling of discomfort" (1998, p. 111) as a potential first indication of an ethical dilemma.

Consider the following three methods to use intuitive responses:

1. Imagine you are at a professional conference and you are asked to stand up in front of a group of colleagues. Would you be comfortable stating your use of this particular professional action in front of the group?
2. Use the "well-lit room" test (Haas & Malouf, 1989). Do you feel comfortable subjecting your choice to the scrutiny of others (Hill, Glaser, and Harden, 1998, p. 114)?
3. If you had a child of your own in a similar situation, would you feel comfortable having your child experience the ramifications of what you are stating or proposing?

If you see yourself being comfortable making these statements in these situations, your actions are probably ethical. However, if you would feel uneasy about making these statements in these situations, you may want to consider further examination of this professional action to evaluate its ethical use.

In the example presented earlier, imagine that an adolescent client's parent comes up to you and asks, "Can you assure the safety of my child your adventure therapy program?" Hopefully you would not answer the question with an unequivocal "yes." The response of the adventure therapist requires an explanation and a listing of the possible benefits and risks in relative comparison to truly help a parent to make an informed decision. Such actions represent how we want to behave with our clients and treat them as individuals. In order to accomplish this, the adventure therapist moves onto the second stage of the decision-making process.

Step 2: Option Listing

When you feel uncomfortable about the ethical decision you are examining at the intuition level, *option listing* becomes the next step in this ethical decision-making process. This step includes listing the potential options the adventure therapist can take, evaluating these options (e.g., the strengths and weaknesses of each listed option), their outcomes, and their potential ramifications (Priest & Gass, 2005). Hill, Glaser, and Harden (1998) recommended brainstorming possibilities when engaging in any sort of cost-benefit analysis for each option, while also considering the practical and prudent values associated with each option (Hass & Malouf, 1989).

Consider again the case example of the parent asking about the safety of his adolescent child and the relative merit of the adventure therapy program. Concerning the "costs in terms of risk" side of this discussion, ethically responsible adventure therapy programs would not only have a program record of annual incidents combined with number of days served with similar clients but also information on the latest trend analyses of incidents and accidents in the field, much like the information found in Chapter 9 on risk management.

If further depth and knowledge is needed, the therapist also should be able to inform the parent and adolescent of the elements of the program that produced the most incidents, accidents, and injuries in programming; what the program did to limit these elements; and what the adolescent could do with the program staff to reduce exposure to these actual risks and the ramifications of particular actions (e.g., limit the effects of contraindications to medicines by being forthright with the program staff, accurately assess the physical fitness all of the adolescents as well as assess any potentially contributing previous physical ailments). Other additional elements of risk management could be shared with the parent in this process, as found in Chapter 9.

Concerning the benefits side of this discussion, ethically responsible presented in Chapter 13 adventure therapy programs would not only have a record of particular outcomes the program has achieved with similar clients and the lasting effect of the treatment program, but also comparative statistics to present to this parent (i.e., treatment comparison statistics of the outcomes of treatment with this adventure therapy program compared to other forms of treatment available for this adolescent). It is important to recognize that findings on the study produced by Gillis, Gass, and Russell (2008) not only aid in the statistical analysis and validation of the program's effectiveness, but also assist in ethical decision-making processes like this one. When making this presentation, it is important to remember that treatment staff have just as much of an ethical duty to try and serve parents and adolescents in vulnerable positions as those parents and adolescents who come from well-resourced backgrounds.

In another example, one practice under seemingly constant ethical examination is the use of escort services to transport unwilling and involuntary adolescents to wilderness therapy programs. Using option listing as an initial technique provides valuable information and a foundation for determining whether such a professional practice in the situation is ethical or not. Note that option listing itself does not provide the answer or decision, but instead outlines and provides the background for the next three steps used to determine whether or not the professional practice is ethical.

Another important consideration with option listing is the type of adventure experience selected for the therapeutic intervention. As the field of adventure programming has evolved, certain standard activities have been found to possess relatively high levels of actual accident rates (e.g., initiative or challenge course elements like the electric fence (Rohnke, 1977) or Hanging Teeter Totter (Rohnke, 1977), wilderness therapy procedures like unaccompanied travel by clients for a final expedition). If the same therapeutic benefit can be achieved in an activity that possesses more actual accident/incident rates, then it should make ethical (as well as any other) sense to use the adventure experience with lower accident/incident rates. For example, if replacing the Hanging Teeter Totter activity with the Whale Watch (Rohnke & Butler, 1995) experience provides the same therapeutic benefit, then certainly the adventure therapist should select the Whale Watch experience.

Step 3: Ethical Rules

Once options are listed, if the client and the adventure therapist are satisfied with the ethical decision, this process ends. However, if more information is needed, the next place to turn for guidance on ethical decisions is to examine if any pre-established ethical rules for particular professional situations exist. It is highly likely other adventure therapists prior to you have previously encountered the ethical dilemma you are facing! As these individuals learned from their experiences, they often wrote down guidelines for others to follow. In mental health, psychological, legal, and medical fields, *ethical rules* have often been established as codes of conduct from the experiences of previous professionals. Professions developed such rules to maintain a certain level of ethical behavior, and the creation of ethical rules is generally considered a developmental benchmark in a particular field's level of professionalism (Priest & Gass, 2005). Some guidelines are presented in Appendix B. Others have been published by the TAPG of the AEE (Gass, 1993; Smith, 2009; see also http://tapg.aee.org/tapg/ethics) and the *Manual of Program Accreditation Standards for Adventure Programs* published by the AEE (Smith, 2009; Williamson & Gass, 1993).

In these guidelines, the ability of professionals to provide appropriate information about the risks as well as the results of therapeutic programming is seen as requisite ethical behavior. Note that such expectations also exist in the ethical codes for psychotherapy, marriage and family therapy, and social work. Given such statements, certainly the expectations for ethical adventure therapy programming around informing clients of potential risks and benefits is quite clear.

Step 4: Ethical Principles

Ethical rules do not exist for all ethical dilemmas. When such guidance does not exist or when ethical rules fail to resolve the particular ethical dilemma, adventure therapists are encouraged to follow pre-established ethical principles. *Ethical principles* are "enduring beliefs about specific modes of conduct or end-states of existence that, when acted upon, protect the interests and welfare of all of the people involved" (Zygmond & Boorhem, 1989, p. 273). Although they are more general than the ethical rules used in Step 3 of this model, ethical principles still provide guidance for adventure therapists when evaluating the options listed in Step 2.

Key to the success of this stage is the appropriate and proactive identification of ethical principles to match clients' needs while still maintaining appropriate intent, objectivity, and perspective. Here again, feminist ethics add a great deal of assistance in such a process by encouraging and reinforcing therapists to consider appropriate ethical concepts such as nonmaleficence and beneficence, as well as the intuitive or feeling concepts such as how practical and prudent solutions are for clients (Hill, Glaser, & Harden, 1998).

In combining the concepts of principle and virtue ethics, Kitchener (1984) identified five ethical principles as the most critical ones for members in the helping professions to follow: autonomy, nonmaleficence, beneficence, fidelity, and justice:

> **Autonomy** means clients have the right to freedom of action and choice as long as their behavior does not infringe on the rights of others. **Nonmaleficence** means that, above all else, no harm is done to people. **Beneficence** means the

focus of a therapist's actions is to do "the greatest good" to contribute to the health and welfare of others. **Fidelity** means to be faithful, keep promises, and be loyal and respectful of people's rights. **Justice** means individuals are treated as equals and implies a concept of fairness. (Priest & Gass, 2005, pp. 292–293)

Of these five ethical principles, the two with the greatest priority are the concepts of nonmaleficence (i.e., "above all else, do no harm") and beneficence ("seek to do the greatest good possible").

Regarding our case study around the concepts of risk and benefits in adventure therapy programming, let us place ourselves back in the mid-1970s with Willi Unsoeld and an appropriately concerned and invested parent asking the question of guaranteeing the safety of their child when participating on the Outward Bound course. Unsoeld did not possess the incident rate statistics that currently exist, nor did he have extensive statistical support for the benefits of programming besides a few tangentially related studies (Clifford and Clifford, 1967; Kelly & Baer, 1968). Using just the two central concepts of ethical principles, the following presents the ethical stance Unsoeld has to work with:

1. Nonmaleficence ("above all else, do no harm"): As stated earlier in Chapter 9, it is impossible to guarantee the safety of any participant in an adventure program. Without statistics to provide accurate comparative figures, you are left to discern what provides the least amount of harm with the adolescent: keeping him or her secure in a juvenile detention center or placing him or her on an unsubstantiated adventure therapy program? When asked such a question, Unsoeld responded as follows:

   It is real, real enough to kill you. And that impresses the kids. You get the students out there; if it's real enough to kill you, it's got to be real. And what is real is relevant.... You emphasize safety in a high-risk operation. You emphasize safety, you don't kill the risk. You emphasize safety as a rational man's effort to survival but we're going to go right ahead and stick our head in the noose ... that's the game. But we're going to be so careful in doing it, at the same time, and that delicate balance, you know, I think it just has to be transmitted, all the time we don't do anything stupid. There is enough out there to get you anyhow. (Unsoeld, 1976, in Hunt, 1990, p. 39)

It is quite possible that someone like Unsoeld could convince others to send the lessons on the adventure therapy program based on passages like the one above, but quite often and even recently, such arguments are being lost in the field.

2. Beneficence ("seek to do the greatest good possible"): As with nonmaleficence, the ethical debate of whether or not to allow the adolescent

to participate in the adventure therapy program comes down to presentations of anecdotal case studies and the belief system of individuals deciding the fate of this client.

As seen in this option listing process and its connection to ethical principles, it becomes much more difficult to justify adventure therapy approaches without the recent work in the field that has been accomplished around comparable incident statistics and research studies evaluating prescribed outcome by participating social systems (e.g., juvenile justice, third-party payers).

Step 5: Ethical Theories

The use of *ethical theories* is the last step in this process, and is only implemented when the previous four steps have not produced a clear result to the ethical dilemma. These theories should be proactively predetermined guidelines on what principles will hold the greatest value in a final decision-making processes. Such a process is obviously quite culturally related—hence the importance of proactively determining what theories will be used to determine the ethical outcomes. Two principles recommended for use by Kitchner (1984) in this process are balancing and universalizability, which are both closely related to the two concepts presented above of nonmaleficence and beneficence. Balancing theory asks you to look at your option list and select the ethical option that brings the least avoidable harm to all parties involved, or produces the greatest happiness for the greatest number (Mill, 1975). Universalizability theory asks you to look at your option list and see if it is possible to apply the same ethical actions across similar situations (e.g., if it is ethical to act one way in a situation, then act that way in similar situations) (Priest & Gass, 2005). If it is possible to make such broad generalizations or implement actions when they can be fairly and broadly applied as a universal law to all similar cases (Kant, 1964), then the behavior being examined holds a more ethical stance.

SUMMARY

In the mental health professions, many of the decisions made with clients are concerned with what is right, best, or appropriate. When one of these decisions is selected as the best answer, fits most appropriately into the relative context of the client's life, and the resulting actions for the client are better than other choices, then we are concerned with ethics. This chapter focused on (1) how adventure therapists should consider preparing themselves for ethical situations, and (2) when adventure therapists find themselves in ethical dilemmas, what should they do, who should they be, and what actions should they take to care for their clients?

Although certainly not the only sources of preparation one can receive, several of the methods used to aid in such a preparation process include: understand your nonnegotiable values, recognize your own value systems as well as those of your clients, know the ethical standards of your profession and use them, practice utilizing ethical decision making by reviewing ethical cases related to your practice, and continually advance your professional practice through continuing education and receiving supervision and feedback while working with clients.

Nonnegotiable values are values you are unable to negotiate or adapt to serve in a positive therapeutic manner for your potential client. These occur when conflicting value systems can be so objectionable or oppositional that a therapist might find it too difficult to negotiate or effectively work on these issues with the client (e.g., the therapist might find a client behavior so oppositional to the therapist's belief system that it would hinder her or his ability to construct a positive therapeutic alliance). It is also very important for adventure therapists to understand their values as well as the values of their clients so they can understand how their values and their clients' values connect or conflict in terms of culture, worldview, and identity factors.

Probably one of the greatest advancements in ethical decision making for adventure therapy was the formulation of ethical guidelines by the AEE. These ethical guidelines were done with the support of allied professional organizations and are broken into seven categories, with an additional four categories recommended for consideration as the field has evolved: competence, integrity, responsibility, respect, concern, recognition, objectivity, service, social justice, dignity and worth of the person, and the importance of human relationships.

The use of case studies can provide another vehicle in the ethical preparation of adventure therapists. Note that the use of case studies is an ethical issue in itself. Primarily done to protect the confidentiality of the client, certain guidelines must be used before utilizing this informative teaching tool.

Most mental health therapies require licensed professionals to maintain if not enhance their professional development through continuing education experiences. Certainly ethical (and effective) professionals using adventure therapy experiences maintain as well as increase their professional development through continual learning and ongoing professional, up-to-date interaction with the field and other colleagues. Adventure therapists also use supervision as a way to grow professionally, deliver more effective therapy, and receive objective feedback to protect the welfare of clients. While traditional supervision models certainly provide one source of professional development, given the experiential nature of adventure therapy, professionals are encouraged to explore integrated models of supervision like the one presented in this chapter.

Regardless of how much preparation an adventure therapist completes, situations will arise that will require the implementation of an ethical decision-making process to determine the best ethical professional practice. This chapter highlighted an ethical decision-making model using the intersecting perspectives of three sources of ethical decision making relevant to the adventure therapy field: principle ethics, virtue ethics, and feminist ethics. The model consisted of five specific steps for making ethical decisions: intuition, option listing, ethical rules, ethical principles, and ethical theory.

FINDING FAMILY BALANCE

Kim Sacksteder

Eric, a 15-year-old adolescent, entered family therapy with his mother after working with us in group therapy for a few months through his school program. Eric was referred to a day treatment program due to oppositional behaviors and aggressive outbursts at home and school. Eric struggled with anxiety, impulsivity, and a lack of coping skills.

Eric's relationship with his mother was very strained. Eric's mother was diagnosed with bipolar disorder and was seeing her own therapist. Eric was frequently frustrated with his mother due to lack of follow through, frequent mood swings, and erratic communication patterns. When Eric's mother was agitated, she often lashed out at Eric, targeting him with criticism and blame for their problems. When she was depressed, Eric was left to care for himself and his 6-year-old brother. This dynamic contributed to Eric's behavior issues, including reinforcing a lack of trust in authority figures and a need to feel in control of situations to manage his anxiety.

We began with a few initial sessions that focused on building their positive regard for one another. In the fourth session, we planned to focus on the dynamics of balance, as this dynamic was central to the family's conflicts. We did not know what would emerge from the session, but we knew selecting activities with this dynamic would bring out the issues we wanted to address and point us toward a solution.

We selected two initiative activities, Turning Over a New Leaf and Key Exchange. Both of these activities required the family to provide some physical support to one another while maintaining their balance. Eric's mother struggled physically with maintaining balance in both of these activities, while Eric was challenged to cope with managing his frustration with his mother's limitations in order to complete the activity.

During the activity, Eric became quite frustrated with his mother's physical challenges and made negative, blaming statements toward her. Eric's mother responded with quiet frustration and a calm manner while continuing to work toward a solution. Eric walked away from the activities a number of times and eventually expressed frustration verbally by stating, "She can't do it." However, Eric eventually calmed down, regrouped, and successfully completed both activities with his mother. We processed the experience, noting dynamics that emerged and behaviors that led to forward movement. In processing the family was able to discuss their limitations: mother's difficulty maintaining balance and Eric's difficulty managing his frustration without outbursts. The family reflected that they had to be able to accept one another's limitations in order to move forward and to explore how to work with one another, instead of becoming stuck in resentment.

From this point forward, the family made significant progress in their relationship and successfully completing treatment. Although they cope with the same limitations, they are currently managing their challenges without significant outbursts and violent behavior. This is an example of what I call adventure therapy.

I began my social work career in a youth crisis shelter at the age of 19. At this time I attended college, completed my undergraduate degree in psychology, and began my graduate program in social work. My work at the crisis shelter allowed me to be very creative in how I approached working with youth. It was a diverse, exciting, and nontraditional environment. Through this work, I found that if I engaged youth in a very active manner (e.g., walks, games, or outings into the community), I was much more able to connect, engage, and motivate them to make changes in their lives.

I grew up on a farm in western Ohio. The challenges of my youth inspired me to want to support other youth who were going through difficult times. My family spent a lot of time outside—at the lake, in the woods, on the river. I found comfort in being out in the woods and around the farm, especially when dealing with difficult situations.

When I put these pieces of information together, it seemed to be a great idea—engage youth in treatment through intentional use of the outdoor environment! I was thrilled with the idea but intimidated by the thought of how to build something and convince others of its validity. I began to do some research and was relieved to discover there was not only precedent for this sort of thing, but there was actually a whole field of people who were already doing it. I began reading everything I could about adventure therapy and made arrangements to do an internship at Camp Mary Orton, where I was eventually hired to build an adventure therapy program.

It was at this point that I discovered AEE and TAPG, and a whole community of adventure professionals who have supported me in my development as an adventure therapist. Twelve years later, I am incredibly grateful for the opportunities I have been given in my career.

Chapter 13

Research and Evaluation
of Adventure Therapy

As we crested the ridge in the late afternoon after an arduous hike, the group of young African American women I (Keith) was leading shook off their heavy packs, sat down on them, and quietly took long drinks from their water bottles. As the water refreshed and cooled, one of the women quietly said, "This is beautiful." My co-leader, a master's level counselor from a nearby Job Corps Center, smiled and said, "It sure is. You see that creek bed way over there? That is where we started walking today." The quiet and reflective responses and smiles that followed told a compelling story of just how far this group had really come on the trip. It seemed like forever ago that we were learning how to load and shoulder a pack, tend to blisters, and set up camp. These basic skills were automatic now, almost like breathing or walking. Our focus now was on where they wanted their lives to be in the next 5 years and what it meant to set, work for, and achieve goals. For these young women who grew up in intense urban environments, this meant graduating from Job Corps, continuing their education, and finding a career that could support them (and in many cases, their children). After a brief period on the ridge, the student leader for the day said, "Well, we better get going if we are going to make camp. That is the only place where we are going to find water tonight." A few groans and grimaces followed, with one group member saying, "Awwww, come on, we got this." Smiles followed as the women loaded up and headed down the trail to camp, where the focus of the day and evening's group talk centered on how to be resilient when confronted with negative peer pressure.

The pre-trip meetings, the wilderness experience, and the intense follow-up programming back at the Job Corps Center to revisit the core lessons learned and to check in with each other was literally life-changing for these young women. None had ever experienced anything like this, and all had a variety of severe emotional and physical trauma they were dealing with in their lives.

Did the program "work" for these adventure therapy (AT) participants? One of the women graduated from Job Corps, went to a nearby technical college, and was working in health care when we contacted her 2 years later. Another woman, full of self-confidence, took issue with something another Job Corps student said and was involved in a brief altercation. Due to a zero-tolerance policy for violence, she was summarily kicked out of the program. The answer to this question is complicated, as it always is, and is the focus of this chapter.

This chapter will provide an overview of issues related to research and evaluation in AT, explain the role that research and evaluation plays in the development of AT theory, and present the current outcomes or effects of AT reported in the literature. The introduction will distinguish key differences between research and evaluation and highlight the importance of asking hard questions that research and evaluation could, and should, address when looking at the effectiveness of any program. A discussion of evidence-based practice follows, including its definition, current initiatives, and its importance. In addition, the various types of research evidence that can inform an evidence-based practice of AT are also reviewed. Next, strategies that can help program designers, practitioners, and researchers be better consumers of research will be presented, including how to read, report, and use research findings in a variety of contexts to facilitate more informed theory development, practice, and research. This chapter concludes with a discussion of future directions, including necessary steps that AT needs to take in order to be considered an evidence-based practice in the eyes of federal funding agencies like the National Institutes of Health and professional associations like the American Psychological Association.

RESEARCH AND EVALUATION: WHAT IS THE DIFFERENCE?

The difference between research and evaluation is one that is confusing to academics and practitioners alike. Moreover, research and evaluation are indeed closely related and should be synergistic with open lines of communication flowing between evaluators and researchers in any given field. That said, what are key differences between research and evaluation? In their classic text *Evaluation*, Rossi, Lipsey, and Freeman (2004) identified five types of program evaluation: needs assessment, program theory, process analysis, impact analysis, and cost–benefit and cost-effectiveness analysis. Using these types of evaluation methods and foci, evaluation seeks to make judgments about a particular program, policy, decision, or initiative by answering questions from stakeholders and evaluators working in concert together. It answers some of the critical questions needed by programmers, including:

1. How effective was the program in meeting its goals and objectives?
2. What was the program theory that was driving the intervention?
3. How did the process work to create change?
4. How cost-effective was the initiative compared to the previous one?

In addition, evaluation is often characterized as being formative or summative in its specific aim. *Formative evaluation* addresses how programs and policies are delivered and implemented (e.g., how are staff delivering the program after being trained on the protocol?). *Summative* evaluation examines the outcomes from such endeavors (e.g., did the program work to reduce antisocial behavior in youth?). When answering these questions, evaluation is specific to the population, program, or policy being evaluated, and the findings are *not* generalized to a larger population. In recent years, the evaluation literature has exploded with the concurrent call for more formalized evaluation procedures in a variety of contexts, including health, education, and economic impact.

Representing a related but different focus, research attempts to answer specific questions and test hypotheses that go beyond a certain program or policy in order to generalize to a larger population or set of conditions. Because of this, research has significant requirements and controls placed on it in in order to achieve the desired goal of arriving at findings that have strong external validity, or the ability to be generalizable to other populations. In doing so, theory is developed through applying outcomes to similar populations, situations, and conditions. A good theory is one that allows a researcher to accurately predict what an outcome might be for a given set of conditions for a certain population. This process involves the use of stringent experimental designs that must be adhered to throughout the period of the study. For example, a classic experimental design would involve random selection into one of the three groups, where one group would receive treatment A, another treatment B, and a third group a control condition or baseline condition. The researcher would put stringent controls on each treatment condition and look for differences in the results. This study would have strong internal and external validity because of the use of a randomized assignment process and stringent controls as to the conditions. If differences were found in outcomes from the study, the results could be generalized to a similar population under similar conditions.

In the evaluation world, if one treatment process was not going well for a particular group, it would not be ethical to simply let the process continue until the study period ended. Changes would be made after reviewing the situation (formative evaluation) and the resulting outcomes would then be evaluated as to whether they worked or not for the particular group (summative evaluation).

Recent advancements in evaluation include the utilization-focused evaluation model proposed by Patton (2008) that states evaluations should be judged on their usefulness to the programs or entity being evaluated. To accomplish this, the evaluation process must be rigorous and adaptable from the beginning of the process to the very end, with input from the stakeholders and evaluators throughout the process. Evaluation by its very nature needs to be flexible and responsive to a variety of factors, primarily the stakeholders and those affected by the evaluation. That said, evaluation is not conducive to rigorous study methods such as experimental designs with stringent controls, nor should it be.

Despite these clear distinctions, research and evaluation are often confused with one another. Part of the reason for this is that there is no place where research stops and evaluation begins, and there is great disagreement in the field as to what constitutes "rigorous" research. It is not the purpose of this chapter to argue the merits of one type of research methodology over the other, nor enter the debate on whether qualitative or quantitative research can best advance the field. However, it is important to note that most of the "research" in AT reported in peer-reviewed journals and other outlets more closely resemble evaluation because of its focus on singular programs and contexts, and because most of the studies have not utilized stringent controls like experimental designs and random assignment. The ramifications of this will be discussed in subsequent sections of evidence-based practice and the section on what we know about the likely outcomes from AT programs. Except where distinction is important and clear, research and evaluation will be used somewhat interchangeably throughout this chapter.

IMPORTANCE OF ASKING THE HARD QUESTIONS

Blindly accepting a treatment, intervention, or program as being effective has grave consequences with profound impacts on the people they were designed to help in the first place. Most large-scale social programs implemented to help a specific population are supported by a variety of factions that all have a stake in the program's success, including the designers, policy makers, funders, practitioners, and, in some cases, the program participants themselves. This high-stakes game often leads to casual acceptance of a program, with supports saying that a particular program would never have been funded if it did not work, causing the proverbial tail to wag the proverbial dog. Classic examples abound when carefully examining programs like Scared Straight and the Drug Abuse and Resistance Education Programs (DARE), and in larger movements like the self-esteem movement in education in the 1970s. These programs are presented as case examples to ask a preliminary question of AT researchers and practitioners: What similarities and differences do the implementation, development, evaluation, and support of AT programs have with these case examples and what does that mean to the field?

I (Keith) remember being mesmerized by a documentary I saw on the Scared Straight program being widely implemented across the United States in the 1970s (Shapiro, 1978). At-risk youth who had committed their first offense were referred to the program and led into prisons for the day to experience the harsh reality of life in prison. Tattooed inmates screamed at the youth and told them get their acts together or they would end up in prison for life. The idea that was wildly popular and heavily funded was that the scared straight youth would return home and never again engage in acts of criminality. However, a randomized controlled trial (RCT) of the initial program found that the Scared Straight condition actually led to an *increase* in posttreatment arrests when compared to a no-treatment control condition (Lilienfield, 2007). A meta-analysis of seven studies showed that the Scared Straight interventions increased the odds that an adjudicated youth would reoffend by a ratio of between 1.6 and 1.7 to 1 (Petrosino, Turpin, & Buehler, 2003). Not only did the program not work, but it made the youth *better* reoffenders, which is called the iatrogenic effect (Weiss et al., 2005).

The DARE program was a drug and alcohol prevention program that involved uniformed officers teaching schoolchildren about the risks of drug use, while also promoting social skills necessary to stave off the inevitable negative influences of peer pressure that precede experimentation. DARE was also widely popular and received significant funding despite the fact that most research on the program indicated that is was largely or entirely ineffective (MacKillop, Lisman, Weinstein, & Rosenbaum, 2003). In many cases, the more rigorous RCTs indicated that programs based on teaching youth to resist social influences actually increased alcohol and other drug use (Werch & Owens, 2002).

Finally, several prominent psychologists have critically examined self-esteem as construct and an arbitrary marker for reasoned behavioral effects that result from increasing or enhancing someone's self-esteem. In the most comprehensive review to date, Baumeister, Campbell, Krueger, and Vohs (2003) asked the question: Does high self-esteem cause better performance, interpersonal success, happiness, or healthier lifestyles? The reason this question is so critical is because of the near consensus movement in the 1970s to promote self-esteem as a tool to work with schoolchildren struggling with academic success, and because the construct has been widely studied in AT and it is widely recognized that AT programs do indeed enhance self-esteem and self-concept. The more important question is what good does it do to enhance someone's self-esteem? What measurable behavioral, emotional, or cognitive benefits come from this? According to Baumeister et al., the research indicates that higher self-esteem was not shown to impact school performance in youth or job performance in adults; predict the quality or duration of relationships; or prevent youth from smoking, drinking, taking drugs, or engaging in early sex. In fact, if anything, higher self-esteem fosters experimentation, which may increase early sexual activity or drinking.

The lessons learned from these case studies are directly relevant to AT. Namely, widely popular and interesting social programs were assumed to be effective until rigorous research uncovered hidden truths and costs of such programs on youth. Not only were they not working, but they actually had negative effects on the vulnerable youth they were trying to protect. The ethical implications are enormous and heed a warning to practitioners and researchers that until research and evaluation has rigorously and consistently showed positive results, one should not make any assumptions as to the efficacy of programs. Moreover, measures like self-esteem, which are held in such high regard as having the ability to impact through programming, may not produce meaningful results to clients, and some cases may also be harmful.

The importance of research and evaluation in AT is critical to its development as a field. Practitioners and academics alike need to be willing to ask the hard questions, including the one asked in Chapter 3:

> What treatment, by whom, is most effective for this individual with that specific problem, under which set of circumstances? (Paul, 1967, p .111)

The answers to this question should drive the practice of AT, making it an evidence-based practice. Becoming an evidence-based practice is the ultimate goal of any health- or education-driven program or intervention. Before we move on to how research-based evidence can inform the practice of AT and what types of research methods and findings constitute the "best" evidence, a brief introduction and overview of the movement of evidence-based practice in medicine and psychology is presented to highlight key issues of what has become a critical feature of healthcare systems and policy.

EVIDENCE-BASED PRACTICE

Evidence-based practice in psychology emerged from the movement of evidence-based medicine, which has been on the forefront of advocating for a process that improved patient outcomes by informing clinical practice with relevant research (Sox & Woolf, 1993). The approach to using evidence-based medicine, as defined by Sackett, Rosenberg, Gray, Haynes, and Richardson (1996, pp. 71–72), pertains to the "conscientious, explicit and judicious use of current best evidence in making decisions about the care of individual patients." The American Psychological Association Task Force on Evidence-Based Practice (2006, p. 273) integrated this approach into psychological practice by defining EBP as the "integration of the best available research with clinical expertise in the context of patient characteristics, culture and preferences." The practice of EBP then requires a synergistic effort between practitioners and researchers to share critical insight, innovative practice, and findings between one another to arrive at what is termed *best practices*. In an ideal world, researchers should be well versed in how findings may be implemented in applied psychological settings, and practitioners should have a strong background in research methodology. The debate about which type of evidence is best is an active and interesting one, with each side presenting compelling arguments. Regardless of which side of the debate you agree or disagree with, the key issue for practitioners, evaluators, and researchers in AT is to realize that EBP in AT requires an appreciation and an integration of the multiple source of scientific evidence. The goal of such an endeavor is the enhancement in the delivery of AT to clients in a way that is mutually respectful, and in collaboration with the multiple stakeholders, which includes clients, practitioners, researchers, evaluators, policy makers, and other related mental health professionals.

In addition to enhancing AT practice, other reasons for stakeholders in AT to strive for EBP include seeking funding and support for the design, implementation, and evaluation of AT interventions. Federal health agencies, such as the Substance Abuse and Mental Health Services Administration (SAMHSA) and the Office of Juvenile Justice and Delinquency Prevention (OJJDP), each have a registry of evidence-based programs that are promoted to the public and in many cases, funded by the agencies. SAMSHA's database is called the National Registry of Evidence-based Programs and Practices (NREPP) (see Appendix D), which includes evidence-based programs that have been reviewed and rated by independent reviewers. The purpose of the registry is to "assist the public in identifying approaches to preventing and treating mental and/or substance use disorders that have been scientifically tested and that can be readily disseminated to the field" (SAMSHA, 2010). The registry is a voluntary, self-nominating system in which intervention developers elect to participate. The OJJDP has developed a Model Program Guide which is referred to as "a user-friendly, online portal to scientifically tested and proven programs that address a range of issues across the juvenile justice spectrum (OJJDP, 2010). In many cases, state agencies, private foundations, insurance companies, and others will not fund a program, intervention, or treatment, unless it is an evidence-based program on one of these registries. Therefore, the movement toward being recognized as evidence-based is both an ethical and a practical concern for AT. In recent years several initiatives have been undertaken to move AT into the realm of an evidence-based practice in line with therapeutic models, such as cognitive-behavioral therapy, and programs and interventions that use proven strategies, such as victim-offender mediation and restorative justice.

In an effort to operationalize EBP in AT, Gass (2007) created a 10-step rubric illustrating the application of EBP research elements (see Appendix D). These steps cover the areas of comparison to federal EBP models like SAMHSA and OJJDP, case studies and clinical samples, research design, cost-benefit analysis, results reporting, training models, power of research design, instrumentation, cultural variability, treatment/intervention fidelity, background literature support, replication, and length of treatment effectiveness assessed. Many of these areas represent what the future of AT research should strive for if it follows the evidence-based research paradigm.

WHAT WE KNOW AND DON'T KNOW

This section examines research in AT that specifically focused on: adventure or challenge-based courses of a variety of lengths and wilderness therapy interventions, in which nature and wilderness expeditions are reasoned to play a key factor in effectuating change in clients. It is not the purpose of this section of the book to debate definitions in the field—although it is an important debate, and one that has distinct and serious ramifications when considering research. Where needed, interpretations will be made to classify reviewed studies into one of these types of AT programs. Before key literature in these areas is reviewed and conclusions are developed, key issues associated with research in the field are discussed: (1) the black box effect, and 2) the unusual limitations and challenges experienced by researchers in AT.

The Black Box Effect in AT Research

Simply put, the black box effect in AT research refers to studies that are reported in scientific refereed journals that refer to the AT intervention in simplistic and incomplete terms that leave the reader wondering exactly what occurred in the intervention. For example, it may seem that the participant enters the program (or black box), a period of time ensues while in the box, and then out of the box comes a new person, ready to take on the world (see Bunge, 1963). This discussion also invokes tenets of the Heisenberg principle, which posits that the more we research, learn, measure, critique and know about a certain phenomena (looking into the black box), the more that phenomenon actually changes, creating an obvious paradox. To apply the principle to AT, the more we peer into the black box, the more we may know about AT, but that understanding may not be in line with what AT actually is in applied settings—which is the center of an important debate about whether we should peer into the black box at all. There are those who say, "I don't really care how AT works; I know it does, and we should just leave it at that." The more poking and prodding we do to understand how it works, the more we change it, and it loses its magic. Then there are those who say, "We need to understand the mechanisms and various aspects of the black box to know which may be most important and why."

The argument withstanding, it is important for researchers, evaluators, and consumers of research to do the best they can to report, describe, and ascertain the key aspects of the intervention being reported or discussed. This can be very challenging for authors and consumers of research. For example, when submitting journal articles, we have received reviews that have asked us to shorten the program description and focus more on reviewing similar studies that have focused on similar outcomes. Others have asked us to elaborate at length about the intervention because it is unfamiliar. For example, in Russell (2003b), three pages were allotted to illustrating the organization and structure of outdoor behavioral healthcare programs, including a description of the basic tenets of the theoretical foundations that are reasoned to make them effective. In another publication (Russell, 2005), I (Keith) was asked by the editors to trim down the section on expeditions, in which I described how a wilderness-based intervention called Wendigo Lake Expeditions operating in Ontario, Canada, worked for young offenders. A 48-day expedition was boiled down to a brief one-paragraph explanation of the activities that youth engage in, and a broad description of natural consequences. The nuances and key aspects of the expedition are literally lost in translation, and up to the interpretation of the reader.

By continuing to do the best we can to describe and illustrate what the AT intervention is, how it may work, and the theoretical assumptions that guide it, we allow researchers and practitioners to ask the hard questions, replicate research studies where possible, and continue the dialogue that can shed light on the black box that is AT.

Challenges and Limitations in Adventure Therapy Research and Evaluation

There is much work to do in AT research and evaluation. Most meta-analyses and reviews of literature (see Table 13.1) point out methodological shortcomings and state that it is difficult to draw conclusions on the effects of AT because of the lack of program description and limited information available in most published studies.

When first reviewing the Focus column of these key reviews and meta-analyses in Table 13.1, it is evident that each study made important assumptions about the types of programs being reviewed and the outcomes associated with them. Note that while nearly all of the studies involve adventure programming, few of the studies exclusively focus on adventure or wilderness therapy. Winterdyck and Griffiths (1984) reviewed "wilderness experience programs" for young offenders, while Burton (1981) reviewed "Outward Bound and related programs." This re-emphasizes the definition discussion presented earlier, highlighting a critical shortcoming of the field when reviewing research: seemingly no two interventions or programs are the same.

Wilson and Lipsey (2000) asked this question in their meta-analysis: Are wilderness challenge programs effective in reducing antisocial and delinquent behavior? They answered with a qualified yes and suggested that "the results of

TABLE 13.1 Key Meta-Analyses and Reviews of Literature in Adventure Therapy

Author	Year	Type	Focus
Gibson	1979	Literature review	Therapeutic aspects of wilderness programs
Burton	1981	Review of literature	Review of outcomes on Outward Bound and related outcomes
Wynterdyk & Griffith	1984	Review of literature	Effects of wilderness experience programs on delinquent youth
Ewert	1987	Review of literature	Overview of research in experiential education
Bandoroff	1989	Review of literature	Wilderness therapy for delinquent youth
Cason & Gillis	1994	Meta-analysis	Outdoor adventure programming for adolescents
Friese, Pittman, & Hendee	1995	Annotated bibliography	Review of studies on the use of wilderness or personal growth, therapy, and education
Hattie, Marsh, Neill, & Richards	1997	Meta-analysis	Outcomes in adventure education and therapy
Moote & Wadarski	1997	Review of literature	Review of studies on life skills in adventure education and therapy
Easley, Passineau, & Driver	1990	Review of literature	Review of studies on the use of wilderness or personal growth, therapy, and education
Hans	2000	Meta-analysis	Review of studies on locus of control
Wilson & Lipsey	2000	Meta-analysis	Wilderness challenge programs for delinquent youth
Bunting & Donley	2002	Meta-analysis	Challenge and ropes courses
Moore & Russell	2002	Annotated bibliography	Review of studies on the use of wilderness or personal growth, therapy, and education
Gillis & Speelman	2008	Meta-analysis	Challenge and ropes courses in educational and therapeutic settings

this meta-analysis be interpreted chiefly in a formative manner" (p. 8) because of the methodological shortcomings. Namely there are very few randomized studies included in the meta-analysis and most, if not all studies, suffer from having an inadequate sample size to have sufficient statistical power to make distinct conclusions. Hattie et al. (1997) came to conclusions similar to the findings of Wilson and Lipsey and stated in their assessment of the literature that "methodologies have ranged in quality, and even the outcomes range from dubious to extravagant" and that there is a great deal of variability between different studies, different programs, and different individuals (p. 77). AT programs seem to have a difficult time conducting studies that have sufficient rigor, including randomized assignment to treatment, the use of comparison control groups, and large enough sample sizes to make findings more conclusive. Reasons for this include that most studies are based on convenience samples of a single program, are of existing programs serving paying clientele (thus researchers "get in the way"), and that most group sizes or programs are rather small, making larger sample sizes difficult to obtain.

OUTCOMES RESEARCH IN ADVENTURE THERAPY

Table 13.1 illustrates many of the seminal reviews of literature in AT. Despite the limitations noted above, conclusions can be drawn about the effects of adventure programming on a variety of clients who were involved in some type of AT program or intervention. These reviews and meta-analyses show that past studies have focused on two *primary* effects on participants: (1) the positive and significant development of self-concept from participation in an AT intervention, and (2) the development of adaptive and social skills due to the unique group-based treatment milieu. Other studies have examined the effects of AT on recidivism in criminal behavior and are also reviewed. There are very few studies related to the effects of AT on substance abuse and dependence, which are the primary outcomes on which current AT practice is focused (highlighting the need for future research in this area). Each of these are reviewed and followed by a section on recent research highlighting current research directions. The section will conclude with recommendations for further research. It is noted that the majority of research on AT has focused on adolescents ages 12–18. Unless otherwise noted, it is assumed that the focus of the research was on adolescents.

Adventure Therapy and Self-Concept

Adolescents continuously compare and contrast their behavior with that of their peers and develop their sense of self based on the feedback they receive. An adolescent who is struggling with an externalizing mental health problem (as opposed to an internalizing issue such as depression or anxiety), whether it is attention-deficit/hyperactivity disorder or a behavioral disorder, typically uses a group of normative peers rather than other peers to make these self-assessments of worth or ability in forming their self-concept. Because of this unique dynamic, adolescents in mental health crisis can often develop negative views of themselves. These negative views, manifest in low levels of self-concept, are associated with the presence and continuation of self-destructive behaviors in adolescents. Because this is also a time when adolescents naturally seek risk, adventure, and excitement, the ability to assess the risks and benefits attached with their behaviors is crucial. Adolescents in crisis are often poor judges, which can lead to developing problems with the law, dropping out of school, becoming increasingly aggressive, and increased substance use. Because of these and other related factors, much of the research in AT has focused on the degree to which AT programs enhance the participant's self-concept.

Early studies on self-concept noted that AT programs significantly enhance the self-concept of adolescents by presenting challenges that are developmentally appropriate, in that they are concrete, attainable, and increase in difficulty and challenge as the intervention progresses (Bandoroff & Scherer, 1994; Gibson, 1981; Hazelworth, 1990; Kelly & Baer, 1969; Kimball, 1979; Kleiber, 1993; Pommier, 1994; Porter, 1975; Weeks, 1985; Wright, 1982). A more recent meta-analysis conducted by Hattie et al. (1997) suggested that past research on self-concept in the AT literature has ignored the advances being made in self-concept research, concluding that early research on self-concept in AT was too simplistic. These earlier studies tended to focus on physical ability, peer relations, general self-concept, physical appearance, academic progress, self-confidence, self-efficacy, and self-understanding (Hattie et al., p. 48).

Marsh, Richards, and Barnes (1984) assessed several dimensions of self-concept in their study of nondelinquent youth and demonstrated that these various dimensions of self-concept can be changed through a 26-day Outward Bound wilderness challenge program. The various dimensions of self-concept are related to different environments (peer relations and school) or task-specific behaviors. Based on the work by Marsh (1990), researchers in AT have begun to identify these multiple dimensions of self-concept, and adapt and link the specific goals of AT interventions to these measures of self-concept. Hans (2000) compiled studies for a meta-analysis on the specific outcome of locus of control in adventure programming that resulted in a nonstandardized mean difference effect size of 0.38. Russell, Hendee, and Cooke (1998) found that increases in self-concept from participation in a wilderness program led to increased student performance in the Federal Job Corps program as well as reduced the likelihood they would leave the program early before completing their educational and vocational training.

Despite reported successes, systematic reviews of self-concept research emphasize the lack of a theoretical basis in most studies, the poor quality of measurement instruments used to assess self-concept, methodological shortcomings, and a general lack of comparable or consistent findings (Gillis, 1992; Hattie et al., 1997; Winterdyk & Griffiths, 1984). Hattie et al. (1997, p. 67) stated that the "greatest effects of the adventure programs in the area of self-concept domain were for independence, confidence, self-efficacy, and self understandings, and they were further enhanced during follow-up periods." When integrated with their findings that longer, wilderness-based programs with therapeutic intent also showed higher effect sizes, a compelling argument can be made that these types of AT programs have the potential to enhance specific self-concept domains of participants.

Addressing some of the above limitations, specifically by including only those studies that identified control groups, possessed sufficient sample sizes, and reported quantitative measures, Gillis and Speelman (2008) conducted a meta-analysis of 44 studies related to the effects of challenge courses on a variety of participants. The results suggested studies with a therapeutic focus ($d = 0.53$) had robust effect sizes in general, with medium effect sizes reported for outcomes focusing on self-efficacy ($d = 0.48$), behavioral observations ($d = 0.37$), personality measures ($d = 0.29$), and self-esteem or self-concept ($d = 0.26$) (p. 127). The highest effect sizes were reported for middle school age children ($d = 0.46$), and adults ($d = 0.80$), for programs that were 21–30 hours in length. These results suggest the potential that challenge courses have for being used as a tool in AT interventions with individuals, groups, and families for the development of self-concept.

Adventure Therapy and Social Skills

Much of the research on AT has focused on adolescents and their maladaptive behaviors in relation to self and others. Research has shown that adolescents in mental health crisis report significant deficits in social competence (Achenbach & Edelbrock, 1981). Social competence is the collection of behaviors that adolescents develop in the context of their family, peer, and other personal relationships. A key indicator of psychological, social, and emotional health is an adolescent's perceived and real effectiveness in social interactions or social competence. Delinquent and self-destructive behavior is often a manifestation of social skill deficits that can be changed by teaching alternate prosocial behaviors. Thus, many AT programs focused on the development of social skills and research have examined the degree to which participants learn and apply these skills in posttreatment environments.

Early research in AT sought to evaluate the effects of AT on a variety of pro-social skill development. Gibson (1981) determined that interpersonal competence of participants in an Outward Bound program was increased following the experience. Porter (1975) noted a decrease in defensiveness and a large increase in social acceptance. Kraus (1982) concluded that wilderness therapy aids emotionally disturbed adolescents in reaching various therapeutic goals, including a reduction in aggressiveness towards others. Weeks (1985) noted an improvement in participant interpersonal effectiveness in relating to others through learned social skills. In a more recent study, Sachs and Miller (1992) reported that a wilderness experience program had positive effects on cooperative behavior exhibited in the school setting following completion of a wilderness program. This study used direct observation of behaviors in a school setting following the intervention to form this conclusion. Hattie, Marsh, Neill, and Richards (1997, p. 69) distinctly stated "for social competence, cooperation, and interpersonal communication it certainly appears that adventure programs affect the social skills of participants in desirable ways."

Using both qualitative and quantitative methods, Russell (2003a, 2003b, 2005) showed that AT (in this case, long-term expedition-based wilderness therapy) resulted in improvements in adolescents' social skills; these improved interpersonal relations were practiced and refined throughout the treatment process. The group milieu led to a deeper level of sharing in group counseling sessions, which were then related to family and peer environments (Russell, 2003a). All of the study participants noted a desire to work on their relationships with their family, specifically their desire to communicate better with their family members through the sharing of their feelings. Similar results showed clinically significant improvement in the Interpersonal Relation subscale on the Youth-Outcome Questionnaire (Y-OQ). These clinically significant reductions were maintained at 12 months posttreatment and in a 2-year follow-up. Russell (2006c) also identified social skill development as a result of AT in a study that examined the effects of a wilderness therapy program on adjudicated youth. Again using the Y-OQ, significant improvements were found in interpersonal relations, which was also corroborated with student feedback.

A review of the effects of AT programs on social skill development suggests that such programs influence the development of more socially adaptive and cooperative behavior. Clark, Marmol, Cooley, and Gathercoal (2004) examined the effects of a 21-day wilderness therapy program on DSM-IV Axis I, II, and IV concerns of troubled adolescents. The study sought to better identify treatment effects related to personality disorders of 109 adolescent clients included in the study. They demonstrated that the 21-day expedition-based wilderness therapy intervention resulted in statistically significant improvement on immature defense and maladaptive behavior scores, and on dysfunctional personality patterns, expressed concerns, and clinical syndromes scores. Results on maladaptive behaviors and treatment effects were similar to those found by Russell (2001) in an outcome study that included 858 subjects admitted for treatment at eight participating AT programs. Because this research focused on adolescent maladaptive behaviors, which are driven by an inability to relate to self and others, it serves as an important study in demonstrating the potential of wilderness therapy to treat personality disorders, which "take a huge emotional and financial toll on individuals, families and society, and they are notoriously difficult to treat" (p. 227).

Adventure Therapy and Substance Abuse

There are few studies reported in the literature on AT effects on clients with histories of drug and alcohol abuse. Three studies report reduced substance abuse from treatment. Gillis and Simpson (1992) noted a positive behavior change and positive effect on relapse from an 8-week residential treatment program with a wilderness component for drug-abusing adolescents. Bennet et al. (1998) found that a therapeutic camping program was more effective at reducing the frequency of negative thoughts and reducing alcohol craving when compared with a residential drug and alcohol treatment model. They also noted a reduction in alcohol use 10 months after the program. Russell (1999) studied 12 case studies 4 months after completion of a wilderness program and found that three cases (25%) had self-reported that they had relapsed on drugs and alcohol, which were corroborated with parent interviews, while the other nine (75%) had not relapsed.

Russell (2008) sampled 774 participants in one of five expedition-based residential AT programs that had a median length of 49 days. The study population was predominantly Caucasian males between ages 16 and 17, who were reasoned to be from middle class socio-economic backgrounds. An interesting characteristic of this treatment sample was that 92% of the youth completed treatment; this is very high for adolescent substance use treatment delivery models, which typically report completion rates of 80% or less (Winters, 1999). The study suggests that expedition-based AT programs had positive effects on the reduction of substance use. This study also assessed the youth's motivation to change using the University of Rhode Island Change Assessment Scale (Prochaska & Di Clemente, 1983) and found that though the majority of clients were very unmotivated at admission to treatment, at discharge they had shifted to an awareness of problem issues in their lives and had begun to actively work on these problems. Thus, this type of program was effective for unmotivated youth who otherwise may have not wanted to enter treatment, or were even unaware that their behavior had become a problem. The 6-month follow-up assessment of substance use frequency suggested that the adolescents in both outpatient and residential aftercare settings had significantly reduced the frequency of substance use, especially the more serious narcotics, following the intervention. The study did conclude that the majority of adolescents in the sample were still actively using substances, but to a significantly lesser degree than they were at admission.

Youth seeking AT treatment seem to need something different, an approach that traditional residential or outpatient talk therapy cannot provide (Russell, 2008). Finally, some positive outcomes were noted but should be treated with caution due to the limitations inherent in the study: namely, that there was no comparable control group used, and that the only data available was self-reported by adolescents. Together, these findings suggest that AT treatment should continue to be evaluated, developed, and identified.

Adventure Therapy and Recidivism

Considerable attention in research on AT has been given to the effects of the treatment on adjudicated youth, who are characterized as younger than the age of the majority who have violated the law or committed a status offense and have been processed through the juvenile justice system in some way. A review of the criminology literature reveals only a few studies published on the effects of AT programs on recidivism and related outcomes (not boot camps; for more on this distinction, see Russell, 2006b). A review of studies in the 1970s and 1980s linked wilderness programs with reduced recidivism, reduced frequency of deviant behaviors, and fewer arrests (Winterdyk & Griffiths, 1984). Greenwood and Turner (1987) compared 90 male graduates of the VisionQuest adjudicated program with 257 male juvenile delinquents who had been placed in other probation programs, and found that VisionQuest graduates had fewer arrests. Further evidence in support of VisionQuest's effectiveness is provided in a study by Goodstein and Sontheimer (1987). A study by Castellano and Soderstrom (1992) evaluated the effects of the Spectrum Wilderness Program, a 30-day Outward Bound type of wilderness challenge program, on the number of post-program arrests. They found it reduced arrests among graduates, which lasted for about 1 year after the program. At this point, the positive program results began to decay to the point where they were no longer apparent.

Russell (2006c) examined the Wendigo Lakes Expedition program in Ontario, Canada, which was developed to help young offenders specifically address many of the issues underlying their antisocial behavior. The program integrated principles of positive youth development with adventure programming and wilderness expeditions to help young offenders learn and practice prosocial skills in a safe and nurturing environment. The study evaluated 57 youth, with an average age of 15 years, who stayed in the program for approximately 100 days. In general, study participants evaluated Wendigo Lakes Expedition favorably, felt safe while at the facility, and felt they learned valuable lessons from the experience. In addition, youth also noted on exit interviews that the program helped them in dealing with frustrations and developing and working on interpersonal skills, which reflected two primary goals of the program—to help youth deal with their anger appropriately and to learn to get along better with others.

Gillis, Gass, and Russell (2008) evaluated Project Adventure's Behavior Management through Adventure (BMtA) program for young offenders in the Georgia Juvenile Justice system. The results of the study showed that the BMtA program participants experienced significantly lower rates of re-arrest at 1, 2, and 3 years following release when compared to adjudicated youth in an outdoor therapeutic camping program and in a specialized substance-use treatment program. There also were statistically significant differences between time from release until re-arrest for the BMtA program and the two comparison programs. The findings in this study demonstrated the promise, adaptability, and potential for AT programs that use the BMtA approach and called for more clarity concerning the range and types of AT programs and their reasoned treatment differences. The study also highlighted the importance of understanding intervention/treatment fidelity in AT programs, particularly regarding program settings and key clinical factors.

Walsh and Russell (2010) evaluated the outcomes of an AT program for adjudicated youth. Although this study had limitations, namely due to restrictions placed on data that could be collected from the control group, and it was difficult to compare the control and treatment group on psychosocial measures, it did offer insight into contemporary types of AT programming for adjudicated youth. This study evaluated the Wilderness Endeavors Program, a correctional-based wilderness and adventure program for youthful offenders in the state of Minnesota. The results of the study showed that male program graduates, who averaged 16 years of age, demonstrated significant increases in *self-efficacy* and *hope* (as measured by the Children's Hope Scale (Snyder, 2003).) as a result of completing the program. The results also indicated no significant differences on reoffense rates between the treatment group and a control group of youth who were placed in alternative correctional programs. Recidivism rates were approximately 44% for the treatment group and 42% for the control groups. Further analysis revealed that *hope* was the only psychological domain that was significantly associated with those participants who did not recidivate. Therefore, it appears that hope could be a robust psychological trait; those individuals with high levels of hope for the future are more likely to be self-efficacious and may have a stronger ability to make positive adaptations to adversity.

Conclusions from Literature Review

In reviewing studies of the effects AT has on self-concept-related measures, social skills, substance abuse, and recidivism, several conclusions can be drawn. First, it appears that AT programs are a good fit developmentally for youth who are reluctant to engage in treatment due to the barriers and stigma associated with traditional treatment alternatives. Also of note is the broader application of AT to other demographics, including young adults, persons with disabilities, and other groups. Second, many of the studies in this review are plagued with methodological weaknesses mentioned above, including a lack of randomized assignment to treatment groups and a lack of control groups. Coupled with this conclusion, however, is the noted increase in refined and standardized client assessment, and process and outcome measures. This includes more specific measures of self-efficacy and social skills, more elaborate assessment of the psychosocial factors associated with substance use, and more illustrative measures of recidivism. Third is the repeated call from researchers to offer more complete and thorough descriptions of programs so that AT and its subsequent effects on participants can be more clearly understood. The logic is that if the program or treatment is ill-defined, then it is difficult to compare one study to the next. Finally, more research is needed on AT as an intervention, specifically research that begins to isolate and identify what it is about AT that creates changes in individuals, behavior, cognition, or emotional states. Lessons from a recent metaanalysis of after school programming can serve as a guide as we move forward with our research in AT. Durlak & Weissberg (2007) conducted a meta-analysis of 73 after school programs (with a control group) designed to identify which programs were successful at increasing personal and social skills. They found that effective programs were S-A-F-E. In the training process, the programs found to be successful were Sequential - they used a coordinated sequential set of activities and they used Active forms of learning? In the content delivery the programs were Focused—they had at least one component devoted to the specific skills they were measuring and they were Explicit in how they targeted these skills. Thus the acronym **SAFE** represents an effective double entendre for adventure therapy. We want to be both physically and psychologically safe, and by being sequenced, active, focused and explicit we can also increase the chances of getting the outcomes we desire.

RECENT TRENDS IN ADVENTURE THERAPY RESEARCH

Two recent publications reviewed in this search (Frishman, 2006; Moler, 2008) addressed the theory of AT. Frishman (2006) used a theoretical lens of postmodern philosophy to explore shared meaning between the fields of adventure and postmodern therapies and termed the intersection of these two theoretical areas the *adventure-journey perspective*. The key elements of this perspective provide a frame for examining how adventure, when seen as a journey, involves the collaborative use of experiential educational practice, development of generative metaphors, risk-taking, and dialogical processing of experiences for therapeutic purposes. The fact that only one publication in this review was theoretical in nature reflects a noted finding from several reviews of literature that have concluded that AT lacks a common theoretical frame in which to distinguish the practice from other treatment approaches. More research is needed in this area.

Taylor, Segal, and Harper (2010) believe that AT has been rightly criticized for not recognizing the ecological paradigm of therapy conducted in wild nature. To address this, the paper includes principles from integral systems theory to offer adventure therapists a map to piece together various elements of AT theory into a coherent whole. They concluded that wilderness is a crucial co-facilitator in the change process and should be integrated into discussions of AT theory.

Two articles specifically addressed policy issues in AT, focusing specifically on understanding the range of AT services in the state of Maine (Lynch, 2005) and the practitioner-directed movement to establish AT as an evidence-based treatment model (Harper, 2010). Lynch sought to identify and assess how many of the 191 mental health agencies in the state of Maine used AT services in the treatment of their clientele. The results of the survey suggested that 33% of all agencies used AT to some degree. The barriers to further use included psychotherapists' perceptions of the utility of the services, the agencies' access to required resources, and the availability of appropriately trained staff to conduct AT programs. This is one of the few studies found in the literature to evaluate the use of AT across a continuum of services and to identify barriers to AT treatment services by clientele. Harper (2010, p. 52) critically evaluates the movement to establish AT as an evidence-based approach and instead suggests the following:

> Theoretical understanding and an articulation of evidence [in AT] needs to be located in the context of client/student characteristics, program design and objectives, cultural understanding, and so forth. From there, more specific program models may explore their curricular or therapeutic applications—again, supported theoretically—to test for validation, effect, and causality.

Durr (2009) studied the effects of an adventure experience on the subjective well-being of participants based on the perceived level of challenge that the experience offered. The results of the study showed that optimal challenge experiences are better than nonoptimal experiences at producing positive effects if the challenge was assessed by the participants immediately after participation. The study is important because it addresses predicted and actual levels of challenge as assessed by the participants and neutral observers and the relationship that these had with outcomes.

Jelalian et al. (2010) examined the effects of a cognitive behavioral treatment approach integrated with AT on youth ages 13–16 years and who were between 20% and 80% overweight. The youth were randomly assigned to one of two treatment conditions: the AT treatment or a cognitive-behavioral group treatment that included aerobic exercise. The results showed that average weight loss did not differ significantly between groups at the conclusion of treatment. Significant differences in maintaining the weight loss were noted at 10 months posttreatment, with the AT group showing significantly more maintained weight loss. The authors also found a significant age by treatment group interaction, concluding that older adolescents who participated in AT demonstrated more than four times the weight loss of older adolescents assigned to the cognitive-behavioral therapy and exercise regimen. The authors concluded that peer-based AT is a promising adjunct to standard cognitive-behavioral weight control intervention for adolescents, and may be most effective for older adolescents.

Moler (2008) examined the effects of AT on women who had experienced trauma. AT was defined as an active type of therapy that often involves ropes courses, problem-solving games, and cognitive dissonance that I processed in group settings by professionally trained therapists. This qualitative study included two forgiveness measures and two open-ended questionnaire sessions to determine what effect AT had on forgiveness. The findings indicated an increase in the understanding of the forgiveness process as well as the amount of forgiveness each participant felt towards the person she was forgiving. Norton (2010) used a case study approach to examine wilderness therapy as an intervention for adolescents experiencing depression. The clinical case study suggested that wilderness therapy an be an effective and appropriate intervention for adolescent depression that can promote positive self-image and enhanced coping skills.

Tucker and Rheingold (2010, p. 260) called for more attention to be made to fidelity research in AT, defining fidelity as "the consistency and quality in which interventions and programs are being implemented in reference to their prescribed model." They concluded the paper by saying that AT interventions and programs need to be defined more accurately, including how practitioners are trained and supervised. These practices should become a norm rather than an exception. Finally, Bettmann and Tucker (2011) examined shifts in adolescents' attachment relationships with parents and peers during a 7-week wilderness treatment program. The results showed not only that adolescents reported decreased anger and increased emotional connection towards parents, but also that trust and communication with parents had become troubled at the conclusion of treatment. The authors discuss the complexity of parent–adolescent relationships in the context of out-of-home care and point to the importance of continued research in this area.

SUMMARY

A variety of journals from various disciplines are publishing articles on AT, including medical, mental health, social work, and education journals. This shows a growing interest in the use of AT as an intervention to create change in individuals. Second, there are some authors concerned with the theoretical development of AT; they are seeking to integrate a wide variety of variables and theoretical constructs to existing models of AT. It is clear that more theoretical development and testing is needed to more clearly articulate what AT is and how it works. Third, research and evaluation of AT process and outcome is expanding to include a wider variety of clientele and application, including more rigorous research designs and methodology. This was shown in several studies that evaluated the effects of AT on obesity, seriously ill children, women survivors of trauma, and college students.

Finally, it is clear that healthy discourse around establishing AT as an evidence-based treatment is occurring and will continue into the future as more practitioners, policy makers, mental health professionals, and researchers critically examine AT practice and its subsequent outcomes. This discourse is healthy and will shape how AT continues to develop as a treatment of choice for affected individuals.

BUILDING TRUST

Rachael Wood

A 6-year-old boy was referred to the county mental health clinic for individual counseling because of aggressive and unusual behaviors that he was exhibiting in his foster home that were jeopardizing his placement (e.g., fighting with his brothers, urinating in corners, eating out of the trash). He had lived his entire life in a pickup truck with his parents and two younger brothers until he was placed in foster care. His contact with anyone outside his family had been minimal and he had been taught by his parents not trust anyone. Because I had 6 months at most to work with him, I felt it was important to begin building trust immediately.

For our second session, I took him to a local park that had a playground structure consisting of a series of decks, steps, ladders, and slides. He agreed to be blindfolded and I told him that I could lead him safely through the playground structure using vocal prompts. At first, he wanted to try to find his way on his own (still blindfolded). I allowed him to make an attempt but stayed close enough to spot him, making sure he would not fall or hurt himself.

After only a few seconds and a couple of shuffling steps forward, he reluctantly admitted he needed my help and allowed me to guide him. He had never been to school and it soon became evident that he did not understand certain commands, such as "move toward me." Despite this disadvantage, we managed to get him through the structure successfully and he liked it so much that he elected to try it several more times. He followed a different route each time and then took a turn guiding me. After this session, he began to talk openly with me about his feelings and eagerly engaged in any activity I presented. In that one session, we accomplished a level of trust that may have taken weeks of play or talk therapy to reach. The ability to use one meaningful activity to achieve a therapeutic goal that could take weeks of traditional talk or play therapy to accomplish is what I consider adventure therapy.

I became an adventure therapist while working as a mental health counselor with foster children at Santa Cruz County Children's Mental Health, my first job out of graduate school. I had studied social work and enjoyed doing therapy with children, but felt that something was lacking in the approaches I had learned. Combined with the limited amount of time in which I had to help my clients make lasting behavior changes in order to successfully reunite with their families, I really needed a new approach. Then one of my coworkers introduced me to AT and I was hooked immediately. I loved it because it was fun and because I could help my clients accomplish their goals in a significantly shorter amount of time. Plus when I used it with families, every member of the family was able to participate in some way, regardless of their age or level of education. Since I usually had only three or four sessions with the families as a whole, being able to meet treatment goals quickly was extremely important.

I continued to use AT working as a case manager for adolescent boys at a residential drug and alcohol treatment center. Most recently, I have introduced it to the clinicians I oversee in my current job as a supervisor of an outpatient mental health program at a community clinic.

Chapter 14

The Future of Adventure Therapy

This chapter discusses several possibilities on the future of adventure therapy. Part of this chapter is informed by an online survey conducted in April 2011 with 53 respondents who shared their thoughts on the current strengths, weaknesses, opportunities, and threats (SWOT) of adventure therapy. This chapter also includes issues related to access: access of clients to adventure therapy programs, access of programs to federal land, and access of programs to external fiscal support to participate in such treatment programs (e.g., Medicaid). This chapter also builds on the training competencies in Chapter 10 of this book, suggesting training paths for becoming an adventure therapist along with the trials and triumphs of working in the field. The increasing use of technology in the field is discussed, along with some thoughts about what the adventure therapy field might look like in the near future and what factors may impact this viewpoint.

Gass (1993a, p. 415) previously asked: "Will adventure therapy remain on its present course, return to being an application of other therapies, or will it emerge as a profession unto itself?" In this discussion, he highlighted issues related to internal professionalism, training, risk management, recognition by others, and adherence to ethical standards. Since Gass first asked these questions and pointed to pitfalls as well as possibilities for adventure therapy, many elements of the field have changed—while many others have remained the same. The elements that have changed will be the focus of this chapter, with the clarity of hindsight combined with the foresight of questions to accompany future predictions.

In 2004, Gass presented the keynote address at the annual conference of the National Association of Therapeutic Schools and Programs, using the rise and fall of corporate adventure training programs as a potential path for what might happen to adventure therapy programs if practices remained unchanged.

Gass noted the following five reasons why corporate adventure training programs' impact on corporate training diminished in quite a dramatic manner:

1. Failure of evidence-based outcome and procedures (e.g., beneficial cost-benefit analysis returns, positive return on investment)
2. Inability to proactively implement appropriate risk management procedures for the specific needs of this population (in this case, cardiac issues of older clients not used to physical activity)
3. Flood of low-quality programs and lack of market differentiation
4. Competition/backlash from traditional sources of management training
5. Inability to grow as a field in a systemic, collaborative manner and offer continuously new material (e.g., looking for short-term return with little focus of long-term investment in the field, failure to produce "the latest/hottest thing")

Gass (2004) challenged the audience to develop risk management plans and related procedures that would demonstrate AT programs' professionalism, care, and concern for clients (e.g., plans for how programming fit into each client's continuity of care). He additionally compelled programs to look at definitions of effectiveness and examples of model programs, and to stand on the shoulders of others who shared their processes and outcomes for public scrutiny. He encouraged programs to invest a minimum of 3% or greater of their net income into the research and development of their programs' practices, focusing on matching the evolving value structure of the broader mental health and educational systems (e.g., the Department of Education [DOE] and the Substance Abuse and Mental Health System Administration [SAMHSA]). Russell, Gillis, and Lewis (2008) found more than 95% of respondents to a survey said their program—past or present—had conducted some form of treatment outcome evaluation, while 4% indicated they had not. The most frequent type of evaluation conducted by 55% of participating programs was the use of internally developed instrumentation conducted by program staff. A smaller percentage (12%) noted they conducted evaluations in the past through an external organization, but that outcomes were not tracked regularly. Programs were also asked if they regularly contacted families after completion of treatment, and if so how often (e.g., periodically) and at what time in relation to discharge. Almost 90% of all programs said they did contact families and that the average time after completion of treatment was 3.5 months.

The findings regarding evaluation are surprising given the evidence-based environment where mental health programs operate. Most programs continue to use internal evaluations with program-developed instruments. Given that adventure therapy is largely a demand-driven treatment alternative, it is critical to note that an estimated 20,000 clients and their families annually turn to adventure therapy programs, despite the fact that they remain relatively untested. Unfortunately, more issues have emerged and proliferated to their present status today, becoming more troublesome for the adventure therapy field.

STRENGTHS, WEAKNESSES, OPPORTUNITIES, AND THREATS

In 2011, an online survey was conducted of the adventure therapy community by H.L. "Lee" Gillis (through http://www.surveymonkey.com) between March 27, 2011 and April 7, 2011. They were asked about the threats and opportunities in the future of adventure therapy (see Table 14.1). From these responses, several themes emerged, and they are discussed in the following sections.

Client Access to Treatment

As noted in the Chapter 2, there was tremendous growth of wilderness and adventure programs for adjudicated youth, and later for hospitalized adolescents, in the late 1970s through 1990s. Many states poured money into modified Outward Bound programs for adjudicated youth after the publication of Kelly and Baer (1971) showed decreases in recidivism rates and lower costs from wilderness programs than from traditional incarceration. Wilson and Lipsey's (2000, p. 11) meta-analysis challenged many of the findings of wilderness expeditions used for incarcerated youth due to the poor research methodology and inadequate sampling of subjects:

> Perhaps the most important finding of our meta-analysis is that additional randomized studies of wilderness challenge programs, especially those with therapeutic enhancements, are clearly justified by the promising findings of the studies reviewed here. A larger body of evidence will be necessary before it will be possible to generate conclusive results about the effects of these programs and the influence of study methodology on the size of the effects actually observed using different methods.

Unfortunately the larger body of evidence for therapeutic challenge programs mentioned by Wilson and Lipsey (2000) never emerged for adjudicated youth, youth in need of help for substance abuse, or similar clients in mental health treatment. The control-based military style boot camp models used in juvenile justice, although ineffective, were often mistakenly combined in the minds of policy makers with challenge programs. As a result, and in light of reduced state budgets and a mandate of many states for using only evidence-based programs, adventure programming for adjudicated youth have waned in the past 20 years.

TABLE 14.1 Strengths, Weaknesses, Opportunities, and Threats in the Future of Adventure Therapy (AT)

Construct	Element	Example Quotes from Survey
Strengths		
Integrates existing evidence base	Theoretical	Integrate the Adventure Therapy (AT) experience into an already existing treatment plan
Intense and engaging therapeutic milieu	Theoretical	It is immediate and provides a platform to challenge oneself in the moment; it is intense
Nature as restorative	Theoretical	Clients can access the benefits of talk therapy while also connecting with the restorative properties of nature
Concrete and tangible	Theoretical	Offers the opportunity for clients to actually act out and see concrete therapeutic gains or changes
Offers alternative and novel approach	Theoretical	It occurs in a novel environment which helps draw out the authentic person as it places them outside habitual/learned experience so it disarms the self-protective strategies to deflect/avoid the challenging situation
Conducive to multiple learning styles	Process	Works with people for whom an analytic style of learning or processing is not natural or productive
Extreme resistance/low motivation	Process	Offers the ability to engage into therapy notoriously difficult–to-engage populations, for example, males, behavioral disorders
Adventure experience metaphor	Process	Uses the outdoors as metaphor for the reality of clients' current situations
Observe tangible behaviors	Process	Provides immediate examples of healthy and unhealthy behaviors and choices
Flexible and adaptive	Process	Flexible, creative treatment in a non-pathologizing environment that capitalizes on a student's strengths
Activity task self-development	Process	Reinsert teens into the healthy adolescent stages of development
Therapeutic relationship	Process	Allows for strong therapeutic relationships to develop between group members and the facilitator
Not manipulate nature/ natural consequence	Process	You cannot manipulate nature. There is nothing more rewarding for dealing with personal issues, no matter on what level, than doing it in the wilderness.
Self-regulation/ awareness outcomes	Outcome	It provides clients with boosts in self-esteem, capacity for self-regulation, authentic community experiences, social and leadership skills, relapse prevention skills, and a meaningful rite of passage.

TABLE 14.1 Strengths, Weaknesses, Opportunities, and Threats in the Future of Adventure Therapy (AT) (Continued)

Construct	Element	Example Quotes from Survey
Develops resilience	Outcome	Nonstigmatizing modality that promotes and enhances normal psychological and social development and builds resilience and protective factors that mitigate future psychological disorder
Interpersonal/ communications	Outcome	Teaches communication skills, problem solving, coping mechanisms, and cooperation
Physical activity benefits	Outcome	Ability to promote change in clients in a variety of ways (physical, emotional, behavioral)
Family systems communication	Outcome	For wilderness (therapy) to grow and expand, the involvement of family is critical. Families are more and more detached because of "screen time" and wilderness is the perfect antidote for this.
Weaknesses		
Definitionally challenged	Theory	It is difficult to communicate what we do to people outside the field. I think people outside the field have a hard time getting past the outdoor piece to understand the therapeutic intention behind the outdoor piece.
Weak research base	Research	Compared to other modalities, research is still lagging in terms of number of outcomes and ongoing projects.
Lack of researchers	Practice/ theory	Only a handful of professionals advancing the academic aspect of the field, arguing the same points for the last 15 or more years
Lack of awareness	Practice	Lack of awareness among the general and clinical populations is probably the greatest weakness because it results in fewer people knowing about it as well as gives more space for misinformation (i.e., the confusion of boot camps with adventure therapy).
Lack of good reputation	Practice	Programs evaluated are often lumped with boot camp programs thereby diluting reputation and research. We are often a field that provokes fear/mystery within a broader mental health field and our strategies and modalities are looked at as cavalier, extreme, and scary.

continued

TABLE 14.1 Strengths, Weaknesses, Opportunities, and Threats in the Future of Adventure Therapy (AT) (Continued)

Construct	Element	Example Quotes from Survey
Lack of diversity in services offered	Practice	Too much emphasis on intervention and group process without sufficient attention to the therapeutic effects of nature immersion itself
Cater to higher socioeconomic status clients	Practice	It is expensive. On that note, it is limited to those who can pay for it.
Aftercare is challenging	Practice	It is difficult to follow clients after they complete programs due to the variety of aftercare situations they enter.
Poor supervision of field staff	Practice	Relatively low level of supervision of those in direct contact with the clients
Lack of licensed programs	Practice	Poor regulation and standardization of programs (still) to this day. Most are not covered by insurance or IEP funding despite research.
Professional organizations proliferate	Practice	Too many professional organizations for such a small field; both OBHIC and NATWC are a long shot from the AMA, and AEE has become primarily a conference business.
Low risk tolerance	Practice	Liability concerns and costs have caused all programs to restrict risk to a point where the experience is becoming less authentic.
Lack of adequately trained staff	Practice	Many untrained, inexperienced professionals claiming to provide therapy when they are not licensed to do so

Opportunities

Research networks	Research	Continued discussions with APA, NASW, and other peer organizations to get input and establish professionalism
Research	Research	Spreading research about our work to the public to gain support not only for what it is that we do but for *where* we do it as well, protecting these resources, both human and environment
Need for a brand	Practice	Good programs do great work. With better public relations, adventure therapy can remain a vital link in families getting healthier.
Become more accessible	Practice	Discover ways to include participants who can't afford to participate in these programs. These are the clients who need it the most.

TABLE 14.1 Strengths, Weaknesses, Opportunities, and Threats in the Future of Adventure Therapy (AT) (Continued)

Construct	Element	Example Quotes from Survey
Join with after school programs	Practice	Can be (and is with some) paired with school programs in summer to enhance and prepare students for traditional academics, thus becoming more of a preventative measure instead of a reactionary measure
Expanding beyond programs for youth	Practice	We don't just have to work with adolescents, men's and women's groups, veteran groups, cancer survivors, etc. You can make a 3–4 night trip a very powerful trip.
Aftercare	Practice	Engage families in the treatment to a large extent in an effort to maintain change after programs end.
Creativity	Practice	Freedom to design novel approaches
Threats		
Bad public relations	Practice	The abuse of wilderness therapy as a modality by unscrupulous, unethical, unskilled people whose primary motivation is seeing the student/family as the source of high financial returns. I think the nature of private healthcare can lead to marketing and growing margins and market share with negative results.
Funding	Practice	Generally not understood as a modality and tends to be regulated by those who maintain an archaic notion of what it may actually be
Communication of what we do	Practice	I think that there is a bad rap in the community of what wilderness therapy is all about. Lack of understanding of what true wilderness therapy is, in my opinion, the biggest threat.
Deaths in programs	Practice	Unfortunate death or injury not understood well outside of the industry
Government regulation	Practice	State government attempts at control may also not see the entire picture and may be creating more problems. We know there are plenty of programs that actually make things worse, that are a part of the problem. As a profession, if we are policing ourselves and our profession, we can help the government govern.

continued

TABLE 14.1 Strengths, Weaknesses, Opportunities, and Threats in the Future of Adventure Therapy (AT) (Continued)

Construct	Element	Example Quotes from Survey
Lack of creativity	Practice	What is defined as the state-of-the-art in AT is determined by educational consultants and others who have never actually had to spend any real time with students in the wilderness setting.

IEP = Individual Educational Plan; OBHIC = Outdoor Behavioral Healthcare Industry Council; NATWC = The National Association of Therapeutic Wilderness Camping ; AMA = American Medical Association; AEE = Association for Experiential Education; APA = American Psychological Association; NASW = National Association of Social Work.

In addition to the formative challenge to the value of adventure programming for juvenile offenders was the introduction of misinformed meta-analyses. The aforementioned analysis by Wilson and Lipsey (2000), and later the cost-benefit policy analysis by Aos, Miller, and Drake (2006), proclaimed that it is unclear how therapeutic elements of specific programs effectively and consistently produced change. The use of adventure programming also failed to show it was cost effective in treating young offenders.

These conclusions drawn by Aos, Miller, and Drake (2006), Brown, Borduin, and Henggeler (2001), and Wilson and Lipsey (2000) all served to exacerbate misperceptions of adventure therapy by misinterpreting treatment fidelity and failing to differentiate adventure programming aimed at behavior management versus outdoor programs used for recreation with youth. For a more valid understanding, it became imperative for researchers and policy makers to differentiate between adventure therapy programs centered on behavior management and recidivism outcomes from other adventure programs designed to provide recreational camping for juvenile offenders. In addition, many of the studies used to substantiate—or more often castigate—adventure therapy were theses and dissertations lacking methodological rigor (e.g., no control groups) and treatment fidelity (e.g., many programs were conducted by the researchers themselves).

Cost-benefit analyses certainly attract the attention of politicians, who by definition are policy makers. The lack of clear effectiveness and evidence, along with the sometimes misperceptions and confusion that these youth are "just having fun," can lead to funding cuts for reputable programs. Latessa (2004) questioned the transfer of learning in adventure therapy to real-life situations. Two decisions may support how misperceptions and confusion can lead to program closure. In 2010, Project Adventure's Georgia site was closed, in part due to decreased referrals, decreased funding, and rising staff costs (due to requirements of master's-level mental health degrees). The Woodson Wilderness Challenge (formerly Camp Woodson) in North Carolina also reportedly failed to demonstrate beneficial cost effectiveness figures sufficient for that state's General Assembly to continue its funding (North Carolina Department of Juvenile Justice and Delinquency Prevention, 2011).

Decreases in funding by managed care and insurance companies for the hospitalization of adolescents in the late 1980s and early 1990s actually resulted in the rapid proliferation of many wilderness therapy programs (Santa, 2007) and a substantial growth in publications and workshops on innovative ways to use adventure therapy with multiple diagnostic categories, especially substance use. Conversely, as these insurance companies began to charge per service (instead of for a whole course of inclusive treatment), many inpatient hospitals began to dismantle their challenge ropes courses due to a lack of funding along with the absence of an evidence base for adventure therapy programs.

Chapter 2 discussed the growth of private pay adventure therapy, along with the advent of outdoor behavioral healthcare (see http://www.obhrc.org), which primarily occurred in response to negligent deaths from poorly run (and unprofessionally staffed) programs that advertised themselves as "wilderness therapy." In the age of the Internet, using the search term "wilderness therapy programs" currently results in around 13,000 hits. Families may approach the referral process in this way. They often make contact with a program to gather information if they find it on the Internet, or hear about it from a friend or colleague.

A parent, guardian, or mental health professional also might approach a consultant to help match their youth's issues with an appropriate program. A consultant's job is to determine whether a short-term (30–60 days) program or a longer-term residential treatment (6–24 months) is needed given the background information provided. The assumption is that local mental health options have been explored and most likely exhausted. It is also assumed the youth is not actively suicidal—although they may have previous suicidal ideation or even suicidal attempts. Many times when parents are seeking wilderness therapy programs, they report they have "tried everything." Russell (2008) noted:

> Three-quarters (75%) of all clients in (his) sample had tried at least some form of outpatient counseling, defined as a periodic visit to a mental health professional to help address problems the adolescent was experiencing while still residing in a home environment. A much smaller percentage (23%) had tried inpatient treatment services, defined as some type of clinical residential setting to address any problems the adolescent was experiencing.

There appear to be an increasing number of referrals for youth who know they have issues and want help, or parents who are looking for a productive summer experience to augment the therapeutic work they are doing at home. In more extensive interviews with the referring parent or guardian (or mental health professional working with the family), the consultant gathers past psychological reports, a self-report of the youth being assessed (if possible), educational records, and financial information. If drugs were involved, some professional analysis of the level of dependence would be conducted to determine if medically supervised withdrawal was needed. It is not uncommon for youth to experience a spike in anxiety when entering a program, and determining the youth's ability to handle this spike is necessary for a successful placement.

Most consultants provide at least two options of placements for families to investigate. This is done while recognizing that families in crisis may want the consultant to make the decision for them. When asked what mental health diagnoses would result in excluding wilderness treatment as an option, thought disorder symptoms are closely evaluated to see if a wilderness setting would be appropriate, and ruled out if there is a concern that the stress of wilderness would exacerbate symptoms or tip the client into more serious mental illness. Substance-induced symptoms are closely evaluated and a determination is made if an inpatient chemical dependence treatment program would not be more appropriate, although sometimes a 30-day inpatient program followed by wilderness may be recommended for more resistant clients. Trauma, eating disordered behaviors, and neurobiological disorders are also evaluated in conjunction with other issues to see if wilderness therapy is appropriate. There may be complications of placement due to wishes of grandparents or noncustodial birth parents who doubt whether an out-of-home placement is needed.

In 2011, the cost of private pay wilderness therapy programs ranged from $250–$500 per day with a minimum stay of 5–6 weeks and an average stay of 10 weeks (Paula Leslie, personal communication, May 2011). Russell, Gillis, and Lewis (2008) found an average charge per day was $278, with a range of $0 (payment provided by an alternative source, such as a foundation) to $450. Given the per diem charge of treatment, it is possible to calculate the total revenues generated by wilderness therapy programs currently operating. Using the *median* number of clients served and lengths of stay, annual revenues of $96 million are generated (95 clients a year × 56 days × $278 per day × 65 programs). Using the *average* number of clients served and lengths of stay, annual revenues of over $300 dollars are generated (165 clients a year × 107 days × $278 dollars per day × 65 programs). The average cost of treatment has increased since 2001, and the percentage of costs covered by third-party payment has declined, thus placing the burden of treatment costs on parent consumers. In 2001, the authors go on to say, it was reported that the average daily cost of treatment was $161 ($242 when adjusted to 2007 dollars), whereas this study reports an average daily cost of $278. Interestingly, it appears as though treatment lengths are getting longer, even though different definitions have been used. If an average treatment length of 45 days is applied to the inflation adjusted 2001 daily cost of treatment, the total treatment cost would be $10,890. If the 2006 daily treatment cost is applied to an average treatment length of 45 days, the total cost of treatment would be $12,510. Obviously longer programs are significantly more expensive. This point raises the point that incremental changes in daily cost translate into significant costs to consumers, which in this case are primarily parents with little external support. For access to this level of wilderness therapy families must have deep pockets—or access to them.

It is critical for clients entering private pay adventure therapy programs match the client and his or her issues with a program, or therapist within a program who has specific skills with the diagnosis of the client. One example (and there are many) of such a professional is Paula Leslie, MA, LCPC, of Erkis Consulting, (Personal Communication, March 2011) who visits the programs she refers students to and spends at least 24 hours at each program, including an overnight in the field. According to Leslie, an educational consulting professional can learn much about how a program operates from observing the last events of the evening and the first events of the morning.

Visiting programs and attempting to get the best match is not always possible, but no one wants the youth to get worse when going into treatment. Note this is possible and documented in the literature as an iatrogenic effect (Weiss et al, 2005), in which clients exit a program with more negative resources than positive ones, and are more likely to learn more bad habits and dysfunctional behaviors than healthy and functional ones while in the program.

One of the weaknesses and potential threats identified in the SWOT survey analysis presented in Table 14.1 was the limitation of wilderness and adventure therapy programs that only cater to "privileged" families. Indeed, Aleta Meyer (personal communication, April 2010) who works in Washington, DC, when describing wilderness therapy programs to a colleague in a government funding agency, was met with the remark that this was a "boutique industry." So neither end of this continuum—whether viewed as a discipline-based boot camp for youth or a boutique industry catering to the youth of the rich and famous—accurately portrays the field. It is up to all with a passion for adventure therapy to help provide youth, adults, parents, caregivers, therapists, teachers, and especially policy makers with an accurate and evidence-based picture of how this effective approach changes lives—especially the lives of youth and young adults who are reluctant or resistant to change from traditional therapy techniques.

Access to the Land

Access of clients or potential clients to programs can sometimes be a challenge for the field. The loss of the use of wilderness areas, especially federal lands, potentially poses a risk to a program's ability to operate.

When permits for wilderness access are denied, many programs literally have no place to go. Wells (2011) discussed the Bureau of Land Management's

Secretarial Order 3310, which controls access to "wild lands," explaining how some interpretations of this act could prevent wilderness therapy programs from operating in crucial backcountry areas. A likely scenario would be that programs might have an access permit to a certain area, but be denied the ability to use motorized vehicles or helicopters from conducting rescue operations (on the rare chance they were needed), preventing them from being able to conduct their business in a safe and ethical manner.

Oversight and Regulation Issues

One respondent to the survey mentioned earlier in this chapter used an ink-blot image to describe how the general public viewed adventure and wilderness therapy. Some people (especially the general public, including legislative policy makers) still do not distinguish adventure therapy programs from discipline-based boot camps, even though the distinctions are clear. Russell (2006b, p. 64) outlined these differences as follows:

> In direct contrast to boot camps, consequences of client actions while on the trail were not met with harsh and cruel punishment in the form of marathon hikes and food deprivation, but are experienced through natural cause and effect associated with wilderness living and often mediated in a group context. Moreover, staff in these programs did not force participants to change their behavior for their betterment. Staff were seen as patient and let natural consequences first work to help clients work on self care, and then when the client was ready, engaged them in uncovering the reasons for their being in treatment. Each of these points was also supported with client references. Finally, staffs were not viewed as the enemy or commander, as would likely be the case in a boot-camp environment. Rather, they are seen as patient, supportive, easy to talk to, and caring.

The U.S. Government Accounting Office (GAO, 2007, p. 1) produced a report to

> (1) verify whether allegations of abuse and death at residential treatment programs are widespread and (2) examine the facts and circumstances surrounding selected closed cases where a teenager died while enrolled in a private program.

The GAO report and testimony before Congress was entitled "Concerns Regarding Abuse and Death in Certain Programs for Troubled Youth" (Kutz & O'Connell, 2007). The GAO defined the programs under scrutiny in this report as "wilderness therapy programs, boot camps, and academies, among other names" that "provide a range of services, including drug and alcohol treatment, confidence building, military-style discipline, and psychological counseling for troubled boys and girls with a variety of addiction, behavioral, and emotional problems" (p. 1). The GAO report focused *solely* on private-pay programs and was in reference to a request put forth by the House Committee on Education and Labor to investigate allegations of abuse and neglect reported in these programs. The information presented and conclusions generated in the report were startling, and include incidents of abuse and neglect reported in several states. Of particular relevance to this chapter were the conclusions put forth by the GAO that little is known about this industry, as there is no one entity providing information or oversight, be it allegations of abuse and neglect, or the number and types of programs operating. It is important to note that programs operated by state agencies or operated under state contracts were excluded from this study. Nevertheless, the GAO report led to House Bill (H.R. 911) Stop Child Abuse in Residential Programs for Teens Act of 2009, which was referred to the U.S. Senate Committee on Health, Education, Labor, and Pensions—where, that year, it "died" in committee.

Some of the issues the law tried to address have been detailed in several articles by a group of researchers called Alliance for the Safe, Therapeutic, and Appropriate Use of Residential Treatment (ASTART), with a particular focus on mistreatment and abuse of youth in residential care (Behar, Friedman, Pinto, Katz-Leavy, & Jones, 2007; Friedman et al., 2006; Pinto, Friedman, & Epstein, 2005). These articles make a case for regulations to stop abuses occurring primarily underline at unlicensed and unregulated facilities. They advocate adoption of policies recommended by the American Bar Association (2007) that included closing facilities that cannot provide evidence of their efficacy.

Many of the deaths cited in the GAO report were a result of staff neglect and misuse of physical restraint—a direct result of inadequate background and training for work with challenging youth. In 2011, Congressman George Miller (D-CA) introduced a bill to prevent and reduce the use of physical restraint and seclusion in schools, and for other purposes. Many programs that advertised themselves as offering therapy did not have a therapist on staff. Training and hiring in adventure therapy programs has changed considerably from the dates of the deaths cited in the GAO report, yet the academic and professional training and certifications required to practice adventure therapy are still not clear. Clearly positive outcomes in adventure therapy, much like surgery or psychotherapy, are related to the skill of the therapist or surgeon. Training paths in adventure therapy are not clearly demarcated as they are in medicine, social work, or psychology. How does one become an adventure therapist?

TRAINING: HOW DO YOU GET THERE FROM HERE?

Students and recent graduates often ask how they can become an adventure/wilderness therapist. It would be a simple answer if there were several programs to choose from that had a clear mental health focus, leading the student to become a licensed mental health practitioner while also offering adequate training in wilderness/adventure skills. The field does not have a straight pathway like medical school, for which a student is able to leave the bachelor's degree (that contains some specific prerequisite courses for applying to medical school), attend medical school, participate in residency and serve as an intern, pass recognized assessments ("boards"), and be granted a license to practice. There are mental health programs in professional counseling, social work, marriage and family therapy, psychology, and psychiatry that can lead one toward state licensing as a mental health practitioner. We feel this qualification is necessary (but not sufficient) to calling oneself an adventure therapist.

Due to the changing landscape of programs in the past decade and what might occur in the decades following the publication of this text, we will not recommend specific programs to obtain training, although we are beginning to see master's-level programs where one can obtain specific training in adventure therapy (e.g., the University of New Hampshire). Instead, what is offered is a broad pathway to becoming an adventure therapist. As noted above, this pathway includes obtaining a recognized and licensable mental health degree, although this may not be the first stop along the path.

We recommend working as field staff or as a guide in an adventure therapy program that has a clinical focus and licensed mental health practitioners on staff early in one's career path. This experience is invaluable in determining if this approach to treatment is one that appeals to you. Once one has worked for several years in the field and obtained the requisite (and often literal) "muddy boots" of credibility needed, the next step would be to secure an advanced mental health degree that qualifies one for a license to practice mental health. We will not make recommendations as to which mental health degree best fits with adventure therapy, as each has its strengths and prejudices. We instead encourage exploration of which professional identify fits with one's own personality and belief systems. The bottom line is that to call oneself a therapist, one must have a degree that leads to a mental health license in the state where one is working. As Davis Berman and Berman (1994, p. 141) stated:

> Staff who provide for the mental health needs of the clients should meet the same rigorous standards that would apply in other settings. Thus counseling and/or psychotherapy should be provided by professional mental health staff who are trained and licensed in accordance with state statutes and national standards.

We also believe the path to becoming an adventure therapist should include experience in placements other than adventure therapy (perhaps more "traditional" placements for youth) including, but not limited to, private practice, community mental health, therapeutic boarding schools, therapeutic camps, residential treatment, and psychiatric hospitals. Such a breadth of experience can help the practitioner learn traditional approaches that may or may not be valid placements for adventure therapy participants either prior to or following treatment. In addition, the training path we recommend helps one learn the tools, theories, and experiences that make these other environments effective. Knowing what these traditional approaches offer also helps in understanding how and why adventure therapy can be effective.

More master's and doctoral programs are sorely needed where students can study and practice mental health treatment using adventure therapy techniques. We have downloaded titles of theses and dissertations with the terms *adventure therapy* and *wilderness therapy* in the title that we conducted in a program that trained mental health professionals. Although there are a handful of these manuscripts each year, sadly few of them make it to a peer-reviewed publication for wider dissemination. In addition, and perhaps more telling, rarely can one find the same university or major professor who has served to advise the master's or doctoral student. This unfortunate fact is one major reason there has not been a one-time, let alone sustained, grant-funded research in adventure therapy practice. One can only dream of an adventure therapy "lab" graduate students can apply to, study in, produce research from, and spawn protégées who go forth with multiple funded research projects in adventure therapy.

SUSTAINING PROFESSIONALS IN ADVENTURE THERAPY

Bunce (1998) presented a workshop at the First International Conference on Adventure Therapy in Perth, Australia, where she focused on burnout of staff in adventure therapy settings. Many students who read this article, even today, note they read many of the benefits of adventure therapy for the participants, but they rarely see the challenges addressed of working long hours with difficult clients over many days.

Bunce (1998) found professionals working in adventure therapy settings had feelings of incompletion concerning their clients' weekly goals. She also reported the experience of transient work relationships due to the turnover in the field. This turnover can be by design in open continuous flow programs or by default in closed, set timeframe, seasonal programs. Bunce documented the following issues of countertransference:

1. Staff developing inappropriate relationships with clients or even mimic maladaptive behaviors of their clients while on expeditions.
2. Staff encountering problems with finding and keeping intimate relationships while involved with work.
3. Staff losing feelings of control.
4. Staff developing a lack of self-confidence.
5. Staff growing in fear and insecurity for being exposed as inadequate.

Marchand, Russell, and Cross (2009) investigated field staff in adventure therapy programs and empirically confirmed many of the characteristics Bunce (1998) identified. These authors found most staff were typically under 30 and single. Those who were in relationships partnered with other staff or persons in related fields. Perhaps misery or support loves company! The authors found that even with the high cost of training there was no reliable data on turnover rates of staff, although nearly one half of those surveyed had been in their jobs less than 5 months.

Recommendations from Marchand, Russell, and Cross (2009) included a call for programs to do the following:

- Helping staff maintain balanced lifestyles and healthy living situations
- Offering stress-reducing opportunities for feedback, counseling, meditation, and exercise
- Being honest in hiring by stressing both the pros and the cons of working in the field, especially when working with troubled and manipulative youth
- Connecting new staff with mentor staff to help normalize, guide, and enlighten
- Being open to the therapeutic benefits of pets in the wilderness and work to consider reasonable and responsible policies to take advantage of this bond

The care and nurturing of staff in adventure programs is not a well-researched area, but one that must be examined for the health of the profession. In addition, more studies on what hiring attributes might predict an effective and healthy staff member are sorely needed. This is not a place for "trial by fire."

TECHNOLOGY

Since Gass (1993) questioned and challenged the field, there has been an explosion of technology. In fact, the Internet was on only two years old when he offered his challenges. The "bag phones" of 20 years ago are now being replaced with smartphones that allow GPS, the ability to capture video, and download e-books. These are just a few of the applications that are impacting, or have the potential to impact program practices in AT in the near future. The community standard whereby all of one's professional peers are engaging in a practice may determine how programs embrace or eschew technology. If your competitors have satellite phones in the wilderness, why don't you? Does the battery-powered smartphone GPS replace the ability of staff to know map and compass skills? Do iPads and e-book readers allow information to be taken into the field that previously would have been restricted by weight?

Should field staff be allowed to take their personal cell phones into the wilderness? Should field staff be allowed to send text messages when off duty but still in camp? Can the smartphone or iPad provide a mechanism to capture, store, and transmit treatment notes back to base camp to allow for continuous supervision and billing of client services? Can the smartphone's camera allow field staff to take pictures of rashes, burns, or questionable first aid incidents so they can be relayed back to the base camp medical staff for a determination of whether a participant should come out of the field or stay in and follow the treatment recommended? How might social networking (e.g., Facebook) be used ethically for follow-up with clients in wilderness programs? Should clients be able to contact field staff and therapists after they have completed treatment? Can parents join together online to support one another as their youth are involved in treatment or help those who are contemplating treatment? If programs do not embrace social networking for them, might "crowd sourcing" of information about their program hurt their reputations unjustly?

These questions pale against the many future incidents we cannot even imagine as technology changes, improves, and allows for new innovations. The debate of how much the wilderness is compromised by technology will remain, however, and is a debate that should continue.

SUMMARY

There are many questions that stem from this chapter that will need to be addressed in the future. The question that began this chapter—will adventure therapy remain or return to being an application of other therapies or will it emerge as a profession unto itself? (Gass, 1993, p. 415)—remains unanswered, including:

- Will government control of reporting structures for any alleged or real incidents in residential treatment come to fruition and provide hardships that shut down adventure therapy programs?
- Will land access become so restrictive for those who take groups into the wilderness that the programs have no place to go and thus have to close?
- Will wilderness therapy go the way of corporate adventure and price itself out of the market, becoming the "boutique industry" it does not want to be?
- Will clear academic and internship training paths in adventure therapy emerge for social workers, professional counselors, marriage and family therapists, psychologists, and psychiatrists?
- Will there be lifelong career paths in adventure therapy that extend to direct care practitioners beyond their 20s that do not have to involve going into administration?

- Will technology enhance our safety in the wilderness or become an attractive nuisance?
- Will social networking provide ongoing support for participants and parents of adventure therapy clients so that there is sustained positive aftercare that supports changes made while in treatment?
- Will there be more widespread acceptance of adventure therapy as a valid, research-supported treatment?
- Will multiple graduate training opportunities exist for budding adventure therapists who can help refine this prevention and treatment approach for a variety of diagnoses and funded opportunities help researchers provide undeniable evidence of this powerful approach to treatment?
- Can each of us who read this book make a commitment to influence public policy to be open to accepting adventure therapy as a viable approach to healing and health?

It only takes a spark—to ignite a sustained flame—from many passionate professionals and eager students joining together to offer valid answers to these questions!

AIN'T BUT ONE WAY OUT

Nicole Lovato

A referred group of teens ranging from 15 to 18 years were on their second program with us. They come from a small community and have been in a drug court program ranging from 1 week to 3 months. Our first program had been difficult. Getting the clients to participate in activities had been a bit of a challenge and when we asked them to reflect on it, it seemed like that was asking for too much. The following is what happened on their second program.

A maze of rope had been strung up and connected to a series of trees for them as an activity. The goal was for them to find "their way out." They were not allowed to talk to each other. They would be informed when they had come to the end and exit out of the maze. The clients were also blindfolded. As they made their way around and around the maze, some students were beginning to become frustrated and annoyed. Other clients were just quietly looking and feeling around the maze. Staff on the sidelines were constantly saying, "If you need help, I'm here to help." The first student that found the way out was completely dumbfounded to learn that the way out was to ask for help. Some participants that had found the way out chose to stay out; others went back in to help the remaining individuals find the way out. As it was getting toward the end of activity and time was running out, more and more people were asking for help. Only one was left on the maze when time had been called.

Not quite sure if they would even talk about the experience, we ended up spending a good 45 minutes discussing it. We analyzed the experience from numerous angles, many different metaphors, and every bit of learning they gained from that experience. One student expressed the group's stubbornness and how that had led them into their current situation. Even though he knew he had been going in circles for the whole time, he was not going to give up. He also did not want to ask for help because "I could do it on my own, I didn't know where the end was, but I was going to try and get there." He commented that one of the learnings for him was "to not have too much pride and allow others who have been in a similar situation to help me." This was the same student who was the last one left in the maze.

For many clients the maze became a metaphor for them being in drug court, not exactly sure how to get out and stay out of the program. Although staff always offered help to them, it was not always taken. In retrospect, this activity really centered their attention and investment on understanding the purpose of our program and providing them with the resources we were there to offer. As we continued with the next four programs, they were more willing and open to reflect on our experiences. Not asking for help can be one of the most difficult lessons life has to offer. Being able to teach difficult lessons in a safe environment with consequences people can learn from is what I call adventure therapy.

As a freshman at an Indian boarding school in Santa Fe, I began experimenting, first with drugs, then alcohol. In both instances, I was suspended and placed in an intensive residential guidance program. This program took misbehaving teens to the Santa Fe Mountain Center. Part of the center was a program that primarily works with the Native American population in New Mexico, using adventure as a tool to learn life skills. This is where I learned that I could make a career in this field. I saw facilitators working there who were from my own pueblo. I remember asking them "You guys get paid to do this?" From that day on, I knew that's where I wanted to work. I began to make changes in my life; I was getting better at school, my circle of friends changed, and I was done with drugs and alcohol. Upon graduation from high school, I applied to the center—not knowing how to be an experiential educator, just knowing that I wanted to do it. To my surprise, I was hired. Being a participant and then an employee at the center gave me a sense of confidence that led me to pursue bigger adventures, like a 28-day NOLS backpacking course and an apprentice-ship on an 18-foot Chinese Junk. I sailed the seas for almost 2 years learning about the coral reefs of the oceans, how to scuba dive, and how to be a part of a world outside my reservation. When I returned to land, I came back to the center stronger, more experienced, and passionate about the work I would continue to do for the next 6 years.

As a Native woman, it has become so important to me to help my people. Experiential education is the best way that I know how to teach. It is the way we as Native people have always learned, whether through stories, people, thoughts or ideas. I believe in the power of adventure therapy because it has changed my own life path. I can only hope to do the same for others.

Risk Management of Adventure Therapy Programs

Gass (2003) presented 25 guidelines to use in the analysis of adventure therapy programs at the Third International Adventure Therapy Conference. Directly based on similar principles to Association for Experiential Education's accreditation program, the following 25 items are offered as a beginning overview to assist in the construction, or use as a verification checklist, of an adventure therapy program risk management system.

1. **Do you have a written set of policies and procedures?**

   Program documents communicate to staff expected practices and standards for activities posing risk to the health and well-being of clients and staff. This documentation can be specifically written by and for the adventure therapy program, or adapted from other reputable sources. It should include policies or protocols governing practices, or guidelines on accepted practices and curriculum materials (e.g., procedures involving medical screening, assessment, treatment, behavior management, record keeping, individualized treatment plan, supervision). All staff should be familiar with and have access to written risk management procedures and associated guidelines. These procedures are part of the larger risk management plan. Policies and procedures should apply to staff and clients alike.

2. **Do you have a written emergency action plan for all adventure therapy activities?**

   An emergency action plan includes, but may not be limited to, the following:
   - Site-specific considerations
   - Search-and-rescue protocols
   - Location and contact information for emergency medical facilities

- Emergency care/first aid protocols
- Notification protocols (e.g., rescue groups, next-of-kin contact person, local authorities, media person)

3. Does your program have a functioning risk management committee?
Your program should have a committee with an appropriate representative mix of individuals to cover all areas of risk management. This includes, but may not be limited to, lawyers, medical personnel, and outside technical skill advisers. This committee should meet regularly (once or twice a year) to review all facets of the program.

4. Does your program prepare an annual risk management report? Does your program make changes based on the findings of this report (e.g., trends, training needs, incidents as a predictor of future areas of inappropriate risk exposure)?
Adventure therapy programs should have systems in place for managing risk and sanctioning practices. This often means that incident data is collected, analyzed, acted upon, and reported. For the benefit of the adventure therapy field, programs are encouraged to submit their data to risk management databases of appropriate professional organizations on an annual basis.

5. Does your program engage in scheduled internal and external risk management reviews?
During risk management reviews, targeted aspects of the program are examined and a written review is presented along with a verbal presentation to program personnel and supervisors. A final written report is prepared with recommendations, suggestions, and observations focusing on any necessary or suggested program changes aimed at increasing quality and managing risk appropriately. Copies of any internal or external reviews/reports should be made available to the organization's insurance company and legal counsel.

6. Does your adventure therapy program have all staff and clients go through appropriate admissions and medical screening processes?
Programs should acquire appropriate information from staff and clients to facilitate medical screening so informed decisions can be made regarding their ability to participate. No clients or staff should be allowed to participate in activities that possess a reasonable likelihood of causing harm to themselves or others due to a medical or physical condition. Medical forms should clearly state that failure to accurately complete all portions of the form could result in injury or compound the extent of an injury.

7. Does your program address additional participant health concerns specific to each activity, including the management of medications?
Certain health concerns make clients more susceptible to injury, or sometimes contraindicate actual preventative efforts. For example, if a participant is on certain psychotropic medications, the interaction with certain environmental conditions (e.g., heat regulation systems) are

understood and addressed, and participation in adventure experiences is adapted or eliminated.

8. **Does your program to inform clients and their guardians of the nature and goals of the program, its requirements regarding physical activity and behavior, and the consequences of not meeting these requirements?**
   Programs must take steps (written and verbal) to disclose the nature of the program, its physical requirements, and the rules of behavior. These conditions must be accepted, agreed upon, and followed.

9. **Does your program inform clients and guardians of potential risks and strive to have clients acknowledge and assume the program's inherent risks?**
   Programs should have clients (and parents/guardians of minors) sign documents were risks associated with the program are identified, acknowledged, and assumed. These risks include inherent risks that can be reasonably anticipated. Such provisions may appear in an assumption and acknowledgment of risk for, or be part of a release/waiver form.

10. **If your organization allocates legal liability for injuries or losses suffered by clients, does it do so by means of appropriate agreements?**
    Programs should take steps to appropriately allocate responsibility and/or liability for injuries or losses related to program activities. Note government statutes or regulations sometimes limit the use of these documents. Releases and related documents should be reviewed and approved by the program's legal counsel regarding enforceability and consistency with the program's philosophy and intent. (For example, a program may choose not to be released for its negligence). Specific examples include, but may not be limited to, release of liability, acknowledgment and assumption of risk, waiver of claims, agreement to indemnify and/or defend, and other documents.

11. **Does your program maintain adequate types and levels of insurance coverage?**
    Whether our commercial policy or self-insurance, your coverage must adequately meet local, state, and national requirements where your programs operate. Policies should be reviewed periodically by a knowledgeable insurance professional. Specific examples of insurance include, but may not be limited, to general liability, automobile, marine, property damage, workers compensation, professional liability, sexual abuse liability, and staff medical coverage.

12. **Does your program have a policy of no drug use during programs (other than those prescribed by a physician and used accordingly) by clients as well as employees on duty?**
    Programs have established an appropriate set of procedures to follow when administering medications in the field. Illegal and inappropriate drug use is prohibited for clients and staff.

13. **Does your program have an emergency medical protocol and an established system for calling upon emergency medical services in the event of a serious or life-threatening injury or illness? Are your staff skilled and trained in carrying out these protocols?**

    Programs have established and reliable emergency medical protocols, including a communications plan with emergency phone numbers for specific areas of operation and contact with emergency medical services in the event of an accident requiring outside expertise for medical care. Methods for communication working in the particular programming area are used. This may, or may not, include cell or satellite phones, two-way radios, CB radios, locator devices, and GPS. In remote areas where these services are not practical, clients are informed, understand, and agree to this condition.

14. **Does your program have a search and rescue protocol and establish system for calling upon rescue services, if needed, in the event of a lost or missing person? Are your staff skilled in carrying out this protocol?**

    Programs need to have procedures to reduce the possibility of clients becoming lost or separated from the group, and there is a plan of supervision in place if this happens. Clients and staff are informed and taught what to do if clients become lost or separated from the group. Staff must know what to do if they need a level of rescue that is of greater magnitude that can be reasonably expected from the program. Staff must know how to implement the program's protocol for search and rescue procedures, including air or watercraft assistance if applicable.

    Elements of this protocol may include, but may not be limited to, instructions to clients to prevent becoming lost or separated; instructions to participants on what to do if lost or separated; organizing a search (e.g., locations, methods, boundaries, rendezvous times, communications); documentation; criteria for determining the need for outside assistance; procedures for hasty, general, and fine searches; and what to do if the group is delayed or behind schedule.

    For example, with solo' experiences there are emergency "secondary" systems are in place. Each solo participant has appropriate signaling capabilities (e.g., a whistle) for emergency notification, and knows the proper protocols for its use. For longer solos, a visual check in system is established and followed according to predetermined procedures. Even though risk management measures are in place to reduce the possibilities of clients from becoming separated or lost, the program also has contingency plans for these occurances in place.

15. **Does your program have appropriate evacuation protocols? Are staff skilled and practiced in carrying out this protocol?**

    Program staff need to know how to evacuate clients under any circumstances of programming, or have others evacuated clients in need of higher levels of care. Appropriate equipment for evacuation is available as needed. Protocols may include procedures for initiating and carrying out of accusations by fixed wing aircraft, helicopter, or watercraft as appropriate.

16. **Does your program have a notification protocol that is used in the event of an emergency or accident?**
Program staff must understand the notification protocol to be followed in the event of an emergency or accident (e.g., communications with family, officials, news media).

17. **Are appropriate and adequate emergency and rescue equipment available at the site of each activity?**
Adequate emergency care and rescue equipment is available and present for all activities. Emergency care kits and appropriate emergency equipment are available and routinely checked. Repair kits and appropriate spare items are available for trips beyond the facility or road-head. Clothing, shelter, and roads are provided for activities conducted behind the facility or road-head. In the event of an injury, illness, or extreme changes in the weather, staff have the skills and equipment to survive until a return to the road to can be achieved.

18. **Are participants properly prepared for emergencies and inform the appropriate emergency skills and procedures for each activity?**
All participants should be informed of the risk management an emergency procedures for each activity (e.g., evacuation routes, contingency plans, available rescue and medical support). Emergency skills and procedures are taught to participants so they understand what to do in the event of an emergency.

19. **Does the program have appropriate design staff to client ratios for each activity?**
There are accepted ratios of staff to clients for all activities based on the nature of activity, the participant profile, and the type of environment. Programs provide appropriate staff: client ratios depend upon these and other relevant factors.

20. **Does the program make reasonable efforts to conform to all applicable government laws and regulations?**
Examples of this could include laws and guidelines pertaining to facilities/national parks, hazard communication, and exposure control for blood-borne pathogens.

21. **Do appropriate forms and documents exist and they are located in proper/accessible locations?**
Examples of this could include:
- Administrative forms: for example, mission, goals, and a random objectives; marketing materials; licenses and permits; participant information/admission and orientation; releases and related documents; specific risk management plans; personnel policy and

procedures; personnel files (e.g., resumes, applications, documentation staff training, copies of certifications, evaluations; equipment purchases and maintenance logs; equal opportunity employment statement (appropriately posted)
- Health forms: for example, staff medical history and data, clients' medical history and data, released for emergency medical treatment, first aid supplies list
- Emergency materials: for example, incident report form, program notification protocol, media protocol, search and rescue/evacuation report form, missing person report form, staff notification of next-of-kin information, client notification of next-of-kin information

22. **Does your program use appropriate therapeutic methods for specific client behavioral issues? And are your adventure therapy staff trained and qualified to use these techniques?**
The therapeutic methods employed to address client issues should represent the current best practices of the field. Staff delivering these methods should be trained, qualified, certified/licensed, and supervised in these specific techniques. This includes managing adverse psychological reactions, nonviolent crisis intervention, and therapeutic holds (physical restraints) when appropriate.

23. **When clients are involuntarily enrolled either through legal mandates or parental admission, are appropriate steps taken to ensure clients ethical rights as well as client participation?**
In certain situations (e.g., judicial mandates, incarceration, parental admission) clients are admitted into adventure therapy programs against their will/choice. In these situations care is taken to maintain client ethical rights as well as involve them in therapeutic choices whenever possible and appropriate.

24. **Does your program possess a formal plan and administration of supervision for staff?**
A formal and scheduled plan of supervising staff working with clients and therapeutic situations is maintained and properly administered. This plan may include, but may not be limited to, individual as well as group supervision. Appropriately trained supervisors deliver the supervision.

25. **Is your adventure therapy staff appropriated trained in the therapeutic methods for their clients, the adventure experiences they are using, and are they "cross trained" in adventure therapy procedures?**
The most effective adventure therapy professionals are the ones who select and adapt adventure experiences on the basis of how they "interact" with client issues, background, presenting problems, and associated clinical hypotheses. Adventure therapy techniques such as appropriate

facilitation guidelines, framing, debriefing, full-value contracting, challenge by choice, and solution-oriented approaches have been shown to make critical differences in the immediate as well as long-term benefits of adventure therapy for clients. Adventure therapy staff know how to use these procedure appropriately.

Adventure Therapy Competencies

1. TECHNICAL COMPETENCIES

The areas of practice with technical competencies cover three subsections:

1. Content and instructional knowledge of particular adventure programming skills in those areas where adventure therapy is practiced
2. Risk management protocols related specifically to adventure therapy populations and settings
3. Environmental practices

As adventure therapists become more proficient in this area of professional practice, one key indicating factor is their ability to integrate therapeutic strategies and adventure experiences in an effective and appropriate manner.

Emerging Adventure Therapist	Competent Adventure Therapist	Exemplary Adventure Therapist
• Supports senior-level adventure therapists in adventure therapy protocols • Follows established written protocols and procedures • Attends professional training opportunities to advance skills in these areas • Possesses minimum qualifications for leading particular adventure experiences • Possesses pre-site experience in particular programming area • Ensures participants always have access to appropriate equipment, nutrition, hygiene resources for particular environment	• Matches the instructor criteria for outdoor/wilderness/adventure therapy • Independently possesses all expected qualifications of their responsibilities • Is aware of latest developments of professional practice in adventure programming related to adventure therapy • Participates in ongoing training to maintain proficiency status • Ensures consistency between written protocols and actual practices	• Possesses instructor trainer skill sets and teaching capabilities • Conducts professional training opportunities for other professionals • Uses learning opportunities from clients to advance the field in new and innovative ways • Proactively works on upgrading and maintaining personal proficiency in these technical areas • Seeks innovative ways to integrate therapeutic strategies and adventure experiences and shares results with other professionals

Rating scale: Check all statements above in all three categories that describe the competency level of the adventure therapist regarding technical assessment. Check one box below indicating the adventure therapist's overall level of competency related to technical competencies in adventure programming:

☐ Emerging ☐ 2 ☐ Competent ☐ 4 ☐ Exemplary

TECHNICAL SKILLS COMPETENCIES

1. *Activity-specific content knowledge:* Rationale for program, possesses appropriate skill level and knowledge of particular adventure skill area, proper activity selection, location/site selection, staffing, supervision, qualifications, forms, nutrition, hygiene, emergency planning and procedures, clothing and equipment, warmup activities, activity protocols, activity briefing, instructional/therapeutic strategies, time control plans, transportation issues, site-specific trip planning procedures

2. *Risk management protocols:* Emergency medical skills for a particular environment, knowledge of drug/environment contraindications, risk management plans and procedures, evacuation procedures, general search protocols, crisis/fatality protocols, crisis debriefing, documentation, forms, medical information forms, exposure to blood

3. *Environmental practices:* Related to Leave No Trace principles (LNT, 2011) for a specific environmental area; plan ahead and prepare, traveling camp on durable surfaces, dispose of waste properly, leave what you find behind, minimize campfire impacts, respect wildlife, be considerate of other visitors and cultural value systems.

2. FACILITATION/PROCESSING COMPETENCIES

These areas of practice are used to enhance the effectiveness of the adventure therapy experience, assist clients in finding direction and sources for functional change, and create changes that are lasting and integrated into the clients' lives.

Emerging Adventure Therapist	Competent Adventure Therapist	Exemplary Adventure Therapist
• Possesses beginning level of processing skills	• Tailors specific processing technique to clients' needs	• Creates individually designed therapeutic techniques/processes for specific clients for their specific needs
• Monitors group behavior and presents general guidelines for growth in the adventure therapy experience	• Monitors group and individual behaviors	• Proactively promotes positive group development through engaging and creative facilitative processes
	• Develops specific guidelines for growth for this specific group and their needs	

continued

Emerging Adventure Therapist	Competent Adventure Therapist	Exemplary Adventure Therapist
• Directs clients toward areas of generic functional change • Considers how adventure therapy experience will integrate into clients' lives after experience • Refers difficult clients to supervisor or senior staff	• Develop specific areas of functional change and goals for each individual client • Prepares specific concepts and mechanisms to integrate change from adventure therapy experience into clients lives after the experience • Selects facilitation model that best fits each particular client's needs • Delivers treatment with empathy • Uses appropriate techniques with resistant and difficult clients • Creates strong connections for integration of treatment gains into clients' lives once they finish adventure therapy experience	• Designs adventure therapy experiences that address group and individual needs simultaneously • Creates processing techniques enabling clients to lead and develop their own personal growth • Enables clients to utilize strengths they bring therapy in therapeutic interventions and solutions

Rating scale: Check all statements above in all three categories that describe the competency level of the adventure therapist regarding facilitation/processing. Check one box below indicating the adventure therapist's overall level of competency related to facilitation/processing competencies in adventure programming:

☐ Emerging ☐ 2 ☐ Competent ☐ 4 ☐ Exemplary

Facilitation/Processing Competencies

a. Effective listening
b. Goal setting and monitoring
c. Providing/overseeing feedback processes
d. Debriefings/reflection (verbal and nonverbal)
e. Transfer and integration of client change
f. Experiential learning methodology and knowledge

g. Processing skills
h. Group development/process skills
i. Conflict/crisis management
j. Creating group norms/full value contracting
k. Challenge by choice
l. Facilitation guidelines and models
m. Nonverbal methods of facilitation

3. ORGANIZATIONAL/ADMINISTRATIVE COMPETENCIES

These areas of practice are concerned with the organizational structure surrounding the adventure experiences used by the adventure therapist. This competency area recognizes that even the best adventure therapist cannot be effective in an organization that is dysfunctional and does not adequately support the client or therapists in their efforts.

Emerging Adventure Therapist	Competent Adventure Therapist	Exemplary Adventure Therapist
• Follows adventure activity standards set forth by the field	• Accredited by AEE, JCAHO, COA, or other appropriate accrediting agency for adventure therapy	• Program contributes to accrediting process or advancing the standards of the field of adventure therapy
• Follows ethical standards of the field for programs	• Proactively informs clients of ethical standards of the field	• Contributes outcome and risk management data to national databases
• Written policies and procedures	• Conducts risk assessment for all program operations	• Conducts program evaluation or research on program effectiveness
• Adequate supervision is provided for particular client group	• Receives feedback from established risk management committee	• Is involved in the exchange of program information to advance the field
• Appropriate permission, access permits, and licenses for operation	• Clearly written administrative crisis management plan	
• Awareness of potential risks and hazards where activities are conducted		

continued

Emerging Adventure Therapist	Competent Adventure Therapist	Exemplary Adventure Therapist
• Adequate insurance coverage • Conducts program reviews on periodic basis • Clear policy regarding alcohol and illicit drug use in program • Proper client screening is conducted • Established emergency action plans proactively developed for serious incidents and lost person protocols • Clear medication protocols established • Appropriate transportation policies and procedures in place	• Proactively have critical incident personnel engaged • Clients are informed verbally and by writing of inherent risks of adventure activities	• When appropriate with wilderness programs, trains clients to reduce inherent risks of activity • Belongs and contributes to national organizations designed and tested to advance the field • Engaged in multiple processes of ensuring the long-term benefit of staff • Actively involved in supporting other programs, particularly those working with disadvantaged clients

Rating scale: Check all statements above in all three categories that describe the competency level of the adventure therapist regarding organizational/administrative structure. Check one box below indicating the adventure therapist's overall level of competency related to organizational/administrative structure competencies in adventure programming:

☐ Emerging　　☐ 2　　☐ Competent　　☐ 4　　☐ Exemplary

Organizational/Administrative Competencies

a. Logistical skills/trip planning

b. Activity standards

c. Ethical standards

d. Policy and procedures

e. Supervision: appropriate staff, client ratios

f. Access issues

g. Risk management planning

h. Insurance

i. Program reviews
j. Appropriate policies
k. Client screening
l. Emergency action plans: serious incidents, lost person protocols
m. Medication protocols
n. Transportation protocols
o. Accreditation
p. Advancing the field

4. CONTENT/CONCEPTUAL KNOWLEDGE COMPETENCIES

This competency refers to the ability of the adventure therapist to use specific models, practices, philosophies, and applications of adventure therapy for the particular needs of treatment issues with clients. Special attention is paid to the specific and diverse contexts of various clients (e.g., social, cultural, systemic, ethnic, gender, sexual orientation).

Emerging Adventure Therapist	Competent Adventure Therapist	Exemplary Adventure Therapist
• Aware of a variety of adventure therapy models and current practices • Aware of how client context effects the application of various adventure therapy models • Knowledgeable of various strengths and weaknesses of several adventure therapy models (e.g., indications and contraindications for specific client use)	• Proficient in using a variety of adventure therapy models • Understands how to implement adventure therapy models based on client context • Understands strengths and weaknesses of various adventure therapy models and can adapt models based on client needs and therapeutic objectives	• Adapts a variety of adventure therapy models for specific needs of each individual client • Develops new versions of adventure therapy models based on continued practice and applications and findings with specific clients in treatment

continued

Emerging Adventure Therapist	Competent Adventure Therapist	Exemplary Adventure Therapist
• Possesses current understanding of where adventure therapy models fit into current behavioral healthcare strategies • Uses adventure therapy models and practices the same with all clients • Uses adventure therapy models and practices but is largely unaware of supporting research of such practices	• Only uses particular elements of adventure therapy models when indicated • Adapts adventure therapy models and practices based on diverse needs of particular clients • Aware of supporting research of adventure therapy models and practices and adjusts treatment accordingly	• Strives to link adventure therapy practices to evolving evidence-based practices and "kernels" of key concepts of effectiveness • Advocates and makes professional presentations on the effectiveness of adventure therapy models and practices • Conducts research on adventure therapy models and practices and the effects on treatment for specific populations

Rating scale: Check all statements above in all three categories that describe the competency level of the adventure therapist regarding conceptual and content knowledge of adventure therapy. Check one box below indicating the adventure therapist's overall level of competency related to conceptual and content knowledge of adventure therapy:

☐ Emerging   ☐ 2   ☐ Competent   ☐ 4   ☐ Exemplary

Content/Conceptual Competencies

a. Adventure therapy foundations: Experiential learning, rationale for using adventure experiences in therapy
b. Adventure therapy models: Transfer of learning, solution-oriented facilitation, indications and contraindications of use, integration with other models in mental health, group development
c. Adventure therapy change process: The use of experience, reflection, framing, facilitation processes, change processes with client, and programming depth, etc.
d. The independent and interdependent uses of wilderness, nature, urban, and challenge in adventure therapy with specific populations
e. Metaphor and adventure therapy
f. Adventure therapy theories, techniques, and specific application of therapeutic techniques
g. Systemic understanding and applications of using adventure therapy

h. Understanding of behavioral healthcare delivery system intersecting with adventure therapy
  i. Current uses and effectiveness with adventure therapy practices

5. THERAPEUTIC ALLIANCE BUILDING COMPETENCIES

The focus of this competency area is the ability of the adventure therapist to co-construct an effective therapeutic alliance with clients. The building of this positive form of therapeutic relationship incorporates the use of natural environment elements and adventure programming concepts.

Emerging Adventure Therapist	Competent Adventure Therapist	Exemplary Adventure Therapist
• Meets clients at appropriate time • Orients clients to therapeutic setting • Covers appropriate intake procedures • Ensures clients complete necessary intake procedures • Informs clients of appropriate rules and regulations and acquires their signature on being informed of this process • Ask clients if they have any questions • Finds commonalities with client	• Establishes rapport with clients • Provides proper emotional validation for client • Provides feelings of support for client • Creates appropriate feelings of safety and security in adventure therapy group • Steers clients away from counterproductive behavior toward beneficial outcome behavior • Properly assesses client therapy objectives • Creates contracts or agreements on necessary tasks to be completed to reach therapeutic objectives • Forms connections built on appropriate trust, confidence, and belief that adventures therapy experiences will bring client closer toward problem resolution	• Uses natural environment to strengthen therapeutic relationship • Uses adventure experiences to strengthen therapeutic relationship • Uses natural consequences to rectify inappropriate behaviors • Involves clients in structuring behavioral norms for therapy when appropriate

Rating scale: Check all statements above in all three categories that describe the competency level of the adventure therapist regarding competencies creating therapeutic alliances in adventure therapy. Check one box below indicating the adventure therapist's overall level of competency related to creating therapeutic alliances in adventure therapy:

☐ Emerging   ☐ 2   ☐ Competent   ☐ 4   ☐ Exemplary

Therapeutic Alliance Building Competencies

a. Joining and connected skills

b. Emotional validation techniques

c. Create appropriate feelings of safety, support, and security in adventure therapy group

d. Dealing with counterproductive behavior toward beneficial outcome behavior

e. Creating contracts or agreements on necessary tasks to be completed to reach therapeutic objectives

f. Appropriate boundary settings

g. Rapport building

h. Forms connections built on appropriate trust, confidence, and belief that adventures therapy experiences will bring client closer toward problem resolution

i. Use natural environment and adventure experiences to strengthen therapeutic relationship

j. Use natural consequences to rectify inappropriate behaviors

k. Involve clients in structuring behavioral norms for therapy when appropriate

6. ASSESSMENT COMPETENCIES

Assessment includes the examination of clients in mental health settings through adventure experiences and supportive documentation for screening and creating potential interventions.

Emerging Adventure Therapist	Competent Adventure Therapist	Exemplary Adventure Therapist
• Follows established written assessment procedures	• Considers both a macro and micro perspective in assessment planning	• Uses assessment as part of building a therapeutic alliance as well as integrating interventions and planning for positive transfer of learning once adventure experiences completed

- Makes structured and basic professional interpretations/hypotheses of assessment material
- Develops 1-2 possible insights into potential treatment interventions
- Uses assessment primarily prior to treatment and interventions (e.g., diagnosis, delivery)
- Documents necessary information
- Assists in crisis situations
- Relies on supervision to formulate comprehensive and accurate client assessment

- Understands how to use adventure therapy models for therapeutic assessment (e.g., CHANGES, GRABBS)
- Understands how to diagnosis and design particular assessments using adventure therapy
- Interprets client behaviors in adventure therapy experiences and link them to specific client needs
- Views assessment not only as a procedure done prior to treatment, but also as a process done throughout client treatment
- Identifies more than one hypothesis as a rationale for client behavior
- Accesses more than one source of information for corroborating certain behaviors (e.g., affect, behavior, cognition, relationships)
- Manages crisis situations
- Uses assessment to join with clients, build therapeutic alliance, and design treatment
- Seeks out supervision and feedback when necessary for alternative perspectives on assessment and interpretation

- Analyzes and interprets data to build multiple tenable hypotheses of client behavior in meetings
- Collaborates with supporting professionals to confirm hypotheses and assessment
- Documents assessment findings and treatment reports and appropriate manner
- Inventories all sources of information on clients' behavior (e.g., affect, behavior, cognition, relationships)
- Ability to change direction of an adventurous therapy experience during the actual experience based on immediate and new client assessment information
- Understands client processing/learning preferences and how they interact with assessment and intervention processes

Rating scale: Circle all statements above that best describe the competency level of the adventure therapist regarding client assessment. Check one box below indicating the adventure therapist's overall level of competency related to client assessment:

☐ Emerging   ☐ 2   ☐ Competent   ☐ 4   ☐ Exemplary

Assessment Competencies

a. Knowledge of adventure therapy assessment procedures (e.g., CHANGES, GRABBS)
b. Collect important information on the context of the client
c. Develop multiple hypotheses regarding client response during adventure experiences for intervention recommendations
d. Appropriately document client responses and behaviors
e. Screen for potential client contraindications to adventure experiences, including physical abilities and injuries, contraindications with medications
f. Identify and determine integration strategies for client when adventure experience is completed

7. INTERVENTION COMPETENCIES

Intervention competencies focus on the implementation of adventure therapy treatment strategies and processes to produce functional client change in an appropriate, culturally relevant, lasting manner.

Emerging Adventure Therapist	Competent Adventure Therapist	Exemplary Adventure Therapist
• Possesses knowledge of a singular approach to adventure therapy	• Possesses a working knowledge of, as well as experience with, several effective treatment strategies with adventures therapy	• Encases entire adventure therapy experience in a specific culturally relevant intervention for a particular client
• Aware that cultural differences affect adventure therapy approaches	• Adapts adventure therapy treatment approaches to cultural perspectives of clients	• Strengthens the therapeutic alliance as intervention proceeds
• Conducts adventure therapy in natural and/or wilderness settings	• Understand how to use natural environment and wilderness settings to expand treatment effectiveness	• Supports clients as they in advance through interventions
• Uses adventure therapy experiences to speak for themselves to help clients change	• Understands when and how to use challenging experiences with appropriate populations, and adapts this approach with contraindicating clients	• Adapts adventure therapy experiences with clients' stages of change
• Believes risk is good, and places clients in challenging situations to develop positive change		• Works with natural environment in a synergistic manner to enhance treatment

- Aware of contraindication with some drugs and certain environmental factors in wilderness settings
- Uses assessment data select relevant adventure therapy experiences
- Regularly checks in with clients to see how they are doing
- Talks with clients about how they would use insights from the adventure therapy experience in their futures

- Competently uses adventure therapy experiences to foster functional change with clients
- Uses assessment data to select and frame isomorphic connections to adventure therapy experiences
- Continually assesses client's readiness, abilities, and integration processes as the change process occurs throughout the adventure therapy experience
- Designs integration strategies for clients to use for implementing change processes in the future

- Co-constructs challenges in adventure therapy experiences with client, making each experience individualized for particular client needs
- Assessment data connects directly to intervention strategies
- Interventions serve as next assessment process for clients
- Client changes are well integrated into their future lives

Rating scale: Check all statements above in all three categories that describe the competency level of the adventure therapist regarding intervention competency in adventure therapy. Check one box below indicating the adventure therapist's overall level of competency related to intervention competency in adventure therapy:

□ Emerging　　□ 2　　□ Competent　　□ 4　　□ Exemplary

Treatment Delivery Competencies

a. Reframing
b. Culturally sensitive treatment/intervention delivery
c. Metaphors
d. Solution-oriented therapy
e. Behavior management skills
f. Systems theory consideration
g. Emergency procedures in place
h. Working with difficult clients
i. Specific treatment competencies for specific client populations
j. Understands application of various styles, techniques, and protocols related to specific therapeutic populations

k. Conflict resolution
l. Group processing
m. Crisis management
n. Stages of change

8. THERAPEUTIC MONITORING COMPETENCIES

Therapeutic monitoring competencies focus on the continual connection to clients involved in adventure therapy programming, including ongoing evaluation of therapy, maintenance of treatment gains, ongoing treatment planning, and termination.

Emerging Adventure Therapist	Competent Adventure Therapist	Exemplary Adventure Therapist
• Stays updated in clients' therapeutic processes	• Constantly assesses clients therapeutic process	• Client treatment plan contains detailed and informative material on client progress, future assessment, and future interventions
• Informally checks in with other therapists on clients	• Formally and informally connects with client on therapeutic progress and future plans for therapeutic work	• All members of client treatment team are fully aware of change processes with each individual client
• Responds to other treatment providers when asked about client progress	• Continually evaluates treatment effectiveness to adjust interventions and plan for future changes	• All members of treatment team fully understand adventure therapy and assist in the ongoing treatment planning when using adventure experiences
• Evaluates treatment effectiveness upon completion of program and discharge	• Works with clients to integrate change and transfer changes into clients' lives	• Integration into clients future lives and termination from treatment are seen as celebrations
• Talks with clients about what they are going to do after termination of therapeutic services	• Works with clients to devise a continuum of care and ability to integrate functional changes into this care system	
• Understands basic concepts of continuum of care		

- Documents treatment process as requested in organizational protocol

- Documents client progress for therapeutic uses, therapist and organizational evaluation, and potential outcome based research when approved and appropriate

- Treatment gains are maintained, if not enhanced, over time due to maintenance strategies and integration/transfer processes

Rating scale: Check all statements above in all three categories that describe the competency level of the adventure therapist regarding therapeutic monitoring with adventure therapy. Check one box below indicating the adventure therapist's overall level of competency related to therapeutic monitoring with adventure therapy:

☐ Emerging ☐ 2 ☐ Competent ☐ 4 ☐ Exemplary

Therapeutic Monitoring Competencies

a. Client progress
b. Determining treatment effectiveness upon program completion/discharge
c. Transfer of learning/integration of change into clients' future
d. Documentation of treatment process throughout program
e. Constant assessment processes
f. Evaluating program effectiveness
g. Follow-up strategies

9. DOCUMENTATION COMPETENCIES

Documentation competencies focus on the accurate appraisal of all steps in the adventure therapy process, including but not limited to screening and intake; participant forms, such as agreement to participate, waiver, and informed consent; assessment and treatment plans; clinical progress reports and notes; referral and termination/discharge records; and other pertinent documentation forms for client benefit.

Emerging Adventure Therapist	Competent Adventure Therapist	Exemplary Adventure Therapist
• Ensures all required paperwork is completed in a timely manner • Protects clients' rights with appropriate privacy and confidentiality with all records and paperwork • Files paperwork and appropriate manner • Conducts documentation processes under the guidance and assistance of their supervisor • Documents all paperwork following agency protocol and associated federal, state, and professional regulations	• Completes and stores required client paperwork in the manner required by agency, federal, state, and professional regulations (e.g., HIPAA) • Uses picture work to help chart client progress as well as assess and develop client treatment plans and objectives • When appropriate, discusses purposes of documentation with clients to further treatment objectives and integration of change to client's future	• Completes, stores, and presents overall package of documentation in a comprehensive manner • Documentation is prepared in such a manner that with client permission it can be used for training staff as appropriate • Documentation is easily retrievable for use when referrals are requested from other agencies • Documentation clearly meets all agency, federal, state, and professional requirements

Rating scale: Check all statements above in all three categories that describe the competency level of the adventure therapist regarding documentation competency in adventure therapy. Check one box below indicating the adventure therapist's overall level of competency related to documentation competency in adventure therapy:

☐ Emerging   ☐ 2   ☐ Competent   ☐ 4   ☐ Exemplary

Documentation Competencies

a. Admission procedures and assessment of client strengths and capabilities
b. Screening, intake, orientation, obtaining consent
c. Understand psychological and physiological background elements of particular issue/disease/affliction
d. Case management
e. Appropriately use client background and history
f. Proper, timely, and appropriate documentation and communication
h. Meet federal, state, and professional requirements for documentation and associated paperwork
i. Use appropriate resources for clients

10. PROFESSIONALISM COMPETENCIES

Professionalism competencies focus on the expected professional behavior of an adventure therapist.

Emerging Adventure Therapist	Competent Adventure Therapist	Exemplary Adventure Therapist
• Aware of federal and state regulations of professional practice and program operation	• Ensures adherence to federal and state regulations on professional practice	• Provides advocacy and information to advocate for advancement of adventure therapy in federal and state areas of recognition
• Basic understanding of professional research on adventure therapy	• Integrates recent research findings and advances of adventure therapy to enhance professional practice	• Assists or leads efforts to conduct research on the field of adventure therapy
• Uses supervisor's feedback to improve practice	• Involved with peer feedback and supervision to improve professional practice	• Receives feedback and supervision of professional practices to further treatment effectiveness
• Involved in appropriate continuing education and professional development practices	• Promotes ethical standards and guidelines in professional practice and professional interaction with other colleagues in public	• Supports in the training of allied professionals to help understand adventure therapy concepts
• Obtains appropriate professional licenses and certifications	• Designs programs with social justice and multicultural issues in mind	• Gives presentations at adventure therapy conferences as well as allied related fields
• Follows ethical standards and guidelines identified by professional practice		• Serves as a model for other programs and professionals, particularly in areas of innovative practice, rigorous research, social justice, and multicultural issues
• Aware of social justice issues and multicultural influences on treatment and programming		• Serves as a model for ethical behavior and seeks to enhance new interpretations of ethical practice of adventure therapy

Rating scale: Check all statements above in all three categories that describe the competency level of the adventure therapist regarding professional development in adventure therapy. Check one box below indicating the adventure therapist's overall level of competency related to professional development with adventure therapy:

☐ Emerging   ☐ 2   ☐ Competent   ☐ 4   ☐ Exemplary

Professionalism Competencies

a. Cultural and ethical sensitivity

b. Social justice knowledge

c. Legal issues

d. Ethics, standards: adheres to professional ethics

e. Research and program evaluation knowledge

f. Ongoing training and development, continuing education

e. appropriate use of supervision

Adventure Therapy Ethics

ETHICAL GUIDELINES FOR THE THERAPEUTIC ADVENTURE PROFESSIONAL GROUP (TAPG) OF THE ASSOCIATION FOR EXPERIENTIAL EDUCATION (AEE)

Competence

Professionals strive to maintain high standards of competence and their work. They recognize the boundaries of their particular competencies and understand the potential limitations of adventure activities. Professionals exercise reasonable judgment and take appropriate precautions to promote the welfare of clients. They maintain knowledge of relevant professional information related to the use of adventure experiences and they recognize their need for ongoing education. Adventure therapists make appropriate use of professional, technical, and administrative resources that serve the best interests of participants in their program.

Boundaries of Competence

1. Professionals provide services only within the boundaries of their competence, based on their education, training, supervision, experience, and practice.
2. Professionals provide services involving specific practices after first undertaking appropriate study, training, supervision, and/or consultation from persons who were confident in those areas or practices.
3. In those areas where generally recognized standards for preparatory training do not yet exist, professionals take reasonable steps to ensure the competence of their work and to promote the welfare of clients.

4. Professionals seek appropriate assistance for their personal problems or conflicts that may impair their work performance or judgment.

Continuing Training

Professionals are aware of current information in their fields of activity and undertake ongoing professional efforts to maintain the knowledge, practice, and skills they use at a competent level.

Integrity

Professionals seek to promote integrity in the practice of adventure therapy. In these experiences, they are honest, fair, and respectful of others. In describing or reporting their qualifications, services, products, fees, and research, adventure therapists do not make statements that are false, misleading, or deceptive. Professionals strive to be aware of their own belief systems, values, needs, and limitations and the effect of these on their work.

Interaction with Other Professionals

In deciding whether to offer or provide services to those already receiving services elsewhere, professionals carefully consider the potential client's welfare. Professionals discuss these issues with clients in order to minimize the risk of confusion and conflict, consult with other professionals when appropriate, and proceed with caution and sensitivity.

Professionals do not engage, directly or through agents, in uninvited solicitation of services from actual or potential clients or others who, because of particular circumstances, are vulnerable to undue influences (e.g., respecting client relationships).

Supervision

Professionals delegate to their employees, supervisees, or students only those professional responsibilities that such persons can perform competently. Within the limitations of their institution or other roles, professionals provide proper training or supervision to employees or supervising. Professionals also take reasonable steps to see that such persons perform these services responsibly, competently, and ethically.

Professional Responsibility

Professionals uphold ethical principles of conduct, clarify the rules and obligations, accept responsibility for their behavior and decisions, and adapt their methods to the needs of different populations. Professionals consult with, refer to, and cooperate with other professionals and institutions to the full extent needed to serve the best interests of clients. Professionals are concerned about the ethical professional conduct of their colleagues. When appropriate, they consult with colleagues in order to avoid unethical conduct. Because of its direct negative influence on clients as well as on the field, professionals are strongly urged to report alleged unethical behavior to appropriate and pre-scribed channels. Professionals are ethically bound to cooperate with profes-sional associations' inquiries concerning ethical misconduct.

Basis for Professional Judgments

Professionals have an adequate basis for their professional judgment and actions that are derived from professional knowledge.

Initiation and Length of Services

Professionals do not begin services for clients where the constraints of limited contact will not benefit them. Professionals continued services only as long as it is reasonably clear that clients are benefiting from that service.

Concern for the Environment

Professionals conduct adventure experiences in a manner that has minimal impact on the environment. Professionals do not conduct adventure experiences or perma-nent damage to wilderness environments will occur as a result of programming.

Respect for Clients Rights and Dignity

Professionals respect the fundamental rights, dignity, and worth of all people. They respect the rights of clients to privacy, confidentiality, and self-determination. Professionals strive to be sensitive to cultural and individual differences, includ-ing those due to age, gender, race, ethnicity, national origin, religion, sexual orientation, disability, or socioeconomic status. Professionals do not engage in sexual or other harassment or exploitation of participants, students, trainees, supervise these, employees, colleagues, research subjects, or actual or potential witnesses or complainants in investigations and ethical proceedings.

Policy Against Discrimination

Professionals do not discriminate against or refuse professional services to anyone on the basis of age, gender, race, ethnicity, national origin, religion, sexual orientation, disability, or socioeconomic status.

Ethic of Empowerment

Professionals respect the rights of clients to make decisions and help them to understand the consequences of their choices. Professionals assist clients in charting the course of their own lives. They respect the rights of clients to make decisions affecting their lives but also demonstrate an equal concern for the rights of others.

Describing the Nature and Results of Adventure Therapy

When professionals provide services to individuals, groups, or organizations, they first provide the consumer of services with appropriate information about the nature of such services and the rights, risks, and responsibilities. Professionals also provide an opportunity to discuss the results, interpretations, and conclusions with clients.

Informed Consent

Professionals respect clients' rights to refuse or consensus services and activities. Clients must be well informed of the fees, confidentiality, benefits, risks, and responsibilities associated with these services and activities prior to participation. Professionals make reasonable efforts to answer clients' questions, avoid apparent misunderstanding about the service, and avoid creating unrealistic expectations in clients. Professionals inform clients of the relevant limitations of confidentiality as early as possible and the foreseeable uses of the information generated through their services. In the case of clients who are minors, parents and/or legal guardians must also give informed consent for participation. Professionals obtain informed consent from participants, parents, or guardians before videotaping, auto recording, or permitting third-party observation.

Fees

Professionals charged appropriate fees or services. Fees are to disclose to the clients at the beginning of services and are truthfully represented to clients and third party payers. Professionals are not guided solely by a desire for monetary reimbursement. They are encouraged to contribute a portion of their professional time for little or no personal advantage.

Advertisement

Professionals accurately represent their confidence, training, education, and experience relevant to their practices. This practice includes using

- Titles that inform clients and the public about the true and accurate identity, responsibility, source, and status of those practicing under that title.

- Professional identification (e.g., business card, office sign, letterhead, or listing) that does not include statements that are false, fraudulent, deceptive, or misleading.

Distortion of Information by Others

Adventure therapists make efforts to prevent the distortion or misuse of their clinical materials and research findings. Professionals correct, whenever possible, false, inaccurate, or misleading information representations made by others concerning their qualifications, services, or products.

Public Opinions and Recommendations

Because of their ability to influence and alter the lives of others in the field, adventure therapists exercise special care when making public their professional recommendations and opinions (e.g., public statements and testimony).

Concerns for Welfare

Adventure therapists are sensitive to real and ascribed differences in power between themselves and their clients, and they avoid exploiting or misleading other people during or after professional relationships.

Professional Relationships

Professionals provide services only in the context of their defined professional relationship or role.

Dual Relationships

Adventure therapists are aware of their influential position with respect to clients and avoid exploiting the trust and dependency of such persons. Because of this, adventure therapists make every effort to avoid dual relationships with clients that could impair professional judgments (e.g., business or close personal relationship with participants). When dual relationships exist, professionals take appropriate professional precautions to ensure that judgment is not impaired and no exploitation occurs.

Sexual Relationships

Sexual intimacy with participants is prohibited during the time of the professional relationship. Professionals engaging in sexual intimacy with past participants bear the burden of proving that there is no form of exploitation occurring.

Physical Contact/Non-Sexual Contact

Adventure therapy experiences often include various forms of physical contact between professionals and participants or among participants (e.g., spotting, checking climbing harnesses, holding hands). Professionals are sensitive and respectful of the fact that clients experience varying degrees of comfort with physical contact, even when it is offered for safety, encouragement, or support. Whenever possible, professionals inform, explain, and gain consent for usual and customary forms of physical contact. Professionals are aware of individual needs when initiating physical contact, especially if the contact is meant to communicate support (e.g., hugs, pats) and is otherwise not required for a particular activity. Except when safety is a factor, clients have the right to limit or refuse physical contact with professionals or other clients.

Behavior Management

Each program and professional will approach the topic of managing behavior with a concern for dignity and safety for both clients and professionals. Definitions of appropriate and inappropriate behaviors of clients should be made clear to clients before any adventure therapy programming commences.

Professional responses to inappropriate behaviors should be clearly understood by both professionals and clients and carried out in an appropriate manner. There should be clear documentation of staff training and awareness the about program policies concerning the management of unsafe behavior. Policies should never advocate the use of restraint unless client(s) impose a threat to themselves or others. Restraint should never be used as a punishment or a means frighten, humiliate, or threaten a client. Whenever possible, restraint should be avoided and as passive as possible. All behavior management should be accurately documented.

Physical Needs of Clients

Clients will be provided with the necessary water, nutrition, clothing, shelter, and other essential needs they require for the environment where they are living, unless there is a prior mutual consent between clients and professionals and is recognized that this will serve a valid purpose (e.g., solo). At no time during any program will though withholding of these needs be used as a punitive measure.

Physical Treatment of Clients

At no time will clients be asked to perform excessive physical activity as a means of punishment. There should be a direct relationship between the clients' physical activity levels and be objective of the experience.

Appropriate Use of Risk

The actual amount of emotional and physical risk clients experience in adventure therapy activities will be appropriate for the treatment objectives and competence level of clients. Professionals use the appropriate judgment when choosing activities that expose clients to actual or perceived physical and emotional risks.

Assisting Clients in Obtaining Alternative Services

Adventure therapists assist clients in obtaining other services if they are unwilling or unable, for appropriate reasons, to provide professional help. Professionals will not unilaterally terminate services to clients without making reasonable attempts to arrange for the continuation of such services (e.g., referral). Experiences are planned with the intent that decisions made during and after the adventure experience are in accordance with the best interest of clients.

Confidentiality

Adventure therapists respect the right of clients to decide the extent to which confidential material is made public. Professionals may not disclose participant confidences except: (a) as mandated by law; (b) to prevent a clear and immediate danger to a person or persons; (c) where the professional is a defendant in civil, criminal, or disciplinary action arising from services (in which case client confidences may be disclosed only in the course of action); or (d) if there is a waiver previously obtained in writing, and then such information may be revealed only in accordance with the terms of the waiver.

Unless it is contraindicated or not feasible, the discussion of confidentiality occurs at the onset of the professional relationship.

Use of Case Materials with Teaching or Professional Presentations

Adventure therapists only use client or clinical materials and teaching, writing, and public presentations if a written waiver has been obtained in accordance with Principle 5.10 or when appropriate steps have been taken to disguise client identity and assure confidentiality.

Storage and Disposal of Client Materials

Adventure therapists store and dispose of client records in ways that maintain confidentiality. Records should be maintained for minimum of seven (7) years.

Social Responsibility

Adventure therapists are aware of their professional possibilities to the community and society where they work and live. Within the limitations of their roles, adventure therapists avoid the misuse of their work. Professionals comply with the standards stated in the AEE Accreditation program as well as with the particular laws in their particular geographical and professional area. Professionals also encourage the development of standards and policies that serve the interests of clients and the public.

Research Rubric for Evidence-Based Research on Adventure Programs

Rubric Quality	4	3	2	1	0
Evidenced-based research evaluation	Would exceed SAMHSA or USDOE rating for model program	Would receive SAMHSA or USDOE rating for model program	Would receive SAMHSA or USDOE rating for effective program	Would receive SAMHSA or USDOE rating for promising program	Would not receive any SAMHSA or USDOE rating
Case studies or clinical samples included	Two or more case studies/clinical samples included in research	One case study/clinical samples included in research	Hypothetical case study/clinical samples included in research	Direct reference to treatment population is clearly made in an appropriate manner	No connection of findings to treatment population
Experimental Design	Random (true) experimental design	Quasi-experimental design with appropriate comparison group(s) and equal n's	Quasi-experimental design with comparison group(s) but statistical limitations (e.g., ANOVA test violations).	Single group, pre-post test design	Single data collection (e.g., post test only), no comparison group
Benefit-cost analysis	Financial benefits of treatment combined with program costs are compared against other programs offered to clients. Comparisons are calculated in a benefit cost ratio for clients to understand	Financial benefits of treatment combined with program costs are compared against other programs offered to clients.	Financial benefits of treatment combined with program costs are presented.	Program costs are presented.	None completed

Results reporting	Complete and accurate reporting on significance testing, effect size, and cost benefit figures compared to other research studies	Complete and accurate reporting on significance testing, effect size, and cost benefit figures	Complete and accurate reporting on significance testing and effect size	Complete and accurate reporting on significance testing	No significance testing completed
Training models	Clear uniform and tested professional training model presented with methods of validating/certifying adherence to model	Clear uniform and tested professional training model presented	Clear uniform professional training model presented	Reference to guidelines on how to implement intervention program is made	No reference on how to implement intervention program
Power of research design (NAROPA or power calculation)	Research design has enough power to significantly reduce Type II errors	Research design has enough power to reduce most problems with Type II errors	Research design has enough power to reduce some problems with Type II errors	Research design has enough power to reduce minor problems with Type II errors	Research design is destined to fail from the beginning of the analysis due to multiple sources of Type II errors
Instrumentation	Instrument measures variables of the "highest value" in the population being analyzed, possesses well established, and high levels of validity and	Instrument measures variables of the "high value" in the population being analyzed, possesses established levels of validity and reliability	Instrument has been used with population with relative success, established yet somewhat lower levels of validity and reliability scores (e.g., .70)	Instrument has been used with population with mixed success, established yet somewhat lower levels of validity and reliability scores (e.g., .60)	Value of measured variables is limited or unknown, Instrument possesses no established validity or reliability measures. Limited

continued

Rubric Quality	4	3	2	1	0
	reliability (e.g., higher than .90), is appropriate for client group, possesses strong levels of objectivity	(e.g., higher than .80), is appropriate for client group, possesses adequate levels of objectivity			previous use with client group, subjective analysis in reporting scores
Cultural variability	Treatment accounts for differences in SES, gender, language, intellectual abilities, cultural characteristics.	Treatment accounts for four of these characteristics	Treatment accounts for three of these characteristics	Treatment accounts for two of these characteristics	Treatment generalization is limited to specific research population
Treatment/ Intervention fidelity	Clear treatment manual available documenting well-defined and previously tested treatment/ intervention practices, testing procedures in place to verify maintenance of intervention procedures	Treatment manual available but not previously tested	Treatment procedures available for replication but not manualized, no testing to verify maintenance of intervention procedures	Information on treatment limited and not replicable unless further information is acquired	No information on treatment available

Background literature support	Building off of at least two highly similar control group studies or a large series of single-case study designs (e.g., more than 30).	Building off of at least one highly similar control group studies or several single-case study designs	Sound, accurate, and complete review of the literature in this particular area of adventure research that is also integrated with study's findings	Several key pieces of related research presented as a background and integrated with findings	None or inaccurate review of the literature in this area of adventure research
Replication	Treatment program has been replicated in more than two sites with different populations	Treatment program has been replicated in more than one site with different populations	Treatment program has been replicated in more than one site with same population	Treatment program has been replicated in one site with different populations	Treatment program has not been replicated
Length of treatment effectiveness assessed	Effects of treatment analyzed for 3 years or more	Effects of treatment analyzed for more than 1 year	Effects of treatment analyzed for more than 6 months	Effects of treatment analyzed for more than 1 month	Effects of treatment only analyzed immediately after treatment

This research rubric accounts for 10 primary indicators of excellence in evidence-based research, primarily influenced by the United States Offices of Juvenile Justice and Delinquency Prevention (OJJDP) and Substance Abuse and Mental Health Administration (SAMHSA). Initially presented at the 2007 REAP AEE conference, it has been used to evaluate the value of research projects toward supporting evidence-based practices for adventure therapy programs. Examples of research projects evaluated using this system can be found at http://www.chhs.unh.edu/kin_oe/bibliographies.html. The two bibliographies listed here combine to cover the history of empirically-based adventure therapy research through 2007.

Source: Gass, M. A. (2007, March). Evidenced based practice research rubric. Presented at the Third Annual Research and Evaluation for Adventure Programming Symposium. Santa Fe, NM.

ACRONYMS and INITIALISMS

7KMP	Seven Step Kinesthetic Metaphor Process
ACC	Adventures in a Caring Community
AEE	Association for Experiential Education
AMA	American Medical Association
APA	American Psychological Association
APA	American Psychiatric Association
APA	American Psychological Association
ASTART	Alliance for the Safe, Therapeutic, and Appropriate Use of Residential Treatment
AT	Adventure Therapy
BLM	Bureau of Land Management
BMTA	Behavior Management through Adventure
CEU	Continuing Education Unit
CHANGES	Context-Hypothesis-Action which is Novel – Generating – Evaluating- Solutions
COA	Council on Accreditation
CORE	Council on Research and Evaluation
DSM-IV	*Diagnostic and Statistical Manual of Mental Disorders*, Fourth Edition
EBP	Evidence-Based Practice
ENHANCES	Engage–New Hypotheses–Action (which is) Novel–Co-create–Evaluate–for Solutions
GAO	Government Accounting Office
GRABBS	Goals-Readiness-Affect-Body-Behavior-Stage
IEP	Individual Educational Plan
NASMHPD	National Association of State Mental Health Program Directors
NASW	National Association of Social Work
NATSAP	National Association of Therapeutic Schools and Programs
NATWC	National Association of Therapeutic Wilderness Camping
NOLS	National Outdoor Leadership School
NREPP	National Registry of Effective Programs and Practices
OB	Outward Bound
OBHIC	Outdoor Behavioral Healthcare Industry Cooperative
OBHRC	Outdoor Behavioral Healthcare Research Cooperative
OJJDP	Office of Juvenile Justice and Delinquency Prevention
RCT	Randomized Control Trial
REAP	Research and Evaluation of Adventure Programming
SAMHSA	Substance Abuse and Mental Health Services Administration
SWOT	Strengths-Weaknesses-Opportunities-Threats
TAPG	Therapeutic Adventure Professional Group
WOGA	Wilderness Outfitters and Guides Association
WRMC	Wilderness Risk Manager's Conference

References

Abrams, D. (1996). *The spell of the sensuous*. New York: Vintage Books.

Achenbach, T. M., & Edelbrock, C. S. (1981). Behavioral problems and competencies reported by parents of normal and disturbed children aged four through sixteen. *Monographs for the Society for Research and Child Development, 46*(1), 1–82.

Adams, D. (1987). *A path of honor: The story of VisionQuest*. Tucson, AZ: Blue Horse Productions.

Allin, L., & Humberstone, B. (2010). Introducing Journey(s) in adventure and outdoor learning research. *Journal of Adventure Education and Outdoor Learning, 10*(2), 71–75.

Alvarez, A. G., & Stauffer, G. A. (2001). Musings on adventure therapy. *Journal of Experiential Education, 24*(2), 85.

American Association for Marriage and Family Therapy. (2011). AAMFT core competencies. Retrieved from http://www.mftcompetencies.org/page2/page2.html

American Bar Association. (2007). American Bar Association policy requiring licensure, regulation, and monitoring of privately operated residential treatment facilities for at-risk children and youth. *Family Court Review, 45*(3), 414–420.

American Psychological Association. (1994). *Diagnostic and statistical manual of mental disorders* (4th ed.). Washington, DC: Author.

American Psychological Association Task Force on Evidence-Based Practice. (2006). Evidence-based practice in psychology. *America Psychologist,* May/June, 271–285.

Andrews, D. A., & Bonta, J. (1998). *The psychology of criminal conduct* (2nd ed.). Cincinnati, OH: Anderson Publishing.

Aos, S., Miller, M., & Drake, E. (2006). *Evidence-based public policy options to reduce future prison construction, criminal costs, and crime rates*. Olympia, WA: Washington State Institute for Public Policy.

Ashbrook, J. (2003). Mind as a humanizing brain: Toward a neurotheology of meaning. *Religion and Science, 32*(3), 301–320.

Ashby, J. S., Kottman, T., & DeGraaf, D. (2008). *Active interventions for kids and teens: Adding adventure and fun to counseling!* Alexandria, VA: American Counseling Association.

Ashley, F. B. (1990). Ethnic minorities' involvement with outdoor experiential education. In J. Miles & S. Priest (Eds.), *Adventure education* (pp. 369–374). State College, PA: Venture Publishing.

Association for Experiential Education. (1992). *Ethical guidelines of the therapeutic adventure professional group (TAPG)*. Boulder, CO: Author.

Association for Experiential Education. (2011). *Adventure therapy and adjudicated youth.* Boulder, CO: Author.

Bachelor, A., Meunier, G., Laverdiére, O., & Gamache, D. (2010). Client attachment to therapist: Relation to client personality and symptomatology, and their contributions to the therapeutic alliance. *Psychotherapy: Theory, Research & Practice, 47*(4), 454–468.

Bacon, S. (1983). *The conscious use of metaphor in Outward Bound.* Denver, CO: Colorado Outward Bound School.

Bandoroff, S. (1989). *Wilderness therapy for delinquent and pre-delinquent youth: A review of the literature.* Columbia, SC: University of South Carolina.

Bandoroff, S., & Newes, S. (2004). What is adventure therapy? In S. Bandoroff & S. Newes (Eds.), *Adventure therapy: Coming of age* (pp. 1–30). Boulder, CO: Association of Experiential Education.

Bandoroff, S., & Scherer, D. G. (1994). Wilderness family therapy: An innovative treatment approach for problem youth. *Journal of Child and Family Studies, 3*(2), 175–191.

Baruth, L. G., & Manning, M. L. (2003). *Multicultural counseling and psychotherapy: A lifespan perspective* (3rd ed.). Columbus, OH: Merrill.

Baum, L. F. (1900). *The Wizard of Oz.* New York: Schocken.

Baumeister, R. F., Campbell, J. D., et al. (2003). Does high self-esteem cause better performance, interpersonal success, happiness, or healthier lifestyles? *Psychological Science in the Public Interest, 4*(1), 1–44.

Baumeister, R. F., Campbell, J. D., Krueger, J. L., & Vohs, K. D. (2003). Exploding the self-esteem myth. *Scientific American, 292,* 84–92.

Behar, L., Friedman, R., Pinto, A., Katz-Leavy, J., & Jones, W. G. (2007). Protecting youth placed in unlicensed, unregulated residential "treatment" facilities. *Family Court Review, 45*(3), 399–413.

Bell, G. (2009). Thrilling therapy. *Army Times, 70*(5), 4.

Bennet, L. W., Cardone, S., & Jarczyk, J. (1998). Effects of a therapeutic camping program on addiction recovery: The Algonquin Haymarket Relapse Prevention Program. *Journal of Substance Abuse Treatment, 15*(5), 469–474.

Beringer, A. (2004). Toward an ecological paradigm in adventure programming. *Journal of Experiential Education, 27*(1), 51–66.

Berman, M. (1988). *The re-enchantment of the world.* Ithaca, NY: Cornell University Press.

Berry, T. (1988). *The dream of the earth: Our way into the future.* San Francisco: Sierra Club Books.

Bettman, J., & Tucker, A. R. (2011). Shifts in attachment relationships: A study of adolescents in wilderness treatment. *Child and Youth Care Forum.* DOI 10.1007/s10566-011-9146-6.

Boyle, P. (1994). *Scout's honor: sexual abuse in Americas most trusted institution.* Rocklin, CA: Prima Publishing.

Brekke, J. (2005, May 4). *Therapists in the woods.* Retrieved from http://www.strugglingteens.com/artman/publish/article_5124.shtml

Bridgeland, J., Dululio, J. J., & Morison, K. B. (2006). The silent epidemic: Perspectives of high school dropouts. Washington, DC: Civic Enterprises.

Brown, E. (2002, October 14). When rich kids go bad. *Forbes, 170*(8), 140–148.

Brown, S., & Lent, R. (Eds.). (2007). *Handbook of counseling psychology* (4th ed.). New York: Wiley.

Brown, T. L., Borduin, C. M., & Henggeler, S. W. (2001). Treating juvenile offenders in community settings. In J. B. Ashford, B. D. Sales, & W. H. Reid (Eds.), *Treating adult and juvenile offenders with special needs.* Washington, DC: American Psychological Association, (pp. 445–464).

Bruner, J. S. (1966). *Toward a theory of instruction.* Cambridge, MA: Belknap Press of Harvard University.

Buell, L. H. (1981). *The identification of outdoor adventure leadership competencies for entry-level and experience-level personnel.* Unpublished doctoral dissertation. Amherst, MA: University of Massachusetts.

Bunce, J. (1998). Sustaining the wilderness therapist. In *Proceedings of the First International Adventure Therapy Conference.* Perth, Australia.

Bunge, M. (1963). A general black box theory. *Philosophy of Science 30*(4), 346–358.

Bunting, C. J., & Donley, J. P. (2002, January). *Ten years of challenge course research: A review of affective outcome studies.* Poster presented at the 6th Coalition for the Education in the Outdoors Research Symposium, Bradford Woods.

Bureau of Land Management. (2008). Health and safety of participants attending "Wilderness Therapy Programs" or "Residential Treatment Programs for Troubled Youth" on public lands. Retrieved June 14, 2010, from http://www.blm.gov/wo/st/en/info/regulations/Instruction_Memos_and_Bulletins/national_instruction/20080/IM

Burg, J. E. (2001). Emerging Issues in Therapeutic Adventure with Families. *Journal of Experiential Education, 24*(2), 118.

Burlingame, G. M., Wells, M. G., & Lambert, M. J. (1995). *The Youth Outcome Questionnaire.* Stevenson, MD: American Professional Credentialing Services.

Burns, B. J., Hoagwood, K. & Maultsby, L. T. (1998). Improving outcomes for children and adolescents with serious emotional and behavioral disorders: Current and future directions. In M. H. Epstein, K. Kutash, & A. J. Duchnowski (Eds.), *Outcomes for children and youth with emotional and behavioral disorders and their families: Programs and evaluation best practices* (pp. 686–707). Austin, TX: Pro-Ed.

Burns, B. J., Phillips, S. D., Wagner, H. R., Barth, R. P., Kolko, D. J., Campbell, Y., et al. (2004). Mental health need and access to mental health services by youths involved with child welfare: A national survey. *Journal of the American Academy of Child & Adolescent Psychiatry, 43*(8), 960–970.

Burton, L. M. (1981). A critical analysis and review of the research on Outward Bound and related programs. *Dissertation Abstracts International, 47*/04B.

Cameron, S., & turtle-song, i. (2002). Learning to write case notes using the SOAP format. *Journal of Counseling & Development, 80*(3), 286–292.

Carlson, K. P., & Cook, M. (2007). Challenge by choice: Adventure-based counseling for seriously ill adolescents. *Child and Adolescent Psychiatric Clinics of North America, 16*(4), 909–919.

Carroll, L. (1865). *Alice in Wonderland.* New York: Tribeca Books.

Carter, B., & McGoldrick, M. (Eds.). (2005). *The expanded family life cycle: Individual, family and social perspectives.* Boston: Allyn & Bacon.

Cason D., & Gillis, H. L. (1994). A meta-analysis of outdoor adventure programming with adolescents. *Journal of Experiential Education, 17*(1), 40–47.

Castellano, T. S., & Soderstrom, I. R. (1992). Therapeutic wilderness programs and juvenile recidivism: A program evaluation. *Journal of Offender Rehabilitation, 17*(3/4), 19–46.

Catton, W. R. (1969, December 19). Motivations of wilderness users. *Pulp and Paper Magazine of Canada,* pp. 12–26.

Chalquist, C. (2009). A look at the ecotherapy research evidence. *Ecopsychology, 1*(2), 64–74.

Chisholm, M. & Gass, M. A. (2011, April). *Using adventure programming for reintegrating the combat soldier.* Paper presented at the 2011 Research and Evaluation of Adventure Programs (REAP) Conference, Washington, DC.

City Year. (2011). Retrieved from http://www.cityyear.org

Clark, J., Marmol, L., Cooley, R., & Gathercoal, K. (2004). The effects of wilderness therapy on the clinical concerns of troubled adolescents. *Journal of Experiential Education, 27*(2), 213–232.

Clifford, E., & Clifford, M. (1967). Self-concepts before and after survival training. *British Journal of Clinical Psychology, 6*, 241–248.

Cockerill, E., & Witmer, H. (1938). An evaluation of a psychiatric camp for children. *Smith College Studies in Social Work, IX*(3), 199–236.

Cole, E., Erdman, E., & Rothblum, E. D. (Eds.). (1994). *Wilderness therapy for women.* Binghamton, NY: Harrington Park Press.

Constantine, N., Benard, B., & Diaz, M. (1999). *Measuring protective factors and resilience traits in youth: The Healthy Kids Resilience Assessment.* Paper presented at the Seventh Annual Meeting of the Society for Prevention Research, New Orleans, LA.

Cooley, R. (2000). How big is the risk in wilderness treatment of adolescence? *Wilderness Risk Management Conference Proceedings,* Anchorage, AK, pp. 13–18. Retrieved from http://www.nols.edu/wrmc/resources.shtml

Corteo, J., Vallee, W., & Gass, M. (2010). *Staff development model.* Durham, NH: University of New Hampshire.

Corvette, D. (1986). Family feud contributed to downfall of Anneewakee's founder. *The Atlanta Journal,* p. B1.

Corvette, D. (1990). Anneewakee's almost out of the woods.

Council on Accreditation. (2010). *Wilderness and adventure-based therapeutic outdoor services.* Retrieved from http://www.coastandards.org/standards.php?nav-View=private§ion_id=83

Council on Social Work Education. (2008). *Educational policy and accreditation standards.* Alexandria, VA: CSWE

Crisp, S. J. R. (2002). *The Australian Wilderness Adventure Therapy Accreditation Scheme.* Melbourne, Australia: Neo YouthPsych Consulting.

Cushman, P. (1990). Why the self is empty: Toward a historically situated psychology, *American Psychologist, 4*, 599–611.

Davis-Berman, J. S., & Berman, D. (1994). *Wilderness therapy: Foundations, theories and research.* Dubuque, IA: Kendall/Hunt Publishing.

De Hert, M., Dirix, N., Demunter, H., & Correll, C. (2011). Prevalence and correlates of seclusion and restraint use in children and adolescents: a systematic review. *European Child Adolescent Psychiatry,* 1–10.

Dean, A. J., Duke, S. G., George, M., & Scott, J. (2007). Behavioral management leads to reduction in aggression in a child and adolescent psychiatric inpatient unit. *Journal of the American Academy of Child and Adolescent Psychiatry, 46*(6), 711–720.

Deci, E. L., & Ryan, R. M. (2008). Facilitating optimal motivation and psychological well-being across life's domains. *Canadian Psychology, 49*, 14–23.

Delaney, K. R. (2006). Evidence base for practice: Reduction of restraint and seclusion use during child and adolescent psychiatric inpatient treatment. *Worldviews on Evidence-Based Nursing, 3*(1), 19–30.

Dewey, J. (1938). *Experience and education.* New York: Touchstone.

DiClemente, C. C., McConnaughy, E. A., Norcross, J. C., & Prochaska, J. O. (1986). Integrative dimensions for psychotherapy. *Journal of Integrative & Eclectic Psychotherapy, 5*(3), 256–274.

Dobkin, C., & Gass, M. A. (2010). *Dropout prevention program: A dropout prevention program for Denver public schools.* Durham, NH: University of New Hampshire.

Dreikurs, R., Greenwald, B. B., & Pepper, F. C. (1982). *A new approach to discipline: Logical consequences.* New York: Hawthorne Books.

Driver, B., & Tocher, S. R. (1970). Toward a behavioral interpretation of recreation, with implications for planning. In B. L. Driver (Ed.), *Elements of outdoor recreation planning* (pp. 7–91). Ann Arbor, MI: University Microfilms International.

Durlak, J. A., & Weissberg, R. P. (2007). *The impact of after-school programs that promote personal and social skills.* Chicago, IL: Collaborative for Academic, Social, and Emotional Learning.

Durr, L. I. (2009). Optimal challenge: The impact of adventure experiences on subjective well-being. *Journal of Experiential Education, 31*(3), 451–455.

Dynarski, M., Clarke, L., Cobb, B., Finn, J., Rumberger, R., & Smink, J. (2008). *Dropout prevention: A practice guide* (NCEE 2008–4025). Washington, DC: National Center for Education Evaluation and Regional Assistance, Institute of Education Sciences, U.S. Department of Education.

Easley, A. T., Passineau, J. T., & Driver, B. L. (1990). The use of wilderness for personal growth, therapy, and education. Fort Collins, CO: Rocky Mountain Forest and Range Experiment Station.

Eason, A., Colmant, S., & Winterowd, C. (2009). Sweat therapy theory, practice, and efficacy. *Journal of Experiential Education, 32*(2), 121–136.

Eells, E. (1986). *History of organized camping: The first 100 years.* Martinsville, IN: American Camping Association.

Eisen, G. (Producer). (1988, July 10). VisionQuest [Television series episode]. In *60 Minutes.* New York: CBS News.

Embry, D., & Biglan, A. (2008). Evidence-based kernels: Fundamental units of behavioral influence. *Clinical Child and Family Psychological Review, 11,* 75–113.

Emerson, R. E. (1836). *Nature.* Boston: James Munroe and Company. Retrieved from http://www.archive.org/details/naturemunroe00emerrich

Erickson, M. (1952). Deep hypnosis and its induction. In E. Rossi (Ed.), *The collected papers of Milton H. Erickson: Vol. I. The nature of hypnosis and suggestion.* New York: Irvington.

Erikson, E. (1980). *Identity and the life cycle.* New York: Norton.

Etzkorn, K. R. (1965). The social meaning of a form of public recreation. *Sociology and Social Research, 49,* 76–81.

Ewert, A. (1987). Research in experiential education: An overview. *Journal of Experiential Education, 10*(2), 4–7.

Ewert, A., Frankel, J., Van Puymbroeck, M., & Luo, Y. (2010). The impacts of participation in outward bound and military service personnel: The role of experiential training. Boulder, CO: Association for Experiential Education.

Falender, C., & Shafranske, E. (2004). *Clinical supervision: A competency-based approach.* Washington, DC: American Psychological Association.

Ferguson, G. (1999). *Shouting at the sky: Troubled teens and the promise of the wild.* New York: St. Martin's Press.

Fischer, R. L., & Attah, E. B. (2001). City kids in the wilderness: A pilot-test of outward bound for foster care group home youth. *Journal of Experiential Education, 24*(2), 109.

Flavin, M. (1996). *Kurt Hahn's school and legacy.* Wilmington, DE: The Middle Atlantic Press.

Flippo, T., & Warren, K. (2010, April). *Social justice issues.* Presented at the Association for Experiential Education Conference, Peterborough, NH.

Fredrickson, L. M., & Johnson, B. L. (2000). Wilderness: A place for ethical inquiry. In S. F. McCool, D. N. Cole, W. T. Borrie, J. O'Loughlin. (2000). Wilderness science in a time of change conference—Volume 3: Wilderness as a place for scientific inquiry (pp. 177–180). Ogden, UT: U.S. Department of Agriculture, Forest Service, Rocky Mountain Research Station.

Freitas, R. A. (2002). *Death is an outrage*. Retrieved from http://www.rfreitas.com/Nano/DeathIsAnOutrage.htm

Friedman, R. M. (2009, February). Abuse of youth in residential placements: An overview of the problem presentation to "Abuse of Youth in Residential Treatment: A Call to Action." Retrieved from http://astart.fmhi.usf.edu/AStartDocs/overview-abuse-presentation-021909.pdf

Friedman, R. M., Pinto, A., Behar, L., Bush, N., Chirolla, A., Epstein, M., et al. (2006). Unlicensed residential programs: The next challenge in protecting youth. *American Journal of Orthopsychiatry, 76*, 295–303.

Friese, G. T., Pittman, J. T., & Hendee, J. C. (1995). Studies of the use of wilderness for personal growth, therapy, education, and leadership development: An annotation and evaluation. Moscow, ID: Wilderness Research Center.

Frishman, J. S. (2006). The adventure-journey perspective: Postmodern adventure therapy expressed through the Hero's journey metaphor. Ann Arbor, MI: ProQuest Information & Learning.

Frueh, B. C., Monnier, J., Grubaugh, A. L., Elhai, J. D., Yim, E., & Knapp, R. (2007). Therapist adherence and competence with manualized cognitive-behavioral therapy for PTSD delivered via videoconferencing technology. *Behavior Modification, 31*, 856–866.

Galkin, J. (1937). The treatment possibilities offered by the summer camp as a supplement to the Child Guidance Clinic. *The American Journal of Orthopsychiatry, VII*, 474–482.

Gallon, S. and Porter, J. (2011). *Performance assessment rubrics for the addiction counseling competencies*. Oregon Health and Science University: Northwest Frontier Addiction Technology Transfer Center. 2nd edition.

Gass, M. (1985). Programming the transfer of learning in adventure education. *Journal of Experiential Education, 8*(3), 18–24.

Gass, M. (1991). Enhancing metaphor development in adventure therapy programs. *Journal of Experiential Education, 14*(2), 7–13.

Gass, M. (1993). *Adventure therapy: Therapeutic applications of adventure programming*. Dubuque, IA: Kendall/Hunt Publishing.

Gass, M. A. (Ed.). (1998a). *Administrative practices of accredited adventure programs*. New York: Simon & Schuster.

Gass, M. A. (1998b). Client conversation in therapy. Durham, NH: University of New Hampshire.

Gass, M. A. (1998c). The system. *Ziplines, 36*, 52–53.

Gass, M. A. (2004, January). Best practices in adventure therapy in 2004 and 2010. Presented at the 2004 National Association of Therapeutic Schools and Programs conference, Clearwater Beach, FL.

Gass, M. A. (2005). Comprehending the value structures influencing significance and power behind experiential education research. *Journal of Experiential Education, 27*(3), 286–296.

Gass, M. A. (2007, March). Evidenced based practice research rubric. Presented at the Third Annual Research and Evaluation for Adventure Programming Symposium, Beverly, MA. Retrieved from http://www.chhs.unh.edu/kin_oe/2007_symposium.html

Gass, M. A., & Gillis, H. L. (1995a). CHANGES: An assessment model using adventure experiences. *Journal of Experiential Education, 18*(1), 34–40.

Gass, M. A., & Gillis, H. L. (1995b). Focusing on the "solution" rather than the "problem": empowering client change in adventure experiences. *Journal of Experiential Education, 18*(2), 63–69.

Gass, M. A., & Gillis, H. L. (2010). Clinical supervision in adventure therapy: enhancing the field through an active experiential model. *Journal of Experiential Education, 33*(1), 72–89.

Gass, M. A., & Wurdinger, S. (1993). Ethical decisions in experience-based training and development programs. *Journal of Experiential Education, 16*(2), 41–47.

Gibson, P. M. (1979). Therapeutic aspects of wilderness programs: A comprehensive literature review. *Therapeutic Recreation Journal, 13*(2), 21–33.

Gibson, P. M. (1981). *The effects of, and the correlates of, success in a wilderness therapy program for problem youth.* Unpublished doctoral dissertation, Columbia University, New York.

Gillis, H. L. (1992). Therapeutic uses of adventure-challenge-outdoor-wilderness: theory and research. In K. Henderson (Ed.), *Proceedings of Coalition for Education in the Outdoors Symposium.* Cortland, NY: Coalition for Education in the Outdoors.

Gillis, H. L. (1993). Cooking with Gass. In M. Gass (Ed.), *Adventure therapy: Therapeutic applications of adventure programming* (pp. ix–x). Dubuque, IA: Kendall/Hunt Publishing.

Gillis, H. L. (1998). The journey in Oz: From activity-based psychotherapy to adventure therapy. In C. M. Itin (Ed.), *Exploring the Boundaries of Adventure Therapy International Perspectives.* Proceedings of the 1st International Adventure Therapy Conference, Perth Australia.

Gillis, H. L., & Bonney, W. C. (1986). Group counseling with couples or families: Adding adventure activities. *Journal for Specialist in Group Work, 11*(4), 213–220.

Gillis, H. L., & Gass, M. A. (1993). Bringing adventure into marriage and family therapy: An innovative experiential approach. *Journal of Marital and Family Therapy, 19*(3), 273–286.

Gillis, H. L., & Gass, M. A. (2000, November). Supervision in adventure therapy: Bring your best or worst cases to an active, experiential program. Presented at the Association for Experiential Education International Conference, Tucson, AZ.

Gillis, H. L., & Gass, M. A. (2010). Treating juveniles in a sex offender program using adventure-based programming: A matched group design. *Journal of Child Sexual Abuse, 19*(1), 20–34.

Gillis, H. L., Gass, M. A., Clapp, C., Rudolph, S., Nadler, R., & Bandorhoff, S. (1992). Family adventure questionnaire: Results and discussion. In Birmingham, C. (Ed.), *Association for Experiential Education: 1991 Conference Proceedings and Workshop Summaries Book* (29–39), Boulder, CO: *Association for Experiential Education.*

Gillis, H. L., Gass, M. A., & Russell, K. C. (2008). The effectiveness of Project Adventure's behavior management programs for male offenders in residential treatment. *Residential Treatment for Children & Youth, 25*(3), 227–247.

Gillis, L., & Priest, S. (1999, April). Shining a light on adventure therapy competencies. Presented at the 1999 Southeast Regional Conference of the Association for Experiential Education, Jabez, KY.

Gillis, H. L., & Ringer, T. M. (1996). Using adventure groups for personal change: Principles, practice and group process. Presented at 50th Anniversary Conference of Developmental Training Beyond 2000, Brathay, United Kingdom.

Gillis, H. L., & Ringer, T. M. (1999). Therapeutic adventure programs adventure programming. In S. Priest & J. Miles (Eds.), *Adventure Education.* State College, PA: Venture Publications.

Gillis, H. L., & Russell, K. C. (2008). Group-based adolescent treatment: Service delivery and effectiveness, and emerging treatment alternatives. Poster presented at the Annual Convention of the American Psychological Association, Boston, MA.

Gillis, H. L., & Simpson, S. (1992). Therapeutic uses of adventure-challenge-outdoor-wilderness: Theory and research. In K. Henderson (Ed.), *Proceedings of the coalition for education in the outdoors* (pp. 35–47). Cortland, NY: State University of New York.

Gillis, H. L., & Speelman, L. (2008). Are challenge (ropes) courses an effective tool? A meta analysis. *Journal of Experiential Education, 31*(2), 111–135.

Glasser, W. (1965). *Reality therapy: A new approach to psychiatry.* New York: Harper & Row.

Glendinning, C. (1990). *When technology wounds.* New York: Morrow.

Golins, G. L. (1978). How delinquents succeed through adventure-based education. *Journal of Experiential Education, 1*(2), 26–30.

Goodstein, L., & Sonthenhamer, H. (1987). *A study of the impact of ten Pennsylvania placements on recidivism prepared for the Pennsylvania Juvenile Court Judges Commission.* Shippensburg, PA: Center for Juvenile Training and Research.

Government Accounting Office. (2007, October 10). Residential treatment programs: Concerns death and abuse in certain programs for troubled youth. Retrieved October 10, 2007, from http://www.gao.gov/new.items/d08146t.pdf

Government Accounting Office. (2008, April 24). Residential treatment programs: Selected cases of death, abuse and deceptive marketing. Retrieved from http://www.gao.gov/new.items/d08713t.pdf

Green, P. J. (1981). The content of a college-level outdoor leadership course for land-based outdoor pursuits in the Pacific Northwest: A Delphi consensus. Unpublished doctoral dissertation. Eugene, OR: University of Oregon.

Greenhouse, L. (2000, June 29). The Supreme Court: The New Jersey case; Supreme Court backs boy scouts in ban of gays from membership. *The New York Times,* p. A1.

Greenleaf, R. K. (1977). *Servant leadership: A journey into the nature of legitimate power and greatness.* New York: Paulist Press.

Greenway, R. (1995). "The wilderness effect and ecopsychology." In T. Roszak, M. Gomes, & A. Kanner (Eds.), *Ecopsychology: restoring the earth healing the mind.* San Francisco: Sierra Club Books, pp 122–135.

Greenwood, P. W., & Turner, S. (1987). The VisionQuest program: An evaluation. Santa Monica, CA: Rand Corporation.

Gregory, G. (2000, February 12). Deadly discipline. *The Oregonian.*

Haas, L. J., & Malouf, J. L. (1989). *Keeping up the good work: A practitioner's guide to mental health ethics.* Sarasota, FL: Professional Resource Exchange.

Hahn, K. (1960, July). Outward Bound. Presented at the annual meeting of the Outward Bound Trust.

Haley, J. (1993). *Uncommon therapy: Psychiatric techniques of Milton H. Erickson, M. D.* New York: WW Norton & Company.

Hall, R. (1987). Linking resources, learning, and experience in a multicultural world. Unpublished master's thesis. Mankato, MN: Mankato State University.

Hans, T. A. (2000). A meta-analysis of the effects of adventure programming on locus of control. *Journal of Contemporary Psychotherapy, 30*(1), 33–60.

Harper, N. J. (2009a). Family crisis and the enrollment of children in wilderness treatment. *Journal of Experiential Education, 31*(3), 447–450.

Harper, N. J. (2009b). Current insights into wilderness and adventure therapy. Family crisis and the enrollment of children in wilderness treatment. *Journal of Experiential Education, 31*(3), 447–450.

Harper, N. (2010). Future paradigm or false Idol: A cautionary tale of evidence-based practice for adventure education and therapy. *Journal of Experiential Education, 33*(1), 38–55.

Hartig, T., & Evans, G. (1991). Restorative effects of natural environment experiences. *Environment and Behavior, 23*(1), 3–26.

Hattie, J., Marsh, H. W., Neill, J. T., & Richards, G. E. (1997). Adventure education and Outward Bound: Out-of-class experiences that make a lasting difference. *Review of Educational Research, 67*(1), 43–87.

Hill, M., Glaser, K., & Harden, J. (1998). A feminist model for ethical decision making. *Women and Therapy, 21*(3), 101–121.

Hilsenroth, M. J., Blagys, M. D., Ackerman, S. J., Bonge, D. R., & Blais, M. A. (2005). Measuring psychodynamic-interpersonal and cognitive-behavioral techniques: Development of the Comparative Psychotherapy Process Scale. *Psychotherapy: Theory, Research, Practice, Training, 42*(3), 340–356.

Hirsch, J., & Gillis, H. L. (1997). *Food for thought: A workbook & video for developing metaphorical introductions to group activities.* Dubuque, IA: Kendall/Hunt Publishing.

Hoare, C. H. (1991). Psychosocial identity development and cultural others. *Journal of Counseling and Development, 70,* 45–53.

Hogue, A. (2002). Adherence process research on devlopmental interventions: Filling in the middle. *New Directions for Child and Adolescent Development, 98,* 67–74.

Horvath, A. O., & Greenberg, L. S. (1989). Development and validation of the Working Alliance Inventory. *Journal of Counseling Psychology, 36*(2), 223–233.

Horvath, A. O., & Symonds, B. D. (1991). Relation between working alliance and outcome in psychotherapy: A meta-analysis. *Journal of Counseling Psychology, 38,* 139–149.

Human Givens Institute. (2011). Ethics and professional conduct policy: Guidelines on the writing in use of case histories. Retrieved from http://www.hgi.org.uk/casestudyguidelines.html

Hunt, J. (1990). *Ethics in experiential education.* Boulder, CO: Association for Experiential Education.

Hunt, J. (2009). Ethical issues and risk management: Ethically tolerable accidents. Retrieved from http://www.nols.edu/nolspro/pdf/wrmc_proceedings_98_ethically_tolerable_accidents_hunt.pdf

International Adventure Therapy Conference. (2009). History of international adventure therapy conferences. Retrieved from http://www.bacp.co.uk/5iatc/history.php

Itin, C. (1997). Exploring the boundaries of adventure therapy: International perspectives. Paper presented at the First International Adventure Therapy Conference, Perth, Australia.

Itin, C. (2002). The double diamond model of experiential education as a framework. In K. Richards, & B. Smith (Eds.), *Therapy within adventure.* Augsburg, Germany.

James, T. (1980). Can the mountains speak for themselves? Outward Bound. Retrieved from http://wilderdom.com/facilitation/Mountains.html

James, W. (1892). The stream of consciousness. In W. James (Ed.), *Psychology.* New York: World.

Jelalian, E., Lloyd-Richardson, E. E., Mehlenbeck, R. S., Hart, C. N., Flynn-O'Brien, K., Kaplan, J., et al. (2010). Behavioral weight control treatment with supervised exercise or peer-enhanced adventure for overweight adolescents. *The Journal of Pediatrics, 157*(6), 923–928.

Jelalian, E., Mehlenbeck, R., Lloyd-Richardson, E. E., Birmaher, V., & Wing, R. R. (2006). 'Adventure therapy' combined with cognitive-behavioral treatment for overweight adolescents. *International Journal of Obesity, 30*(1), 31–39.

Johnson, B. L., & Fredrickson, L. M. (2000). "What's in a good life?" Searching for ethical wisdom in the wilderness. *Journal of Experiential Education, 23*(1), 43–50.

Johnston, L. D., O'Malley, P. M., Bachman, J. G., & Schulenberg, J. E. (2006). *Monitoring the Future national results on adolescent drug use: Overview of key findings, 2005* (NIH Publication No. 06-5882). Bethesda, MD: National Institute on Drug Abuse.

Jones, S. R., & McEwen, M. K. (2010). *A conceptual model of multiple dimensions of identity.* Retrieved from http://www.drapuig.info/files/A_conceptual_model.pdf

Jordan, A. E., & Meara, N. M. (1990). Ethics and the professional practices of psychologists: The role of virtues and principles. *Professional Psychology: Research and Practice, 21*(2), 107–114.

Kahn, P. H., Jr. & Kellert, S. R. (Eds.). (2002). *Children and nature: Psychological, sociocultural, and evolutionary investigations.* Cambridge, MA: The MIT Press.

Kant, I. (1964). *Groundwork of the metaphysic of morals.* New York: Harper & Row.

Kaplan, R., & Kaplan, S. (1989). *Experience of nature.* New York: Cambridge University Press.

Kaplan, S. (1983). A model of person environment compatibility. *Environment and Behavior, 15,* 311–332.

Kaplan, S. & Berman, M. G. (2010). Directed attention as a common resource for executive functioning and self-regulation. *Perspectives on Psychological Science, 5*(1), 43–57.

Karver, M. S., Shirk, S., Handelsman, J., Fields, S., Gudmundsen, G., McMakin, D., & Crisp, H. (2008). Relationship processes in youth psychotherapy: Measuring alliance, alliance-building behaviors, and client involvement. *Journal of Emotional and Behavioral Disorders, 16*(1), 15–28.

Kaslow, N. (2004). Competencies in professional psychotherapy. *American Psychologist, 59,* 74–78.

Kaslow, N. (2009). President's column. *Psychotherapy Bulletin, 44*(3), 2–5.

Kataoka, S. L., & Zhang, E. (2002). Unmet need for mental health care among U.S. children: Variation by ethnicity and insurance status. *American Journal of Psychiatry, 159*(9), 1548–1555.

Kellogg Foundation. (2004). *Using logic models to bring together planning, evaluation, and action: Logic model development guide.* Battle Creek, MI: W.K. Kellogg Foundation.

Kelly, F., & Baer, D. (1968). *Outward Bound: An alternative to institutionalization for adolescent delinquent boys.* Boston, MA: Fandel Press.

Kelly, F., & Baer, D. (1969). Jesness inventory and self concept measures for delinquents before and after participation in Outward Bound. *Psychological Reports, 25,* 719–724.

Kelly, F. J. & Baer, D. J. (1971). Physical challenge as a treatment for delinquency. *Crime and Delinquency, 17*(4), 437–445.

Kelly, V. A. (2006). Women of courage: A personal account of a wilderness-based experiential group for survivors of abuse. *Journal for Specialists in Group Work, 31*(2), 99–111.

Kemp, T. (2006). An adventure-based framework for coaching. In D. R. Stober & A. M. Grant (Eds.), *Evidence based coaching handbook: Putting best practices to work for your clients* (pp. 277–311). Hoboken, NJ: John Wiley & Sons.

Kennedy, L., & Monrad, M. (2007). *Approaches to dropout prevention: Heeding early warning signs with appropriate interventions. National High School Center at the American Institutes for Research.* Retrieved from http://www.betterhighschools.com/docs/nhsc_approachestodropoutprevention.pdf

Kesselheim, A. D. (1974). *The reason for freezin'.* Paper presented at the Conference on Outdoor Pursuits in Higher Education, Boone, NC.

Ketcham, C. (2007, May). A death at Outward Bound. *National Geographic Adventure,* pp. 49–55.

Kimball, R. (1979). *Wilderness experience program.* Final evaluation report. (No. ERIC ED179327).

Kimball, R. (1983). The wilderness as therapy. *Journal of Experiential Education, 6*(3), 7–16.

Kimball, R. O., & Bacon, S. B. (1993). The wilderness challenge model. In M. Gass (Ed.), *Adventure therapy: Therapeutic applications of adventure programming.* Dubuque, IA: Kendall Hunt Publishing.

Kitchener, K. S. (1984). Intuition, critical evaluation, and ethical principles: The foundation for ethical decisions in counseling psychology. *The Counseling Psychologist, 12*(3), 43–55.

Kleiber, L. C. (1993). *An experiential education intervention for at-risk youth in the eagle county school district.* Denver, CO: University of Denver.

Knight, C. (2006). Integrating solution-focused principles and techniques into clinical practice and supervision. *The Clinical Supervisor, 23,* 153–173.

Knopf, R. C. (1972). Motivational demand of recreation behavior. Unpublished master's thesis. Ann Arbor, MI: University of Michigan.

Krakauer, J. (1995, October). Loving them to death. *Outside Magazine,* pp. 72–82.

Kutz, J. D., & O'Connell, A. (2007). *Concerns regarding abuse and death in certain programs for troubled youth.* Report and Testimony to the Committee on Education and Labor, House of Representatives. Washington, DC: U.S. Government Accounting Office.

Latessa, E. (2004). The challenge of change: Correctional programs and evidence-based practices. *Criminology and Public Policy, 3*(4), 547–560.

Lazarus, A. A. (1981). *The practice of multimodal therapy.* New York: McGraw Hill.

Lazarus, H., & Reaves, A. (1973). *How to get your money's worth out of psychiatry.* Dover, MA: Sherbourne Press.

LeBel, J., Stromberg, N., Duckworth, K., Kerzner, J., Goldstein, R., Weeks, M., et al. (2004). Child and adolescent inpatient restraint reduction: A state initiative to promote strength-based care. *Journal of the American Academy of Child & Adolescent Psychiatry, 43*(1), 37–45.

Leemon, D. (2008). Adventure program risk management report incident data from 1998–2007. Boulder, CO: Association for Experiential Education. Retrieved from http://www.aee.org/files/en/user/cms/WRMC_poster_2008_final.pdf

Lilienfeld, S. O. (2007). Psychological treatments that cause harm. *Perspectives on Psychological Science 2*(1), 53–70.

Lime, W., & Cushwa, C. T. (1969). *Wildlife aesthetics and autocampers in the Superior National Forest.* St. Paul, MN: North Central Forest Experiment Station.

Littell, J. H., Campbell, M., Green, S., & Toews, B. (2005). Multisystemic therapy for social, emotional, and behavioral problems in youth aged 10–17. *Cochrane Database of Systematic Reviews, 3,* CD004797.

Loughmiller, C. (1965). *Wilderness road.* Austin, TX: Hogg Foundation for Mental Health.

Loughmiller, C. (1979). *Kids in trouble.* Tyler, TX: Wildwood Books.

Louv, R. (2006). *Last child in the woods: Saving our kids from nature deficit disorder.* Chappel Hill, NC: Algonquin Books.

Lowe, R., & Guy, G. (1996). A reflecting team format for solution-oriented supervision: practical guidelines and theoretical distinctions. *Journal of Systemic Therapies, 15*(4), 26–45.

Luborsky, E. B., O'Reilly-Landry, M., and Arlow, J. A. (2007). Psychoanalysis. In R. J. Corsini, & D. Wedding (Eds.), *Current psychotherapies* (8th ed, pp. 15–62). Stamford, CT: Brooks Cole Publishing.

Lucas, R. C. (1963). The importance of fishing as an attraction and activity in the Quetico-Superior area. St. Paul, MN: U.S. Department of Agriculture, Forest Service, North Central Forest Experiment Station.

Lung, D. M., Stauffer, G. A., & Alvarez, T. G. (2008). *The power of one: Using adventure and experiential activities in one-on-one counseling sessions.* Bethany, OK: Wood N Barnes Publishing.

Lynch, D. F. (2005). *An examination of the scope and variety of adventure therapy services within the state of Maine.* Ann Arbor, MI: ProQuest Information & Learning.

MacKillop, J., Lisman, S. A., Weinstein, A., & Rosenbaum, D. (2003). Controversial treatments for alcoholism. In S. O. Lilienfeld, S. J. Lynn, & J. M. Lohr (Eds.), *Science and pseudoscience in clinical psychology* (pp. 273–305). New York: Guilford Press.

Marchand, G., Russell, K. C. & Cross, R. (2009). An empirical examination of outdoor behavioral healthcare field instructor job related stress and retention. *Journal of Experiential Education, 31*(3), 359–375.

Marsh, H. W., & Craven, R. G. (2006). Reciprocal effects of self-concept and performance from a multidimensional perspective: Beyond seductive pleasure and unidimensional perspectives. *Perspectives on Psychological Science, 1,* 133–163.

Marsh, H. W., & Richards, G. E. (1990). Self-other agreement and self-other differences on multidimensional self-concept ratings. *Australian Journal of Psychology, 42*(1), 31–45. doi/10.1080/00049539008260103

Marsh, H., Richards, G., & Barnes, J. (1984). Multi-dimensional self concepts: The effects of participation in an Outward Bound program. *Journal of Personality and Social Psychology, 50*(1), 195–204.

Martin, A., Krieg, H., Esposito, F., Stubbe, D., & Cardona, L. (2008). Reduction of restraint and seclusion through collaborative problem solving: a five-year prospective inpatient study. *Psychiatric Services, 59*(12), 1406–1412.

Masten, A., & Reed, M. G. (2002). Resilience in development. In C. R. Snyder, and S. Lopez (Eds.), *Handbook of Positive Psychology* (pp. 74–88). Oxford University Press: New York.

Masters, K., Bellomci, C., Bernet, W., Arnold, V., Beitchman, J., Benson, R., et al. (2002). Practice parameter for the prevention and management of aggressive behavior in child and adolescent psychiatric institutions, with special reference to seclusion and restraint. *Journal of the American Academy of Child & Adolescent Psychiatry, 41*(2, Supplement 1), 4S–25S.

McAvoy, L. (1990). Rescue-free wilderness areas. In J. C. Miles & S. Priest (Eds.), *Adventure education* (pp. 329–334). State College, PA: Venture.

McCue, R., Urcuyo, L., Lilu, Y., Tobias, T., & Chambers, M. (2004). Reducing restraint use in a public psychiatric inpatient service. *The Journal of Behavioral Health Services and Research, 31*(2), 217–224.

McManus, M. A. (2003). *Is the health care system working for adolescents?* Washington, DC, Maternal and Child Health Policy Research Center.

McManus, M., McCarthy, E., Kozak, L. J., & Newacheck, P. (1991). Hospital use by adolescents and young adults. *Journal of Adolescent Health, 12,* 107–115.

McNeil, E. B. (1957). The background of therapeutic camping. *Journal of Social Issues, 13*(1), 3–14.

McPeake, J. D., Kennedy, B., Grossman, J., & Beaulieu, L. (1991). Innovative adolescent chemical dependency treatment and its outcome: A model based on outward bound programming. *Journal of Adolescent Chemical Dependency, 2,* 29–57.

Medrick, F. (1977). Confronting passive behavior through outdoor experience: A TA approach to experiential learning. Upper Darby, PA: U.S. Department of Agriculture, Forest Service, Northeastern Forest Experiment Station.

Merchant, C. (1993). *Major problems in environmental history.* Lexington, MA: D.C. Heath and Company.

Metzner, R. (1995). The psychopathology of the human-nature relationship. In T. Roszak, M. E. Gomes, & A. D. Kanner (Eds.), *Ecopsychology: Restoring the earth, healing the planet* (pp. 55–67). San Francisco: Sierra Club Books.

Meyer, D., & Williamson, J. (2009). Potential causes of accidents in outdoor pursuits, matrix. Retrieved from http://www.nols.edu/wrmc/resources.shtml

Mill, J. S. (1975). *On liberty*. New York: Penguin Classics.

Miller, J. A., Hunt, D. P., & Georges, M. A. (2006). Reduction of physical restraints in residential treatment facilities. *Journal of Disability Policy Studies, 16*(4), 202–208.

Miner, J., & Boldt, J. (1981). *Outward Bound USA: Learning through experience in adventure-based education.* New York: William Morrow & Co.

Minuchin, S., & Fishman, C. (1981). *Family therapy techniques.* Cambridge, MA: Harvard University Press.

Mitchell, V., & Crawford, I. (1950). *Camp counseling.* Philadelphia: W.B. Saunders Co.

Mitten, D. (1994). Ethical considerations in adventure therapy: A feminist critique. In E. Cole, E. Erdman, & E. D. Rothblum (Eds.), *Wilderness therapy for women: The power of adventure.* New York: Harrington Park Press.

Mitten, D. (1996). *The value of feminist ethics in experiential education teaching and leadership.* Boulder, CO: Association for Experiential Education.

Mitten, D. (2002, January). An analysis of outdoor leaders' ethics guiding decisions. Presented at the Coalition for Education in the Outdoors 6th Biennial Research Symposium, Bradford Woods, IN.

Moler, C. L. (2008). *The effects of adventure therapy on forgiveness in women.* Ann Arbor, MI: ProQuest Information & Learning.

Moore, T., & Russell, K. C. (2002). Studies of the use of wilderness for personal growth, therapy, education, and leadership development: An annotation and evaluation. Moscow, ID: University of Idaho-Wilderness Research Center.

Moote, G. T., & Wadarski, J. S. (1997). The acquisition of life skills through adventure-based activities and programs: A review of the literature. *Adolescence, 32*(125), 143–167.

Moreno, J. L. (1972). *Psychodrama, Vol. 1* (4th ed.). Beacon, NY: Beacon House.

Morganstern, J. (1995, January 15). A death in the desert. *Los Angeles Times Magazine.*

Morse, W. (1947). From the University of Michigan fresh air camp: Some problems of therapeutic camping. *The Nervous Child, 6,* 211–224.

Muir, J. (1901). *Our national parks.* Boston: Houghton, Mifflin, and Company.

Murphy, M. J. (1996). *The Wizard of Oz* as cultural narrative and conceptual model for psychotherapy. *Psychotherapy: Theory, Research, Practice, Training, 33*(4), 531–538.

Nadler, R. S. (1993). Therapeutic process of change. In M. Gass (Ed.), *Adventure therapy: Therapeutic applications of adventure programming.* Dubuque, IA: Kendall/Hunt.

Naess, A. (1989). *Ecology, community and lifestyle: Outline of an ecosophy.* Cambridge, MA: Cambridge University Press.

Nash, R. (1982). *Wilderness and the American mind.* New Haven, CT: Yale University Press.

National Association of Social Workers. (2011). *Code of Ethics of the National Association of Social Workers.* Washington, DC: NASW.

National Association of State Mental Health Program Directors Research Institute. (2010). National Public Rates: Age stratification report restraint hours. Alexandria, VA: NASMHPFRI.

National Registry of Evidence-based Programs and Practices. (2010). *About NREPP.* Retrieved from http://www.nrepp.samhsa.gov/about.asp

Neill, J. T. (2003). Reviewing and benchmarking adventure therapy outcomes: Applications of meta-analysis. *Journal of Experiential Education, 25*(3), 316–321.

Neill, J. (2004). The elephant in the black box. Retrieved from http://www.wilderdom.com/research/blackbox2.htm

Newes, S. (2001). Adventure-based therapy: Theory, characteristics, ethics, and research. Retrieved from http://wilderdom.com/SandyNewes.htm

Newes, S., & Bandoroff, S. (2004). What is adventure therapy? In S. Bandoroff & S. Newes (Eds.), *Adventure therapy: Coming of age* (pp. 1–30). Boulder, CO: Association of Experiential Education.

Nock, M. K., Kazdin, A. E., Hiripi, E., & Kessler, R. C. (2007). Lifetime prevalence, correlates, and persistence of DSM-IV oppositional defiant disorder: Results from the National Comorbidity Survey Replication. *Journal of Child Psychology and Psychiatry, 48,* 703–713.

Norcross, J. C. (Ed.). (2011). *Psychotherapy relationships that work* (2nd ed.). New York: Oxford University Press.

Norcross, J. C., Bike, D. H., & Evans, K. L. (2009). The therapist's therapist: A replication and extension 20 years later. *Psychotherapy: Theory, Research, Practice, Training, 46*(1), 32–41.

Norton, C. (2010). Into the wilderness—A case study: The psychodynamics of adolescent depression and the need for a holistic intervention. *Clinical Social Work Journal, 38,* 226–235.

North Carolina Department of Juvenile Justice and Delinquency Prevention. (2011). News and Events: Budget Cuts Force Closure of Swannanoa and Camp Woodson. Retrieved from http://www.juvjus.state.nc.us/news/2011/January/closeSwannanoa-CampWoodson.html.

Nunno, M. A., Holden, M. J., & Tollar, A. (2006). Learning from tragedy: A survey of child and adolescent restraint fatalities. *Child Abuse & Neglect, 30*(12), 1333–1342.

Office of Juvenile Justice and Delinquency Prevention. (2010). *Model program guide.* Retrieved from http://ojjdp.ncjrs.gov/programs/mpg.html

Olsen, L. (1997). *Outdoor survival skills* (6th ed.). Chicago: Chicago Review Press.

Outdoor Behavioral Healthcare Industry Research Consortium. (2010). Incident report for 2009. Durham, NH: Outdoor Behavioral Healthcare Research Cooperative.

Outdoor Behavioral Healthcare Industry Research Consortium. (2011). Durham, NH: Outdoor Behavioral Healthcare Research Cooperative.

Papadopoulos, J. (2000). Building a house from the foundation up: Adventure therapy training in Canada. *The Ontario Journal of Outdoor Education, 12*(4), 9–12.

Patton, M. Q. (2008). *Utilization-focused evaluation.* Thousand Oaks, CA: Sage Publications.

Paul, G. L. (1967). Strategy of outcome research in psychotherapy. *Journal of Consulting Psychology, 31,* 109–118.

Peebles, L. M., Jr. (2007). Improving self-efficacy in college students: A modified adventure therapy program. Ann Arbor, MI: ProQuest Information & Learning.

Perls, F. (1969). *Gestalt therapy verbatim.* Moab, UT: Real People Press.

Petrosino, A., Turpin-Petrosino, C., & Buehler, J. (2003). "Scared Straight" and other juvenile awareness programs for preventing juvenile delinquency. *Annals of the American Academy of Political and Social Science, 589,* 41–62.

Pinto, A., Friedman, R. M., & Epstein, M. (2005). Exploitation in the name of "specialty schooling": What counts as sufficient data? What are psychologists to do? *American Psychological Association: Public Interest Directorate, Children, Youth and Families Division News.* Retrieved from http://www.apa.org/pi/cyf/specialty_schooling.pdf

Pommier, J. H. (1994). *Experiential education therapy plus family training: Outwards Bounds school's efficacy with status offenders.* College Station: Texas A & M.

Porter, W. (1975). *The development and evaluation of a therapeutic wilderness program for youth.* Unpublished masters thesis, University of Denver, Denver, CO.

Portrie-Bethke, T. L., Hill, N. R., & Bethke, J. G. (2009). Strength-based mental health counseling for children with ADHD: An integrative model of adventure-based counseling and Adlerian play therapy. *Journal of Mental Health Counseling, 31*(4), 323–339.

Pos, A. E., Greenberg, L. S., & Warwar, S. H. (2009). Testing a model of change in the experiential treatment of depression. *Journal of Consulting and Clinical Psychology, 77*(6), 1055–1066.

Priest, S. (1984). Effective outdoor leadership: A survey. *Journal of Experiential Education, 7*(3), 34–36.

Priest, S. (1986). *Outdoor leadership in five nations.* Unpublished doctoral dissertation, Eugene, OR: University of Oregon.

Priest, S., & Gass, M. (2005). *Effective leadership in adventure programming (2nd ed.)* Human Kinetics Publishing.

Priest, S., Gass, M. A., & Gillis, H. L. (1999). *Essential elements of facilitation.* Tarrak Technologies.

Priest, S., Gass, M. A., & Gillis, H. L. (2009). *Essential elements of facilitation.* Taipai: Taiwan Outward Bound School.

Prinsen, E. J. D., & van Delden, J. J. M. (2009). Can we justify eliminating coercive measures in psychiatry? *Journal of Medical Ethics, 35*(1), 69–73.

Prochaska, J. O., & DiClemente, C. C. (1983). Stages and processes of self-change in smoking: Toward an integrative model of change. *Journal of Consulting & Clinical Psychology, 5*, 390–395.

Prochaska, J. O., & Norcross, J. C. (2002). Stages of change. In J. C. Norcross (Ed.), *Psychotherapy relationships that work: Therapist contributions and responsiveness to patients* (pp. 303–313). New York: Oxford University Press.

Prouty, D. (1999). Project adventure: a brief history. In J. Miles & S. Priest (Ed.). *Adventure programming* (pp. 93–99). State College, PA: Venture Publishing.

Puchbauer, D. (2007). Outdoor behavioral healthcare for troubled adolescents: A clinical skills training manual for adventure counselors. Ann Arbor, MI: ProQuest Information & Learning.

Quinn, D. (1992). *Ishmael.* New York: Bantam.

Rademacher, E. S. (1928). Treatment of problem children by means of a long-term camp. *Mental Hygiene, XII,* 385–390.

Ragsdale, K. G., Cox, R. D., Finn, P., & Eisler, R. M. (1996). Effectiveness of short-term specialized inpatient treatment for war-related posttraumatic stress disorder: A role for adventure-based counseling and psychodrama. *Journal of Traumatic Stress, 9*(2), 269–283.

Raiola, E. O. (1986). *Outdoor wilderness education: A leadership curriculum.* Unpublished doctoral dissertation. Schenectady, NY: Union Graduate School.

RAND Corporation. (2008). *Invisible wounds of war: Psychological and cognitive injuries, their consequences, and services to assist recovery.* Santa Monica, CA: RAND Corporation.

Ray, S. L. (2008). The experience of adolescent girls participating in an adventure therapy program: A qualitative study. Ann Arbor, MI: ProQuest Information & Learning.

Ringer, T. M. (1994). Leadership competencies: From recreation to therapy. In J. Barrett (Ed.), *Enabling troubled youth* (pp. 29–52). Ambleside, UK: Basecamp.

Ringer, T. M., & Gillis, H. L. (1995). Managing psychological depth in adventure programming. *Journal of Experiential Education. 18*(1), 41–51.

Ringer, T. M. & Gillis, H. L. (1996). From practice to theory: Unearthing the theories of human change that are implicit in your work as an adventure practitioner. Presented at the Association for Experiential Education Annual Conference, Spokane, WA.

Ringholz, R. C. (1997). *On belay! The life of legendary mountaineer Paul Petzoldt.* Mountaineers Books.

Rogers, C. R. (1961). *On becoming a person.* Boston, MA: Houghton Mifflin Company.

Rohnke, K. (1977). *Cowstails and cobras.* Beverly, MA: Project Adventure.

Rohnke, K. (1994). *Bottomless Bag Again!* (2nd ed). Dubuque, IA: Kendall Hunt.

Rohnke, K., & Butler, S. (1995). *Quicksilver.* Dubuque, IA: Kendall Hunt.

Ross, A. (2007). Transformative education: Revisiting the therapeutic milieu to harness the power of culture. *Reclaiming Children and Youth, 16*(3), 5–9.

Rossi, P. H., Lipsey, M. W., & Freeman, H. E. (2004). *Evaluation: A systematic approach* (7th ed.). Thousand Oaks, CA: Sage.

Roszak, T. (1992). *Voice of the earth.* New York: Simon and Schuster.

Roszak, T. (1995). Where psyche meets gaia. In T. Roszak, M. E. Gomes, & A. D. Kanner (Eds.), *Ecopsychology: Restoring the earth, healing the planet* (pp. 1–20). San Francisco: Sierra Club Books.

Rowan, E. L. (2005). *To do my best: James E. West and the history of the Boy Scouts of America.* Las Vegas: PublishingWorks.

Russell, K. C. (1999). *Theoretical basis, process, and reported outcomes of wilderness therapy as an intervention and treatment for problem behavior in adolescents.* Doctoral dissertation, University of Idaho, Moscow, ID.

Russell, K. C. (2001). What is Wilderness Therapy? *Journal of Experiential Education, 24*(2), 70–79.

Russell, K. C. (2003a). A nation-wide survey of outdoor behavioral healthcare programs for adolescents with problem behaviors. *Journal of Experiential Education, 25*(3), 322–331.

Russell, K. C. (2003b). Assessing treatment outcomes in outdoor behavioral healthcare using the Youth Outcome Questionnaire. *Child and Youth Care Forum, 32*(6), 355–381.

Russell, K. C. (2005). Two years later: A qualitative assessment of youth-well-being and the role of aftercare in outdoor behavioral healthcare treatment. *Child and Youth Care Forum, 34*(3), 209–239.

Russell, K. C. (2006a). Depressive symptom and substance use frequency outcome in outdoor behavioral healthcare. Minneapolis, MN: Outdoor Behavioral Healthcare Research Cooperative, College of Education and Human Development, University of Minnesota.

Russell, K. C. (2006b). Brat camps, boot camps, or....? Exploring wilderness therapy program theory. *Journal of Adventure Education and Outdoor Learning, 6*(1), 51–67.

Russell, K. C. (2006c). Evaluating the effects of the Wendigo Lake Expedition program for young offenders. *Journal of Youth Violence and Juvenile Justice, 4*(2), 185–203.

Russell, K. C. (2008). Adolescence substance use treatment: Service delivery, research on effectiveness, and emerging treatment alternatives. *Journal of Groups in Addiction and Recovery, 2*(2–4), 68–96.

Russell, K. C. & Gillis, H. L. (2007). *Stages of change and substance use frequency outcome in adolescent treatment.* Poster presented at the American Psychological Association, San Francisco, CA.

Russell, K. C., & Gillis, H. L. (2010). Experiential therapy in the mental health treatment of adolescents. *Journal of Therapeutic Schools and Programs, 4*(1), 47–79.

Russell, K. C., Gillis, H. L., & Lewis, T. G. (2008). A five-year follow-up of a nation-wide survey of outdoor behavioral healthcare programs. *Journal of Experiential Education, 31,* 1, 55–77.

Russell, K., & Harper, N. (2006). Incident monitoring in outdoor behavioral healthcare programs: before your summary of restraint, runaway, injury, and illness rates. *Journal of Therapeutic Schools and Programs, 1*(1), 70–90.

Russell, K. C., Hendee, J., & Cooke, S. (1998). The potential social and economic contributions of Wilderness Discovery as an adjunct to the Federal Job Corps program. *International Journal of Wilderness, 4*(3), 32–38.

Rust, M. (2004). Creating a psychotherapy for a sustainable future. Resurgence. Retrieved from http://www.mjrust.net/downloads/Seeking%20Health%20in%20an%20Ailing%20World.pdf

Ryan, R. M., Lynch, M. F., Vansteenkiste, M., & Deci, E. L. (2011). Motivation and autonomy in counseling, psychotherapy, and behavior change: A look at theory and practice. *The Counseling Psychologist, 39*, 193–260.

Sachs, J. J. (1992). The impact of a modified wilderness camping program on the social interactions and social expectations of behavior disordered adolescents. *Behavioral Disorders, 17*(2), 89–98.

Sackett, D. L., Rosenberg, W. M. C., Gray, J. A. M., Haynes, R. B., & Richardson, W. S. (1996). Evidence based medicine: What it is and what it is not. *British Medical Journal, 312*, 71–72.

Sacksteder, K. (2010). Introduction to best practices. Retrieved July, 25, 2010, from http://tapg.aee.org/tapg/bestpractices

Sacksteder, K. (2011). Best practices: An introduction. Retrieved from http://tapg.aee.org/tapg/bestpractices.

Samargia, L. A., Saewyc, E. M., & Elliot, B. A. (2006). Foregone mental health care and self-reported access barriers among adolescents. *The Journal of School Nursing, 22*(1), 17–24.

Santa, J. (2007). The history of private residential treatment programs. *Journal of Therapeutic Schools and Programs, 2*(1), 15–25.

Scheidlinger, S. (1995). The small healing group: A historical overview. *Psychotherapy, 32*(4), 657–668.

Schoel, J., & Maizell, R. (2002). *Exploring islands of healing: New perspectives on adventure based counseling.* Dubuque, IA: Kendall Hunt Publishing.

Schoel, J., Prouty, D., & Radcliffe, P. (1988). *Islands of healing: A guide to adventure-based counseling.* Hamilton, MA: Project Adventure.

Sermabeikian, P., & Martinez, D. (1994). Treatment of adolescent sexual offenders: Theory-based practice. *Child Abuse & Neglect, 18*(11), 969–976.

Seymour, S. R. (1976). Outdoor wilderness survival and its psychological and sociological effects upon student in changing human behavior. Unpublished doctoral dissertation. Provo, UT: Brigham Young University.

Shanahan, L., McAllister, L., & Curtin, M. (2009). Wilderness adventure therapy and cognitive rehabilitation: Joining forces for youth with TBI. *Brain Injury, 23*(13–14), 1054–1064.

Shankar, P. R., Field, S. K., Collins, C. L., Dick, R. W., & Comstock, D. (2007). Epidemiology of high school and collegiate football injuries in the United States. *American College of Sport Medicine, 35*(8), 1295–1303.

Shapiro, A. (1978). *Scared straight.* New York: New Video Group.

Shepard, P. (1995). *Nature and madness.* San Francisco, CA: Sierra Club Books.

Sibthorp, J. (2003). An empirical look at Walsh and Golins' adventure education process model: Relationships between antecedent factors, perceptions of characteristics of an adventure education experience, and changes in self-efficacy. *Journal of Leisure Research, 35*(1), 80–106.

Simpson, C. A. & Gillis, H. L. (1998). Working with those who hurt others: adventure therapy with juvenile sexual perpetrators. In C. M. Itin (Ed.), *Exploring the boundaries of adventure therapy: International perspectives.* Boulder, CO: Association for Experiential Education.

Smith, (2009). *Manual of program accreditation standards for adventure programs.* Boulder, CO: Association for Experiential Education.

Snyder, C. R., Hoza, B., Pelham, W. E., Rapoff, M., Ware, L., Danovsky, M., Highberger, L., Rubinstein, H., & Stahl, K. (1997). The development and validation of the Children's Hope Scale. *Journal of Pediatric Psychology, 22*(3), 399–421.

Snyder, C., Lopez, S., Shorey, H., Rand, K., & Feldman, D. (2003). Hope theory, measurements, and applications to school psychology. *School Psychology Quarterly, 18*(2), 122–139.

Sox, H. C. & Woolf, S. H. (1993). Evidence-based practice guidelines from the U.S. Preventive Services Task Force. *Journal of the American Medical Association, 169,* 26–78.

Sperry, L. (2010). *Core competencies in counseling and psychotherapy: Becoming a highly competent and effective therapist.* New York: Routledge Taylor & Francis Group.

Statewide Autism Council. (2004). *Competencies for professionals and paraprofessionals supporting individuals with autism across the lifespan in Virginia.* Richmond, VA: Virginia Department of Education.

Stednitz, L. (1991, June). Aspen achievement academy. Retrieved from http://www.strugglingteens.com/archives/1991/6/oe01.html

Steinberg, L., & Silverberg, S. B. (1986). The vicissitudes of autonomy in ealry adolescence. *Child Development, 57,* 841–851.

Steinert, T., Lepping, P., Bernhardsgrütter, R., Conca, A., Hatling, T., Janssen, W., et al. (2010). Incidence of seclusion and restraint in psychiatric hospitals: a literature review and survey of international trends. *Social Psychiatry and Psychiatric Epidemiology, 45*(9), 889–897.

Stich, T. F. (1983). Experiential therapy. *Journal of Experiential Education, 6*(3), 23–30.

Substance Abuse & Mental Health Services Administration. (2003). A national call to action: Eliminating the use of seclusion and restraint. Washington, DC: U.S. Department of Health and Human Services.

Sudetic, C. (2000, July 6). The struggle for the soul of the Boy Scouts. *Rolling Stone,* pp. 101–106.

Swank, J. M., & Daire, A. P. (2010). Multiple family adventure-based therapy groups: An innovative integration of two approaches. *The Family Journal, 18*(3), 241–247.

Swann, W. B., Chang-Schneider, C., & Larsen McClarty, K. (2007). *American Psychologist. 62*(2), 84–94.

Swiderski, M. J. (1981). *Outdoor leadership competencies identified by outdoor leaders in five western regions.* Unpublished doctoral dissertation. Eugene, OR: University of Oregon.

Szalavitz, M. (2006). *Help at any cost.* New York: Penguin Group.

Tanielian, T., & Jaycox, L. H. (Eds.). (2008). Invisible wounds of war: Psychological and cognitive injuries, their consequences, and services to assist recovery. Santa Monica, CA: RAND Corporation.

Taylor, A. F., Kuo, F. E., & Sullivan, W. C. (2001). Coping with ADD: The surprising connection to green play settings. *Environment & Behavior, 33*(1), 54–77.

Taylor, D. M., Segal, D., & Harper, N. J. (2010). The ecology of adventure therapy: An integral systems approach to therapeutic change. *Ecopsychology, 2*(2), 77–83.

Thoreau, H. D. (1971). *Walden.* Princeton, NJ: Princeton University Press.

Trepka, C., Rees, A., Shapiro, D. A., Hardy, G. E., & Barkham, M. (2004). Therapist competence and outcome of cognitive therapy for depression. *Cognitive Therapy and Research, 28,* 143–157.

Tucker, A. R., & Rheingold, A. (2010). Enhancing fidelity in adventure education and adventure therapy. *Journal of Experiential Education, 33*(3), 258–273.

Tyler, J. L., Ziedenberg, J., & Lotke, E. (2006). *Cost effective corrections: The fiscal architecture of rational juvenile justice systems.* Washington, DC: The Justice Policy Institute.

U.S. Department of Defense. (2008). Warrior adventure quest helps soldiers return to normalcy. Retrieved from http://www.defense.gov/news/newsarticle.aspx?id= 51348

U.S. Department of Defense. (2009a). Army leaders struggle with soldier suicide rate. FDCH Regulatory Intelligence Database. Washington, DC: Author.

U.S. Department of Defense. (2009b). New fitness program helps soldiers maximize potential, general says. FDCH Regulatory Intelligence Database. Washington, DC: Author.

U.S. Department of Defense. (2010). 'Outdoorsmen' breathe life into war. FDCH Regulatory Intelligence Database. Washington, DC: DOD.

U.S. Department of Education. Retrieved from http://ies.ed.gov/ncee/wwc

U.S. Department of Health and Human Services, Maternal and Child Health Bureau. (2005). *The national survey of child health, 2003.* Retrieved from http://www.acf.hhs.gov/

Utah Division of Administrative Rules (2007). Outdoor youth program licensing standards. Retrieved October 26, 2007 from http://www.rules.utah.gov/publicat/code/r501/r501-08.htm.

Unsoeld, W. (1974). Spiritual values in wilderness. Paper presented at the Association for Experiential Education Conference, Estes Park, CO.

Van Gennep, A. (1960). *The rites of passage.* Chicago: The University of Chicago Press.

Volkow, N. D. (2011). Physical activity may prevent substance abuse. NIDA Notes, March 2011. Retrieved from http://www.drugabuse.gov/news-events/nida-notes

Vorrath, H. H., & Brendtro, L. K. (1985). *Positive peer culture.* Piscataway, NJ: Transactions Publishers.

Wachtel, P. (1989). *The poverty of influence.* Philadelphia: New Society.

Waller, J. & Peller, J. (1992). *Becoming solution-focused in brief therapy.* NY: Bruner-Mazel.

Walsh, M., & Russell. K. C. (2011). An exploratory study of a wilderness adventure program for young offenders. *Ecopsychology, 2,* 211–229.

Walsh, V., & Gollins, G. (1976). *An exploration of the Outward Bound process.* Denver, CO: Outward Bound Publications.

Warren, K. (2008). A call for race, gender, and class sensitive facilitation in outdoor experiential education. In K. Warren, D. Mitten, & T. A. Loeffler (Eds.), *Theory and practice of experiential education.* Boulder, CO: Association for Experiential Education.

Warren, K., Mitten, D., & Loeffler, T. (Eds.). (2008). *Theory and practice of experiential education* (4th ed.). Boulder, CO: Association for Experiential Education.

Warren, K., Sakofs, M., & Hunt, J. S. (1995). *The theory of experiential education.* Dubuque, IA: Association for Experiential Education.

Watts, S. T. (2003). *Better an honest scoundrel: Chronicle of a western lawman.* Victoria, Canada: Trafford Publishing.

Weeks, S. (1985). *The effects of Sierra II, an adventure probation program, upon selected behavioral variables of adolescent juvenile delinquents.* Unpublished doctoral dissertation, University of Colorado, Boulder, CO.

Weiss, B., Caron, A., Ball, S., Tapp, J., Johnson, M., Weisz, J. R. (2005). Iatrogenic effects of group treatment for antisocial youths. *Journal of Consulting and Clinical Psychology, 73*(6), 1036–1044.

Wells, L. (2006). Incident monitoring in outdoor behavioral healthcare programs: before your summary of restraint, runaway, injury, and illness rates. *Journal of Therapeutic Schools and Programs, 1*(2), 126–136.

Wells, L. (2011). Parent empowerment. Retrieved from http://parent-empowerment-blog. com/2011/02/28/wilderness-therapy-challenged-by-new-wilderness-characteristics-government-regulations/

Werch, C. E., & Owen, D. (2002). Iatrogenic effects of alcohol and drug prevention programs. *Journal of Studies on Alcohol, 63,* 581–590.

White, W. (2008). A mighty change: the influence of Larry Dean Olsen on the evolution of wilderness therapy. *Journal of Therapeutic Schools and Programs, 3*(1), 8–19.

Wilcoxon, S. A., Remley, T. Gladding, S. T., & Huber, C. H. (2007). *Ethical, legal, and professional issues in the practice of marriage and family therapy (3rd ed)*. Upper Saddle River, NJ: Pearson.

Wilderness Act of 1964. Public Law 88-577, 16 U.S.C. 1131-1136, 88th Cong., 2nd Session, 1964.

Williamson, J., & Gass, M. A. (1993). *Manual of program accreditation standards for adventure programs*. Boulder, CO: Association for Experiential Education.

Wilson, E. O. (1984). *Biophilia*. Cambridge, MA: Harvard University Press.

Wilson, S. J., & Lipsey, M. W. (2000). Wilderness challenge programs for delinquent youth: A meta analysis of outcome evaluations. *Evaluation and Program Planning, 23*(1), 1–12.

Winterdyk, J., & Griffiths, C. (1984). Wilderness experience programs: reforming delinquents or beating around the bush? *Juvenile and Family Court Journal, Fall,* 35–44.

Winters, K. C. (1999). Treating adolescents with substance use disorders: An overview of practice issues and outcomes. *Substance Abuse, 20*(4), 203–225.

Woodbury, L. (1991, August). Catherine freer wilderness survival school. Retrieved July 12, 2010, from http://www.strugglingteens.com/archives/1991/8/np01.html

Wright, A. (1982). *Therapeutic potential of Outward Bound process: An evaluation of a treatment program for juvenile delinquents*. Unpublished doctoral dissertation, Pennsylvania State University, College Station.

Yalom, I. (1995). *The theory and practice of group psychotherapy.* New York: Basic Books.

Zeig, J. K. (1994). The evolution of psychotherapy revisited. In J. K. Zeig (Ed.), *The evolution of psychotherapy: The second conference* (pp. xi–xvi).

Zelov, R., & Gass. M. A. (2011, January). *Research and NATSAP: How did we get here? Why do we need it? What do we know? And what are we doing about it?* Presented at the National Association of Therapeutic Schools and Programs Conference, Tucson, AZ.

Zygmond, M. J., & Boorhem, H. (1989). Ethical decision making in family therapy. *Family Process, 28,* 269–280.

Author Index

Subject Index